Racing & Football Outlook

FLAT RACING
GUIDE 2015

Statistics • Results
Previews • Training centre reports

Contributors: David Baxter, Richard Birch, Nick Deacon, Steffan Edwards, Katherine Fidler, Dylan Hill, Tony Jakobson, Kel Mansfield, Steve Mellish, John O'Hara, Ben Osborne, Stuart Redding, Martin Stevens, Richard Williams

Designed and edited by Nick Watts and Dylan Hill

Published in 2015 by Raceform Ltd
27 Kingfisher Court, Hambridge Road, Newbury RG14 5SJ

A catalogue record for this book is available from the British Library.

ISBN 978-1-909471-88-7

Printed by CPI Group (UK) Ltd, Croydon, CRO 4YY

RACING & FOOTBALL | **OUTLOOK**

Est. 1909

Contents

Introduction		4
Profiles for punters	Hugo Palmer	6
	David Elsworth	11

2015 Preview

Ante-post	16
Racing & Football Outlook's 30 horses to follow	31
Pedigrees for punters with Katherine Fidler and Martin Stevens	39
Aborigine	43
Jerry M	48
Downsman	52
Borderer	56
Hastings	60
Southerner	63
John Bull	67
Steve Mellish	70
Richard Birch	73
Time Test	76

2014 Review

Group 1 Review	80
Two-year-old Review	92

Statistics, Races and Racecourses

Comprehensive stats for ten top trainers	113
Jockey & trainer standings	153
Group 1 records	159
Big handicap records	172
Fixtures	181
Big-race dates	188
Track facts for all Britain's Flat courses	191

Final furlong

Picture quiz	233
Betting guide & Rule 4 deductions	236
Horse index	238

Est. 1909
RACING & FOOTBALL OUTLOOK

Editor's introduction

YOU don't need to talk to many trainers to realise that our sport was hit hard by the recession, but thankfully the show will always stay on the road as the lure of British racing remains as strong as ever around the world – as the last 12 months has shown.

Investment from Qatar has been huge in recent years and was taken to extraordinary new heights when Goodwood signed a ten-year sponsorship deal with Qatar to bring about a massive increase in prize-money at Glorious Goodwood – which will this year be branded the Qatar Goodwood

Festival for the first time – with £2 million invested in eight key races.

And while some might justifiably claim that such money would serve more good spread around a bit more, you certainly can't level that accusation at Qatar's approach to racehorse ownership.

Sheikh Joaan Al Thani's Al Shaqab Racing and his cousin Sheikh Fahad Al Thani's Qatar Racing have invested fortunes on the course in pursuit of superstars and the number of trainers feeling the benefit has been enormous. How heartening, for example, to see a trainer like John Quinn house a genuine Classic pretender in The

TREVE: Al Shaqab's brilliant flag-bearer will go for a third Arc this year

Wow Signal – already a Group 1 winner as a juvenile since he was bought by Qatar Racing last year.

That said, fortunes on the course have been mixed. Al Shaqab struck gold with Treve and also enjoyed real success with the likes of Toronado and Olympic Glory, but Qatar Racing, for all the cash going around, are still waiting for a real superstar to emerge. Perhaps Elm Park, last year's Racing Post Trophy winner and a serious contender for the Derby, will be the one.

Yet maybe it shouldn't be surprising that money hasn't bought instant success. There are only so many good horses to go around and the two more long-standing powerhouses in the sport – Godolphin and Coolmore – aren't going to disappear.

It's been a rough few years for Godolphin, but Sheikh Mohammed's determination to put things right was emphasised this winter when he paid what must presumably have been a small fortune to tempt top riders William Buick and James Doyle to turn their backs on big jobs to join the Dubai operation.

And Coolmore, of course, just go on and on with a seemingly never-ending supply of top young talent. In fact our ante-post expert Steffan Edwards is predicting an even bigger year for Aidan O'Brien and his team than normal, tipping the Ballydoyle yard to land the 2,000 Guineas and the Derby this year.

Edwards should know. After all, he tipped last year's shock 2,000 Guineas winner Night Of Thunder and advised getting on Oaks heroine Taghrooda when she was a 33-1 shot in the spring.

We've got much more besides our peerless ante-post previews to help you decide where your money's going this season. For starters our regional reporters have scoured the yards in their area to bring you all the best prospects from all over Britain and Ireland, although we've stuck to HQ at Newmarket for our in-depth stable tours with two men at opposite ends of their careers – rising star Hugo Palmer and legendary veteran David Elsworth, both of whom could well be in for stellar years.

Richard Williams has searched far and wide for his list of 30 horses to follow, and

JOHN F KENNEDY: the Derby favourite is one of many top prospects for Coolmore

as well as all that pedigree experts Katherine Fidler and Martin Stevens uncovers the best first-crop sires to follow; there are the unique views of Steve Mellish and Richard Birch; Time Test brings you all the key speed figures; and Dylan Hill guides you through last season's leading form.

Then there are the stats, reams and reams of winner-finding numbers detailing the top trainers and jockeys also broken down course by course so you know who to follow at your local track.

Once again we have every base covered for a year packed with bumper profits, and don't forget to buy your copy of the RFO every week for the very latest news and tips.

Profiles for punters
Hugo Palmer

HUGO PALMER: enjoyed a superb 2014 despite being nervous in the spring

Profile by John O'Hara

HUGO PALMER is one of the most upwardly mobile young trainers in Britain. The Newmarket handler is starting only his fifth season of training yet has already ticked off many of his targets.

Palmer set himself three aims last year. The first was to pass £200,000 in prize-money and he ended up earning more than double that. The second was to train a Group winner, which he did twice in the space of five days with Aktabantay in the Solario Stakes at Sandown and New Providence in the Dick Poole Fillies' Stakes at Salisbury. Only the third aim – to notch a treble – went unfulfilled.

Palmer reflects: "I was very nervous last spring because Making Eyes had retired, Short Squeeze was struggling to find form and Ascription had a year off. Without the stars it was going to be hard, but in the end it was an incredibly exhilarating year."

Palmer's rise is all the more impressive considering he has done it without the background of coming from a racing dynasty or the backing of a single major backer.

Bearing that in mind, it's perhaps little wonder that the trainer he idolised was Martin Pipe, a man who built an empire out of nothing.

"Pipe started from scratch and revolutionised jump racing and his domination of the sport was so rare. I remember he took so much pleasure out of winning small races with poor horses, as much as he did winning Cheltenham races with class acts.

"I remember we had a filly called Mazoula, who was not very big and all she had going for her was a big heart. After four unplaced efforts we managed to find a nursery for her at Wolverhampton over 7f which she won off 57. I couldn't pretend it was like training a Group winner but the job satisfaction as her trainer was huge, because it was much harder for her to win that than Aktabantay to win the Solario."

Palmer's interest in the sport was fuelled by his uncle Justin, who is married to Lucy Wadham.

He says: "At the time he was working for Sheikh Mohammed during the era of the great Lammtarra. I remember around that time a friend slipped out of school to meet me in town and we spent a whole afternoon in a betting shop. I had 60p and he had 40p – a measly pound between us. We put our entire kitty on a horse which won and I think we had about six or seven winners and won about £30 each. Then it was straight to the pub!"

His education within the sport saw him spend three seasons with Hughie Morrison and two with Patrick Chamings before going to Australia to work under Gai Waterhouse's tutelage.

It is Waterhouse he credits as the biggest influence on his career, saying: "I learned so much with Gai and we are still in touch."

As for the coming season, Palmer realises this is one sport in which you cannot afford to rest on your laurels.

AKTABANTAY: Palmer's first Group winner pictured in California before his aborted Breeders' Cup mission

"We start all over again this year," he says, "and although I have a few targets we just want to continue improving.

"I am still looking for that first treble and would like to top the £500,000 mark in prize-money this time. In general my hopes are much broader in that I want to win more of the better prizes and move the business forward. We have expanded over the winter and I am very happy with the bunch of two-year-olds from what I have seen so far."

Indeed, the Palmer team has virtually doubled in strength from "around 35 to 40" to 70, with a very healthy number of juveniles.

Palmer is still searching for a permanent jockey, although that was no problem last year.

He says: "We are in a state of flux with jockey arrangements, as we were last year. I love to use Ryan Moore whenever I can and James Doyle, although it is not always that easy to secure their services. One day it would be great to have our own stable jockey."

The horses

Aktabantay 3yo colt
Oasis Dream – Splashdown (Falbrav)

I fell in love with him from day one and we ended up going beyond what we had planned (370,000gns) to buy him at the sales. Thankfully he did really well last year, winning twice including the Solario. I was actually disappointed he didn't win that more easily and I think he will be better on quicker ground. With that in mind we took him to the Breeders' Cup, but it was a wasted trip as he kicked a wall and injured a foot. He has filled out and looks stronger and more mature and I am looking forward to seeing him back on track. I am sure he will get a mile as he is out of a staying family so he could start in the 2,000 Guineas, although if he doesn't make it the Jersey Stakes at Royal Ascot would be an option.

Ascription 6yo gelding
Dansili – Lady Elgar (Sadler's Wells)

He has been a star for us, winning races at Glorious Goodwood and the St Leger Festival at Doncaster, but he hasn't run since the autumn of 2013. Last year we were preparing him for the Lincoln and trying to push it a bit when he became ill, so we felt it was best for the horse to turn him out in a field for the year and bring him back now. He looks fantastic and we will plan his campaign around the ground as he doesn't want it any quicker than good. He is on a mark of 109 and I think we will start in a Listed race and see if he is up to Group level or has to stick to handicaps. I also wouldn't rule out a trip to France at some time.

Covert Love 3yo filly
Azamour – Wing Stealth (Hawk Wing)

She is a big filly and because of that we didn't do a lot with her last year. She ran once when fifth at Lingfield in October which was much as I had expected. She had a great break and has really grown into herself. I would be disappointed if she weren't up to winning a maiden over a mile and she could get further.

Extremity 4yo gelding
Exceed And Excel – Chanterelle (Indian Ridge)

He had a terrific season last year, winning three times including at Glorious Goodwood off a mark of 84. On his final start he ran in the Cambridgeshire and we thought he would go well, but he pulled off a shoe off and was never in the race. He will go for some top mile handicaps such as the Hunt Cup and the Betfred Mile, but he is bred to stay further and could step up in trip again at some point. I hope he improves enough to take to Dubai next year.

Home Of The Brave 3yo colt
Starspangledbanner – Blissful Beat (Beat Hollow)

He is an exciting horse who showed us a huge amount of spark right from the very early days as a yearling. He did well last year, winning easily at Newmarket and finishing third in the Sirenia when things didn't go right for him. He was a light and wiry two-year-old and has done well over the winter. He needs plenty space and a galloping track, so with that in mind the Free Handicap at Newmarket is going to be his starting point this season. I can't see why he won't get 7f and possibly a mile if he learns to settle.

Lobster Pot 4yo filly
Dylan Thomas – Classical Flair (Distant Music)

She was our only two-year-old who could work with Short Squeeze a couple of years ago, but she took a long while to come to hand last year and then later we found a

NAILBITER: Extremity (far side) gets up to win at Glorious Goodwood last year

breathing problem. She has had that operated on and I hope there is plenty of improvement in her. She is very well handicapped and I think she could end up a couple of stone ahead of her mark.

New Providence 3yo filly
Bahamian Bounty – Bayja
(Giant's Causeway)

She's a very athletic filly and won three times last year, including the Group 3 Dick Poole Fillies' Stakes over 6f at Salisbury, before a good third to Lucida in the Rockfel when she just didn't get home over the extra furlong. We will try again over 7f in the Fred Darling as Newbury has a less stiff finish than Newmarket and I might then consider the French Guineas as she might be suited by a slow pace and a sprint finish.

Not Never 3yo gelding
Notnowcato – Watchoverme (Haafhd)

He is a big-framed horse who took a long time to come to himself and I was nervous about running him last year, but his owner told me to get on with it and she was right as he won on his second run in a maiden at Redcar by a head. It is hard to know how good the maiden was, but it was probably decent as the second, third and fourth were all Godolphin horse and his mark of 81 looks reasonable. He has done well over the winter and could be one to consider for the King George V Handicap at Royal Ascot.

Only Joking 3yo filly
Aussie Rules – Cliche (Diktat)

Early last year she was up there with Aktabantay as our leading lights but she didn't go on like he did despite winning what was probably a weak maiden at Thirsk by eight lengths. She needs soft ground and perhaps while we waited for some cut she started to grow. James Doyle said she felt weak after her last run at Newmarket even though she didn't look it. She has come back much stronger, so much so she was almost unrecognisable. I think she will get a mile easily enough and we might aim her at the valuable fillies' handicap at Ascot's first Saturday meeting in May. She would get in off a light weight off a mark of just 74 and if there was some dig then she could be interesting.

She's Mine 4yo filly
Sea The Stars – Scribonia (Danehill)

I have got two new fillies from John Oxx's yard – the other is called Royal Empire – and this was the one he felt had the most potential. She has had Group 1 entries, so that tells you what he thought of her. She is beautifully bred, being a half-sister to Gile Na Greine and Cuis Ghaire, but she had terrible foot problems in Ireland which held her back. They look good now and hopefully we can get the best out of her.

Short Squeeze 5yo gelding
Cape Cross – Sunsetter (Diesis)

He found life hard for much of last year as he had gone up from 75 to 106 when winning three times in 2013, but he won the mile handocap at York's Ebor meeting for the second successive year and is still improving. He started the year in Dubai so he will have a break and probably be back in July for Goodwood and then a third crack at York. If all goes to plan then the Woodbine Mile would be a great late target. He is part-owned by Australians and will be heading there at the end of the year unless I can persuade them otherwise!

Silvery Blue 3yo filly
Paco Boy – Blue Echo (Kyllachy)

She twice ran well on the all-weather before winning a 6f maiden on turf at Redcar. Like all Paco Boys she shows enormous heart and doesn't know when to lie down. She will stay sprinting, although some people feel she will get further which would give us more options. She has wintered well and will win more races.

Spanish Squeeze 3yo colt
Lope De Vega – Appetina (Perugino)

Putting it simply, he is the most exciting horse I have had. We thought he might be among the very best two-year-olds last year, but he was plagued with sore shins and we didn't get him out until late September when he was a very good third at Newmarket before winning well at Kempton over a mile. He was given a mark of 88, which was a pleasant surprise. I think he is much better than that – in fact I am sure he is a Group horse. He has strengthened up a lot and looks a real miler, but in time he could get a lot further.

Spirit Of Sound 3yo filly
Invincible Spirit – Sound Of Summer (Fusaichi Pegasus)

We still think a lot of this filly even though ahe disappointed on her only run at Haydock last year when we expected her to nearly win. She subsequently injured her knee, but she has had a chip removed and has come through it well.

Ziggurat 3yo colt
Tagula – Visual Element (Distant View)

He's a lovely unraced horse. He was very nearly ready to run in a 7f maiden at the July meeting last year when he injured himself on the gallops and had to take the rest of the year off. He has since grown an enormous amount and is going nicely. I feel he could be a top handicapper in time and it wouldn't surprise me if he developed into a Britannia type.

If I had to pick out one of my two-year-olds to follow, it would be a Poet's Voice colt called Gimlet. I am a big fan of his sire and he is a good mover who finds everything very easy at home. He could be one for the first half of the season. I have an unnamed Arcano colt out of Manuelita Rose who is a stand-out among the early types, and I also have a couple of potentially nice early fillies called Magical Path and Nidnod, who have plenty of speed. Fiftyshadesofpink is a Pour Moi filly with a pedigree to die for and I also have Aktabantay's half-brother by Rock Of Gibraltar, who is no less nice than his sibling – a bit bigger and scopier though not as muscular. Sheriff is a gorgeous big colt for the backend.

Profiles for punters
David Elsworth

DAVID ELSWORTH: reaping the rewards of his success with Justice Day

Profile by Dylan Hill

DAVID ELSWORTH is revelling in what he calls an "unexpected bonus" in the twilight of his magnificent career.

Elsworth, 75, is training 14 well-bred two-year-olds this year for Robert Ng, a Hong Kong property developer who shares a personal wealth of $11.5 billion with his brother Philip, as a result of his success with Ng's horses over the last two seasons.

"Charlie Gordon-Watson called me a couple of years ago to say Mr Ng wanted to buy Justice Day from me, which he did," Elsworth explains. "I did well with that horse so last year he sent me two more, Justice Good and Justice Well. We won with both of them as well, so this year he sent me 12 more yearlings and I've also bought a couple for him.

"I've never actually met him, but I do remember speaking to him on the phone early last year about one of the horses he had sent me. He asked how the horse compared to Justice Day and I told him, 'He's just as good,' so that horse became Justice Good, we named the other Justice Well and we'll name the others in the same way, although we'll run out of words eventually!"

More than living up to his name, Justice Good could well prove to be the best of the bunch. Off the track since finishing fourth in last season's Coventry Stakes, he has Elsworth hugely excited ahead of the new season and is being aimed at the 2,000 Guineas, with the trip Elsworth's only concern.

Arabian Queen is another potential Classic contender as she had problems on her last two starts having claimed the notable scalp of High Celebrity in the Duchess of Cambridge Stakes.

A British Classic would be the icing on the cake in terms of Elsworth's career. He's had many near misses and even trained Island Sands, who won the 2,000 Guineas for Godolphin in 1999, as a two-year-old, but so far his only Classic victory came in Ireland with In The Groove.

However, he refuses to dwell on what would complete his CV. Indeed, asked if he has any ambitions he has yet to achieve, he jokes: "Yes, but she's still married to her husband!"

More seriously, Elsworth adds: "Every time you get a new crop of yearlings you hope one of them could be a Derby horse. The best I've done was third with Mighty Fly and I'd like to think I've had a lot better than him. Seattle Rhyme was a big, fine horse who won the Racing Post Trophy, but he got injured in his Derby year. Then Norse Dancer was only beaten two lengths even though he couldn't handle the track – he was last at Tattenham Corner."

Even if there is a burgeoning great ready to finally break Elsworth's duck, they will have to go some to match his greats of the past such as the mighty Desert Orchid and dual Champion Chase winner Barn-brook Again. Asked to compare the pair, Elsworth says: "Desert Orchid wanted it more. He just had that edge. He was tough and you could run him eight or nine times a season year after year - handicaps, two miles to three and a half. They don't do that now! People could relate to him as they got to see him every Saturday.

"Floyd was another who would die for you and Persian Punch was just a slogger but what a slogger! You look back at his third in the Melbourne Cup and it was a hell of a run, going halfway around the world at the end of a long season.

"I could bore you all day talking about these horses!" Elsworth says, and it's not just his own greats that get his passion flowing as he continues: "If you compare all the Gold Cup winners I think Denman was the best. He was up against a real champion in Kauto Star that year and he galloped him into submission. He also won two Hennessys under top-weight so he's probably the only horse since Desert Orchid to have done something like that. Arkle was brilliant, don't get me wrong, but the only good horse he beat was Mill House and he'd been beaten fair and square by that horse in the Hennessy. In his other Gold Cups he was beating the same horses in fields of three and four."

Talk of the past inevitably leads to discussion of Whitsbury, the tiny Hampshire village where Elsworth enjoyed his glory days, and he admits to finding Newmarket more difficult. However, he benefits from his Egerton House Stables – next door to Martyn Meade's overflow yard – being on the outskirts of the quiet side of town, well away from Warren Hill. Elsworth does most of his work on the Cambridge Road Polytrack, saying: "I just take the two-year-olds up to Warren Hill for the experience when they're almost ready to run."

The yard is alongside the National Stud and the July Course, where Elsworth has a tremendous record with his 15 winners in the last four years returning punters a £39 profit to £1 level stakes. Given his proliferation of two-year-olds, it would be no surprise if many of the track's top-class juvenile races in the summer stayed pretty close to home.

The horses

Arabian Queen 3yo filly
Dubawi – Barshiba (Barathea)

We really fancied her when she won the Duchess of Cambridge Stakes at Newmarket last season and she didn't get anything like the credit she deserved. It was all about how she got first run, but the French filly [High Celebrity] had every chance to go past her and couldn't. She had won her maiden and run a really good race to be sixth in the Queen Mary before that as she was drawn on the wrong side and still beaten less than three lengths by Anthem Alexander and Tiggy Wiggy. After that she disappointed in the Sweet Solera, but it turned out she was in the early stages of an infection. Her nose streamed after the race and she had problems with her sinus, which happened again in the winter so we've had it fixed properly now. In the middle of all that came her run in the Cheveley Park and she is much better than that. She will start off over a mile and we're thinking of the 1,000 Guineas. On pedigree she ought to get further, although you couldn't be sure as she has so much speed.

Burning Thread 8yo gelding
Captain Rio – Desert Rose (Green Desert)

He's a decent sprinter who won last season for Tim Etherington off 90 and is now lower than that. I got him for £19,000 and I'd like to think I can turn him into a Stewards' Cup horse. He likes firm ground.

Cascades 3yo filly
Montjeu – Seattle Ribbon (Seattle Dancer)

She's out of a half-sister to Seattle Rhyme. She ran in four maidens last year and was never better than fifth, which was disappointing. I know she's better than that and I hope she will do better this year.

Dashing Star 5yo gelding
Teofilo – Dashiba (Dancing Blade)

He hasn't won since June 2013 but ran well in defeat on all seven runs last season. He has been so consistent but

ARABIAN QUEEN: Elsworth feels she deserved more credit for Newmarket win

because of that he doesn't get any leeway from the handicapper – last season he ran in big-field handicaps every time and was never out of the first five. We ran him over 2m on the all-weather in January when he was below his best, but the upside is that it might help with his handicap mark.

Highland Castle 7yo gelding
Halling – Reciprocal (Night Shift)

He could have been top-class, but he has had his problems. He missed 18 months with injury after his three-year-old season in 2011 and last year we felt he wasn't finishing his races off. Then we noticed he was making a noise on the gallops so we gave him a breathing operation and as things stand he seems a bit better now. He's also come down to his lowest ever handicap mark so hopefully he should be able to win again. I will also consider hurdling as he's a brilliant jumper.

Justice Day 4yo gelding
*Acclamation – Rock Exhibition
(Rock Of Gibraltar)*

He's just a pony but is a very good little sprinter. He was third in the Middle Park as a two-year-old and then last season he won good races at Haydock and Ascot as well as finishing second in a Group 3 at Newbury. He loves soft ground and wants to get his toe in, so because of that I might go to France with him – we did try it once last season but the ground was too bad even for him. He has a bit to find at the top level, but I hope he will raise his game again with another year on his back. He's best in a very strongly run 5f.

Justice Good 3yo colt
Acclamation – Qui Moi (Swain)

This is a seriously good horse who reeks of class. He won twice last season at Windsor as well as dead-heating at Newmarket and then he was fourth in the Coventry Stakes on his last run. We were going to run him in the July Stakes next, but just as I was about to declare him we found

JUSTICE DAY: smart little sprinter

he had a problem behind which we have dealt with. He is fine now and has done really well over the winter. We'll look at the Craven Stakes and the 2,000 Guineas for him as he's certainly good enough, but I just don't know if he will stay the mile. He's out of a Swain mare who won over 1m2f, but he's a quick horse and I can't remember his sire, Acclamation, getting a top-class miler.

Justice Well 3yo gelding
Halling – Porthcawl (Singspiel)

He won what turned out to be a strong maiden at Newmarket – the second and third both did well in much better races later in the season – but he ran only once more when fifth in the Chesham. He didn't like the firmish ground and came back with a bit of a problem as he wasn't right behind. I was never really happy with him after so we decided to have him gelded and wait for this year. He's probably a miler.

La Superba 3yo filly
Medicean – La Spezia (Danehill Dancer)

She was well beaten in two maidens in Ireland last season for Paul Hickey, but she ran well to be midfield the second time. She's been sent to me and she looks a nice filly. She could go for the fillies' maiden at the Greenham meeting in April.

Master The World 4yo gelding
Mastercraftsman – Zadalla (Zaha)

He's a nice horse. He came to me last season from Gerard Butler's yard after winning a Newmarket maiden and we even ran him in the 2,000 Guineas to start with. He didn't run to that level as he's a bit of a character and we tried him in a visor and cheekpieces, but he still won over a mile at York. We have had him gelded now which should help and he's definitely got a heritage handicap in him. He might even be one for the Cambridgeshire.

Melodious 3yo filly
Cape Cross – Gower Song (Singspiel)

We threw her in at the deep end for her debut last season in a big sales race at Newmarket, but she fell out of the stalls and was only eighth. She did much better next time when going close at Kempton and she could have won. She should be a sure thing for a maiden and she's another I might aim at the fillies' maiden at the Greenham meeting.

Merdon Castle 3yo colt
Acclamation – Siren's Gift (Cadeaux Genereux)

He's a good sprinter and should have beaten Kool Kompany at Windsor last season – we gave him too easy a lead and were beaten half a length when in hindsight we should have kicked on and made the running. He ran only once more last year in the Windsor Castle as he had a problem with one of his knees. He came back on the all-weather in January and ran really well at Lingfield considering he had been out for so long before winning at Chelmsford and finishing second at Lingfield again. He'll be aimed at the all-weather finals day, but long-term we see him as a good turf horse. I'd like to think he could be a Group horse.

Speculative Bid 4yo gelding
Excellent Art – Barzah (Darshaan)

We got him from Gerard Butler's yard last season and managed to win a maiden with him at Doncaster in May on heavy ground. He then came fifth at Newmarket on his handicap debut off 82, but after that he had his issues and didn't run again. He's fine now and has been gelded.

Yorkshire Dales 3yo gelding
Vale Of York – Rock Exhibition (Rock Of Gibraltar)

He's a half-brother to Justice Day and will be a good horse. He ran in a couple of maidens last season and showed some promise both times. He's been gelded since then.

*As I've said, I've got a big team of two-year-olds and some really nice ones. One of the proper sharp types is by Zebedee out of Chantilly Beauty and he might be a Royal Ascot horse. At the other end of the scale I've got a lovely Dylan Thomas colt out of Shanghai Girl who will be more of a three-year-old, although you never know – perhaps he'll end up in the Racing Post Trophy! I've got two nice Dream Ahead fillies – one of them is out of Celestial Dream, from the family of Lochsong, while the other one is out of Dorothy Dene and more of a stayer. Among the others are the half-sister to Arabian Queen by Fastnet Rock, an Acclamation colt out of Fashion Rocks, who is a Rock Of Gibraltar mare so makes him the same cross as Justice Day, and a New Approach colt out of Maziona, who is a sister to our St Leger runner-up The Geezer, called **The New Master**.*

RACING & **Est. 1909**
FOOTBALL **OUTLOOK**

Ante-post preview by Steffan Edwards

2,000 Guineas

WITH the bookies going 10-1 the field, the temptation is to look for value down the lists, but I actually think it's towards the top of the market that the prices are more attractive.

For example, double-figure odds about **Faydhan** could look a gift after he returns in one of the trials. A $500,000 yearling, his stable knew he was special before he made his debut as he was sent off at odds-on despite being up against the Charles Hills-trained Dutch Connection, who had already run with credit on his debut at Salisbury.

Faydhan hammered him by six lengths and, while he was sidelined by a leg injury for the rest of the campaign, Dutch Connection went on to advertise the form over and over again, winning his maiden easily and taking the Acomb before a fair third in the National Stakes.

John Gosden, who was so keen to play down expectations with Kingman at two, has described Faydhan as "exceptionally brilliant", which is quite a statement. But he also said he's fragile, which is what scares me from an ante-post perspective.

I don't think it would be a surprise if, like Kingman, he won the Greenham and went to Newmarket a lot shorter in the betting than he is now, but there's also the ques-tion of the mile (connections were consid-ering the Gimcrack after his maiden win), and a strongly run race might just find him out, as arguably it did with Kingman last year.

The next task is to try to figure out who will represent Ballydoyle in the race.

The likes of **War Envoy** and **Smuggler's Cove**, who are probably way down the pecking order, give Aidan O'Brien a good line to a number of the British-trained run-ners and he's sure to hold a strong hand.

I think we can dismiss **John F Kennedy**, as O'Brien's already intimated that he'll be going the Ballysax/Derrinstown route to the Derby, while on breeding **Sir Isaac Newton** also looks a Derby candidate.

Ol' Man River is a bit trickier as he didn't look short of pace last year and his dam won two Guineas, but he is by Montjeu and, for all his success at stud, Camelot is the only horse he has ever sired to win a Group 1 over a mile beyond their juvenile season in the northern hemisphere, and he only just scraped home from a bad field in a soft-ground, slow-time Guineas.

Gleneagles looks a natural candidate for the race. He ran plenty last year, win-ning the National Stakes and Prix Jean-Luc Lagardere (subsequently disqualified) on his final two starts. As he's a brother to Irish 1,000 Guineas winner Marvellous, a mile shouldn't be an issue, but he's an early January foal and I just wonder if we've already seen the best of him.

The one from the stable who interests me is **HIGHLAND REEL**. Before he won his maiden at Gowran Park by 12 lengths, only four other O'Brien-trained two-year-olds had won 7f-1m maidens by ten lengths or more this century.

Two of them went on to become dual Classic winners, namely Galileo and Alexandrova, while Battle Of Marengo, who went off second-favourite and finished fourth in his Derby, and Dante runner-up Freemantle were the other two.

There was substance as well as style to his maiden win as the third, Hall Of Fame, went on to beat John F Kennedy next time out and then ran respectably in Group company behind Gleneagles, while the fourth won his maiden in good style next time out.

It was a bit of a surprise to see the Vintage Stakes chosen as Highland Reel's next race as it's not really a race O'Brien has targeted in the past, but he won it easily, quickening away at the finish despite

not really having had the race run to suit, and he took a while to pull up afterwards.

He didn't run again, but all is well with the horse and at the beginning of this year O'Brien said that he has a lot of speed and comes to hand very easily, which can't be a bad thing when trying to ready one for the Guineas, and he nominated the Newmarket Classic and the St James's Palace Stakes as his targets, which suggests he sees him as a miler through and through.

Joseph O'Brien has been reported as describing him as an "absolute machine" and he looks the best of the Ballydoyle runners to me.

I can easily forgive **Ivawood** his defeat in the Middle Park on account of the soft ground, but he was a physically imposing juvenile and I fear others will have caught up with him over the winter.

He also has the stamina question to answer, as he's by the speedy Zebedee. The dam's side of his pedigree is more encouraging, but he was quite a free-going sort last year and I have my doubts about him getting home.

The champion two-year-old **Belardo**

HIGHLAND REEL: easily wins the Vintage Stakes at Goodwood last season

RICHARD PANKHURST: gives John Gosden strong back-up to Faydhan

Criterium International at Saint-Cloud late in the season, is another who might need deep ground to be seen at his best.

Even though he's now owned by Godolphin, **Richard Pankhurst**, who ran away with the Chesham, gives Gosden another bullet to fire.

He wasn't seen again after Royal Ascot (heat in a knee prevented him from running in the Champagne Stakes and the ground was against him in the Dewhurst), but his form was boosted on several fronts. Runner-up Toscanini went on to finish second in the National Stakes; the third, Dick Whittington, took the Phoenix Stakes; and the fourth, Nafaqa, won in Listed company and chased home Elm Park in the Royal Lodge. The Craven looks an ideal starting off point for Richard Pankhurst and he could easily be a serious runner.

Fannaan would be a major Guineas hope in most stables, but I get the impression he might just be Gosden's third string such is the strength in depth of the stable. He's won his two starts easily and could be very good, but with the Guineas in mind I don't like it that he's a May foal as you have to go back to 1992 and Rodrigo de Triano for a horse that young to have won the race.

Despite being bred to stay, **Charming Thought** will have the stamina question to answer and the record of Middle Park winners in the Guineas hasn't been good for years.

The Wow Signal was apparently sick after the Lagardere, so he can be forgiven that disappointing run. His previous defeat of **Hootenanny** in the Prix Morny reads well enough, but both were out early at two and don't really strike me as likely Guineas winners.

Parish Boy, already a winner over 1m1f at two, is likely to appreciate further than a mile this season, while Racing Post Trophy winner **Elm Park** looks another who will need middle distances to shine.

Zawraq is interesting. He defeated the well-regarded Sir Isaac Newton on his debut and Dermot Weld has a high opinion of him. The problem is that Weld just doesn't bring his horses over for the Guineas very often. Grey Swallow, who finished fourth

impressed in winning the Dewhurst, beating the progressive **Kodi Bear** by two lengths, but how reliable is that form?

The favourite **Estidhkaar**, who'd given him weight and a beating in the Champagne Stakes, ran poorly and it was later discovered that he'd sustained a hairline fracture in one of his hocks. I'd argue that the next two in the betting, Smuggler's Cove and **Maftool**, didn't run to their best in the soft ground, and there's also the question of whether the first-time hood sparked improvement from the winner which may not be repeated. Belardo is one I could only consider near the day if it looked like the ground was going to come up testing.

Vert De Grece, who bolted up in the

back in 2004, was his last runner in the race, so it's hard to take a position now. If it becomes clear that he plans to travel over then the hint should be taken.

Lope De Vega made quite an impression as a first-season sire last year, not only siring the champion two-year-old Belardo but also a number of maiden winners who fit into the 'could be anything' category, with Endless Drama and Flaming Spear, both owned by Qatar Racing, and Consort among the more interesting.

Endless Drama, trained by Ger Lyons, was an impressive winner on his debut, has plenty of size and scope and should do well from two to three.

Flaming Spear, who is in the hands of Kevin Ryan, won the York maiden his stable had won with The Grey Gatsby in 2013 before succumbng to an injury.

Consort, trained by Sir Michael Stoute, took a Newmarket maiden that's worked out really well, with stacks of winners coming out of the race.

Convey, another impressive Stoute-trained maiden winner, has a real miler's pedigree, being by Dansili out of a Mr Prospector mare. He quickened up smartly and took a while to pull up after winning on the Kempton Polytrack, but the opposition might not have been that strong so he

still has a bit to prove.

The same goes for the Richard Hannon-trained **Moheet**, who overcame greenness to run away with a Salisbury maiden on his debut, as that form hasn't worked out either, but he was one of the stars of the Craven breeze-ups, cost 800,000gns and it's clear that his trainer holds him in high regard, so it'll be interesting to see if he returns in a Guineas trial or heads down the Derby route, as his pedigree is inconclusive distance-wise.

When it comes to potential challengers from France, as usual it's the Prix Djebel that will be the guide, with all 11 runners this century taking in that particular trial beforehand.

The standout candidate at the moment is **Full Mast**, who won the Lagardere on the disqualification of Gleneagles. A keen-going sort, he should be suited by a strong pace on the Rowley Mile, and on breeding he should bounce off fast ground. However, he's another who's a May foal, so he's not for me.

The best of Andre Fabre's milers could be **Make Believe**, who's by Makfi and closely related to Grade 1 winner Dubawi Heights. He's 2-2 so far and could be interesting if he shows up at Maisons-Laffitte in the first week of April.

2,000 Guineas							Newmarket, 4 May
	Bet365	Betfred	Betway	Boyles	Coral	Hills	Lads	PPower
Gleneagles	10	7	10	8	10	8	8	6
Faydhan	10	10	9	9	10	10	8	10
Ol' Man River	10	10	11	10	8	8	10	10
Highland Reel	10	10	11	10	8	10	12	10
Ivawood	12	12	12	12	10	10	10	10
John F Kennedy	10	14	10	12	10	8	12	16
Belardo	14	16	16	12	12	12	14	14
Charming Thought	16	16	16	16	16	16	16	16
Richard Pankhurst	14	16	20	20	20	14	20	20
Convey	20	20	20	25	20	25	20	16
Fannaan	25	20	22	20	16	25	25	-
Estidhkaar	20	25	20	16	25	25	20	25
Zawraq	20	25	25	20	20	25	-	25
The Wow Signal	25	25	22	20	-	16	-	25

each-way 1/4 odds, 1-2-3

Others on application, prices correct at time of going to press

FOUND: may well turn up at Newmarket undercooked with a long year ahead

1,000 Guineas

N CONTRAST to the 2,000 Guineas, the fillies' version has a clear favourite, but prices around 3-1 about the Prix Marcel Boussac winner **Found** make no appeal whatsoever.

For starters, Aidan O'Brien has said that, while she'll be aimed at the Guineas first, she'll be better suited to the Oaks. That view is backed up by her pedigree as she's a sister to Magical Dream, who was at her best over 1m2f-1m4f at three, finishing placed in Group company.

It's also worth bearing in mind that Aidan O'Brien's two winners of this race (Virginia Waters and Homecoming Queen) were unheralded rather than high-profile two-year-olds and came into the reckoning for Newmarket only after winning the 1,000 Guineas Trial at Leopardstown.

As a Group 1 winner at two, I can't see Found having a run before the Guineas, and with a long season ahead there's a danger she'll turn up a little undercooked.

The same goes for stablemate **Words**, who wasn't seen again after winning a maiden in June that worked out particularly well. Like Found, she's probably more of an Oaks filly.

Together Forever, who won the Fillies' Mile, is less certain to be a middle-distance type as she's a half-sister to Lord Shanakill. It therefore wouldn't surprise me if she did best of these fillies at Newmarket, yet history suggests that not running in a trial might cost her.

The O'Brien dark horse is **Qualify**. She had plenty of racing at two, but O'Brien only learned how to ride her in her last two starts when she was switched from front-running to being held up for a late run. She won a Group 3 at the Curragh in a good time and would have been placed at the Breeders' Cup had she enjoyed anything approaching a clear run.

On paper she looks pretty exposed, but being ridden patiently in a strongly run mile on fast ground should suit her, and it will be interesting to see if she's the one from the yard who gets the chance to stake her claim in the trial at Leopardstown.

Tiggy Wiggy was the star two-year-old of last year, scooting up in the Super Sprint, then following up in the Lowther and Cheveley Park. Richard Hannon plans to campaign her with the Guineas in mind, but it really is hard to imagine such a speedy filly stretching out successfully to a mile. It can be done, as Attraction showed, but her victory was the exception.

I quite like the chances of one who finished behind her at Newmarket as **High Celebrity** didn't have much go her way in her two visits to Britain last year.

In the Duchess of Cambridge Stakes the ground came up unexpectedly soft, which was all against her, and she was too keen off a slow pace and couldn't catch Arabian Queen, who led throughout.

Then in the Cheveley Park, although the ground was in her favour, she again found herself in a race with no pace, didn't settle and faced an impossible task in trying to close down a high-class rival who had had an easy time of it in front.

In between, she'd looked very impressive in winning a Group 3 at Chantilly and

I think she's just the type to be suited by a strongly run fast-ground Guineas, being delivered late from off the pace. Her debut win came over 7f and, while her subsequent starts came over shorter, her pedigree suggests she has the potential to get a mile this year.

She looked a filly with plenty of scope last year, is just the type to improve from two to three, and her trainer Andre Fabre holds her in high regard.

Having said all that, Maxime Guyon reported she got unbalanced in the Cheveley Park, and while she wouldn't be the first to struggle with the undulations on her first visit, it appeared to put a little doubt in Fabre's mind about whether to return for the Guineas. I expect she will, as she's more likely to get fast ground and a good pace at Newmarket than at Longchamp, but I'd like confirmation she's coming over before backing her.

In the 16 years since the Rockfel Stakes was upgraded to a Group 2 it's produced five Guineas winners and five runners-up. It's also thrown up five Irish Guineas winners over that time, only one of whom was doubling up after taking the English version beforehand. It's therefore a race to take very seriously, and last year's winner

QUALIFY (right): the Aidan O'Brien dark horse having flourished in the autumn

LUCIDA: has been compared favourably to Finsceal Beo by trainer Jim Bolger

LUCIDA looks another potential Guineas winner to me.

Having stayed on really well at the end of the Moyglare when going down by a neck to **Cursory Glance**, who misses the Guineas through injury, she was sent off a short price to go one better in the Rockfel despite the stable being out of form at the time. There was a moment in the race when she looked in a spot of bother as she came off the bridle, just as she had done in the Moyglare, but once she hit the rising ground she kicked into gear and came home strongly, clocking a smart time in the process.

Afterwards, her trainer Jim Bolger was in two minds about bringing her back for the Fillies' Mile, and perhaps in hindsight he wishes he hadn't as the ground was too soft for her and it was a messy race tactically. I wouldn't read too much into that defeat, and on the plus side she's now a bigger price for the Guineas than she was after the Rockfel.

By Shamardal out of a Street Cry mare, she will be suited by a mile this year and Bolger has compared her favourably with his previous Guineas winner Finsceal Beo.

Fadhayyil, the Rockfel runner-up, is also worth considering. She was very green when winning her maiden at Salisbury and again showed signs of inexperience at Newmarket. After travelling well, she quickened smartly but then wandered about a bit in front and the winner came past her in the closing stages.

She has bags of scope for improvement and Barry Hills, who appears to rate her highly, suggested she'd go straight to the Guineas. While she looks like she'll probably stay, her pedigree puts doubts in my mind, because her sire has done better with sprinters than milers so far, the majority of her siblings' wins have come at up to 7f and her dam was a 5f sprinter. On balance, I think she'll be beaten for stamina.

Raydara quickened up well to beat Lucida in the Debutante Stakes and has the pedigree for the job, but Mick Halford rarely brings horses over to Britain. She does need fast ground, though, so that might persuade him to travel.

Anthem Alexander has a sprinting pedigree and is unlikely to take part according to her trainer Eddie Lynam, but the stable still has cosy May Hill winner **Agnes**

Stewart to rely on. She's likely to stay a bit further in time, but there was plenty to like about her win at Doncaster and her second in the Fillies' Mile and she holds sound claims. She's priced about right.

Malabar wasn't beaten far in the Moyglare and didn't get the clearest of runs in the Marcel Boussac. She doesn't have a huge amount to find and is bred to improve from two to three so shouldn't be completely dismissed.

Likely couldn't have been more impressive on her debut at Carlisle in May when slamming subsequent Group 2 winner Mattmu by five lengths over the minimum trip, but injury intervened and she wasn't seen again. Connections think a bit of her and, given the German stamina on the dam's side of her pedigree, there's hope there that she'll get a mile. It'll be interesting to see how she gets on if she returns, as has been suggested, in the Nell Gwyn.

Among other interesting unexposed sorts are David Wachman's **Queen Nefertiti**, who wasn't seen again after winning her maidens in June; **Lady Correspondent**, who should be fully effective over a mile and could also start in the Nell Gwyn according to John Gosden; and **Sympathy**, another who should relish the trip.

Having said all that, given that 31 of the last 33 Guineas winners had Group race form at two, these types are probably best passed over.

Beautiful Romance, **Al Naamah** and **Jack Naylor** are likely to be more effective over middle distances, while a mile might just stretch **Muraaqaba** and **Terror**.

There was a lot to like about the way **Irish Rookie** travelled through her races when scoring twice on the Rowley Mile last autumn, and her trainer Martyn Meade has said she's another likely to reappear in the Nell Gwyn with a view to running in the Guineas. She has to improve but it's not impossible to see her making the leap.

I'd expect the Boussac runner-up **Ervedya** to stay in France, but Criquette Head-Maarek is talking about bringing **Fontanelice** over. She was trained in Italy last year, winning each of her four starts including two Group 3s, and it will be interesting to see how she fares if, as expected, she returns in the Prix Imprudence.

Also bear in mind that the form of **Lady Eli**, the impressive Breeders' Cup Juvenile Fillies Turf winner, stacks up really well through the likes of **Sunset Glow**, **Osaila** and **Prize Exhibit**. There's no indication that Chad Brown intends bringing her over from the United States, but she would be a fascinating contender if making the trip.

1,000 Guineas

Newmarket, 5 May

	Bet365	Betfred	Betway	Boyles	Coral	Hills	Lads	PPower
Found	7-2	3	11-4	3	3	3	3	3
High Celebrity	12	10	10	10	8	10	8	12
Lucida	16	16	14	12	14	16	14	10
Together Forever	14	16	14	14	16	14	14	16
Agnes Stewart	20	20	20	20	20	16	20	20
Tiggy Wiggy	20	25	25	25	16	16	20	16
Malabar	25	25	20	16	20	20	20	25
Words	25	25	25	20	20	25	16	20
Fadhayyil	25	-	25	-	20	25	-	25
Queen Nefertiti	25	25	25	-	-	-	-	20
Qualify	-	-	22	-	-	25	-	-
Osaila	25	33	25	20	20	20	25	20
Sympathy	33	25	25	25	25	-	25	-
Lady Correspondent	33	-	25	-	20	25	-	33

each-way 1/4 odds, 1-2-3

Others on application, prices correct at time of going to press

Derby

AIDAN O'BRIEN has sent out the last three winners of the Derby so it makes sense to start with his runners when looking for this year's winner.

John F Kennedy is favourite and it's easy to see why as he won the same Group 3 race at Leopardstown that Australia won on his final start at two, and he's clearly bred to get the Derby trip, being a brother to Yorkshire Oaks winner Tapestry.

However, I'm not sure he's as far ahead of some of his stablemates as the prices would suggest this season, taking in the Ballysax and the Derrinstown, has not been the route taken by the yard's recent winners.

O'Brien has expressed reservations about whether **Ol' Man River** will get 1m4f and he might be right on that as his dam Finsceal Beo was at her best over a mile, although Montjeu usually imparts plenty of stamina. As I'm not sure his form amounts

to a great deal either, for all that O'Brien was effusive after his Beresford win, that stamina doubt is enough to put me off him.

Highland Reel has the potential to stay on paper, but he's shown plenty of pace so far in his career and it's clear from O'Brien's comments that he sees him as a miler. The same undoubtedly goes for **Gleneagles**, whose pedigree backs up that view.

Giovanni Canaletto was very green but still quickened up smartly to win his maiden, and it's easy to see this brother to Ruler Of The World improving in leaps and bounds over the winter.

He'd need supplementing if he were to run at Epsom, but that's no bar and it wouldn't be a surprise if he took a trip to Chester for a trial, just like his brother did, as it'll teach him plenty.

He makes the shortlist, but of even more interest is **SIR ISAAC NEWTON**, who will begin the season as a maiden but showed more than enough in defeat on his debut

GIOVANNI CANALETTO: big potential improver who has to be on the shortlist

SIR ISAAC NEWTON (left): beaten on his debut but lost nothing in defeat

in a late Leopardstown maiden to be of serious interest for the Derby.

The horse who beat him, **Zawraq**, was described by his trainer Dermot Weld as potentially high-class and a candidate for a Guineas, so it was no disgrace to be beaten by him for a bit of speed given the steady early gallop. O'Brien also hinted that his horse may just have been beaten by a fitter rival.

In any case, this brother to Oaks runner-up Secret Gesture, who cost a staggering 3,600,000gns, is clearly highly regarded and, in pulling seven lengths clear of the rest on his debut, he showed he's got the talent to be a contender at Epsom. A maiden should be a formality, and it'll be interesting to see which path they take to the Derby afterwards, but wherever he goes I expect him to be hard to beat.

Unfortunately challengers to Ballydoyle are thin on the ground, with **Elm Park** much the best of them.

Andrew Balding's charge kept improving last season and rounded off the year with wins in the Royal Lodge and Racing Post Trophy. He was impressive enough and is bred to improve for middle distances this year, but Aloft chased him home at Doncaster and I'd be surprised if he was in the top half-dozen of Derby candidates at Ballydoyle.

Criquette Head-Maarek is best known for her success with fillies, but she has a good bunch of three-year-old colts this year, including Group 1 winners Full Mast and Epicuris.

Full Mast will be a miler, but **Epicuris**, a winner of the Criterium de Saint-Cloud over 1m2f in heavy ground last autumn, is one for middle distances.

If his trainer, who has said it's her dream to win the Derby, decides to bring him over, he could be a big player at Epsom as he looks sure to stay 1m4f on pedigree and should also appreciate better ground, being by Rail Link out of an Observatory mare, but at the moment it looks like the Prix du Jockey-Club is the favoured target

Another potential contender from

MOHEET: an exciting colt but a doubtful stayer at Epsom

France is Andre Fabre's **Eternal**, who won his maiden in fine style at Saint-Cloud in November.

There were five races run over the mile distance that day and he clocked by far the fastest time of the lot, and being a half-brother to Amralah, who won over 1m4f at three, he should be fully effective over the Derby trip. Once again, though, connections may opt to stay in France.

Chemical Charge is unbeaten in two starts and ought to stay all right, but I'd rather see what he can do in a trial first, while **Parish Boy** should get the Derby trip but I don't think his form is strong enough.

Golden Horn and **Vert De Grece** don't look stayers on breeding, and neither does **Moheet**, despite being by High Chaparral, as there's plenty of speed on the dam's side of his pedigree. He does look exciting, though.

Ten furlongs is likely to be the limit for **Consort**, **Convey** and **Richard Pankhurst**, while **McCreery** is another who should be at his best over distances short of the Derby trip.

Christophermarlowe already has experience of Epsom, winning a four-runner conditions race there in the autumn, but I doubt he'll have the class to win there in June.

Derby

Epsom, 1 June

	Bet365	Betfred	Betway	Boyles	Coral	Hills	Lads	PPower
John F Kennedy	**6**	**6**	**6**	**6**	**6**	**6**	**6**	**6**
Ol' Man River	**8**	**8**	**8**	**8**	**8**	**8**	**8**	**8**
Highland Reel	11	10	**12**	10	10	10	**12**	**12**
Elm Park	**14**	12	**14**	12	**14**	**14**	**14**	12
Gleneagles	**14**	12	**14**	**14**	**14**	10	**14**	**14**
Epicuris	16	-	18	16	16	**20**	16	16
Giovanni Canaletto	**20**	**20**	18	14	**20**	**20**	**20**	16
Sir Isaac Newton	**20**	**20**	**20**	**20**	**20**	**20**	14	**20**
Jamaica	20	16	20	20	25	16	16	20
Zawraq	**25**	**25**	**25**	-	-	-	-	-
Christophermarlowe	20	25	25	20	25	25	**33**	**33**
Richard Pankhurst	25	25	25	**33**	-	**33**	25	-
Parish Boy	**33**	-	28	-	-	**33**	-	**33**
Consort	**33**	-	**33**	**33**	-	**33**	-	**33**

each-way 1/4 odds, 1-2-3

Others on application, prices correct at time of going to press

TAGHROODA: our man tipped her at 33-1 last year and has two at similar odds

Oaks

FOUND tops the Oaks market, which is only right as her chance is there for all to see. Her Marcel Boussac win was a top-class performance and she's only bred to do better over middle distances at three.

She's not much of a price, though, and the trend in recent years has been for the Oaks to be won by an unexposed sort rather than one with Group race form as a juvenile.

In the last eight years, six of the winners had done no more than run in maidens at two, five of them winning one, so if ever there was a market in which to take a chance on one or two at long odds it's the Oaks.

The first one I'm interested in is **GOODYEARFORROSES**, who was a shock 33-1 winner on her debut at Leicester, finishing strongly to deny a couple of well-fancied fillies from good yards.

The kneejerk reaction is to assume it was a fluke, but I'm not so sure. The time was 0.81sec faster than that clocked by Sir Michael Stoute's **Sympathy**, who looked impressive in the other division, and it was the quickest of the four races run over the course and distance that day. The runner-up, **Redstart**, representing Ralph Beckett, won easily on the all-weather next time out, while the third, **Star Of Seville**, trained by John Gosden, bolted up by six lengths at Doncaster on her next start and is now only 20-1 for the Oaks.

Trained by Rae Guest, who's had some smart fillies down the years, she's by Azamour out of a Galileo mare called Guilia, whom Guest also trained. Just like Goodyearforroses, she won her one start at two, and then at three she was a close second in the Fillies' Trial at Newbury before finishing fifth in the Oaks.

Stamina shouldn't be an issue given

LOAVES AND FISHES: could hardly have looked any better at Haydock

her pedigree, but the fact she was able to beat a couple of useful rivals over 7f at two shows she's not short of speed either. She might just have been underestimated.

Guest has also been lucky enough to have had **What Say You** transferred to his stable from Karl Burke's yard. She won a Newmarket maiden that's worked out well and didn't run badly in the Rockfel on her final start. Being a sister to Martin Chuzzlewit, who stayed at least 1m4f, she gives the stable a potential second string.

The second flyer I'm going to take is with **LOAVES AND FISHES**, who won her maiden at Haydock in September.

In contrast to the race won by Goodyearforroses, the form couldn't have worked out much worse and she clearly beat trees, but it was hard not to be taken by the way she travelled and quickened, and it's probably fair to say she could have won by treble the official margin had Adam Kirby wanted.

Her trainer Clive Cox was buzzing afterwards and, having trained her dam Miracle Seeker to win the Lingfield Oaks Trial, in which she beat subsequent Oaks winner Look Here into second, he was justifiably excited at the prospect of having another potentially smart filly on his hands.

Being by Oasis Dream, she wouldn't be sure to get the Oaks trip, but her dam did stay 1m6f so she should be fine.

A case can be made for Aidan O'Brien's Fillies' Mile winner **Together Forever** staying, but her speed won her that tactical Group 1 and she's a half-sister to Lord Shanakill, who just about got a mile, so she's worth opposing.

Stablemate **Words** is far more interesting after making a strong impression when winning on her debut at the Curragh in June. She beat subsequent Group 2 winner Raydara into second that day, and back in fourth was stablemate Qualify, who later won a Group 3.

A sister to Nevis, who won the Lingfield Derby Trial, she's bred to win the Oaks, but her absence from the track since that debut is worrying.

Another who went missing in the second half of the campaign was Jim

Bolger's **Pleascach**. He'd described her as his filly for the Classics when she won at Leopardstown in early July, but she didn't run again and that was also before Lucida came along.

The pick of the Godolphin fillies looks to be **Beautiful Romance**, who won a back-end Doncaster maiden by nine lengths. It's possible her margin of victory is a little misleading because the ground was riding pretty soft and hers was one of three races on the card won by six lengths or more, and she might have just handled it better than others. Even so, she was very impressive, and being by New Approach out of a 1m4f Group 3 winner, she should relish the Oaks trip.

Joseph O'Brien said **Easter** could be an Oaks filly after she won on her second start. She's a sister to a French 1m5f winner so ought to stay all right.

Perhaps the most interesting of the Ballydoyle fillies yet to race is **Truth**, who cost €1,000,000 and is closely related to Irish Oaks winner Chicquita. She could be one to look out for in an early-season maiden.

David Wachman has a couple of possibles in **Queen Nefertiti** and **Legatissimo**. The latter is probably the most interesting, being by Galileo out of a sister to Fame And Glory.

Banzari seemed to relish the soft ground when taking a Nottingham maiden in October. She's by Motivator so it wouldn't be a surprise if she needs give underfoot to show her best.

Cartier is another who might well appreciate some dig, being by Montjeu out of a Linamix mare.

Bargain buy **Jack Naylor** has ground to make up on Found on her Boussac form, but she promises to be suited by middle

LEGATISSIMO: by Galileo out of a sister to Fame And Glory so bred for Epsom

distances and might prove a stronger stayer than **Agnes Stewart**, who isn't short of toe. **Timba** also looks to have more speed than her dam, who won over 1m4f, while Martyn Meade has floated the idea of **Irish Rookie** heading to the Prix de Diane after the Guineas, which suggests he has doubts about her staying 1m4f.

Forte should stay given she's a sister to Oaks winner Talent, but she is a keen sort and that might find her out in the best company.

Crystal Zvezda is a half-sister to Crystal Capella and Hillstar, who have both won over 1m4f in Group company, and she could be Sir Michael Stoute's strongest candidate, although the maiden **Moonlight Sonata**, who's closely related to Western Hymn and should have won on her second start when collared on the line by the William Haggas-trained Toujours L'Amour, might also be in the mix.

There was plenty of schadenfreude about in some quarters when the Andre Fabre-trained **Al Naamah**, who's a sister to Oaks winner Was and cost a whopping 5,000,000gns as a yearling, was beaten handily by her pacemaker in a Group 3 at Chantilly in September. I don't believe she ran her race that day and it's worth remembering how good she looked on her debut when cosily beating a filly who went on to win a Listed race next time out. She could easily bounce back and would have to be respected if her connections decided to bring her over.

Recommended bets

2,000 Guineas
Highland Reel 2pts 12-1
(Ladbrokes)

1,000 Guineas
Lucida 2pts 16-1
(generally available)

Derby
Sir Isaac Newton 2pts 20-1
(generally available)

Oaks
Loaves And Fishes 1pt 40-1
(Betfred)

Goodyearforroses 1pt 50-1
(bet365, Betfred)

Oaks

Epsom, 31 May

	Bet365	Betfred	Betway	Boyles	Coral	Hills	Lads	PPower
Found	**5**	4	**5**	9-2	4	**5**	4	4
Together Forever	12	**16**	14	16	14	14	14	12
Words	**16**	**16**	**16**	**16**	**16**	14	**16**	**16**
Star Of Seville	16	**20**	18	-	12	16	**20**	16
Pleascach	**20**	**20**	18	16	**20**	-	**20**	**20**
Beautiful Romance	**20**	16	**20**	-	**20**	**20**	**20**	**20**
Agnes Stewart	20	20	22	16	**25**	-	-	**25**
Queen Nefertiti	20	20	22	20	20	-	**25**	**25**
Al Naamah	20	25	20	16	16	**33**	14	16
Jellicle Ball	22	**33**	20	-	20	25	-	25
Crystal Zvezda	**33**	**33**	-	-	25	25	**33**	-
Loaves And Fishes	**40**	**40**	-	-	25	33	25	-
Goodyearforroses	40	**50**	-	-	33	40	33	-

each-way 1/4 odds, 1-2-3

Others on application, prices correct at time of going to press

Est. 1909
RACING & FOOTBALL OUTLOOK

Richard Williams' horses to follow

AGGRESSION 3 br c
Marju – Radha (Bishop Of Cashel)
1-

Here's a colt who could go a long way in the sprinting division this season. He had only one start last year as he had a dirty lung and was sick, but he got to the track in December and caught the eye in a 5f maiden at Dundalk. He made a mess of things coming out of the stalls, but he got up close home to win by a neck and had quite a bit in hand. After the race his trainer said he had been concerned about his fitness, so it was an even more meritorious effort, and he was duly snapped up by Qatar Racing a few days later. He is unlikely to race beyond 6f.

Michael O'Callaghan, Curragh

AGNES STEWART 3 b f
Lawman – Anice Stellato (Dalakhani)
1212-

An easy winner of a 7f Fairyhouse maiden in July and second in a Group 3 that same month, Agnes Stewart went on to win the Group 2 May Hill Stakes at Doncaster in September. It was probably a sub-standard May Hill but she collected the prize in efficient style. Her last race was Newmarket's Fillies' Mile in which she was narrowly beaten by Together Forever, the soft ground not really helping. With her dam a 1m4f winner, she has the look of an Oaks contender.

Edward Lynam, Dunshaughlin

ANGEL VISION 3 b f
Oasis Dream – Islington (Sadler's Wells)
4-

Sir Michael Stoute often leaves something to work on with his two-year-old fillies and this one wasn't knocked about on her Salisbury debut in September when she came fourth. The fifth horse won at Newbury next time out and the winner, Fadhayyil, was runner-up in the Rockfel. I have always liked Ballymacoll Stud produce and this daughter of the great Islington (dual Yorkshire Oaks and Breeders' Cup winner) is another who can go places.

Sir Michael Stoute, Newmarket

31

ANTHEM ALEXANDER 3 ch f
Starspangledbanner – Lady Alexander (Night Shift)
61132-

The rivalry between this filly and Tiggy Wiggy was one of the features of last season and the score was 2-1 in the British filly's favour. Anthem Alexander held off her rival by a neck in the Queen Mary Stakes at Royal Ascot but was beaten into third and second by the Richard Hannon speedster in the Lowther Stakes and the Group 1 Cheveley Park. Eddie Lynam, the trainer of those top sprinters Sole Power and Slade Power, plans to keep his filly to sprint distances with Royal Ascot's new Group 1 for three-year-olds the big target.

Edward Lynam, Dunshaughlin

CAPPELLA SANSEVERO 3 b c
Showcasing – Madam President (Royal Applause)
11125314-

This colt was an early starter at two, racking up a hat-trick in small fields before coming over to Royal Ascot for the Coventry Stakes in which he finished second. He had perhaps done enough for the time being when a disappointing fifth soon after, but he returned to win a Group 3 either side of finishing third and fourth in the Group 1 Phoenix Stakes and Middle Park. That form shows he is a thoroughly likeable, consistent sort capable of holding his own in the best company. Expect to see him racing in Britain and Ireland and rewarding those who follow him.

Ger Lyons, Dunsany

CONNECTICUT 4 b c
New Approach – Craigmill (Slip Anchor)
311139-

Unraced at two, Connecticut won a couple of handicaps before being upped in grade for the Melrose Handicap at York over 1m6f. Luca Cumani often aims a good three-year-old at this race – it is one he has won twice since 2004 – but it was not to be this time as he came a close third to Vent De Force and it's possible he may not have seen out the trip. Though he was below his best next time at Newmarket, he's been handled with great patience by Cumani and, with only six runs under his belt, the best is yet to come.

Luca Cumani, Newmarket

CONSORT 3 gr c
Lope De Vega – Mundus Novus (Unbridled's Song)
1-

This colt won the 7f maiden at Newmarket on Rockfel Stakes day, making all the running and lengthening coming out of the Dip to win by two and three-quarter lengths. The runner-up, Hathal, didn't run again that season, but the third, Spanish Squeeze, is very highly regarded by Hugo Palmer and won next time out, as did the fourth. Consort looked a real bull in the paddock, deep-girthed and muscular. This 150,000gns yearling is a half-brother to three winners including Steer By The Stars and he should carry the Highclere colours to Group success.

Sir Michael Stoute, Newmarket

CONVEY 3 b c
Dansili - Insinuate (Mr Prospector)
1-

Convey was sent off 4-6 favourite for a 7f Kempton maiden in October on the strength of his homework and justified that confidence in style, winning by five lengths. He has a lot going for him including the right connections (Khalid Abdullah and Sir Michael Stoute) and some choice parents. Dansili was Europe's fifth leading sire of 2014 and responsible for 1,000 Guineas winner Miss France, while Insinuate has produced four winners. Convey is not entered in the Classics but could well be Group standard.

Sir Michael Stoute, Newmarket

EDGE OF SANITY 6 b h
Invincible Spirit – Saor Sinn (Galileo)
152281-

You wouldn't think it possible to improve a horse who had left Jim Bolger's yard but Brian Ellison seems to have done just that with Edge Of Sanity. The six-year-old switched yards midway through last year having failed to win in his last three handicaps, yet on his second run for Ellison he won the 2m handicap at York's Ebor meeting. Most big staying handicap are on this horse's radar and the Northumberland Plate, a race his trainer has admittedly would be very special to win given he was born in Newcastle on Plate day, is the chief target.

Brian Ellison, Malton

ELM PARK 3 b c
Phoenix Reach – Lady Brora (Dashing Blade)
31111-

It was a terrific effort by Elm Park to win two of last season's biggest juvenile races, the Royal Lodge Stakes and the Racing Post Trophy. The plan is to go for both the 2,000 Guineas and the Derby and, while Royal Lodge winners have had a lean time of it recently, Racing Post Trophy winners have done extremely well, notably Camelot, who won both Classics. Some have him down as a soft-ground horse but the going at Newmarket for the Royal Lodge was good to firm. Expect him to hold his own against the best.

Andrew Balding, Kingsclere

ENDLESS DRAMA 3 b c
Lope De Vega – Desert Drama (Green Desert)
1-

Endless Drama won a Naas maiden by five and a half lengths in October and it wasn't just one of those occasionally meaningless backend Irish maidens run in heavy autumn ground. The going was good to yielding, the time was respectable and he showed an eyecatching turn of foot when given the office. This is a big colt who was given lots of time to grow and has plenty of size and scope. He's another who was quickly snapped up by Qatar Racing and trainer Ger Lyons is eyeing up a Guineas trial as a starting point.

Ger Lyons, Dunsany

EPICURIS 3 b c
Rail Link – Argumentative (Observatory)
111-

This unbeaten French colt had caught the eye with his efficient Group 3 success at Longchamp in October and it was only natural that he should go off odds-on for the Group 1 Criterium de Saint-Cloud in November. This time he looked commanding as he galloped through the heavy ground, making all. The race has never thrown up an Epsom Derby winner since promoted to Group 1 status in 1987, but it has been won by Darshaan and Fame And Glory. Epicuris would certainly be a contender at Epsom or he could be a major player for the Prix du Jockey-Club.

Criquette Head-Maarek, Chantilly

FORGOTTEN RULES 5 b g
Nayef – Utterly Heaven (Danehill)
111-

Unraced at two and three, this gelding served notice of serious ability when winning a Punchestown bumper in April by 13 lengths. It's usually one of the most telling bumpers on the calendar and Forgotten Rules turned it into a procession. Dermot Weld decided to send him down the Flat route and he duly hacked up in a small race at Galway before landing the Group 2 Long Distance Cup at Ascot in October. The ground was heavy that day and he did well to overcome it. Weld has nominated the Ascot Gold Cup as this season's target and he is a worthy favourite.

Dermot Weld, Curragh

FOUND 3 b f
Galileo – Red Evie (Intikhab)
131-

Found beat 14 others on her Curragh debut over a mile and was then dropped back a furlong for the Group 1 Moyglare Stud Stakes, coming third to Cursory Glance and Lucida, beaten a neck and half a length. The latter went on to win the Group 2 Rockfel Stakes while Found herself went on to take the Prix Marcel Boussac in tremendous style by two and a half lengths on good ground. Even though it looks like we have have an above-average crop of three-year-old fillies, Found looks easily the best of the middle-distnace prospects and is a worthy Oaks favourite.

Aidan O'Brien, Tipperary

GM HOPKINS 4 b g
Dubawi – Varsity (Lomitas)
11143-

The world opened up for GM Hopkins the moment he passed the post first in the Silver Cambridgeshire, but it didn't quite play out that way because he never threatened in two subsequent races (mile handicaps at York and Nottingham) for which he was favourite. However, the ease with which he dominated at Newmarket suggests he is well worth persisting with this year. He was made Lincoln favourite as soon as the entries were made and it would be no surprise if he turned out to be considerably better than a handicapper.

John Gosden, Newmarket

INTRANSIVE 3 b c
Dansili – Imroz (Nureyev)
921-

Ninth to John F Kennedy on his debut at the Curragh over a mile, Intransive dropped down a furlong and stepped up seven places to finish runner-up in a Roscommon maiden in September. He looked a lot sharper three weeks later when he went to Gowran Park for a 16-runner maiden over a mile in which he made all and was pushed clear to prevail by two lengths. The runner-up was Aloft, who franked the form by going on to finish in the same spot in the Racing Post Trophy. This is a well-bred colt with a bright future.

Dermot Weld, Curragh

JACK NAYLOR 3 b f
Champs Elysees – Fashionable (Nashwan)
521113-

This filly achieved a mid-summer hat-trick before being outclassed by Found and Ervedya in the Prix Marcel Boussac. The three-timer began with a Roscommon maiden and moved on to a Group 3 at Leopardstown and a Listed race at the Curragh. In the Curragh race her Group 3 penalty meant she had to give 5lb to everything else, including the third horse, Together Forever, who went on to win her next three culminating in the Fillies' Mile. Jack Naylor looks like being a middle-distance Group filly.

Jessica Harrington, Moone

KINGSTON HILL 4 gr/ro c
Mastercraftsman – Audacieuse (Rainbow Quest)
82414-

The Racing Post Trophy winner, Derby second and St Leger hero is hardly an unexposed sort, but there is surely plenty to come from this likeable sort who has only raced eight times. It was perhaps his last effort, when fourth to Treve in the Arc, that caught the eye most. It came just three weeks after he had won the St Leger and he defied the worst draw and ground (officially good) that might not have suited given he had missed previous engagements when conditions were deemed to be too quick. He will be hard to beat on soft ground.

Roger Varian, Newmarket

LIGHTNING MOON 4 b c
Shamardal – Catch The Moon (Peintre Celebre)
111-

Unraced as a two-year-old, Lightning Moon won all three of his races last year. He took a Haydock handicap by six lengths and then had a four-month layoff before returning to Ascot for the Bengough Stakes. This time the winning distance was only a neck, but it was a very good effort considering he ran free early on. Plans to run at Champions Day were shelved after a setback, but he will be stepped up to that sort of level this year, starting in the Duke of York Stakes. His trainer is also convinced he will stay 7f.

Ed Walker, Newmarket

MY TWINKLE 3 b f
Sea The Stars – What A Picture (Peintre Celebre)
5-

This could be a nice filly for Christopher Tsui, the owner of My Twinkle's sire Sea The Stars. She is a half-sister to five winners including three with black type, most notably the 2011 Godolphin Mile runner-up Mufarrh, and she cost 230,000gns as a yearling. She ran only once last year in a mile maiden at Gowran Park and was fifth to Together Forever, never getting on terms once the pace quickened. However, she will have learned a lot from that and, given her pedigree, she surely has a lot more to offer.

John Oxx, Currabeg

OOTY HILL 3 gr c
Dubawi – Mussoorie (Linamix)
1-

Ooty Hill turned up at Newmarket in October with a bit of a reputation and was sent off 7-2 for a ten-runner 7f maiden full of horses from top yards. He travelled beautifully and wasn't fazed when leant on by a rival in the closing stages, coming home two and a quarter lengths clear. Roger Charlton confirmed that the win had come as no surprise after the race as he had been working so well at home, and he added that his best trip this year will be from 1m-1m2f. He's well bred, scopey and could be anything.

Roger Charlton, Marlborough

OL' MAN RIVER 3 b c
Montjeu – Finsceal Beo (Mr Greeley)
11-

This fellow made €2.85m as a yearling so it was no surprise that he won both his starts last year, most notably the influential Beresford Stakes over a mile at the Curragh when he dismissed five rivals with authority. The Beresford has been won by Sea The Stars and St Nicholas Abbey in the last ten years and Ol' Man River could be just as good. By Montjeu out of a mare who won three Guineas, his optimum distance could be 1m2f, but that's not to say he wouldn't have the speed for the 2,000 Guineas or the stamina for the Derby.

Aidan O'Brien, Tipperary

PARISH BOY 3 gr c
New Approach – Requesting (Rainbow Quest)
511-

The winner of the Eyrefield Stakes on his third start, here's a colt that Jim Bolger views as both a Guineas candidate and a middle-distance sort. The Eyrefield is a Listed race run over the testing trip of 1m1f, and Parish Boy missed the break but still beat Aidan O'Brien's Order Of St George with a bit in hand. The time was also good – the fastest recorded since the race moved to Leopardstown in 1995. While the Godolphin colt might fall just short in the Classics, he should at least be Group standard.

Jim Bolger, Coolcullen

PORTAGE 3 b c
Teofilo – Galley (Zamindar)
21-

Beaten a neck by Aidan O'Brien's East India on his debut at the Curragh in July, Portage returned there two months later to take a 21-runner maiden, also over 7f. This time he was impressive, lengthening his stride and asserting in the final furlong to win going away by a cosy half-length. He looked thoroughly at home on the good to firm ground, which suggests he might be well suited by travelling to Britain during the summer. Wherever he goes, though, he should be competing at Group level and could prove a feather in the cap for Godolphin.

Michael Halford, Doneany

RAYDARA 3 b/br f
Rock Of Gibraltar – Raydiya (Marju)
2141-

This Aga Khan filly came second to Words on her debut in one of the hottest fillies' maidens of the season at the Curragh on Irish Derby weekend. A routine success in a Leopardstown maiden came next and two subsequent runs in Group company underlined the fact that she was a work in progress as she finished fourth to Jack Naylor when ridden prominently yet then beat Lucida in the Group 2 Debutante Stakes under more patient tactics. She is a proven Group filly with a liking for fast ground.

Michael Halford, Doneany

RICHARD PANKHURST 3 ch c
Raven's Pass – Mainstay (Elmaamul)
41-

A bit green on his Newmarket debut, Richard Pankhurst was mentally and physically sharper when returning for the Chesham Stakes at Royal Ascot. Clearly the best horse in the race, he quickened up to put it to bed in a few strides. The two horses he beat, Toscanini and Dick Whittington, proved classy, the latter winning the Group 1 Phoenix Stakes. Injury put paid to the rest of the season, during which time he was bought by Godolphin. He remains with John Gosden, the man who bred him and trained his sire Raven's Pass.

John Gosden, Newmarket

SECRET PURSUIT 4 b f
Lawman – Secret Melody (Inchinor)
2112501-

This filly established herself at Listed level last year and has the scope to make her mark at Group level this year. Having won a Lingfield maiden and a Nottingham handicap, she went to Chester's May meeting for a 1m4f Listed race, finishing second. She ran two poor races after that so Marcus Tregoning gave her a break and brought her back for a winning return in the Listed Prix Solitude at Saint-Cloud in November. With a preference for soft ground, Secret Pursuit is worth siding with when those conditions prevail.

Marcus Tregoning, Whitsbury

TENDU 3 b f
Oasis Dream – Arabesque (Zafonic)
715-

Tendu broke the 6f juvenile course record at Kempton on her second start, storming away in the Khalid Abdullah colours. She was so impressive that connections even decided to supplement her for the Cheveley Park Stakes, but that proved a bridge too far as she could never get on terms with the likes of Tiggy Wiggy. Still, for such an inexperienced filly to finish fifth, beaten three and a half lengths, was no disgrace at all. A full sister to Gimcrack winner Showcasing, she is a sprinter through and through and should do well this year.

John Gosden, Newmarket

TERUNTUM STAR 3 ch c
Dutch Art – Seralia (Royal Academy)
212817-

There are few better trainers of sprinters than Kevin Ryan and this colt could be another off the production line. The way he landed a 6f nursery at Haydock in September marked him down as a speedster to follow and the third horse won next time out. The ground might have been too soft when he was well beaten after that. With Astaire and Hot Streak in the same stable, Teruntum Star won't be Ryan's best sprinter, but he starts the year on a very handy mark of just 93 and should be followed.

Kevin Ryan, Hambleton

ZAWRAQ 3 b c
Shamardal – Sundus (Sadler's Wells)
1-

This once-raced colt won what was probably one of the better Irish maidens of last season, a 7f contest at Leopardstown. He faced Ballydoyle's hugely expensive Derby hope Sir Isaac Newton and saw him off in determined fashion. The pair dominated the field of 11 to such an extent that Sir Isaac Newton was seven lengths clear of the third. Dermot Weld said afterwards that he had expected Zawraq to win, calling him "potentially high-class", and the Hamdan Al Maktoum colt will probably start off in a Guineas trial.

Dermot Weld, Curragh

Top ten horses

Connecticut	**Kingston Hill**
Convey	**Ol' Man River**
Forgotten Rules	**Portage**
Found	**Richard Pankhurst**
GM Hopkins	**Zawraq**

Est. 1909
RACING & FOOTBALL OUTLOOK

Pedigrees for punters

W E'RE about to see the first crops of the 2012 intake of new stallions hit the track, **write Katherine Fidler and Martin Stevens.**

The intake was relatively small compared to recent standards – just 19 joined the ranks, well below the 36 who retired to stud last year – but here are some who could warrant a betting interest early on.

Canford Cliffs
Tagula – Mrs Marsh (Marju)

At the time of his retirement, Canford Cliffs was described by Richard Hannon Snr as the best the had trained and punters can expect to see a fair few by the sire emerging from East Everleigh under the tutelage of Hannon's son.

A crack two-year-old himself – he was a runaway winner of the Coventry Stakes and beaten just half a length into third in the Prix Morny – Canford Cliffs put a slightly spluttering start to his three-year-old season behind him when landing the Irish 2,000 Guineas by three lengths.

That was to be the first of five straight Group 1 victories over a mile, the winning sequence halted only when Richard Hughes and his mount crossed swords with the unbeatable Frankel.

Retired to Coolmore Stud at five, the son of Tagula was awarded a high-class book of 184 mares, including 29 black-type winners. Among those mares were juvenile Listed winner Alexander Alliance, Breeders' Cup Juvenile and Santa Anita Oaks heroine Eliza – the dam of three two-year-old black-type performers – Queen Mary Stakes winner Gilded and Temple Stakes Stakes winner Look Busy, suggesting the

CANFORD CLIFFS: was sent 29 black-type winners

sire should be represented by a number of classy, but potentially precocious, first runners.

Dick Turpin
Arakan – Merrily (Sharrood)

Dick Turpin formed the second part of Richard Hannon Snr's crack miling duo of 2010 and 2011, beating Canford Cliffs when first in the Greenham Stakes and second in the 2,000 Guineas and filling the same place behind his stablemate in the St James's Palace Stakes before going on to win the Group 1 Prix Jean Prat and Premio Vittorio di Capua.

A son of Arakan, the sire of champion juvenile Toormore, he was relatively well-received at the sales, with 37 yearlings selling for a high of 70,000gns.

However, he will not be represented by as numerically strong a first crop as some of this year's freshman sires, having covered 86 mares in 2012 with 66 producing a foal.

Nevertheless, the signs they could prove precocious are promising, with 29

juveniles registered in training by early February – including three in the care of Richard Hannon.

One to watch could be the filly out of Molecomb Stakes winner Misty Eyed, in training with James Tate but unnamed at the time of writing.

Dream Ahead
Diktat – Land Of Dreams
(Cadeaux Genereux)

Dream Ahead was one of many top performers who were in the unfortunate position of being born in 2008 – the same year as Frankel. The winner of his first three starts at two, including the Prix Morny and Middle Park Stakes, Dream Ahead was comprehensively beaten into fifth in the Dewhurst Stakes behind the world-beater, filling the same position in the following season's St James's Palace Stakes.

However, a return to sprint trips revealed his true colours, and after helping Hayley Turner to a first Group 1 win in the July Cup, he added two more top-flight victories to his tally when landing the

DREAM AHEAD (right): a top-class sprinter who got a very smart book of mares

LILBOURNE LAD (right): could provide a few big-priced early winners

Haydock Sprint Cup and defeating the great Goldikova in the Prix de la Foret.

With such classy performances under his belt, Dream Ahead was rewarded an equally smart first book of mares, including the dams of Immortal Verse, Free Eagle and Havana Gold. Top sprint runners and producers also abound – Lady Alexander, the dam of Dandy Man and Anthem Alexander, Flanders, the dam of G Force, and Listed-winning juveniles Chinese Wall and Polly Perkins all made a visit to Ballylinch Stud in 2012.

The resulting 111 foals include Cry Of Joy and King Of Dreams, both of whom are in the care of their sire's trainer David Simcock and could be precocious types to look for.

Lilbourne Lad
Acclamation – Sogno Verde
(Green Desert)

Lilbourne Lad was typical of the tough and consistent juveniles for whom Richard Hannon Snr was famed, winning three of his eight starts including the Group 2 Railway Stakes, beaten just three-quarters of a length when second in the Middle Park and never finishing out of the first four.

Retired to stud at three, Lilbourne Lad proved a popular pick, covering a book of 131, from whom 93 foals were born. While the mares may not have been as strong as others mentioned here, winning producers are in no short supply, including Christmas Tart, the dam of Queen Mary Stakes runner-up Hoyam.

More notable, however, is the number of his offspring already named and/or registered in training early in the year, suggesting he should be well armed for an early campaign. Trainers preparing to send out Lilbourne Lad runners include Marco Botti, Robert Cowell, Richard Fahey, Charlie Hills and, of course, Richard Hannon.

Throw in the fact his sire Acclamation is himself a noted sire of two-year-olds, and this lesser-known name could provide a few bigger-priced winners.

41

Pour Moi
Montjeu – Gwynn (Darshaan)

Pour Moi was a progressive performer who broke his maiden late in the October of his two-year-old season and won the Derby at three, and he has a stout pedigree to boot, so expect his first runners to appear from late summer onwards and to flourish in the autumn.

Coolmore raced the son of stamina influence Montjeu and stand him at stud, so they will be aiming to help get him off to a good start. It could therefore pay to follow their colt out of 1m Group 3 winner Marjalina, who cost 210,000gns at the sales and is with Aidan O'Brien, and another colt out of 1m Listed winner Gipson Desert, bought for €170,000 and in Andre Fabre's care. Both are unnamed at the time of writing.

Pour Moi covered 148 mares – 55 of them black-type performers – in his first season, resulting in a crop of 95 to go to war with.

Another with an interesting pedigree is Kitty For Me, whose dam has produced six winners from six runners including the high-class filly Purr Along. Kitty For Me is with Purr Along's first trainer William Muir.

Zoffany
Dansili – Tyranny (Machiavellian)

There was a real buzz around the yearlings by Zoffany at last year's sales. No fewer than 96 horses from his first crop, conceived at a fee of €7,500, sold for an average of around £50,000. That suggests they look the part at least.

Zoffany has strength in numbers with 131 foals from his first crop but, as his lower fee indicates, he didn't receive the same depth in quality as some others. Around ten per cent of his first book of mares were black-type performers, whereas the figure for Pour Moi, for example, stands at 37 per cent.

He still has some choicely bred two-year-olds, including a half-sister to Coventry Stakes and Prix Morny winner The Wow Signal who cost £150,000 and is

with that colt's trainer John Quinn, and a half-brother to middle-distance Group 3 winner Forces Of Darkness in the care of Aidan O'Brien after being bought for 350,000gns.

As a two-year-old Zoffany broke his maiden over 6f in April and won the Phoenix Stakes over the same distance, so he should inject a certain amount of precocity into his stock.

However, he also developed into a high-class miler at three and also has stamina strains in his pedigree so not all his two-year-olds will necessarily be early birds.

A few others to look for . . .

Craven Stakes winner and Racing Post Trophy runner-up **Elusive Pimpernel** initially retired to the small Islanmore Stud, where he was primarily supported by his owner Cristina Patino, mirroring the successful launch of the owner's earlier sire Big Bad Bob. The son of Elusive Quality stands for just €1,000, so received a book lacking the strength and depth of some of his peers, but he nevertheless covered plenty of winning producers. His first crop numbers 55.

Group 1-winning juvenile **Roderic O'Connor**, another to be shown a clean pair of heels by the indomitable Frankel in the 2,000 Guineas, went on to land the Irish equivalent next time out – and as such was awarded a smart book of 135 mares in 2012. Counted among them are the dams of Breeders' Cup Juvenile winner Vale Of York and 2,000 Guineas fancy Ivawood, but expect his runners to become more prevalent towards the end of the season.

Poet's Voice is the best juvenile to date by the excellent Dubawi, so the debut of his first two-year-olds are eagerly anticipated. There was a near-frenzy at the yearling sales for his first stock, with 67 of 69 offered selling for an average of more than £100,000. A number of high-profile trainers will be sending out his stock, including Ed Dunlop, John Gosden, Sir Michael Stoute and his own trainer Saeed Bin Suroor.

BELARDO: finally reproduces his brilliant home form as he wins the Dewhurst

Newmarket by Aborigine

ROGER VARIAN really arrived on the big stage last season, landing his first Classic triumph with **Kingston Hill**, and his St Leger hero stays in training at four with the Prix de l'Arc De Triomphe as his big autumn objective.

From the time Kingston Hill rounded his juvenile campaign off with his scintillating Racing Post Trophy success, his sights were set on the Derby.

After a satisfactory run in the 2,000 Guineas, he did his connections proud at Epsom, finding only Australia too good for him. He then made no mistake in the St Leger, coming with a powerful late run to beat Romsdal by a length and a quarter.

It was then across to Paris for the Arc and, despite a dreadful draw, he ran a magnificent fourth to Treve.

Varian will find a suitable mid-season race for him to get him ready for the King George before putting him away for another attempt at Arc glory.

Varian also has some genuine 2015 Classic hopes with **Belardo** likely to go for the 2,000 Guineas on the Rowley Mile.

I had not often been more excited by a two-year-old's work before he made a winning debut at Yarmouth in the summer. The Lope De Vega colt also won a Listed race at Newbury before disappointing next time out. Varian reached for a hood when he stepped him up into Group 1 company in the Dewhurst and it helped him reproduce his brilliant home form in public.

I don't think he has been given enough credit for his great escape when he was boxed in at Bushes Hill before producing a blistering turn of foot to get out and beat Kodi Bear by two lengths.

Varian has a serious 2,000 Guineas

back-up in the shape of **Vert De Grece**, who made short work of his opponents in the Criterium de Saint-Cloud on his first start for the yard after arriving from Ireland. There is every chance that he will return to France for the Poule d'Essai des Poulains.

At one stage Varian was in with a great chance of bidding for a Newmarket Guineas double as his speedy filly **Cursory Glance** had earned herself a place at the head of the 1,000 Guineas market.

She achieved that position thanks to following up a winning Kempton debut by landing the Albany Stakes at Royal Ascot.

After finishing second to the flying Tiggy Wiggy in the Lowther Stakes, she battled home in the Group 1 Moyglare Stud Stakes at the Curragh.

Unfortunately she suffered an injury early this year, but Varian tells me it was only minor and he is optimistic about her chances of being ready for the Coronation Stakes at Royal Ascot. It is interesting that he also reckons she may get beyond a mile, giving him more options in the second part of the season.

WILLIAM HAGGAS regularly boasts a tremendous strike-rate and, though **Mutakayyef** has won only once from seven attempts, he could be the stable star.

Backward as a juvenile, he had just one run in 2013 before proving his mettle last year by winning a maiden on soft ground at Sandown. Though he did not add to that success, he was a half-length second to Berkshire in the Darley Stakes and third to Air Pilot in a Listed race on the Rowley Mile. The Sea The Stars colt will be a revelation, especially if he gets the faster ground that brings out the best in him.

Haggas always enjoys a tilt at the Lincoln and this year's contender is **Mange All**.

The Zamindar gelding won a maiden at

MUTAKAYYEF: finishes second behind Berkshire and will be adding to his tally

LIGHTNING MOON (right): just gets the better of Danzeno in a thriller at Ascot

Beverley in June and then added a decent Sandown handicap. However, it was his fourth to GM Hopkins in the Silver Cambridgeshire that most caught my eye as he won the race on the stands' rail.

The fact he gets beyond a mile will stand him in good stead in the hectic cavalry charge over the Doncaster mile on his way to the Royal Hunt Cup.

HUGO PALMER is one of a thriving pride of young lions on the heath at Newmarket. **Aktabantay's** Solario win at Sandown helped put Palmer on the map and the three-year-old should pick up more races, as should the tough handicapper **Short Squeeze**.

There could be a top-notcher lurking in the wings inthe shape of **Spanish Squeeze**. On his second and final outing he crushed Legend's Gate by a length and three-quarters at Kempton and his gallops indicate that he is a very exciting prospect.

ED WALKER is also an upwardly mobile young 'un as befits someone who rents a couple of yards from Lady Cecil at Warren Place!

The first part of 2014 was something of a struggle, but Walker's patience started paying dividends in the autumn, particularly with **Lightning Moon**.

The Sharmadal colt was unbeaten in his three starts, showing a remarkable amount of toe for a son of Peintre Celebre.

He was sidelined by injury after wins at Salisbury and Haydock, but Walker's belief in his ability was reflected by the fact he made a winning return in the autumn in the Group 3 Bengough Stakes at Ascot.

Walker has indicated that he will use the Duke of York as a launching pad to the July Cup and other Group 1 sprints.

Walker is also sweet on his three-year-old filly **Invisible Gold**, who got a maiden win under her saddle at Kempton and took advantage of a favourable handicap mark to land a hot York nursery.

Though she ran below-par in a valuable sales race at Newmarket, it will ensure she starts proceedings off a good mark and the plan is to take her forward into Listed territory.

CHARLIE FELLOWES scored with his first ever runner last year with Barbary, and though things went quiet for a while he finished with a flourish thanks to **Wet Sail**, who heads the team this year.

A win at Salisbury preceded a sound second to the brilliant Limato in a Listed race at Ripon before a bad draw and fast ground put paid to his bid for Breeders'

Cup Juvenile glory in Hootenanny's race at Santa Anita.

Now back on home shores, Wet Sail could find the new Three-Year-Old Sprint Series tailormade for him.

Stablemate **This Is The Day** won two of her final three starts and Fellowes believes she has a bit in hand of the handicapper. He talks of her in terms of a Listed filly.

Also stick with Fellowes's six-year-old **Accession**, who has the ability to justify a challenge for big sprints such as the Wokingham and Stewards' Cup.

CHRIS WALL goes into battle without his stalwart Premio Loco, now enjoying retirement at his regular jockey George Baker's base in Berkshire.

Though it will take a great deal to fill the void, the signs are that **Royal Altitude** is a burgeoning talent. This was clear from his easy 5l win from Eatsleepracerepeat at Wolverhampton. His early work would

ACCESSION: Charlie Fellowes' sprinter is up to races like the Wokingham and the Stewards' Cup

suggest the handicapper has let him in lightly.

Cloud Seven is another Wall three-year-old with talent. A slow maturer, he was second to a John Gosden hotpot on his third and final run and is ready to move up the ladder over 1m2f and beyong.

MARK TOMPKINS does not have as many horses as usual but he may have unearthed a money-spinner in **Humphrey Repton**, who is a handsome son of Virtual. He indicated there was more in the tank when staying on to be sixth to Captain Revelation over 6f at Pontefract. He will be a dark horse to follow having strengthened appreciably over the winter.

JAMES EUSTACE regularly comes up with good winners for us and his consistent handicapper **Sandy Cove** has more wins in his locker.

Less obvious is the lightly raced **Chief Spirit**, who has had just two runs but made my notebook on both occasions.

Like his sire, Norse Dancer, he is a fine, strong indivdual, and the way he rounded his season off with a third to Chemical Charge at Salisbury gave his connections something to dream about. He will use a maiden as a stepping stone to better things.

On the handicap front, stablemate **Ice Slice** is expected to add to her Newbury and Nottingham wins on the soft ground she relishes.

I must also put in a good word for the filly **Nufooth**, who is settling in well at Park Lodge Stables having come from Richard Hannon's yard.

CHARLIE McBRIDE soldiers on skilfully with his handful of horses and I recommend you keep an eye open for **Kawaii**. The Myboycharlie filly was 12th of 12 in a Newmarket maiden, but she will leave that form far behind in due course.

Hot off the Heath
Humphrey Repton
Lightning Moon
Mutakayyef

Ireland
by Jerry M

AUSTRALIA rescued what would otherwise have been a moderate season by *AIDAN O'BRIEN'S* extraordinary standards, but there seems to be a never-ending production line of blue-blooded Classic prospects at Ballydoyle and as ever there are a number of exciting youngsters to watch from Ballydoyle this year.

O'Brien hasn't had fewer Group 1 wins in Britain than last year's five since 2004, but Arc day in France showed that he has at least a couple of superstars in waiting.

Gleneagles was a victim of one of the Longchamp stewards' more curious decisions as he was demoted to third in the Prix Jean-Luc Lagardere having been first past the post, but his performance confirmed that he was a seriously classy juvenile as well as being tough and durable.

It says a lot about those qualities that, having already landed the National Stakes at the Curragh, he was still well enough after Longchamp that O'Brien also left him in the Dewhurst at the five-day stage before deciding Gleneagles could call it a day for the season.

Gleneagles is a full brother to Irish 1,000 Guineas winner Marvellous, who looked a non-stayer at Epsom, so although he's by Galileo he looks more like another Henry-thenavigator, a horse capable of being a major player in the 2,000 Guineas before taking in all the top mile races and perhaps stepping up to 1m2f later in the campaign.

The inside word at Ballydoyle was that their best juvenile last season was **Ol' Man River**, so it will be fascinating to see how he fares.

The second foal of crack miler Finsceal Beo, he won twice over that trip last season without really coming out of first gear, including when strolling home in the Beresford Stakes.

He may start in the 2,000 Guineas, but

whatever happens it would be no surprise to see him head to Epsom as O'Brien's main hope for a fourth successive Derby win.

John F Kennedy is likely to head to the Ballysax and the Derrinstown en route to Epsom while Highland Reel is expected to stick to a mile, and both also have the potential for further progress.

However, bookmakers have them pretty much where they want them and two dark horses among O'Brien's team of three-year-olds are **Giovanni Canaletto** and **Sir Isaac Newton**.

The Ballydoyle boys tend to know what they have at home and it nearly always pays to keep faith when one of their juveniles is beaten at odds-on first time out, as happened with this pair.

Giovanni Canaletto has already gone on to win as he landed his second start at Leopardstown, powering six and a half lengths clear despite looking green when asked to pick up. O'Brien had been considering the Racing Post Trophy for him even after his debut defeat, which bodes very well, and as a full brother to Ruler Of The World – and half-brother to Duke Of Marmalde – he could be a leading middle-distance performer, although he would need supplementing for Epsom.

Sir Isaac Newton ran into another fine prospect, Zawraq, when second on his only start last year and there was no shame in that as he's bred for longer distances than the winner so wasn't suited by a steady gallop and still pulled seven lengths clear of the rest. He cost €3.6m as a yearling and it would be no surprise if he proved a Group 1 colt this year.

Found was O'Brien's other star performer at Longchamp on Arc day as she ran away with the Prix Marcel Boussac and she certainly sets the standard among the juvenile fillies.

FREE EAGLE: returned in stunning fashion on Irish Champions Weekend

Out of dual Group 1 winner Red Evie, the Galileo filly had been only third in the Moyglare, but she ran green when asked to quicken that day. That's understandable as it was only her second start and the extra furlong of the Boussac also helped – the trip had also been a mile when she made her winning debut.

She just might be good enough to land a blow in the 1,000 Guineas, but it's over middle distances that her future lies and as such she looks a strong favourite for the Oaks. It also bodes well that stablemate **Together Forever** won the Fillies' Mile as Found had comfortably beaten her first time out and is certainly the better filly.

Words is the dark horse among O'Brien's fillies. She didn't run again after winning her maiden at the Curragh in June, but that victory came in arguably the strongest maiden run all year as she had three black-type fillies behind her.

She's out of O'Brien's Irish Oaks winner Moonstone, both of whose previous progeny won at Listed level, and she should take high rank over middle distances.

O'Brien doesn't quite have his usual strength with older horses – **Adelaide**, returning to Ireland after his latest stint in Australia, and exciting sprinter **Due Diligence** are the exceptions – but that is where *DERMOT WELD* steps in.

Weld had a remarkable 2014, with his best tally of winners in Ireland for 20 years plus big winners at Royal Ascot and British Champions Day, and three hugely exciting older horses lead his team.

Free Eagle will have all the top middle-distance races on his agenda and it will take a very good horse to beat him.

Regarded as a Derby horse even before he made his debut as a two-year-old, he missed the Classics due to injury but returned in the spring to win by 7l at Leopardstown and finish a close third in the Champion Stakes.

He should be able to leave that form well behind in time – he's a laid-back horse who is hard to get fit at home so had plenty to work on first time out and then found the ground too soft at Ascot – which is a frightening thought for his rivals.

Weld's top-class mare Pale Mimosa was sold in December, but he had already unearthed an even better stayer in **Forgotten Rules**.

It was an extraordinary achievement for him to win the Long Distance Cup at Ascot after only two previous runs, one of those coming in a bumper. That lack of experience told in the way he hung across his rivals and caused carnage in making his winning move, but he still put the race to bed well and was clearly the best horse.

Bookmakers soon made him favourite to win the Supreme Novices' Hurdle, but Weld always had a Flat campaign in mind as he thinks he can win some top staying

BROOCH (noseband): another potential Group 1 older horse for Dermot Weld

prizes and he has every chance of emulating his 2010 Ascot Gold Cup winner Rite Of Passage.

Weld also has Group 1 ambitions for unbeaten filly **Brooch**.

The four-year-old has been handled with typical patience, not making her debut until last July, but once hitting the track she progressed rapidly through the ranks and won a strong Group 3 at Gowran Park on her third and final start.

She should prove best at around 1m2f, which brings races like the Pretty Polly and Nassau into the equation, but it's worth bearing in mind that she only just got away with good to firm ground at Gowran and would prefer it softer.

Weld could have a smart three-year-old in **Zawraq**, who claimed what is likely to prove a major scalp in Sir Isaac Newton when winning his maiden at Leopardstown over 7f. He will start in a Guineas trial and could well get further, being by a Sadler's Wells mare who won over 1m2f and has produced two other 1m2f winners.

JIM BOLGER enjoyed great success for Godolphin with Dawn Approach a couple of years ago and that has been rewarded with Sheikh Mohammed's operation increasing their interest in the Bolger yard,

most notably with a couple of interesting three-year-olds.

Lucida flopped on soft ground in the Fillies' Mile, but she had already proved herself on the Rowley Mile when landing the Rockfel Stakes and will head to the 1,000 Guineas with solid place prospects provided the ground is fairly quick.

Parish Boy won twice last year, including a Listed race over 1m1f. Bolger intends to start him off over a mile, but there's a lot of stamina in his pedigree – two half-sisters won over at least 2m – and it's surely over middle distances that he will prove best.

Bolger has a habit of throwing his best horses in at the deep end and that was the case with **Pleascach** when she finished fourth on her debut in a competitive Group 3 at the Curragh. Comfortably off the mark in a maiden in her only subsequent start, she is bred to thrive over middle distances (her dam won over 1m2f) and looks a good prospect.

EDDIE LYNAM enjoyed a sensational season thanks to the exploits of his star sprinters Slade Power and Sole Power, who swept all before them in the Group 1 sprints in Britain.

Sole Power is back for more and

Lynam has another budding speedster in **Anthem Alexander**, who won last year's Queen Mary before finding only Tiggy Wiggy too good at York and Newmarket. She will stick to sprinting and has the new Group 1 sprint for three-year-olds at Royal Ascot as her aim.

Lynam can also train middle-distance performers and he gets the chance to prove the point with **Agnes Stewart**.

The Lawman filly showed a real turn of foot to win the May Hill at Doncaster and it was just soft ground that probably blunted her speed in the Fillies' Mile.

Although she could return to Newmarket for the 1,000 Guineas, she is out of a Dalakhani mare who won over 1m4f so expect her to get better and better as she steps up in trip.

GER LYONS had a couple of speedy two-year-olds in his team last year and there could be more to come from **Ainippe** and **Cappella Sansevero** in decent sprints, but **Endless Drama** is the really exciting prospect in the Lyons team.

He was seen only once last year but made a big impression, winning a Naas maiden in October by five and a half lengths. It looked a decent maiden and the runner-up was in turn well clear of the rest.

Endless Drama looks to have all the size and scope needed to make a serious three-year-old and Lyons feels the same, pointing him towards a Guineas trial early in the year.

MICK HALFORD has waited a long time for another Group 1 horse to come along after he lost his Racing Post Trophy winner Casamento to Godolphin in 2010 and he might just have found one in **Raydara**.

The Aga Khan's Rock Of Gibraltar filly, whose half-sister Rayda rattled off a four-timer at around 1m4f last summer, could perform similar feats over middle distances at a higher level having won the Debutante Stakes on her final start last season.

Hold-up tactics worked a treat that day after she had been ridden too forcefully before that, but ground might well be important as Halford wasn't keen on subjecting her to anything softer later in the year – all four of her runs were on good to firm.

Invincible Irish
Gleneagles
Giovanni Canaletto
Free Eagle

ENDLESS DRAMA: has got Ger Lyons dreaming of Classic glory this year

Berkshire by Downsman

ONE of the major differences between training in Newmarket and the Wessex Downs is the presence in our region of a healthy number of yards with their own private training facilities.

Steeped in history, the likes of Beckhampton and Manton near Marlborough, Kingston Warren at Lambourn and Park House Stables at Kingsclere bring a sense of tradition and a dash of colour to the Flat racing scene without living in the past or surviving on past glories.

All are doing well in these fast-changing times, primarily because their proprietors have managed to keep up with the best the training centres can offer in the way of facilities, and one of the most upwardly mobile in 2014 was *ANDREW BALDING*.

Balding has enjoyed success ever since he took over from his father Ian in 2003, including Classic success, but last season was a record-breaker for the 42-year-old

trainer, with over 100 winners and nearly £2 million in prize-money.

The undoubted star of the show was the two-year-old **Elm Park**, whose breeding is Balding to the very core. By the stable's star middle-distance performer Phoenix Reach, he is out of a mare trained by Andrew who was sired by Ian's National and Dewhurst Stakes winner Dashing Blade.

Not surprisingly, he was bred at the family's Kingsclere Stud, and for the first three outings of his two-year-old career he was owned by the Kingsclere Racing Club, run by Andrew's sister Clare, evoking memories of the great Mill Reef when he was an easy winner of a Listed event at Salisbury in the 1971 Derby winner's famous black and yellow cross colours.

The manner of that win prompted his big-money purchase by Qatar Racing, in whose colours he won the Royal Lodge and become the first horse for 32 years to follow up in the Group 1 Racing Post Tro-

NABATEAN: one of a raft of Andrew Balding horses to note for this campaign

phy. He displayed a high-class turn of foot to win both races and gave the impression he was improving fast, and the signs are that he has continued to progress during the winter

Balding has the 2,000 Guineas in mind, and the fact he has won on all types of surfaces suggests he will be a live player, but the mile may just be a bit sharp and the Derby could be his best shot at a Classic.

Master Apprentice was another Park House two-year-old to try his luck at the highest level, but his trip to Saint-Cloud at the backend was disappointing. He is much better than that and looks worth following in 2015.

Make It Up won two of his first three starts, earning a tilt at the Group 3 Somerville Tattersall Stakes, but he withered away after making much of the running to finish well down the field. He should be stronger this season and should make up into a smart three-year-old.

Cosmic Ray is another son of Phoenix Reach and can build on his low starting point.

Two maidens who shouldn't be long in winning are **High Admiral**, who caught the eye on his only start at Kempton, and **Equitanus**, who started favourite on his debut – normally an encouraging sign for a Balding juvenile – and was placed on his only subsequent outing at Salisbury.

Balding has a great ability to improve older horses and special mention must be made of **Here Comes When**, who ended the campaign with a brilliant win in the Group 2 Challenge Stakes at Newmarket. A Group 1 success cannot be ruled out this term and he should be most effective when there is some cut in the ground.

Secret Hint is a lightly raced four-year-old capable of climbing higher after her excellent win over 6f at Doncaster on her final start. She starts the season with a workable rating of 88, but the main object of the exercise will probably be to grab some black type.

Spectator won over 1m6f at Doncaster on his final start of the campaign, showing he has stamina in abundance on the soft ground, and there will be plenty of opportunities for him in good staying handicaps.

MUHAARAR (right): the Gimcrack winner looks set for a Guineas trial

Similar races will be on the agenda for the unexposed **Nabatean**, while **Montaly** and **Royal Warranty** are two others to note from the yard.

CHARLIE HILLS enjoyed another successful season and, while his better three-year-olds appear to have something to find at the top level, it would be no surprise if they made the step forward.

Commemorative is a favourite of mine and followed a good win at Doncaster with an all-the-way success in the Autumn Stakes at Newmarket before he was over the top for his Breeders' Cup challenge. He's powerfully made and should make up into a classy three-year-old.

Strath Burn suffered from foot problems throughout the second half of last season and is better than he showed. The new three-year-old sprint at Royal Ascot could be a target.

A Guineas trial is a likely option for **Muhaarar,** who came out best in a tough duel to win the Gimcrack but was not quite at his best in the Middle Park when he hung throughout and did not fire as his work suggested he would. Expect better in 2015.

Hills also says he is very happy with his Acomb Stakes winner **Dutch Connection**, who should find some good opportunities this year.

Heatstroke finished last when Dutch Connection won a good maiden at Goodwood, but he improved significantly to win a maiden at Kempton on his only other start. There could be mileage in his mark of 87, especially as the Kempton fifth is now rated 98.

Salt Island created a very good impression when hosing up on his debut at Windsor, but he was troubled with dirty scopes for much of the rest of the season and is sure to make up for lost time.

Pharmaceutical was a big positive when he made a winning debut on the sand at Lingfield in the depths of winter and he is expected to do very well when the turf season moves into gear.

Mention should also be made of another debut winner, **Aces**. His close third in the Group 2 Champagne Stakes at Doncaster was a cracking effort for such an inexperienced horse.

Dancetrack and **Dark Profit** were weak two-year-olds who look much stronger now, with the latter particularly well handicapped.

Hills has a couple of nice unraced three-year-olds and is really looking forward to getting **Hakam** into action. A son of War Front, he was troubled by a knee problem among other things last season, but those troubles are hopefully behind him.

Ledbury also had one or two frustrating hold-ups last year. He carries the colours of Qatar Racing and should have no problem winning his maiden.

Unlike 2013, the Faringdon Place colts were much stronger than the fillies last season, but there were still a few names from the distaff side to be mentioned.

Pride of place goes to **Atab**, who won only a minor maiden at Leicester but did it in authoritative fashion from the front and quickened up nicely. Much more is expected during her second season.

Nawaasy saw action only once, finishing third in what looked an ordinary affair, but she was green and looks likely to improve substantially.

Kodiva was a shade disappointing in not losing her maiden tag, but she finished third at Listed level on her final start and gives the impression she will be a better three-year-old.

Two very smart females head up the list of Hills-trained older horses with **Just The Judge** and **Kiyoshi** back for another season.

However, perhaps the most interesting of the older brigade is **Cable Bay**, a high-class two-year-old who was dogged by problems last season.

He finally showed something of his best when second in the Group 2 Challenge Stakes on his final start and connections have been delighted with him during the winter. He has been kept on the move throughout and the niggling injuries seem to be behind him.

Al Kazeem spearheads *ROGER CHARLTON'S* assault on 2015 and the Beckhampton trainer is to be congratulated on his training of the 2013 Eclipse winner after he returned to training in the wake of a disappointing time at stud.

He will pay his way again, as will the progressive miler **Captain Cat**.

Among Charlton's three-year-olds, the well-bred **Ooty Hill** is top of my list after showing an emphatic burst of speed to win his only start at Newmarket. He has progressed through the winter and should progress as the season goes on.

The same comments apply to Thistle Bird's half-brother **McCreery**, who won his only start last year at Newbury and also created a very favourable impression.

Skate is a half-brother to class sprinter Mince among others and he was consistent as a two-year-old, finishing off with a good win in a decent event at Haydock.

Few three-year-olds can be better bred than **Accra Beach**, who is a half-brother to Group 1 performers Cityscape and Bated Breath. He has something to prove after being beaten at 1-4 on his second and final start, but he remains worth following.

Acolyte's final run at York was all wrong and he looks on a nice mark, as does **Judicial**, who won all three of his starts last year and looks ideal for some of those valuable 6f three-year-old handicaps.

CABLE BAY (left): dogged by problems last season but should flourish now

Bold and **Scooner** are two more Juddmonte-bred maidens to look out for, while **Libbard**, a half-sister to Dark Leopard, is a scopey filly who should stay well.

Finally we come back to Lambourn and *CLIVE COX*, who gets better with every passing season and has a first-rate prospect for the 2,000 Guineas.

Second on his debut at Newbury in May, **Kodi Bear** then won two races either side of a very unlucky effort in the Coventry at Royal Ascot and ended the season with a second to Belardo in the Dewhurst.

This may leave him a little short of Elm Park in terms of achievement, but he has done very well physically and the signs have been promising since he started cantering towards the end of January.

Louis De Palma is more speedily bred than Kodi Bear and he could have the new Group 1 sprint for three-year-olds on his agenda.

He has not raced since chasing home the high-class Ivawood in the Richmond at Goodwood, but he has progressed very well during the darker months and his trainer knows exactly what it takes to produce Group 1-winning sprinters.

Loaves And Fishes justified plenty of stable confidence when he won his maiden over a mile at Haydock in September. As he's by Oasis Dream out of Cox's classy middle-distance mare Miracle Seeker, it will be interesting to see what his best trip is, but you can bet his trainer will get it right. He is another exciting prospect.

Shalimah disappointed in the mud on his final start but is better than that performances suggests and his rating of 81 looks a sound launch point, while **Ice Lord** is a maiden to note following a very good debut effort at Doncaster.

Of the fillies, **Rosalie Bonheur** is the pick. She won each of her three outings as a two-year-old but none by very far, which makes her very difficult to assess. What we do know, however, is that she is tough and genuine.

The North by Borderer

NORTHERN trainers enjoyed triple Group 1 success last year and local followers will be pleased that sporting connections are keeping their charges in training.

KEVIN RYAN'S **The Grey Gatsby** was the region's star and was named the joint third-best horse in the world recently, a ranking he earned with wins in the Prix du Jockey-Club and the Irish Champion Stakes.

Connections swerved end-of-season targets when the ground became too testing, but he should take plenty of beating in the prestigious middle-distance races this year.

The future looks bright at Hambleton, with several young prospects coming through, and **Flaming Spear** is one to note.

He raced just once last season as he suffered a hairline fracture after his debut, but he had already made a good impression when striking at York in July, a race was also used by Ryan to introduce The Grey Gatsby, and this horse could be similarly talented.

Sir Domino is another maiden winner to keep on the right side of. He finished second at Redcar in October and had little trouble going one better ten days later, making all in a 6f maiden at Leicester and easing home two lengths clear.

The French-bred colt is related to some decent performers and should make his mark at a higher level, probably over 7f-1m, although he clearly doesn't lack pace.

Weld Al Emarat has been a slow learner, but he started to repay his connections' faith when making a belated debut at Southwell in December. The son of

THE GREY GATSBY: gets up to beat Australia in the Irish Champion Stakes

BROWN PANTHER: scoots home in the Irish Leger for Tom Dascombe

Dubawi was clueless in the early stages but he picked off rivals when the penny dropped and won despite showing more signs of inexperience on the run-in.

He has a long way to go before justifying a Derby entry, but at this stage he has endless potential and there should be plenty more races in him when he reappears on turf in the new season.

DAVID O'MEARA is the rising star of the region thanks to his remarkable success with purchases from other yards, one of which saw him break through at the top level last year as **G Force** won the Haydock Sprint Cup.

The four-year-old left Richard Hannon after defeat in his sole juvenile outing but made giant strides for his new yard, with his emphatic victory at Haydock the clear highlight. Nothing went to plan at Ascot on his final outing but he is proven at the highest level now and will be a leading contender in all the top sprints.

That Is The Spirit came up a little short when his sights were raised in the second half of 2014, but he won his first three starts and looks the sort who can improve with another winter under his belt. He seems ideally suited by 7f and there are

nice prizes in him over intermediate trips.

TOM DASCOMBE was responsible for the region's other Group 1 success last term as **Brown Panther** finally nailed a big one, the apple of Michael Owen's eye making the most of a canny ride from Richard Kingscote to land the Irish St Leger by more than six lengths.

Connections are now keen to add a 1m4f Group 1 and he will probably have an international campaign, but he will deserve serious respect when appearing on these shores and is a former winner of the Goodwood Cup.

Dascombe will be delighted if any of his youngsters get anywhere near Brown Panther's exploits but there are some exciting prospects at Manor House Stables, including **Seve**.

The son of Exceed And Excel showed plenty of speed when winning his debut at Chester in June, getting away from the stalls quickly and finding plenty when challenged. Half-brother Ballesteros was a top-class sprinter at the peak of his powers and this one has clearly inherited plenty of that ability.

Archie also won his only run last summer. He has always been highly regarded

JUMEIRAH GLORY (left): winning at Ascot as he benefited from being gelded

at home and showed why when taking his debut at Haydock in June.

The runner-up Medrano ended 2015 with an official rating above 100 and fellow horse-to-follow Freight Train was down the field, so that form has a solid look to it. He stayed well to win that 7f heat but his pedigree suggests he wouldn't be guaranteed to stay much further.

MARK JOHNSTON again broke the 200-winner mark last year. His connection with Godolphin means he will lose a few of the nicer young ones, and he also suffered a blow when Alex My Boy was sold to Germany, but he owns **Sur Empire** and should be able to find a race or two for her.

She is a half-sister to three winners and made an encouraging debut at Lingfield in October, chasing home two more experienced rivals and only losing second in the dying strides. She was found to be lame after that effort and connections will be hoping she can recover to fulfil her undoubted potential.

Freight Train is another who had his issues last year and wasn't seen after June, but the son of Manduro won easily at Doncaster on that occasion, justifying the market confidence shown both that day and on his debut 16 days earlier.

His dam Sigonella has produced several winners, including a couple who recorded black type in France, and he may be the sort who can run up a sequence with the bare form of his two efforts suggesting the handicapper can't be too harsh.

The other northern big gun is *RICHARD FAHEY*, who had perhaps his most successful season in 2014.

The winners are guaranteed to flow again, with **Grandad's World** one who is sure to contribute.

The son of Kodiac easily justified favouritism at Pontefract in August and probably ran about as well as could be expected in a valuable sales race in his only subsequent start, finishing on the heels of 102-rated Lexington Times in ninth despite being the least experienced runner in the field. He is a big horse and should have plenty more to offer as he matures.

Zuhoor Baynoona found the likes of Tiggy Wiggy too hot to handle in the Cheveley Park but showed plenty of ability at Musselburgh on her final start, blasting four lengths clear of her rivals in what had looked a tight little conditions race. There is enough stamina in her pedigree to think that an extra furlong or two should be well within her range and she could easily find some valuable black type this summer.

Stablemate **Jumeirah Glory** improved after a gelding operation last summer, winning at Epsom and then finding 1m just beyond him at Ayr in September. A break should have allowed him to fill out his frame a bit more and he has the ability to win off his current mark of 80.

MICHAEL DODS enjoyed a good campaign, with **Mecca's Angel** the star.

She won four times and showed she is a very smart sprinter when making a successful step up to Group 3 company at Newbury in September. Connections will be hoping for a wet summer because she likes give underfoot, and she can take another step forward when getting her conditions.

Dragon King is another Dods charge who likes soft ground. He won his debut at Newcastle in May and ran better than the final result suggests at Redcar on his only other start. The ground was a bit too fast and he didn't help himself by taking a strong pull, so it was to his credit that he only gave best in the final furlong.

A handicap mark of 75 should be well within his capabilities.

North of the border *KEITH DALGLEISH* continues to enhance his reputation and will be keen to get past last year's 67 winners.

Jacob Black moved to Carluke last winter and won three of his five starts for Dalgleish. He can be hard to catch when able to dominate and is better than he showed at Ayr on his final start when there was plenty of competition for the early lead.

Wee Frankie was below-par in his final two starts, but 1m4f was too far at Hamilton in August and he pulled too hard when contesting a decent Ayr handicap four weeks later. He is still lightly raced and his pedigree suggests he may still turn out better than his current mark of 86.

If the ability is there, you can be assured that his promising young trainer will be able to find it.

Angels of the north
Mecca's Angel
That Is The Spirit
Flaming Spear

MECCA'S ANGEL: hoses up at Newbury and will be a great sprinter this year

The West by Hastings

RICHARD HANNON deserved all the plaudits for being crowned champion trainer in his first season as licence holder at the Everleigh and Herridge yards. In 2014, he totalled 206 winners on British turf and all-weather combined, amassing over £4.7 million in win and place prize-money.

One of the principal contributors was ace miler **Night Of Thunder**, who provided Hannon with a Classic win at the trainer's first attempt when defying odds of 40-1 in the 2,000 Guineas at Newmarket.

Subsequent placings behind Charm Spirit in the Prix du Moulin at Longchamp and QEII at Ascot proved that win was no fluke. He's since bypassed a trip to the Dubai Carnival in preparation for the upcoming turf campaign at home and, given his consistent profile at the very highest level, he will be a danger to all in the top mile races this summer.

Having sent out 114 juvenile winners in Britain last season, Hannon has a strong team of three-years-olds to look forward to.

The pick of a quality bunch is **Tiggy Wiggy**, whose remarkable campaign was crowned when she was named Cartier's champion two-year-old filly, emulating the yard's previous winners Lyric Fantasy and Lemon Souffle.

As a juvenile, she emerged early on as a classy type, making all in a Kempton maiden and a Salisbury conditions event. She then punched her Royal Ascot ticket by bounding clear in the Listed National at Sandown.

Although then narrowly denied in the Queen Mary, she hasn't looked back since, striking in the Weatherbys Super Sprint at Newbury and smashing the juvenile course record when too quick for subsequent Group 1 Moyglare heroine

OSAILA: could be each-way value for the 1,000 Guineas at Newmarket

Cursory Glance in the Lowther at York.

That lethal mix of quality and phenomenal pace helped her round off a near-flawless campaign by once again exacting revenge on the Queen Mary winner Anthem Alexander in the Group 1 Cheveley Park at Newmarket.

Although she undoubtedly possesses plenty of speed, connections believe she will stay beyond 6f and a crack at a Guineas trial, possibly the Fred Darling at Newbury, will determine whether she'll be campaigned towards the Classics or sprints. Whichever route is taken, she looks sure to make a massive impact.

Another likely 1,000 Guineas candidate is the highly regarded **Osaila**.

She looked a bit special when winning twice over 6f in July, quickening to ready successes in a novice race at Doncaster and a Group 3 at Ascot. She was far from disgraced in a prominent fifth when upped into Group 1 company at the Curragh and then made the most of a drop in grade when plundering a valuable sales race at Newmarket.

A closing third in the Juvenile Fillies Turf on the Breeders' Cup card at Santa Anita when last seen proved both her stamina and class on the international stage.

With conditions to suit and even better to come, she might well represent some each-way value at Headquarters in May.

Hannon could also have a say in the outcome of the 2,000 Guineas thanks to the exceptional talent **Ivawood**, who produced fireworks when dismantling Group 2 opposition on lively ground in the July Stakes at Newmarket and Richmond Stakes at Goodwood.

Once again he travelled like a smart horse when only just inched out by Charming Thought in the Middle Park at Newmarket, his turn of foot appearing to be blunted a fraction by the deeper underfoot conditions.

Back on better ground, it shouldn't be long before he gets the top-flight success his ability deserves, possibly in the opening British Classic in May.

Estidhkaar is another exciting prospect held in the highest regard by his top connections. He began to live up to the hype when wininng a Newbury maiden and, with confidence up, he went on to beat Group 2 rivals more decisively in both the Superlative Stakes at Newmarket and the Champagne at Doncaster.

Although he failed to live up to market confidence when only fourth in the Dewhurst, he didn't travel well in the race and was later diagnosed with a hairline fracture of his hock. He possesses the scope to leave that defeat behind him this season, particularly once upped to a mile.

Smaih, a son of former stable star Paco Boy, is also expected to pick up his share of black type for Hannon this summer.

Last October, the €190,000 yearling conjured a personal best when notching a third juvenile success in a Group 3 on soft ground at Newbury.

He could well make a successful return over that Berkshire course and distance in the Greenham, a race won six times by the Hannon yard. He's proven on good or softer going and, with positive experiences already in the locker, he ought to scale greater heights at three.

Another three-year-old to follow is **Marsh Hawk**, who was thought good enough to supplement for the Fillies' Mile

SMAIH: won a Group 3 at Newbury and will be back there for the Greenham

following a runaway win in a 7f conditions event at Newbury. However, having set a false pace, she was left a sitting duck in the prestigious Newmarket Group 1 and can be forgiven for surrendering the lead in the final furlong.

Although proven with cut in the ground, she shouldn't be troubled once tackling faster summer conditions.

It shouldn't be long before Hannon's unbeaten **Elysian Flyer** successfully graduates into Group company.

In October, he unleashed a potent turn of foot to pass the Flying Childers runner-up Astrophysics in a match for a Salisbury conditions event. He has yet to be seriously threatened in three starts and deserves a crack at better opposition in the months to come.

Peacock made the perfect start when staying on well to bag a Newmarket maiden and hasn't looked out of place in Listed races over 7f since, not least when finishing strongly in third behind Nafaqa and impressive Mill Reef hero Toocoolforschool at Doncaster in September.

It's hard to pick holes in that form and, with a likeable temperament and more to offer once upped in trip, there's every chance he'll be back in the winners' circle before long.

Basateen has a very bright future. He was too green to do himself justice when third on his introduction on soft ground at Newbury. He was wiser next time out at Doncaster and duly surged eight lengths clear to win in a decent time on a sounder surface. He was then too keen when just third in the Group 3 Acomb at York.

He can only improve with maturity and, once learning to settle, he should pick up a valuable race or two for Hannon.

Sugar Lump can make up into a useful handicapper.

As a two-year-old, he showed the benefit of a promise-filled debut second in a Nottingham maiden in June when going one better under a hands-and-heels ride from Richard Hughes at Salisbury shortly afterwards.

He possesses the scope to step up again this season and, with a mark of 78, could well be on a viable figure.

Likely improver **Wajeeh** revealed plenty of positives when, despite being carried wide on the bend, he responded well for pressure to readily land a Lingfield maiden on Polytrack in early February.

He will be race-fit for the turf campaign ahead and is another of Hannon's team expected to make his presence felt once joining the handicap ranks.

Ya Hade Ye Delil ought to be a shoo-in to get off the mark in a maiden before going on to better things.

The 525,000gns yearling is a half-brother to Group 2 winner Spacious and shaped with considerable promise behind much more experienced rivals, including subsequent winner Shadow Rock, in a 1m1f Goodwood maiden in September.

Stamina won't be an issue for him and, with some experience under the belt, he can start paying back that hefty price tag.

Among Hannon's older brigade, a possible Cup horse worth checking out is **Windshear**.

The classy handicapper stepped up to finish second in Group 3 company at Newmarket and Goodwood last July and, not for the first time, he shaped as if stamina was key when keeping on for fourth behind Kingston Hill in the St Leger at Doncaster in September.

It wouldn't take a great leap forward to enter calculations for the Ascot Gold Cup in June.

Also likely to enjoy a career-best campaign is the progressive **Yaakooum**, who made it four wins from his final six starts in 2014 when nosing out Fun Mac in a warm 1m4f handicap at Goodwood in October.

He acts best on good or softer, and although up 4lb for that Goodwood success, he can find the improvement needed to keep on the winning trail.

Western wonders
Estidkhaar
Marsh Hawk
Tiggy Wiggy

The South by Southerner

GRANTED some luck, *RALPH BECKETT* could enjoy one of his best seasons to date. The Kimpton trainer has a nicely balanced team with a solid group of older horses, a very talented three-year-old squad and a juvenile intake he describes as "a terrific bunch".

Classy five-year-old **Secret Gesture**, who signed off last term with a solid fifth in the Fillies & Mares Turf at the Breeders' Cup, has been kept in training.

The daughter of Galileo is very consistent, and given the way she was staying on at Santa Anita and in several of her other races last year – all at around 1m2f – it would be no surprise to see the 2013 Oaks runner-up return to 1m4f.

Air Pilot went from strength to strength last season having missed 2013 through injury.

Off the mark at the second attempt in a maiden, the six-year-old soon progressed beyond handicap company, following a fine second to subsequent John Smith's Cup winner Farraaj at Epsom with an easy

win at Newbury that earned him an 18lb rise.

As a result his final two outings were in Pattern races at Newmarket, where he was a close third to Berkshire in the Group 2 Darley Stakes over 1m1f in October and a ready winner of a 1m2f Listed contest at the start of November.

With just seven races behind him, Air Pilot could easily improve again. He is effective on good ground but relishes some cut and goes well fresh.

Fellow six-year-old **Niceofyoutotellme** also goes well after a break. His record first time out reads 2211 and he was beaten only half a length in both the seconds.

He dead-heated for second in the Cambridgeshire and is at his best on a straight track when the ground is quick.

Beckett is hopeful that **Rideonastar** will make up into a useful middle-distance handicapper this season.

The four-year-old was brought along steadily last term. After three modest effort in maidens, he took a big step forward on his only other outing when landing a 1m4f

AIR PILOT: spreadeagled a competitive field to graduate to Pattern level

handicap on heavy going at Windsor in October. It wasn't the strongest of races, but he showed a good attitude in the testing conditions despite still looking green.

Chemical Charge looked an exciting prospect on his two starts as a juvenile. The Sea The Stars colt made his debut in the same maiden at Salisbury in early October as Beckett's 2009 Oaks heroine Look Here and, like her, he ran out an impressive winner. He then proved far too good for three rivals in a novice race over a mile at Lingfield in November.

The plan this term is to start him off in a conditions race and, if all goes well, then tackle a Derby trial.

Great Glen is another three-year-old colt with vast potential. The handsome son of High Chaparral finished fourth on his debut in a mile maiden at Newmarket in October, looking likely to win until getting worn down close home. He was still beaten just half a length and the winner, Aloft, franked the form when second in the Racing Post Trophy next time.

Great Glen, who was put away to strengthen up over the winter after that run, also holds a Derby entry.

Encore D'Or is held in such regard that connections were considering the Middle Park last season before deciding to give this long-striding colt more time to mature.

He won a 6f maiden at Wolverhampton in October by seven lengths and Beckett is convinced that soft ground was the reason he needed that long to break his duck.

Perrault showed considerable promise on his sole juvenile outing when finishing second to Milky Way. The Rip Van Winkle colt should get 1m2f and seems likely to enjoy a profitable campaign.

Master Of Irony overcame greenness to make a winning debut in a 7f maiden at Lingfield in December. The Makfi colt has a good deal of scope and he should develop into a useful handicapper.

Pacify was another to win on his only start last year, staying on well to lead close home in a mile maiden at Kempton in November.

Magic Dancer had a couple of outings over 1m½f at Windsor on easy ground at the backend of last season. The colt lost

out by a nose to Rocky Rider before going one better with a comfortable all-the-way success is a similar event three weeks later. He saw out the trip well both times, but there's a lot of speed on the dam's side of his pedigree and he has plenty of pace so Beckett will have options over a variety of trips.

Forte sits at the top of the pecking order among Beckett's fleet of talented three-year-old fillies.

A never-nearer third in a 7f Kempton maiden on her debut in August, she readily opened her account at the same track in another maiden over a mille in October. She found the step up to Group 1 class in the Fillies' Mile at Newmarket ten days later too much for her, but if she improves as much from two to three as her Oaks-winning sister Talent did, she will be right at home in the best company this term.

Camagueyana could also be very smart as Beckett was delighted this half-sister to the retired Cubanita, who was a great servant for the yard, was able to win as a juvenile.

The manner in which she pulled clear to land a mile maiden at Kempton in November left the impression she will thrive when moving up to middle distances this year.

As a half-sister to the useful 2m winner Chocala out of a dam who won a Listed race over 1m4f, **Bellajeu** should also appreciate stepping up in trip this season.

The Montjeu filly progressed nicely last year and failed by just a nose to open her account on her final appearance in a mile maiden at Newbury in October.

Back in fourth that day was stablemate **L'Ingenue**, who was sent off 4-1 favourite for her debut. A combination of inexperience and ending up on the slowest ground counted against her, but the daughter of New Approach will stay at least 1m4f this year and should have little trouble landing a maiden before moving up in grade.

Redstart and **Engaging Smile**, comfortable winners of divisions of the same 7f Kempton maiden in November, are two more lightly raced fillies who should do well this season.

Carntop is one of the more interesting two-year-olds Beckett has charge of. The

LIGHTNING THUNDER: should have benefited from a long winter break

Dansili colt hails from a top-class family and is very closely related to the Arc winner Rail Link, though given his middle-distance pedigree he is unlikely to be a precocious type.

In contrast, **Point Of Woods** is bred to make his mark at two. The colt is by the Gimcrack winner Showcasing out of Queen Mary winner Romantic Myth.

The Acclamation colt **Sacrament** is another with plenty of speed in his pedigree who looks a likely first-season winner.

Toumar, **Sightline** and **Tangba** are a trio of juvenile fillies which catch the eye on pedigree, while **Pillar** and **Short Work** are a couple of colts who are bred to be well above average.

OLLY STEVENS wasn't quite able to match the exploits of his rookie season but still enjoyed a good campaign last year.

It could easily have been even better as **Lightning Thunder** was beaten just a neck by Miss France in the 1,000 Guineas at Newmarket before filling the same spot on desperate ground in the Irish 1,000 Guineas three weeks later.

Those exploits left their mark, so it was decided to give the Dutch Art filly a good long break to recharge her batteries with the intention of returning for a selective campaign this season.

Peace And War justified her trainer's faith in her by producing a storming late run to land the Grade 1 Darley Alcibiades Stakes over 1m½f on the dirt track at Keeneland in October.

The victory qualified her for the Breeders' Cup, but an injury prevented her running at Santa Anita.

Further American raids are planned for Peace And War this season with the Kentucky Oaks, Coaching Club Oaks, Spinster Stakes and Breeders' Cup all under consideration.

Indeed, Stevens is unafraid to travel his horses wherever they have a chance of winning and has already made a successful raid this year on Switzerland, where **Burning Blaze** left his rivals eating snow as he blitzed clear in a conditions race at St Moritz in early February.

Closer to home, **Hungerford** opened his account at the second time of asking in workmanlike fashion in a mile maiden at Lingfield in January. The three-year-old has size and scope and should develop into a useful a handicapper.

Stevens is hoping **Lightning Spear** will turn out to be better than a handicapper.

The four-year-old has always been held

65

MILKY WAY (right): could be the best Flat horse Gary Moore has ever trained

in high regard, but he's not been easy to train and has only run twice, winning a Kempton maiden as a juvenile for Ralph Beckett and landing a mile handicap at Nottingham on easy ground for Stevens in October.

Stevens also has a couple of very smart sprinters in **Extortionist** and **Green Door**, both of whom are best over 5f on fast ground.

Extortionist did best last year, winning the Group 3 Coral Charge at Sandown and twice going close at an even higher level, but Green Door was unlucky not to do better as he finished second four times in decent company. Both should pay their way again.

GARY MOORE secured a bargain when paying 32,000gns to acquire **Tall Ship** from Sir Michael Stoute last July.

The Sea The Stars gelding quickly repaid a good chunk of that when landing a 1m3f handicap at Glorious Goodwood and he returned to the same track three weeks later to scoot home in a 1m4f handicap.

The four-year-old has had only seven races and should continue to thrive as he climbs the handicap.

Milky Way was a rather more expensive Moore buy, but sons of Galileo don't come cheap. The Derby entry started to work well in the autumn last year and was sent off a well-backed 4-1 for his debut in October in a mile maiden at Newbury, where he made all the running and always looked like justifying the support. He has the po-

tential to be one of the best Flat horses Moore has trained.

Crisscrossed and **Lightning Charlie** are a couple of nice three-year-olds for *AMANDA PERRETT* to look forward to.

A half-brother to Twice Over, Crisscrossed made a promising start to his career when third in a mile maiden on the Polytrack at Lingfield in November.

Lightning Charlie progressed steadily last year and signed off with a comfortable front-running success in a 6f maiden at Kempton in October. The gelding should make a very useful sprint handicapper this season.

Stable stalwarts **Sirius Propect**, **Tropics** and **Lancelot Du Lac** were again the main standard bearers for *DEAN IVORY* last year, but a new force is emerging at Ivory's Radlett base in **Stake Acclaim**.

He caught the eye when seventh on his introduction in a 7f Newmarket maiden in August and built on that when chasing home Fannaan in a 6f maiden at Haydock the following month. He ended the campaign with a resounding victory in a similar contest at Doncaster and is exciting.

Midlands
by John Bull

I T WAS another great year for *MICHAEL APPLEBY* and there are positive signs that Appleby has enough ammunition to keep the winners flowing.

A tally of 89 winners was another big improvement on Appleby's previous best set in 2013 when he notched 61 successes and, having got cracking early on the all-weather and an additional 20 boxes being built that will give him room for 80 horses, a first century is not out of the question.

Danzeno gave the trainer his first Group success in the Group 3 Chipchase Stakes at Newcastle last June and there are hopes the sprinter may be able to grab a Group 1.

Appleby said: "We'll possibly go for the Duke of York with him first time out and see how he goes from there. We'll be aiming for all the big meetings and all the big sprints. He's a very good horse and looks like he's grown a bit more over the winter. He's best on good ground, or on the quick side of good."

A defence of her William Hill Scottish Sprint Cup crown at Musselburgh is likely to be **Demora**'s first target of the season, with Appleby already considering Dubai for the mare's swansong next winter.

He said: "I think we'll aim her at Musselburgh again first time out and there's also a Listed fillies' race at Bath we wouldn't mind going for to try to get her some black type. I'm thinking about taking her to Dubai next year as she'll be retired after that and go breeding. The track would be ideal as it's a fast 5f and I think she'd go on the dirt as well."

Of the others in the string, Appleby thinks **Donny Rover** may be able to resume last year's progress when he won his final two starts at Newmarket and Nottingham and feels he could be up to Listed class.

Lulu The Zulu is another who might not

DANZENO: Group 1 potential

have finished improving. Now seven, the mare was a revelation last season, going from a mark of 75 to 98, with the highlight a win in a conditions race at Doncaster when beating Top Notch Tonto.

Appleby said: "I think she's still got a lot of improvement in her, she didn't start racing until she was four and we'll try to get some black type with her."

Although Appleby focuses more on older horses, he does have a small team of juveniles, with an unnamed daughter of Dark Angel who is a half-sister to Appleberry (also trained by Appleby) catching the eye.

The trainer said: "She looks quite nice and could be quite forward. I'm not going to rush her but I might aim her at the Brocklesby."

SCOTT DIXON had his best ever year

in 2014 with 35 winners, kicking off with **Cock Of The North**'s Brocklesby success at the Lincoln meeting.

The colt was highly tried for the rest of his juvenile campaign and ran some good races in defeat, notably when beaten only half a length in fourth in a blanket finish in the Group 3 Solario Stakes at Sandown.

Connections are dreaming of Classic glory for 2015 as Dixon said: "He's quite a big, scopey horse and if he's as good as we're hoping he'll be we're not going to mess around. Ultimately the target would be to have a go at the 2,000 Guineas. He'll need to have improved for that to become a viable option and he's likely to have a prep run, possibly at the Craven meeting."

Dixon is also hoping he has another potential Brocklesby winner lurking among the juveniles, adding: "I've got three potential candidates, two I'm quite strong on and one who seems to be improving at a rate of knots. Shares are still available in two and we'd like to win it again."

JAMES GIVEN has plenty of reasons to be optimistic when the turf starts, with last season's flag-bearer **Odeon** on an attractive mark that gives the trainer a plethora of options.

A runaway Redcar maiden win was followed by fourth in the Dante, and although he did disappoint on other occasions, with a tendency to become too buzzed up, he also notched third in the Great Voltigeur Stakes at York. Hopes are high he can improve again in 2015 after being gelded.

Given said: "He's been gelded and I'm hoping that calms him down. Irrespective of his behaviour last year I always felt he was a big horse with a big frame and physically he would be better at four. He's clearly talented and I'm very much lookin forward to him.

"He's on a mark of 100, which looks quite healthy for a horse who was third in the Voltigeur, so we may see if we can take advantage of that early on. He could always run in Listed races and the Further Flight at Nottingham would be an option, although we may look to start over 1m4f."

A Classic trial is the first aim for Listed winner **Russian Punch**, with Given keen to see how far the filly could go.

COCK OF THE NORTH: the Brocklesby winner could be a Guineas horse

CASPIAN PRINCE: Epsom Dash win could point to the future for Tony Carroll

She progressed well as a juvenile, culminating in victory at Newbury in the Radley Stakes, and will head back to the track in April.

"She will probably go for the Fred Darling," Given said. "She is entered in the Irish 1,000 Guineas which is a bit of a windmill tilt, but that could be an option. She went to Newmarket once last year and got unbalanced coming down the hill so we wouldn't be thinking about the Nell Gwyn or anything like that. Being a Listed winner and a filly, you've got to think upwards with her so a Group 3 fillies' race is the obvious target. It may be we end up having our ambitions clipped but at the moment she deserves to be looking at those things."

Given also has Pattern plans for **Pastoral Girl**, who finished second in the Group 3 Princess Margaret Stakes at Ascot last season.

He said: "She is also entered in the Irish Guineas. She was quite a big two-year-old and has matured into herself and done well over the winter and it would be nice to make her a black-type winner."

Of this year's juveniles, Given feels **Cool Silk Boy**, a half-brother to Tiggy Wiggy, could be interesting, saying: "He looks a very strong, powerful, precocious two-year-old type and if he could be half as good as his half-sister we've got a smart horse on our hands."

Unraced Champs Elysees three-year-old **La Fritillaire** was also flagged up by Given. A half-sister to Dandino, whose sire Dansili is a brother to Champs Elysees, the filly has a splendid pedigree.

The trainer said: "She's a lovely specimen and has been with us since December with a view to a good three-year-old campaign."

TONY CARROLL has steadily been raising the quality of horses in his yard and his efforts were rewarded with 56 Flat winners last year.

Carroll has done well with horses picked up at the French sales, notably **Boom The Groom**, who could run at the all-weather championships finals day at Lingfield, and last year's Epsom Dash winner **Caspian Prince**.

That success could prove a springboard for Carroll, because while he has mainly done his business on the all-weather it would be no surprise if he starts making more of an impact on turf and plundering some other big handicaps.

Midlands magic
Cock Of The North
Danzeno
Odeon

Est. 1909
RACING & FOOTBALL **OUTLOOK**

Steve Mellish – the man on the telly

Who will come out on top in the riding stakes?

THE 2014 Flat season didn't have a Frankel – they come around about as often as Halley's Comet – but it was still a good one.

Australia and Taghrooda were above-average Classic winners, Treve was simply superb when bagging her second Arc for Criquette Head-Maarek and in Kingman we had a star.

He suffered his only defeat in the 2,000 Guineas but easy wins at the Curragh, Ascot, Goodwood and Deauville left little room for doubt that here was a tip-top miler.

It's a real shame his season ended in August and his subsequent retirement was even more disappointing as he still had much to give and plenty to prove.

Had he been kept in training, would James Doyle still have jumped ship from Juddmonte to Godolphin? We'll never know.

Doyle was part of a musical chairs game at the end of the year as William Buick also found the lure of Godolphin too much to resist while Andrea Atzeni and Oisin Murphy took over as number one and two riders with Qatar Racing, replacing Jamie Spencer (who announced his retirement before changing his mind) and Harry Bentley.

This is a big year for them all but it's not without risks. Besides Juddmonte, Doyle had a great link with Roger Charlton; Buick left a good job with John Gosden and Murphy's career was progressing quickly with Andrew Balding.

However, it could be argued that the biggest risk has been taken by Atzeni.

He had an arrangement to ride for the increasingly influential Sheikh Mohammed Obaid, was stable jockey to Roger Varian, seemed the rider of choice for Luca Cumani and was fast becoming the go-to jockey for many other trainers.

Number one with Qatari Racing is a potentially great job but he's given up an awful lot to take it.

As for the horses, high on my wish-list for 2015 is a champion sprinter or stayer worthy of their title, but whether we get one or not there will still be plenty of brilliant horses and great action. I can't wait.

Here are five horses it could pay to keep an eye on in 2015. Have a great summer of punting.

Elm Park 3yo colt
31111- (Andrew Balding)

As he won his last four starts including the Group 1 Racing Post Trophy, it can hardly be claimed that Elm Park is a dark horse, but he might still be underestimated.

At the time of writing he's available at 14-1 for the Derby and that looks fair value.

He's shown better form than the three above him in the betting and is bred to improve with time and middle distances.

His sire, Phoenix Reach, thrived when given the opportunity to tackle a mile and a half and Elm Park looks a chip off the old block judging by the way he drew clear at the end of a soft-ground Racing Post.

It's possible he'll contest the 2,000 Guineas before heading to Epsom, but the mile trip is likely to be too sharp for him at three and it's the first Saturday in June when he can show what he's made of.

Encore D'Or 3yo colt
201- (Ralph Beckett)

This good-looking son of Oasis Dream had three races as a juvenile and we already know one important thing about him – he doesn't like soft ground.

That certainly looked the case at Newbury on his second run where he floundered in the mud, coming home a well-beaten 11th.

His runs either side of that – a promising debut at Newmarket on fast ground and his wide-margin romp on the Tapeta at Wolverhampton – show him in an altogether more promising light.

He recorded a good time at Dunstall Park despite his jockey taking things easy in the closing stages and the handicapper may have seriously underestimated him with a mark of 85.

His dam stayed quite well but this is quite a speedy family and trips shy of a mile might prove ideal.

Malabar 3yo filly
241144- (Mick Channon)

Defeats in Group 1 company in Ireland and France at the end of her two-year-old campaign suggests Malabar is just below

ELM PARK: has the form in the book and is bred to improve for a longer trip

top-class but that might be a dangerous conclusion to make.

She was given an awful lot to do in both those races and should most certainly have finished a lot closer. She hasn't got to find much to be a realistic contender in the fillies' Classics and given those defeats she's liable to be a bigger price than she should be.

The 1,000 Guineas trip will be fine in early May and there's enough encouragement in her family to also give her a shot at the Oaks. Mick Channon is likely to campaign her boldly – rightly so given her form – and, Classic or no Classic, she's likely to pick up a big race or two.

Postponed 4yo colt
34311- (Luca Cumani)

Luca Cumani has always been a top trainer and the class of his string has been on the rise again in the past couple of seasons.

He's got several promising types to go to war with in 2015 but possibly none with more potential than Postponed.

He thrived in a typically patient campaign last season winning his last two. The final victory, and his best form to date, came in the Group 2 Great Voltigeur where he beat the subsequent Leger third Snow

Sky with some ease. The step up to 1m4f brought out the best in him as did the decent gallop on a sound surface.

Put away after that with one eye on his four-year-old campaign, he could develop into a high-class performer with all the best middle-distance events on his agenda.

Top Tug 4yo gelding
617- (Sir Michael Stoute)

It will be a big surprise if we've seen the best of this son of Halling yet.

He won on his second start last season, staying on to get the better of the useful Cloudscape in a decent 1m2f handicap on the July course at Newmarket.

He looked certain to improve for a step up to 1m4f and got his chance to confirm this when next appearing at the other Newmarket track more than four months later. However, he was given a rare poor ride by Ryan Moore and finished only seventh. He passed horse after horse in the final furlong having started his run from way back in Norfolk!

The good news is his mark remains unchanged, leaving us with a lightly raced four-year-old (just six runs under his belt) who is well handicapped, trained by a master and is unexposed over middle distances. What's not to like?

MALABAR: no forlorn hope for the 1,000 Guineas having been unlucky last year

Est. 1909

RACING & FOOTBALL OUTLOOK

Richard Birch
Read Richard every week in the RFO

Godolphin set to return to big time – but I'll be focused on lesser lights

HAVING consulted my crystal ball to provide a preview of what's going to happen during the 2015 Flat turf season, one thing stands out – Godolphin's re-emergence as a superpower in British racing.

The last few years have been a total embarrassment by their exceptionally high standards, but something seems to have clicked over the last six months with the horses being campaigned in the right races and Charlie Appleby establishing himself as an excellent young trainer alongside stalwart Saeed Bin Suroor.

Godolphin, of course, remains a global operation whose aim is to win as many Group 1 events around the world as possible and I can see them now moving forward to hoover up plenty of them.

In terms of punting, though, those sort of races interest me about as much as the man who lives in the next street's Twitter account, my modus operandi being to focus on lower-rated horses who remain under the radar.

For example, my main money-spinner last summer was the wonderfully consistent sprinter **Molly Jones**, a mare who simply adores racing on lightning-fast ground at her beloved Bath.

The decision of trainer Derek Haydn Jones to campaign Molly Jones almost exclusively at the Somerset track proved inspired, with the daughter of Three Valleys recording three summer successes on firm terrain, and there is no reason why she cannot land a couple more this term despite a higher mark.

Blessed with a lovely turn of foot, Molly Jones benefits from Bath having no watering system, which means she races on naturally firm ground during periods of little rainfall.

Another course specialist worth latching on to is **Pour La Victoire**.

Tony Carroll's handicapper is a stone better horse at Brighton, as he proved when routing 13 opponents over 7f there in September.

Value for more than the three-quarters-of-a-length winning margin that day – he idles when hitting the front – there will be plenty of opportunities by the seaside for Pour La Victoire this season, and his all-weather form suggests he might have even further improvement on turf when dropped to sprint trips.

William Knight knows the Brighton programme book inside-out and is no doubt already planning an extensive campaign at the Sussex course for **Tunnel Tiger**, a filly who reminds me a great deal of the same trainer's useful mare Beacon Lady.

Two years ago I had the foresight and good fortune to latch on to Beacon Lady at the start of a winning spree that saw her improve out of all recognition on switchback tracks, winning three handicaps at Brighton and one at Epsom.

Tunnel Tiger also looks just the type to make abnormal improvement from three to four. She starts the year on a mark of just 60 and I fully expect her to have improved that rating by 20lb come the end of the summer.

Last Minute Lisa is yet another who comes alive when encountering the gradients of Brighton as well as similar courses such as Epsom and Goodwood.

There will be plenty more opportunities for Sylvester Kirk's mare at those three venues this term and she ought to win two or three handicaps from off the pace; champion jockey Richard Hughes gets on particularly well with her.

Ffos Las doesn't suit every horse, so those who truly thrive at the Welsh track are likely to win more than their fair share. **Greyemkay** is the perfect example, with course form figures of 11422234116.

Richard Price is certain to campaign Greyemkay with several Ffos Las summer handicaps firmly in mind, so expect the gelding's mark to have slipped by the time he visits his happiest hunting ground once again.

Useful hurdler **Handiwork** starts the year on a Flat mark of just 75 and possesses ample scope to add to his eight-length Catterick success last October in staying northern handicaps.

The James Bethell-trained **Kirkman**, hugely impressive winner of a 2m maiden handicap at Beverley last July, is also fancied to make a name for himself in this type of event.

Restricted to just two further runs in

LAST MINUTE LISA: winning at Goodwood last year, the sort of track she loves

ROSALIE BONHEUR (left): a potential Group winner for Clive Cox this season

2014, Kirkman should have strengthened up nicely over the winter and is likely to develop into an 80+ horse from a starting point of just 68.

Another stayer worth following is **Beat The Tide**, who has a likeably high cruising speed.

The son of Black Sam Bellamy promised more than he delivered in seven starts for Michael Dods last season, but as a result he starts on a very fair mark of 72 and the switch to Tim Vaughan, whom he joined after changing hands for 35,000gns at Tattersalls in October, is an intriguing one.

Beat The Tide was bought with hurdling in mind, but one would imagine Vaughan views that Flat rating as eminently workable and I cannot wait for him to turn up in a Class 4 or 5 handicap at the beginning of the campaign on his favoured soft ground.

Double Up caught more eyes than Kylie Minogue's bottom when runner-up to the well-treated Stomp in a 6f Lingfield handicap last May. Given the huge promise of

that performance, it was a major surprise that he failed to hit the target in three subsequent starts, but there were genuine excuses each time.

Roger Varian does particularly well with this sort of lightly raced four-year-old, and it wouldn't be the biggest shock of all time if Double Up made a mockery of a mark of 78 prior to developing into a major contender for one of the big sprint handicaps such as the Wokingham. At the very least, expect him to land a gamble first time out this spring.

Finally, for one who might just prove a class horse, **Rosalie Bonheur** is one to keep on your side.

She entered more notebooks than my local branch of Rymans stock when completing a hat-trick in a Newmarket fillies' nursery in September.

Clive Cox's three-year-old has a wonderful attitude and should make her mark in Group company after landing another handicap this spring.

Est. 1909
RACING & FOOTBALL OUTLOOK

Time Test speed figures

Wonderful Wiggy is a rare talent

I T was a rare year in the juvenile ranks last season as an outstanding crop of fillies outperformed their male counterparts on the stopwatch.

Tiggy Wiggy led the way in blistering fashion. Her peak mark of 112, achieved in winning the Lowther Stakes at York, had her five points clear of Anthem Alexander and Ivawood, with Cursory Glance and Hootenanny the only other juveniles within eight points of her.

Fellow fillies **Anthem Alexander** and **Cursory Glance** also achieved their best marks in the Lowther, but there was plenty to back up the clock in awarding such lofty figures for the race. The trio pulled five lengths clear of the rest, there was real substance to the form with Anthem Alexander having won the Queen Mary and Cursory Glance going on to land the Moyglare, and Tiggy Wiggy was maintaining a constant upward curve to her timeline on her seventh start with the exception of one narrow loss at York three months earlier.

A lower figure was to follow when she won a more slowly run Cheveley Park Stakes, with Anthem Alexander again second, but that showed she had learned to settle and conserve her energy, which gives her at least some hope of seeing out the mile of the 1,000 Guineas.

If that doesn't work out, then she is capable of taking high rank as a sprinter and races like the new Group 1 sprint for three-year-olds at Royal Ascot could be there for the taking.

Lucida is a very likely stayer and she showed her credentials with victory in the Rockfel, returning a highly impressive Time Test figure of 73 in beating the promising **Fadhayyil**. Experence of the Rowley Mile will also stand her in good stead.

Jim Bolger's Godolphin filly blotted her copybook in the Fillies' Mile, but she clearly wasn't herself that day. Indeed, the winner, **Together Forever**, was worth only a figure of 49 and has it all to prove in a more strongly run contest.

The same applies to Prix Marcel Boussac winner **Found**, whose position at the head of the market for both fillies' Classics doesn't tally with the hands of the clock. Her best performance on the clock came in defeat in the Moyglare, leaving the seemingly exposed Group 3 winner **Qualify** with the best Time Test figure among Aidan O'Brien's fillies.

High Celebrity wasn't suited by a slowly run Cheveley Park and had previously returned a highly respectable figure of 70 at Chantilly, so she could be more of a threat.

TIGGY WIGGY: the fastest of an outstanding crop of juvenile fillies last season

One fascinating contender for middle-distance races, perhaps the Oaks, is Alain de Royer-Dupre's **Vedouma**. She was unbeaten in two starts last year, winning last time by six lengths on heavy ground at Chantilly in a tremendous time. Quicker ground is an unknown, but this filly, owned and bred by the Aga Khan, could be anything.

Ivawood was the best two-year-old colt last season, awarded a mark of 77 for his runaway win in the Richmond Stakes when he forced the pace throughout and stormed clear in the closing stages.

His second in the Middle Park wasn't a bad effort either – the winner, **Charming Thought**, also makes the top five with his figure of 72 – but he just lacked the spark of earlier in the campaign. So, too, did another top Richard Hannon juvenile, **Estidhkaar**, on the same day.

If Hannon can bring the pair back to his best, then he would hold a seriously player for the 2,000 Guineas. Certainly their speed figures are head and shoulders above many of their potential rivals such as Faydhan, Gleneagles, Highland Reel, Ol' Man River and Belardo.

Faydhan, though, could be the joker in the pack given he saw the track only once last term. His mark of 58 was excellent for a debutant and he had **Dutch Connection**, who went on to post a very strong 71 in winning the Acomb Stakes, six lengths back in second.

Richard Pankhurst was another who didn't get the chance to fulfil his potential due to injury problems and he is also interesting on the basis of his solid 62 in winning the Chesham when last seen at Royal Ascot.

John F Kennedy, who earned a Time Test figure of 68 for his Group 3 win at Leopardstown, could be the best of Aidan O'Brien's big guns. He is at least proven in a strongly run race, something that cannot be said of **Gleneagles**, **Highland Reel** and, worst of all, **Ol' Man River**.

POSTPONED: clocked an excellent time when winning the Great Voltigeur

Elm Park is another who should be well worth following. He didn't need to be at his best to win the Racing Post Trophy having previously run to a figure of 67 in the Royal Lodge.

The best Time Test figure in any division last season was posted by **Telescope** in the King George, although that's only because Taghrooda's fillies' allowance meant she was carrying 3lb less.

Another Ascot race that produced outstanding marks was the Champion Stakes, and that could have more of an impact on 2015 because of the presence of **Free Eagle** in third.

Dermot Weld's four-year-old had missed virtually all of his Classic season, returning just a month earlier with a six-length victory at Leopardstown, so to push Noble Mission and Al Kazeem to a length and a half in such a good time – Free Eagle earned a figure of 85 with the first two on 89 – on only his second start of the year bodes very well for his future.

Whether he would have been able to get the better of Australia in a vintage Derby is another matter, with Aidan O'Brien's superstar returning a mark of 89, and it's Epsom runner-up **Kingston Hill** who may well set the standard in the 1m4f division on 86.

Others to watch include **Postponed**, who ran to a figure of 80 when winning the Great Voltigeur, and **Arab Spring**, who did the same when completing a four-timer in handicap company and is much better than he showed on his only subsequent outing.

Over slightly shorter trips **The Grey Gatsby** might well be hard to beat, although it's worth noting Australia didn't run to his Derby level in their two clashes and The Grey Gatsby's best performance on the clock came when landing the Prix

Top two-year-old colts of 2014

	Horse	Speed rating	Distance in furlongs	Going	Track	Date achieved
1	**Ivawood**	**77**	**6**	**GF**	**Goodwood**	**July 31**
2	Hootenanny	76	5	GD	Ascot	June 17
3	Estidhkaar	73	7	GS	Newmarket	July 12
3	Maftool	73	7	GD	Kempton	Sept 25
5	Charming Thought	72	6	SFT	Newmarket	Oct 17
6	Dutch Connection	71	7	GF	York	Aug 20
7	El Suizo	70	5.5	VSFT	Chantilly	May 13
7	Muhaarar	70	6	GD	York	Aug 23
7	Toocoolforschool	70	7	GF	York	Aug 20
10	Basateen	69	7	GF	York	Aug 20
10	Jungle Cat	69	6	GD	York	Aug 23

Top two-year-old fillies of 2014

	Horse	Speed rating	Distance in furlongs	Going	Track	Date achieved
1	**Tiggy Wiggy**	**82**	**6**	**GD**	**York**	**Aug 21**
2	Anthem Alexander	77	6	GD	York	Aug 21
3	Cursory Glance	76	6	GD	York	Aug 21
4	Lucida	73	7	GD	Newmarket	Sept 26
5	Qualify	71	7	GF	Curragh	Sept 28
6	Fadhayyil	70	7	GD	Newmarket	Sept 26
6	High Celebrity	70	5	GS	Chantilly	Sept 9
8	Newsletter	68	5	GF	Ascot	June 18
9	Souvenir Delondres	66	6	SFT	Chantilly	Oct 10
10	Vedouma	65	8	HVY	Chantilly	Nov 25

du Jockey-Club.

Nothing stood out in terms of time over a mile last season with Kingman's highest figure coming in defeat in the 2,000 Guineas behind **Night Of Thunder**, who was a worthy winner in a searching test.

Rising French star **Solow** is fascinating in this division having won five out of six last season and returned a fine figure of 82 when winning a Group 3 at Deauville by five lengths, after which he justified favouritism in the Prix Daniel Wildenstein on Arc weekend.

Although his stablemate Slade Power matched him in winning a pair of Group 1 races, **Sole Power** was the real sprint champion last season. He won the King's Stand and the Nunthorpe, with his best figure of 81 coming at York, and was below his best over an extra furlong in the Sprint Cup won by **G Force**.

In fact G Force was some way off being the highest-rated three-year-old sprinter last season, with the hugely exciting filly **Mecca's Angel** (78) leading the way ahead of **Extortionist** (76).

Est. 1909
RACING & FOOTBALL OUTLOOK

Group 1 review
by Dylan Hill

1 **Qipco 2,000 Guineas Stakes (1m)**
Newmarket May 3 (Good To Firm)
1 **Night Of Thunder** 3-9-0   Kieren Fallon
2 **Kingman** 3-9-0   James Doyle
3 **Australia** 3-9-0   Joseph O'Brien
40/1, 6/4F, 5/2. ½l, hd. 14 ran. 1m 36.61s
(Richard Hannon).

A vintage renewal packed with quality but one rendered somewhat unsatisfactory by the field splitting in two and racing wide apart, which contributed to **Night Of Thunder** turning over class acts **Kingman** and **Australia**. Night Of Thunder still did well to survive veering across the track in the final furlong, producing a remarkable burst of speed as he belied his 40-1 odds, and was unlucky not to add to his Group 1 haul. However, Kingman's rider committed far too early, seemingly fearful those on the far side were behind those in the other group, while Australia, though better over further, proved best of those on the stands side in third ahead of **Shifting Power**. Other top-class colts behind included **Charm Spirit**, a big improver having finished fifth, as well as two more who would excel over further in **Kingston Hill** and **The Grey Gatsby**.

2 **Qipco 1,000 Guineas Stakes (Fillies)**
(1m)
Newmarket May 4 (Good To Firm)
1 **Miss France** 3-9-0   Maxime Guyon
2 **Lightning Thunder** 3-9-0   Harry Bentley
3 **Ihtimal** 3-9-0   Silvestre De Sousa
7/1, 14/1, 7/1. nk, ½l. 17 ran. 1m 37.40s
(A Fabre).

A slow gallop played into the hands of those racing prominently, but there's little doubt that, with the possible exception of **Rizeena**, the two best fillies came to the fore with **Miss France** just holding off **Lightning Thunder**. Miss France was beautifully placed to exploit the lack of early pace, but she wandered around and seemed to do little in front, which perhaps masked her superiority as Lightning Thunder challenged fast and late away from her. Moderate pacemaker **Manderley** epitomised the pace bias by holding on to fourth ahead of **Euro Charline**, who was still finding her feet and shaped with real promise in fifth. Rizeena was below her best in seventh ahead of **Vorda**, who did best of those held up, while Aidan O'Brien's pair **Bracelet** and **Tapestry** would both prove better having finished down the field.

3 **JLT Lockinge Stakes (1m)**
Newbury May 17 (Good To Firm)
1 **Olympic Glory** 4-9-0   Frankie Dettori
2 **Tullius** 6-9-0   Ryan Moore
3 **Verrazano** 4-9-0   Joseph O'Brien
11/8F, 9/2, 7/1. 2¼l, 1¾l. 8 ran. 1m 36.98s
(Richard Hannon).

A straightforward win for **Olympic Glory**, who would go on to prove somewhat disappointing until his final win in the Prix de la Foret and wasn't required to run close to that level in seeing off a modest bunch of rivals. Olympic Glory quickened away from **Tullius**, who would have preferred much softer ground, while **Verrazano** needed the run in third.

4 **Tattersalls Irish 2,000 Guineas (1m)**
Curragh (IRE) May 24 (Soft To Heavy)
1 **Kingman** 3-9-0   James Doyle

2 **Shifting Power** 3-9-0   Richard Hughes
3 **Mustajeeb** 3-9-0   Pat Smullen
4/5F, 7/1, 4/1. 5l, 2l. 11 ran. 1m 47.29s
(John Gosden).

Kingman showed his true colours after his Newmarket disappointment as he produced a blistering performance, coping superbly with testing conditions to thrash a couple of very smart rivals. Able to make headway on the bridle as **Shifting Power** set a good gallop, Kingman was unleashed at the furlong pole and showed a stunning turn of foot to storm clear as Shifting Power and Jersey Stakes winner **Mustajeeb** in turn pulled 6l clear of the rest.

5 Etihad Airways Irish 1,000 Guineas (Fillies) (1m)

Curragh (IRE) May 25 (Soft)
1 **Marvellous** 3-9-0   Ryan Moore
2 **Lightning Thunder** 3-9-0   Harry Bentley
3 **Vote Often** 3-9-0   James Doyle
10/1, 100/30F, 4/1. 3l, 4¼l. 11 ran. 1m 45.52s
(A P O'Brien).

There was very little strength in depth to this race with **Lightning Thunder**, who was below her best on soft ground, the only 1,000 Guineas runner to take her chance and none of the first seven from the French version either, and time would show that **Marvellous** had been flattered in looking such an impressive winner. Regarded as a middle-distance type despite ultimately disappointing over longer trips, Marvellous saw her stamina come to the fore in the conditions as she came from

almost last to draw clear of Lightning Thunder, who was in turn well clear of **Vote Often**.

6 Tattersalls Gold Cup (1m2f110y)

Curragh (IRE) May 25 (Soft)
1 **Noble Mission** 5-9-3   James Doyle
2 **Magician** 4-9-3   Joseph O'Brien
3 **Euphrasia** 5-9-0   Gary Carroll
EvsJ, EvsJ, 50/1. 1¼l, hd. 5 ran. 2m 21.71s
(Lady Cecil).

Front-running tactics had proved the key to the talented but infuriating **Noble Mission** earlier in the year and, with conditions hugely favouring him over fast-ground specialist **Magician**, he proved good enough to land this relatively soft first opening at the top level. Noble Mission opened up a clear advantage early in the straight and was always holding Magician, who couldn't produce his usual turn of foot and was nearly beaten for second by 50-1 outsider **Euphrasia** to show the modest level of the form.

7 Investec Oaks (In Memory of Sir Henry Cecil) (Fillies) (1m4f10y)

Epsom June 6 (Good)
1 **Taghrooda** 3-9-0   Paul Hanagan
2 **Tarfasha** 3-9-0   Pat Smullen
3 **Volume** 3-9-0   Richard Hughes
5/1, 9/2, 9/1. 3¾l, nse. 17 ran. 2m 34.89s
(John Gosden).

The emergence of a real star as **Taghrooda** destroyed her rivals in scintillating fashion. Always going well close to the pace, Taghrooda quickened to lead 2f out and drew clear in the

MARVELLOUS (left): flattered at the Curragh as rivals struggled on soft ground

final furlong without needing to be asked for maximum effort. That said, it was hardly vintage opposition with her strongest rival, **Tarfasha**, able to keep on for second ahead of the front-running **Volume**, who became unbalanced in the closing stages, despite looking a patent non-stayer in the Irish Oaks and going on to do better over slightly shorter. Aidan O'Brien relied on **Marvellous** instead of subsequent Group 1 winners Bracelet and Tapestry, but she could manage only sixth.

8 Investec Derby (1m4f10y)
Epsom June 7 (Good)

1 **Australia** 3-9-0		Joseph O'Brien
2 **Kingston Hill** 3-9-0		Andrea Atzeni
3 **Romsdal** 3-9-0		Richard Hughes

11/8F, 15/2, 20/1. 1¼l, 3¼l. 16 ran. 2m 33.63s (A P O'Brien).

A terrific battle between two fine colts as the brilliant **Australia** proved too good for another Classic winner in **Kingston Hill**, with the pair totally dominating a field that admittedly lacked strength in depth. Kept wide out of trouble, Australia made rapid headway once turning for home to hit the front and might even have been idling as Kingston Hill, who had been better placed initially but took much longer to hit top gear, gallantly chased him all the way. It was 3¼l back to **Romsdal**, with an even bigger gap back to **Arod**, who was one of only two subsequent 2014 winners (at 2-9) in the field outside the first two. **Western Hymn** proved the best of the rest but found even good ground too quick for him in sixth, while **Geoffrey Chaucer** was eased after being hampered and losing his action, though the form of his unlucky third in the Derrinstown Derby Trial took a big knock anyway as **Ebanoran** and **Fascinating Rock** were well beaten.

9 Investec Coronation Cup (1m4f10y)
Epsom June 7 (Good)

1 **Cirrus Des Aigles** 8-9-0		C Soumillon
2 **Flintshire** 4-9-0		Maxime Guyon
3 **Ambivalent** 5-8-11		Andrea Atzeni

10/11F, 4/1, 13/2. 2l, 2¼l. 7 ran. 2m 34.86s (Mme C Barande-Barbe).

France provided the only real class in this race as **Cirrus Des Aigles** saw off the subsequent Arc runner-up **Flintshire**. Cirrus Des Aigles had proved himself as good as ever with a spring Group 1 double, most notably when pipping Treve in the Prix Ganay, and followed up with a sixth win at the top level in all, striking for home early and staying on strongly enough to deny Flintshire any chance of pegging him back. Smart mare

Ambivalent was a good third, pulling 3¾l clear of German raider **Empoli**.

10 Queen Anne Stakes (1m)
Ascot June 17 (Good)

1 **Toronado** 4-9-0		Richard Hughes
2 **Verrazano** 4-9-0		Joseph O'Brien
3 **Anodin** 4-9-0		Olivier Peslier

4/5F, 6/1, 9/1. ¾l, 1¼l. 10 ran. 1m 37.73s (Richard Hannon).

The quality of the three-year-old milers, who went on to win every Group 1 at the trip in Europe, meant it proved tough for the older generation to land a blow, but **Toronado** was certainly the best of them, finishing second in the Sussex Stakes and the Prix du Moulin, and managed to grab this chance. Toronado won with plenty in hand, making rapid headway to quicken clear under a patient ride, while a more race-fit **Verrazano** reversed Lockinge form with **Tullius** in fourth.

11 King's Stand Stakes (5f)
Ascot June 17 (Good)

1 **Sole Power** 7-9-4		Richard Hughes
2 **Stepper Point** 5-9-4		Martin Dwyer
3 **Hot Streak** 3-8-12		Jamie Spencer

5/1, 50/1, 3/1F. 1¼l, nk. 16 ran. 58.85s (Edward Lynam).

A second successive win in the race for old favourite **Sole Power**, who was better than ever at seven, perfecting a style of racing that masked much of his superiority. Held together in rear for as long as possible, Sole Power produced a typically stunning turn of foot on his preferred fast ground to win cosily from the sharply progressive **Stepper Point** as less than 2l covered the next seven, with three-year-old **Hot Streak** running particularly well for a young horse in third.

12 St James's Palace Stakes (1m)
Ascot June 17 (Good)

1 **Kingman** 3-9-0		James Doyle
2 **Night Of Thunder** 3-9-0		Richard Hughes
3 **Outstrip** 3-9-0		William Buick

8/11F, 3/1, 33/1. 2¼l, 1l. 7 ran. 1m 39.06s (John Gosden).

Kingman put right his 2,000 Guineas defeat to **Night Of Thunder** as he produced a devastating turn of foot to storm to a comfortable victory. Night Of Thunder was ridden much more forcefully than when producing his best form as he made the running, albeit at a steady gallop, but it would have been hard to see him have any answer to Kingman in any circumstances – especially as others held up could never land a blow – as the champion quickened past him and drew clear. **Outstrip**

LEADING LIGHT: stamina held out as he won a great Gold Cup

and **War Command** finished well from the rear but never had any chance with the first two.

13 Prince of Wales's Stakes (1m2f)
Ascot June 18 (Good To Firm)
1 **The Fugue** 5-8-11   William Buick
2 **Magician** 4-9-0   Joseph O'Brien
3 **Treve** 4-8-11   Frankie Dettori
11/2, 6/1, 8/13F. 1¾l, 1l. 8 ran. 2m 1.90s (John Gosden).

An injury to **Treve** handed an opportunity to one of her rivals and **The Fugue** took full advantage, landing her fourth Group 1 with her best ever performance. The Fugue had just been pipped by **Magician** in the Breeders' Cup Turf in 2013 but seemed to go for home too soon that day and comfortably reversed the form under a more patient ride, quickening clear with a potent turn of foot. Magician returned to his best on quicker ground, battling past Treve, who was found to have pulled muscles in her back after finishing third. **Mukhadram**, unsuited by a less aggressive ride than usual, finished close behind in fourth, pulling 6l clear of the disappointing **Dank**.

14 Gold Cup (2m4f)
Ascot June 19 (Good To Firm)
1 **Leading Light** 4-9-0   Joseph O'Brien
2D **Estimate** 5-8-13   Ryan Moore
3 **Missunited** 7-8-13   Jim Crowley
10/11F, 8/1, 40/1. nk, shd. 13 ran. 4m 21.09s (A P O'Brien).

A magnificent battle saw **Leading Light**, good enough to have won a St Leger, just stretch his class well enough to this longer trip as he saw off defending champion **Estimate** (disqualified later in the year for failing a drug test due to contaminated feed) and another mighty mare in **Missunited**. Estimate, a stronger horse than when winning 12 months earlier, ran a superb race but was just beaten in a better renewal, massively extending her superiority over 2013 runner-up **Simenon**, who was a good fifth, and **Altano**, who had looked unlucky when fifth previously but had his limitations exposed this time in seventh. **Brown Panther** travelled well but didn't quite stay the trip in fourth.

15 Coronation Stakes (Fillies) (1m)
Ascot June 20 (Good To Firm)
1 **Rizeena** 3-9-0   Ryan Moore
2 **Lesstalk In Paris** 3-9-0   C Soumillon
3 **Euro Charline** 3-9-0   Andrea Atzeni
11/2, 15/2, 16/1. ¾l, hd. 12 ran. 1m 40.73s (Clive Brittain).

The dominance of older horses against the Classic generation in this division later in the season exposed the lack of a star among the three-year-olds, but even in the absence of Miss France this was still a competitive contest in which **Rizeena** came out a worthy winner. Rizeena was always prominent and soon forged ahead in the straight, holding off subsequent Grade 1 winner **Euro Charline**, while **Lesstalk In Paris** finished strongly to split the pair but was sadly denied the chance to build on her fine run when dying a week later. **My Titania** was next in a bunch finish that saw just 4l separate the first ten, who included subsequent Group winners **Tapestry**, **J Wonder** and **Kiyoshi**, although all their subsequent wins came over different trips. **Lightning Thunder** was well below her best in ninth.

16 Diamond Jubilee Stakes (6f)
Ascot June 21 (Good To Firm)
1 **Slade Power** 5-9-4   Wayne Lordan
2 **Due Diligence** 3-8-11   Ryan Moore
3 **Aljamaaheer** 5-9-4   Paul Hanagan
7/2F, 5/1, 4/1. 1½l, hd. 14 ran. 1m 12.40s (Edward Lynam).

INTEGRAL: began the domiance of older fillies against three-year-olds over 1m

The best performance at 6f all season as **Slade Power**, placed twice at Group 1 level in 2013, showed he had taken a big step forward in the meantime. Slade Power was much the best of those ridden prominently, doing particularly well to hold off a posse of fast finishers, whereas **Astaire** and **Gordon Lord Byron**, the only other Group 1 winners in the field and also in the firing line from some way out, faded to finish sixth and eighth. **Due Diligence** led those making late progress and would have finished closer but for having to be snatched up as he drifted into the winner close home, while **Aljamaaheer** finished strongly in third ahead of **Music Master**.

17 **Dubai Duty Free Irish Derby (1m4f)**
Curragh (IRE) June 28 (Good To Firm)
1 **Australia** 3-9-0 Joseph O'Brien
2 **Kingfisher** 3-9-0 Colm O'Donoghue
3 **Orchestra** 3-9-0 Seamie Heffernan
1/8F, 25/1, 12/1. 2½l, 2½l. 5 ran. 2m 33.19s
(A P O'Brien).

A stroll for 1-8 shot **Australia**, who had already beaten three of his four rivals easily at Epsom – the best of them managing eighth – and had the race set up for him by his two stablemates ensuring a reasonable gallop. Australia never had to come off the bridle to ease past **Kingfisher** and **Orchestra**, while

Ponfeigh, stepping up in class and trip, didn't quite seem to get home in fourth but still beat **Fascinating Rock**, who may have found the ground too quick.

18 **Newbridge Silverware Pretty Polly Stakes (Fillies & Mares) (1m2f)**
Curragh (IRE) June 29 (Good To Firm)
1 **Thistle Bird** 6-9-10 George Baker
2 **Venus De Milo** 4-9-10 Joseph O'Brien
3 **Just The Judge** 4-9-10 Jamie Spencer
4/1, 7/2, 11/2. 2¾l, ¾l. 8 ran. 2m 5.58s
(Roger Charlton).

A strong race in which the first four had won or been placed at the top level ten times in the past, and **Thistle Bird**, just touched off in the Nassau and the Prix de l'Opera in 2013, duly made a deserved Group 1 breakthrough on her final outing. The late-developing mare was always going well and drew clear of **Venus De Milo**, who ran her best race of a disappointing season, with **Just The Judge** and **Ambivalent** next.

19 **Coral-Eclipse (1m2f7y) Sandown July 5 (Good To Firm)**
1 **Mukhadram** 5-9-7 Paul Hanagan
2 **Trading Leather** 4-9-7 Kevin Manning
3 **Somewhat** 3-8-10 Franny Norton
14/1, 12/1, 100/1. 2l, ¾l. 9 ran. 2m 4.47s
(William Haggas).

Beaten on all eight other runs at Group 1 level, **Mukhadram** finally had his day as he took advantage of several riders giving their mounts far too much to do. The first three held those places throughout, with Mukhadram needing only to quicken past 100-1 pacemaker **Somewhat** before staying on strongly to hold off **Trading Leather**, who also stuck on well but lacked the winner's initial turn of foot. **Kingston Hill** did best of those held up even over an inadequate trip, while **Night Of Thunder** failed to stay and **The Fugue** and **Verrazano**, both making their final appearances, failed to act on the ground (loose on top after a pre-race shower).

20 Qipco Falmouth Stakes (Fillies & Mares) (1m)
Newmarket (July) July 11 (Soft)
1 **Integral** 4-9-7   Ryan Moore
2 **Rizeena** 3-8-12   Olivier Peslier
3 **Peace Burg** 4-9-7   Joseph O'Brien
15/8F, 4/1, 25/1. 2l, ¾l. 7 ran. 1m 41.96s
(Sir Michael Stoute).

Integral managed her first Group 1 win with impressive ease as she proved much too strong for fellow Royal Ascot winner **Rizeena**, coping well on soft ground for the first time. **Peace Burg** ran the race of her life to finish a close third, but the rest were bitterly disappointing, particularly **Sky Lantern**, whose tame fifth was a big sign that she was past her best. **Purr Along** could never challenge and **Kiyoshi** failed to get home.

21 Darley July Cup (6f)
Newmarket (July) July 12 (Good To Soft)
1 **Slade Power** 5-9-6   Wayne Lordan
2 **Tropics** 6-9-6   Robert Winston
3 **Gregorian** 5-9-6   William Buick
7/4F, 66/1, 12/1. 1½l, shd. 13 ran. 1m 12.40s
(Edward Lynam).

A Group 1 double for **Slade Power**, who didn't even need to run to his best with Due Diligence a non-runner, **Aljamaaheer** well below par and none of the field having won a Group 1 outside two-year-old company. Always prominent, Slade Power was soon in total command and easily saw off **Tropics**, who ran a huge race in second. **Gregorian** led those on the near side, finishing strongly as befits a 7f specialist, as did American raider **Undrafted**, whereas **Cougar Mountain**, on only his second run, showed impressive early speed and was a fine fifth considering the other two horses ridden prominently in that group, **Astaire** and **Justice Day**, faded well out of contention.

22 Darley Irish Oaks (Fillies) (1m4f)
Curragh (IRE) July 19 (Good To Firm)
1 **Bracelet** 3-9-0   Colm O'Donoghue
2 **Tapestry** 3-9-0   Joseph O'Brien
3 **Volume** 3-9-0   Kevin Manning
10/1, 13/2, 4/1. nk, nk. 10 ran. 2m 33.68s
(A P O'Brien).

Aidan O'Brien enjoyed a one-two with fillies who had skipped Epsom, but the best of them was beaten as **Tapestry** just lost out to **Bracelet**. Tapestry stumbled out of the stalls, causing her saddle to slip, but she still came desperately close to pulling off a remarkable victory, finishing strongly but not quite reeling in Bracelet, who followed up her victory in the Ribblesdale. **Volume** was better suited by this track than Epsom and was also involved in a desperate three-way finish, with the trio pulling well clear of the rest who included the disappointing **Tarfasha** and **Marvellous**.

23 King George VI and Queen Elizabeth Stakes (Sponsored by Qipco) (1m4f)
Ascot July 26 (Good)
1 **Taghrooda** 3-8-6   Paul Hanagan
2 **Telescope** 4-9-7   Ryan Moore
3 **Mukhadram** 5-9-7   Dane O'Neill
7/2, 5/2F, 12/1. 3l, shd. 8 ran. 2m 28.13s
(John Gosden).

Taghrooda wrote her name into the history books as she became the first three-year-old filly trained in Britain or Ireland to win a 1m4f Group 1 against older males worldwide in the history of the sport, running out a clearcut winner over **Telescope** and **Mukhadram**. Held up off a strong gallop, Taghrooda was strongly ridden to take closer order before powering relentlessly clear in the final furlong. The older challenge was admittedly nothing special, though Telescope was clearly well suited by course and distance having won the Hardwicke by 7l and Mukhadram appeared to see out the extra distance, while the King Edward VII winner **Eagle Top** was next ahead of the below-par **Trading Leather** and **Magician**.

24 Qipco Sussex Stakes (1m)
Goodwood July 30 (Good To Firm)
1 **Kingman** 3-9-0   James Doyle
2 **Toronado** 4-9-8   Richard Hughes
3 **Darwin** 4-9-8   Joseph O'Brien
2/5F, 11/4, 25/1. 1l, hd. 4 ran. 1m 41.75s
(John Gosden).

Another wonderful victory for **Kingman** on

what would prove to be his final race in Britain – he was retired after just one more equally brilliant win in the Prix Jacques le Marois – as he produced a blistering turn of foot to come from last to first in less than 100 yards. Such was Kingman's grip over his rivals by this time that connections of **Toronado** were complicit in allowing the race to be run at a crawl even though it didn't suit their horse at all and, while Toronado was well positioned to strike first, he lacked anything like the speed to match Kingman's dazzling burst. **Darwin** was flattered to finish so close having dictated the early gallop, while **Outstrip** couldn't land a blow.

25 Markel Insurance Nassau Stakes (Fillies & Mares) (1m1f192y)
Goodwood August 2 (Good To Firm)
1 **Sultanina** 4-9-7   William Buick
2 **Narniyn** 4-9-7   Christophe Soumillon
3 **Venus De Milo** 4-9-7   Joseph O'Brien
11/2, 7/4F, 5/2. 1½l, 3l. 6 ran. 2m 6.58s
(John Gosden).

A desperately weak renewal without a single Group 1 winner and any of the leading three-year-olds, giving a chance for **Sultanina** to land her big win. Sultanina outstayed her rivals with a sustained burst in the closing stages, but none of the six runners could finish better than fourth in eight subsequent runs between them in 2014 to emphasise the lack of quality, with French raider **Narniyn** coming up short and **Venus De Milo** below her best.

26 Juddmonte International Stakes (1m2f88y)
York August 20 (Good To Firm)
1 **Australia** 3-8-12   Joseph O'Brien
2 **The Grey Gatsby** 3-8-12 Richard Hughes
3 **Telescope** 4-9-6   Ryan Moore
8/13F, 12/1, 5/1. 2l, 2¼l. 6 ran. 2m 7.35s
(A P O'Brien).

Though a dual Classic winner over 1m4f, **Australia** proved ideally suited by a drop in trip as he produced his best performance in seeing off **The Grey Gatsby**. Australia travelled well and, having quickened into a clear lead, he was always comfortably holding The Grey Gatsby, confirming himself the better horse despite his shock reverse in the Irish Champion. Even so, The Grey Gatsby ran a cracker to back up his Dante and Prix du Jockey-Club victories and might even have finished closer but for being checked when first making his run, still pulling clear of **Telescope**, who just lacked the speed to cope with a drop in trip. **Mukhadram** sustained a

cut leg in finishing a moderate fourth.

27 Darley Yorkshire Oaks (Fillies & Mares) (1m4f)
York August 21 (Good)
1 **Tapestry** 3-8-11   Ryan Moore
2 **Taghrooda** 3-8-11   Paul Hanagan
3 **Tasaday** 4-9-7   Silvestre De Sousa
8/1, 1/5F, 22/1. ½l, 7l. 7 ran. 2m 28.59s
(A P O'Brien).

A memorable clash which brought about **Taghrooda**'s first defeat and, while the vanquished favourite was subsequently found to be in season to perhaps account for a below-par effort, **Tapestry** deserves huge credit for her win. Finally able to show her true colours after nothing had gone right earlier in the campaign, Tapestry tracked the 1-5 favourite and quickened up well to get the better of her in a protracted duel throughout the final quarter-mile, pulling 7l clear of **Tasaday** with even bigger gaps further back.

28 Coolmore Nunthorpe Stakes (5f)
York August 22 (Good)
1 **Sole Power** 7-9-11   Richard Hughes
2 **Stepper Point** 5-9-11   Martin Dwyer
3 **Extortionist** 3-9-9   Ryan Moore
11/4F, 20/1, 14/1. ½l, shd. 13 ran. 57.92s
(Edward Lynam).

A remarkable win for **Sole Power**, who found all sorts of trouble in delivering his typically late challenge but needed barely 50 yards to storm through a wall of horses in front of him, proving himself a true champion as he achieved the most impressive of his four Group 1 wins. **Stepper Point** repeated his runner-up finish from the King's Stand with another fine effort ahead of **Extortionist**, who led a top three-year-old challenge also comprising **Hot Streak** and the unlucky **G Force**, the latter having been badly hampered going for the same gap as Sole Power when staying on. **Moviesta** split that trio in fourth.

29 Betfred Sprint Cup (6f)
Haydock September 6 (Good)
1 **G Force** 3-9-1   Daniel Tudhope
2 **Gordon Lord Byron** 6-9-3 Wayne Lordan
3 **Music Master** 4-9-3   Dane O'Neill
11/1, 6/1, 15/2. ¾l, 1½l. 17 ran. 1m 12.95s
(David O'Meara).

With Slade Power absent and **Sole Power** unsuited by the conditions in fourth, this gave a chance for a new sprinting star to emerge and **G Force** took his chance by proving too strong for the 2013 winner **Gordon Lord Byron**. Initially denied a clear run, G Force burst through once clear and finished strongly enough to reel in even such a staunch stayer as subsequent Ascot winner Gordon Lord Byron. Some late rain turned the ground softer than ideal for **Music Master** and Sole Power, who would have preferred a stronger gallop as well, but they still ran well as the leading quartet pulled clear of the rest.

30 Ladbrokes St Leger Stakes (1m6f132y)
Doncaster September 13 (Good)
1 **Kingston Hill** 3-9-1   Andrea Atzeni
2 **Romsdal** 3-9-1   William Buick
3 **Snow Sky** 3-9-1   James Doyle
9/4F, 13/2, 11/2. 1¼l, 2l. 12 ran. 3m 5.42s (Roger Varian).

A terrific Leger in which several progressive staying types were outclassed by the placed horses from the Derby, with **Kingston Hill** confirming his superiority over **Romsdal**. Kingston Hill was given plenty to do but produced a withering late run to cut down Romsdal, with the winning margin probably not doing him justice. **Snow Sky**, who had the best form from the trials having won the Gordon Stakes and chased home Postponed in the Great Voltigeur, ran exactly to Goodwood form with **Windshear** in third

31 Qipco Irish Champion Stakes (1m2f)
Leopardstown (IRE) September 13 (Good To Firm)
1 **The Grey Gatsby** 3-9-0   Ryan Moore
2 **Australia** 3-9-1   Joseph O'Brien
3 **Trading Leather** 4-9-7   Kevin Manning
7/1, 30/100F, 20/1. nk, 4½l. 7 ran. 2m 3.18s (Kevin Ryan).

A stunning win for **The Grey Gatsby** as he inflicted **Australia**'s only defeat beyond 1m. Jockeyship was the key to the outcome as Australia went for home far earlier than necessary off a breakneck gallop, being forced very wide on the home turn to do so and sacrificing lots of ground, whereas The Grey Gatsby was held up on the inside before being angled out in the straight to run down the favourite in the final furlong. **Trading Leather** reversed Eclipse form with **Mukhadram**, who paid the price for going too quickly in pursuit of the pacemakers, though both finished in front of **Al Kazeem**, who was still finding his

G FORCE: stepped up at Haydock having been hampered in the Nunthorpe

feet after his return from stud.

32 Coolmore Fastnet Rock Matron Stakes (Fillies & Mares) (1m)
Leopardstown (IRE) September 13 (Good To Firm)

1 **Fiesolana** 5-9-5   Billy Lee
2 **Rizeena** 3-9-0   Ryan Moore
3 **Tobann** 4-9-5   Kevin Manning
5/1, 7/4F, 40/1. ½l, ¾l. 10 ran. 1m 38.16s (W McCreery).

A similar outcome to the Falmouth Stakes as **Rizeena** again proved the best three-year-old but ran into a better older rival, this time in **Fiesolana**, who showed a fine turn of foot to get up in the final 50 yards. The pair were by far the class acts at this trip in a field that included only one other Group-winning miler – the unlucky-in-running **Purr Along** – with the bizarre decision to drop **Tapestry** back in trip resulting in her trailing home ninth.

33 Palmerstown House Estate Irish St Leger (1m6f)
Curragh (IRE) September 14 (Good To Firm)

1 **Brown Panther** 6-9-11 Richard Kingscote
2 **Leading Light** 4-9-11   Joseph O'Brien
3 **Encke** 5-9-11   Adam Kirby
14/1, 9/10F, 9/1. 6½l, hd. 11 ran. 2m 57.15s (Tom Dascombe).

After four years of competing in the best staying races and six failed attempts at the top level, **Brown Panther** finally made his breakthrough in spectacular fashion, helped along the way by Richard Kingscote riding his rivals to sleep. More confident in his mount's stamina after he had failed to see out the extra distance of the Gold Cup, Kingscote was the only rider to sit close to pacemaker **Eye Of The Storm** and was 10l clear of the rest when striking for home, an advantage Brown Panther never looked likely to relinquish. **Leading Light** wasn't given a chance but ran on strongly for second ahead of **Encke**.

34 Kingdom of Bahrain Sun Chariot Stakes (Fillies & Mares) (1m)
Newmarket October 4 (Good)

1 **Integral** 4-9-3   Ryan Moore
2 **Miss France** 3-9-0   Maxime Guyon
3 **Fintry** 3-9-0   Mickael Barzalona
7/2C, 7/2C, 7/2C. 1l, nk. 7 ran. 1m 37.52s (Sir Michael Stoute).

Integral proved herself the best female miler

BATTLE ROYAL: Noble Mission and Al Kazeem duel in the Champion Stakes

in Europe as she saw off a three-pronged attack from Andre Fabre's yard led by the 1,000 Guineas winner **Miss France**. Given a superb ride from the front, Integral was always in control and quickened smartly in the final furlong to see off Miss France and **Fintry**, who were both close enough to land a blow but were well held by the line. **Esoterique**, who had just beaten Miss France in the Prix Rothschild when a below-par Integral returned lame, didn't appear to run to form this time in fourth, although that quartet pulled well clear of **Kiyoshi**, who faded late to confirm herself as being best at 7f, and **Sky Lantern**.

35 Qatar Prix de l'Arc de Triomphe (1m4f)

Longchamp (FR) October 5 (Good)

1	**Treve** 4-9-2	Thierry Jarnet
2	**Flintshire** 4-9-5	Maxime Guyon
3	**Taghrooda** 3-8-8	Paul Hanagan

11/1, 16/1, 9/2F. 2l, 1¼l. 20 ran. 2m 26.05s (Mme C Head-Maarek).

A remarkable transformation from **Treve**, who put a nightmare campaign behind her and bounced back to the sort of form that had seen her win the race in such thrilling fashion in 2013. She had won by 5l back then and only **Flintshire** finished within 3l of her this time as she quickened up superbly on the inside and ran out a commanding winner, with Flintshire staying on strongly out of the pack in an honourable second. The three-year-old challenge was weak, The Grey Gatsby's Prix du Jockey-Club romp having hinted at a shortage of top French colts, and **Taghrooda** proved the best of them in third ahead of **Kingston Hill**, who did particularly well from the worst draw. Big Japanese hopes **Harp Star** and **Just A Way** were both given far too much to do, while **Tapestry** and **Ectot** were the biggest disappointments.

36 Qipco British Champions Fillies & Mares Stakes (1m4f)

Ascot October 18 (Heavy)

1	**Madame Chiang** 3-8-12	Jim Crowley
2	**Silk Sari** 4-9-5	Andrea Atzeni
3	**Chicquita** 4-9-5	Joseph O'Brien

12/1, 9/2, 7/1. 2l, ¾l. 10 ran. 2m 38.76s (David Simcock).

A soft Group 1 win but still a big step forward from **Madame Chiang**, who showed that she is a very smart filly in testing conditions having struggled on quicker ground since her Musidora success. **Chicquita** was the outstanding performer in a field lacking a real star, but she blew her chance by hanging across the track having hit the front in the

straight and Madame Chiang took full advantage, staying on strongly from the rear.

37 Queen Elizabeth II Stakes (Sponsored by Qipco) (1m)

Ascot October 18 (Heavy)

1	**Charm Spirit** 3-9-1	Olivier Peslier
2	**Night Of Thunder** 3-9-1	Richard Hughes
3	**Toormore** 3-9-1	Kieren Fallon

5/1, 2/1F, 25/1. ½l, ½l. 11 ran. 1m 46.28s (F Head).

Further evidence that Kingman was far from being the only top-class three-year-old miler as **Charm Spirit** led a clean sweep of the places for the Classic generation, confirming Prix du Moulin form with **Night Of Thunder**, though for the second time he looked fortunate to come out on top. Given too much to do at Longchamp when a fast-finishing third, Night Of Thunder had to be switched several times looking for room this time and could not quite reel in Charm Spirit once in the clear. **Toormore** bounced back to form for the first time since winning the Craven in April, finishing third ahead of **Tullius**, who relished the testing conditions and was beaten only 1l with a much bigger gap back to **Captain Cat**.

38 Qipco Champion Stakes (1m2f)

Ascot October 18 (Heavy)

1	**Noble Mission** 5-9-5	James Doyle
2	**Al Kazeem** 6-9-5	George Baker
3	**Free Eagle** 3-9-0	Pat Smullen

7/1, 16/1, 5/2. nk, 1¼l. 9 ran. 2m 11.23s (Lady Cecil).

A desperately weak race for such a huge spectacle with the likes of Australia, The Grey Gatsby and Mukhadram missing, **Cirrus Des Aigles** well below his best and doubts over the ground for several others, but **Noble Mission** had already proved himself a high-class performer in such conditions and made the most of his big opportunity. Second twice at the top level in France and Germany since his Tattersalls Gold Cup win – though subsequently awarded the Grand Prix de Saint-Cloud due to the winner testing positive for a banned substance after he had just failed to last the 1m4f – Noble Mission made the running and fought back when headed by stud failure **Al Kazeem**, who had yet to show anything like the form of his three Group 1 wins in 2013 but showed plenty of his old sparkle in second. There had been doubts over the exciting **Free Eagle**'s participation until shortly before the race so he might well remain capable of better than his third, though he still ran a cracker to pull clear of **Western Hymn**.

Group 1 index

All horses placed or commented on in our Group 1 review section, with race numbers

Al Kazeem 31, 38	Esoterique 34
Aljamaaheer 16, 21	Estimate 14
Altano 14	Euphrasia 6
Ambivalent 9, 18	Euro Charline 2, 15
Anodin..10	Extortionist 28
Arod...8	Eye Of The Storm...............................33
Astaire 16, 21	Fascinating Rock 8, 17
Australia 1, 8, 17, 26, 31	Fiesolana...32
Bracelet 2, 22	Fintry...34
Brown Panther 14, 33	Flintshire..9, 35
Captain Cat 37	Free Eagle...38
Charm Spirit...1, 37	G Force..28, 29
Chicquita...36	Geoffrey Chaucer...................................8
Cirrus Des Aigles 9, 38	Gordon Lord Byron 16, 29
Cougar Mountain 21	Gregorian 21
Dank...13	Harp Star...35
Darwin..24	Hot Streak..11, 28
Due Diligence...16	Ihtimal...2
Eagle Top..23	Integral 20, 34
Ebanoran...8	J Wonder..15
Ectot 35	Just A Way...35
Empoli 9	Just The Judge 18
Encke...33	Justice Day..21

AUSTRALIA: brilliant colt competed at the top level all season

MUKHADRAM: Eclipse victory was his only one in nine Group 1 attempts

Kingfisher 17
Kingman 1, 4, 12, 24
Kingston Hill 1, 8, 19, 30, 35
Kiyoshi 15, 20, 34
Leading Light 14, 33
Lesstalk In Paris 15
Lightning Thunder 2, 5, 15
Madame Chiang.................................36
Magician..................................6, 13, 23
Manderley 2
Marvellous 5, 7, 22
Miss France..................................2, 34
Missunited 14
Moviesta 28
Mukhadram 13, 19, 23, 26, 31
Music Master...............................16, 29
Mustajeeb 4
My Titania 15
Narniyn 25
Night Of Thunder 1, 12, 19, 37
Noble Mission 6, 38
Olympic Glory 3
Orchestra 17
Outstrip................................12, 24
Peace Burg 20
Ponfeigh 17
Purr Along 20, 32
Rizeena...........................2, 15, 20, 32
Romsdal 8, 30
Shifting Power 1, 4
Silk Sari 36
Simenon..14

Sky Lantern 20, 34
Slade Power 16, 21
Snow Sky 30
Sole Power 11, 28, 29
Somewhat 19
Stepper Point 11, 28
Sultanina 25
Taghrooda 7, 23, 27, 35
Tapestry 2, 15, 22, 27, 32, 35
Tarfasha 7, 22
Tasaday...27
Telescope.....................................23, 26
The Fugue 13, 19
The Grey Gatsby.....................1, 26, 31
Thistle Bird 18
Tobann..32
Toormore...37
Toronado.....................................10, 24
Trading Leather.................19, 23, 31
Treve...13, 35
Tropics 21
Tullius 3, 10, 37
Undrafted 21
Venus De Milo 18, 25
Verrazano.........................3, 10, 19
Volume 7, 22
Vorda...2
Vote Often 5
War Command..................................12
Western Hymn 8, 38
Windshear 30

Est. 1909
**RACING &
FOOTBALL** OUTLOOK

Two-year-old review by Dylan Hill

**1 Coventry Stakes (Group 2) (6f)
Ascot June 17 (Good)**
1 **The Wow Signal** 2-9-1   Frankie Dettori
2 **Cappella Sansevero** 2-9-1 Jamie Spencer
3 **Jungle Cat** 2-9-1   Joe Fanning
5/1J, 6/1, 12/1. 1¾l, shd. 15 ran. 1m 12.99s
(John Quinn).

A dominant performance from **The Wow Signal**, who was always prominent going well and powered clear in the final furlong. It was particularly impressive that he managed to open up by far the biggest gap among the first 12, who were covered by just 5l due to a steady gallop, although doubts remain over his ability against the very best with the bare form no more than fair – **Jungle Cat** and the sixth, **Angelic Lord**, ran to identical form when second and fifth in July Stakes yet were beaten far more comfortably by Ivawood – and his main rivals all below their best. **War Envoy** hung badly in the closing stages, while **Kodi Bear** was crying out for a stiffer test and **Kool Kompany** seemed to resent hold-up tactics.

2 Windsor Castle Stakes (Listed Race) (5f)
Ascot June 17 (Good)
1 **Hootenanny** 2-9-3   Victor Espinoza
2 **Union Rose** 2-9-3   William Twiston-Davies
3 **Mubtaghaa** 2-9-3   Paul Hanagan
7/2F, 100/1, 7/1. 3½l, nk. 24 ran. 59.05s
(Wesley A Ward).

American trainer Wesley Ward had made no secret of the fact that he was aiming his best raider **Hootenanny** for the supposedly weakest juvenile race of the meeting out of eager-

ness to ensure another Royal Ascot winner and the powerful colt duly landed a monster gamble. **Union Rose** was best of the rest as first-time cheekpieces brought short-lived improvement in her, but they were an average bunch with the exception of **Cotai Glory**, who lost all chance when hampered early.

3 Queen Mary Stakes (Group 2) (Fillies) (5f)
Ascot June 18 (Good To Firm)
1 **Anthem Alexander** 2-9-0   Pat Smullen
2 **Tiggy Wiggy** 2-9-0   Richard Hughes
3 **Newsletter** 2-9-0   Shane Foley
9/4F, 7/2, 33/1. nk, ½l. 21 ran. 59.15s
(Edward Lynam).

A top-class contest and the first of three intriguing clashes between **Anthem Alexander** and **Tiggy Wiggy**, who remarkably suffered her only defeat in those meetings in the one in which her blistering speed should have been most favoured by the trip. Instead Tiggy Wiggy hit a flat spot at halfway on the quickest ground she had encountered at this point (although she would cope with good to firm well in the Cheveley Park) and couldn't get up despite clocking the fastest final quarter-mile on the card. Anthem Alexander held on gamely, while **Newsletter**, surely much better than a couple of disappointing performances subsequently, also gave the leading pair a big fright in third and pulled 1¾l clear of the fancied Wesley Ward raider **Spanish Pipedream**.

**4 Norfolk Stakes (Group 2) (5f)
Ascot June 19 (Good To Firm)**
1 **Baitha Alga** 2-9-1   Frankie Dettori

2 **Mind Of Madness** 2-9-1   Ryan Moore
3 **Ahlan Emarati** 2-9-1   Jamie Spencer
8/1, 14/1, 25/1. 1½l, 2¼l. 9 ran. 59.81s
(Richard Hannon).

Baitha Alga had won a very moderate Woodcote Stakes and again wasn't required to run to a level befitting a typical Norfolk as he saw off a field of only nine that lacked strength in depth. Baitha Alga was always prominent and took command over a furlong out, but he failed to beat a single horse in two subsequent outings and only **Ahlan Emarati**, who was checked in his run in third and needed an extra furlong, made any sort of impact at Group level in the future.

5 Albany Stakes (Group 3) (Fillies) (6f)
Ascot June 20 (Good To Firm)
1 **Cursory Glance** 2-9-0   Andrea Atzeni
2 **Sunset Glow** 2-9-0   Victor Espinoza
3 **Patience Alexander** 2-9-0   Adam Kirby
14/1, 7/1, 9/2J. 2l, nk. 21 ran. 1m 13.85s
(Roger Varian).

Three of the first five places were filled by fillies who would be part of a thrilling five-way finish to the Moyglare and subsequent Curragh heroine **Cursory Glance**'s superiority was even clearer over this shorter trip. Possessing the speed to lay up close enough to a good gallop despite having dwelt, Cursory Glance came through to lead in the final 100 yards and was drawing clear at the line. Wesley Ward's **Sunset Glow** was next ahead of **Patience Alexander**, who had looked a star when beating Tiggy Wiggy in a Listed race at York in May but would prove regressive, while

Malabar finished typically strongly in fourth and pulled clear of future rival **Osaila**.

6 Chesham Stakes (Listed Race) (7f)
Ascot June 21 (Good To Firm)
1 **Richard Pankhurst** 2-9-3   William Buick
2 **Toscanini** 2-9-3   Shane Foley
3 **Dick Whittington** 2-9-3   Joseph O'Brien
10/1, 4/1, 15/8F. 3¾l, hd. 14 ran. 1m 27.58s
(John Gosden).

Richard Pankhurst didn't run again as a juvenile, but this performance had already marked out Godolphin's subsequent buy as one of the most exciting seen all year. The form got stronger and stronger as the year went on, with **Toscanini** and **Dick Whittington** going on to prove Group 1 colts, yet neither could get close to Richard Pankhurst as he stormed clear in the final furlong. **Nafaqa** also ran a cracker in fourth having been slowly away on his debut, with the leading quartet pulling 3l clear.

7 GAIN Railway Stakes (Group 2) (6f)
Curragh (IRE) June 28 (Good To Firm)
1 **Kool Kompany** 2-9-3   F M Berry
2 **Ahlan Emarati** 2-9-3   Pat Smullen
3 **War Envoy** 2-9-3   Joseph O'Brien
6/1, 6/1, 5/2. 2l, 1¾l. 7 ran. 1m 12.60s
(Richard Hannon).

A one-two for the British raiders with **Kool Kompany** leading the way as he stormed to a tremendous victory over **Ahlan Emarati**. Kool Kompany seemed to relish a switch to front-running tactics and made virtually all, achieving far more than his increasingly

HOOTENANNY: justified trainer Wesley Ward's confidence at Royal Ascot

I AM BEAUTIFUL (right): flattered by racing prominently in the Grangecon Stud

disappointing performances later in a long campaign with the quick ground possibly aiding his cause. Norfolk third Ahlan Emarati proved much better over an extra furlong as he saw off **War Envoy**, while **Cappella Sansevero** was the big disappointment in fifth.

8 Grangecon Stud Stakes (Group 3) (Fillies) (6f)
Curragh (IRE) June 29 (Good To Firm)
1	**I Am Beautiful** 2-9-0	Seamie Heffernan
2	**Jeanne Girl** 2-9-0	N G McCullagh
3	**Quinta Verde** 2-9-0	Jamie Spencer

12/1, 9/2, 7/1. shd, nse. 11 ran. 1m 12.56s (A P O'Brien).

Front-running tactics paid dividends for **I Am Beautiful**, who just held off **Jeanne Girl** and **Quinta Verde** in a desperate finish. The form behind proved solid, though the first two were helped by racing prominently as they held those positions throughout, showing the quality of Quinta Verde as she finished strongly from the rear, and she had excuses (didn't stay an extra furlong after a long absence when third to Fillies' Mile winner Together Forever) for her defeat on her only subsequent outing.

9 Portland Place Properties July Stakes (Group 2) (6f)
Newmarket (July) July 10 (Good To Firm)
1	**Ivawood** 2-9-0	Richard Hughes
2	**Jungle Cat** 2-9-0	Joe Fanning
3	**Muhaarar** 2-9-0	Dane O'Neill

3/1F, 13/2, 12/1. 2¾l, ½l. 12 ran. 1m 11.02s (Richard Hannon).

The emergence of a real star as **Ivawood** put a solid field to the sword in hugely impressive fashion. **Jungle Cat** and **Angelic Lord** ran exactly to their Royal Ascot form, with the pair split by subsequent Gimcrack winner **Muhaarar** and Dewhurst winner **Belardo**, yet Ivawood was far too good for all of them as he made much of the running even having been slowly away and pulled clear in the closing stages. Belardo admittedly looked badly in need of further as he got going too late.

10 Duchess of Cambridge Stakes (Sponsored by Qipco) (Group 2) (6f)
Newmarket (July) July 11 (Soft)
1	**Arabian Queen** 2-9-0	Ryan Moore
2	**High Celebrity** 2-9-0	Maxime Guyon
3	**Tongue Twista** 2-9-0	J-P Guillambert

4/1, 4/9F, 50/1. 1¼l, 3l. 5 ran. 1m 15.14s (David Elsworth).

There was little strength in depth without any top-five finishers from Royal Ascot and, with class act **High Celebrity** also well below her best, **Arabian Queen** was able to land a soft win. Arabian Queen had run well when sixth in the Queen Mary and didn't need to step up on that as she was given the run of the race in front and wasn't challenged as High Celebrity struggled to pick up in the soft ground. **Parsley** was another who failed to cope with the conditions in fourth.

11 666bet Superlative Stakes (Group 2) (7f)
Newmarket (July) July 12 (Good To Soft)
1 **Estidhkaar** 2-9-1   Paul Hanagan
2 **Aktabantay** 2-9-1   William Buick
3 **Cock Of The North** 2-9-1 Frederik Tylicki
15/8F, 7/1, 9/1. 4½l, 2¼l. 8 ran. 1m 26.73s (Richard Hannon).

A demolition job from **Estidhkaar** as he tore apart a decent field in terrific fashion. Estidhkaar was always prominent and powered clear in the final furlong, exposing stamina failings in several others who perhaps weren't ready to go 7f in testing conditions. While that means the distances may be misleading, it was still a notable achievement to hand out such a drubbing to Solario winner **Aktabantay**, especially as that one also beat **Cock Of The North** far more comprehensively than he would later at Sandown.

12 Rose Bowl Stakes (Sponsored by Compton Beauchamp Estates Ltd) (Listed Race) (6f8y)
Newbury July 18 (Good To Firm)
1 **Limato** 2-9-0   James Doyle
2 **Cotai Glory** 2-9-0   George Baker
3 **Adaay** 2-9-0   Paul Hanagan
11/8, 7/1, 5/4F. 1¼l, 4½l. 5 ran. 1m 11.21s (Henry Candy).

A terrific clash between two of the best juveniles around as **Limato** saw off **Cotai Glory**. The trip played more to Limato's strengths as he quickened clear in the final furlong as Cotai Glory drifted left under pressure, with a return to 5f unlocking his rich potential. Still, the pair pulled well clear of **Adaay**, who was beaten almost twice as far as he had been in the Coventry.

13 Weatherbys Super Sprint (5f34y)
Newbury July 19 (Good)
1 **Tiggy Wiggy** 2-9-1   Richard Hughes
2 **Haxby** 2-8-10   Andrea Atzeni
3 **Fast Act** 2-8-8   Jamie Spencer
5/2F, 10/1, 12/1. 6l, 1¼l. 24 ran. 59.85s (Richard Hannon).

A stunning win for **Tiggy Wiggy**, who topped the weights yet still destroyed a competitive field with a devastating show of raw speed, stepping up significantly on her Queen Mary form. Tiggy Wiggy made all and stormed clear of **Haxby** and **Fast Act**, who wasn't quite at the level he would show later in the

Molecomb and Flying Childers, while **Bond's Girl**, hugely favoured by such races due to her very low purchase price, got going too late in fourth but managed to take advantage over an extra furlong in a similar contest at Doncaster.

14 Jebel Ali Racecourse & Stables Anglesey Stakes (Group 3) (6f63y)
Curragh (IRE) July 19 (Good To Firm)
1 **Dick Whittington** 2-9-3   Joseph O'Brien
2 **Toscanini** 2-9-3   Shane Foley
3 **Rapid Applause** 2-9-3   Fergal Lynch
2/1J, 2/1J, 10/1. ½l, ¾l. 5 ran. 1m 15.33s (A P O'Brien).

Dick Whittington appreciated a slight drop in trip after his Chesham third as he turned around that form with **Toscanini**, winning a shade more comfortably than the margin suggested. **Rapid Applause** might well have given Dick Whittington more to worry about had he not been short of room when making his challenge as he went on to finish strongly in third, but Queen Mary third **Newsletter** looked a non-stayer in fifth.

15 Japanese Racing Authority Tyros Stakes (Group 3) (7f)
Leopardstown (IRE) July 24 (Good To Firm)
1 **Gleneagles** 2-9-3   Joseph O'Brien
2 **Tombelaine** 2-9-3   Pat Smullen
3 **Convergence** 2-9-3   Colin Keane
4/7F, 7/4, 10/1. ¾l, hd. 3 ran. 1m 29.92s (A P O'Brien).

There were only three runners but this was still hugely impressive from **Gleneagles**, who first marked himself down as a very smart colt by sweeping through from last to first even off a moderate gallop. **Convergence** had dictated the pace and went on to win a Listed race next time by 5l, although his form grew increasingly patchy as the year went on.

16 Jockey Club of Turkey Silver Flash Stakes (Group 3) (Fillies) (7f)
Leopardstown (IRE) July 24 (Good To Firm)
1 **Jack Naylor** 2-9-0   F M Berry
2 **Agnes Stewart** 2-9-0   Billy Lee
3 **Qualify** 2-9-0   Seamie Heffernan
14/1, 11/2, 8/1. 1½l, hd. 8 ran. 1m 28.48s (Mrs John Harrington).

Just about the strongest Group 3 run all year as **Jack Naylor** saw off a trio of horses who went on to win at this level or above with the form of her own subsequent victory in the

Flame of Tara Stakes confirming there was little fluke about her beating all of them. Jack Naylor produced a strong run in the closing stages to run down those ridden more prominently, while **Agnes Stewart** could never get on terms having been held up in rear and stayed on into a never-threatening second. The one who didn't show her true running was **Raydara**, who had too much use of her and would comprehensively reverse the form with **Qualify** next time.

17 Princess Margaret Juddmonte Stakes (Group 3) (Fillies) (6f)
Ascot July 26 (Good)
1 **Osaila** 2-9-0   Frankie Dettori
2 **Pastoral Girl** 2-9-0   Joe Fanning
3 **Explosive Lady** 2-9-0   Martin Harley
7/4F, 33/1, 10/1. 2l, 1½l. 8 ran. 1m 14.33s (Richard Hannon).

A strong race for the grade and a comprehensive win for the progressive **Osaila**, who took a big step forward from her Albany fifth when sweeping through the field from last to first. Though soon out of further, Osaila coped better with the unsuitably short trip than another classy filly, **Muraaqaba**, who lacked the pace to mount a serious challenge in fourth but would still have finished

closer but for being impeded in the final furlong, with **Pastoral Girl** and **Explosive Lady**, a much closer third in a strong Two-Year-Old Trophy at Ripon, instead filling the places.

18 Titanic Belfast Winkfield Stakes (Listed Race) (7f)
Ascot July 26 (Good)
1 **Kodi Bear** 2-9-3   Adam Kirby
2 **Disegno** 2-9-3   Ryan Moore
3 **Muhaarar** 2-9-3   Paul Hanagan
2/1J, 7/1, 2/1J. 1½l, ¾l. 6 ran. 1m 27.78s (Clive Cox).

A fine win from **Kodi Bear**, who seemed to take a big step forward on his Coventry fifth as he relished the extra furlong, storming home from the promising **Disegno**. There had been nothing to separate Kodi Bear from **Muhaarar** on a line through Jungle Cat and Angelic Lord, and while that colt was subsequently dropped back in trip, he may well have simply run into two slightly better horses, especially in light of Kodi Bear's second in the Dewhurst.

19 bet365 Molecomb Stakes (Group 3) (5f)
Goodwood July 29 (Good To Firm)
1 **Cotai Glory** 2-9-1   George Baker
2 **Fast Act** 2-9-1   Jamie Spencer

KODI BEAR: better over 7f than when managing only fifth in the Coventry

3 **Beacon** 2-9-1   Richard Hughes
3/1, 10/1, 10/11F. ½l, hd. 8 ran. 57.30s
(Charles Hills).

Returning to 5f brought out the best in leading speedster **Cotai Glory** as he ran out a terrific winner, making all the running and comfortably holding off **Fast Act**. **Beacon** would certainly have finished at least second had he not been hampered when starting to make headway, but Cotai Glory had something in hand, as he would show when a desperately unlucky loser in the Flying Childers. **Muthmir** blew his chances for most of the season by pulling too hard but settled better for once in a first-time hood and ran his best race in fourth.

20 Veuve Clicquot Vintage Stakes (Group 2) (7f)
Goodwood July 30 (Good To Firm)
1 **Highland Reel** 2-9-1   Joseph O'Brien
2 **Tupi** 2-9-1   Richard Hughes
3 **Room Key** 2-9-1   Dane O'Neill
10/11F, 13/2, 20/1. 2¼l, ¾l. 8 ran. 1m 26.81s
(A P O'Brien).

A runaway win for **Highland Reel**, a rare Goodwood raider for Aidan O'Brien, though he proved very little in thrashing a desperate field for the grade and wasn't seen again. **Ahlan Emarati** was by far the strongest of Highland Reel's opponents, but he was stopped in his run when making ground on the inside and looked a weak stayer anyway. Otherwise the form took a string of knocks as the rest of the first six beat just four out of 25 rivals between them in four subsequent attempts at Pattern level.

21 Qatar Bloodstock Richmond Stakes (Group 2) (6f)
Goodwood July 31 (Good To Firm)
1 **Ivawood** 2-9-3   Richard Hughes
2 **Louie De Palma** 2-9-0   Adam Kirby
3 **Jungle Cat** 2-9-0   Joe Fanning
2/5F, 14/1, 5/1. 4½l, nk. 8 ran. 1m 10.09s
(Richard Hannon).

A mighty performance from **Ivawood**, his best of the season, as he defied a 3lb penalty to beat **Jungle Cat** far more comprehensively than he had at Newmarket. Breaking much more sharply than he had previously, Ivawood forced the pace throughout yet still proved strongest in the final furlong as he drew clear of Jungle Cat, who paid the price for trying to match strides early as he was caught for second close home by **Louie De Palma**. **Fox Trotter** ran well as he was beaten by just a short-head for third, but **Moonraker**

didn't see out the trip.

22 German-Thoroughbred.com Sweet Solera Stakes (Group 3) (Fillies) (7f)
Newmarket (July) August 9 (Soft)
1 **Muraaqaba** 2-9-0   Dane O'Neill
2 **Calypso Beat** 2-9-0   Pat Smullen
3 **Winters Moon** 2-9-0   Silvestre De Sousa
7/1, 10/1, 15/8F. 1¾l, 1l. 7 ran. 1m 28.04s
(Mark Johnston).

A much stiffer test of stamina proved the key to significant improvement in **Muraaqaba**, who won a strong race for the grade in terrific fashion when powering through the soft ground in the final furlong having been outpaced earlier. Muraaqaba drew clear of **Calypso Beat**, who had won a fair Listed race over 6f at the course previously, while subsequent Fillies' Mile third **Winters Moon** and Listed winner **Alonsoa** were next ahead of **Arabian Queen**, who had little chance with her flattering Group 2 penalty. The sixth, **Stroll Patrol**, also franked the form when finishing a much closer third in another Group 3 at Salisbury next time.

23 Keeneland Phoenix Stakes (Group 1) (6f)
Curragh (IRE) August 10 (Soft)
1 **Dick Whittington** 2-9-3   Joseph O'Brien
2 **Kool Kompany** 2-9-3   Richard Hughes
3 **Cappella Sansevero** 2-9-3   Colin Keane
6/1, 8/11F, 13/2. ½l, shd. 6 ran. 1m 14.55s
(A P O'Brien).

Soft ground led to three non-runners and robbed the race of much quality, with **Dick Whittington** scrambling home from a pair who were well beaten in similar conditions in the Middle Park. Dick Whittington was well held by **Kool Kompany** on a line through Rapid Applause, but he had won over further and that proved decisive as he outstayed Kool Kompany in the final furlong, while **Cappella Sansevero** was also in the mix as he bounced back to form. The trio pulled 2l clear of the filly **Beach Belle** with front-running **I Am Beautiful** failing to last home on soft ground.

24 Bathwick Tyres St Hugh's Stakes (Listed Race) (Fillies) (5f34y)
Newbury August 15 (Soft)
1 **Bronze Maquette** 2-9-0   Shane Kelly
2 **Al Fareej** 2-9-0   Martin Harley
3 **Parsley** 2-9-0   Pat Dobbs
10/1, 16/1, 4/1. 1¾l, 1l. 9 ran. 1m 2.76s
(Gary Moore).

A competitive race on paper but one in

which few fillies acted on the soft ground, meaning **Bronze Maquette** was flattered by her clearcut win. Bronze Maquette had progressed steadily to win a nursery off 83 on her previous start and powered clear in the final half-furlong, but she was well beaten twice subsequently to suggest she had reached the limit of her ability whereas the next three – **Al Fareej**, **Parsley** and **Accipiter** – all went on to do better in significantly quicker conditions.

25 Tattersalls Acomb Stakes (Group 3) (7f)
York August 20 (Good To Firm)
1 **Dutch Connection** 2-9-1   William Buick
2 **Toocoolforschool** 2-9-1   Ben Curtis
3 **Basateen** 2-9-1   Paul Hanagan
16/1, 33/1, 6/4F. hd, 1¼l. 10 ran. 1m 22.32s (Charles Hills)

Plenty of bubbles were burst in this race, but time would tell that **Dutch Connection** and **Toocoolforschool** had been vastly underrated. Dutch Connection made relentless progress in the straight and wore down the long-time leader Toocoolforschool before emerging with credit behind the top-class Gleneagles next time, while Toocoolforschool, though flattered by his win in the Mill Reef, was again a good second to the smart Nafaqa. **Basateen** and **Jamaica** were the fancied horses turned over just behind them.

26 Pinsent Masons Lowther Stakes (Group 2) (Fillies) (6f)
York August 21 (Good)
1 **Tiggy Wiggy** 2-9-0   Richard Hughes
2 **Cursory Glance** 2-9-0   Andrea Atzeni
3 **Anthem Alexander** 2-9-3   Pat Smullen
15/8F, 11/4, 5/2. 1½l, ½l. 9 ran. 1m 8.90s (Richard Hannon)

An outstanding contest fought out between two subsequent Group 1 winners, with the 6f trip favouring the speedy **Tiggy Wiggy** over **Cursory Glance**. Tiggy Wiggy was always travelling comfortably in front and found plenty more in the final furlong, seeing off Cursory Glance, a stronger stayer who did superbly to split Tiggy Wiggy and Queen Mary winner **Anthem Alexander** in such a sharp test. Anthem Alexander was the only one of the first three lumbered with a 3lb penalty but, as the Cheveley Park showed, she wouldn't have been able to match Tiggy Wiggy anyway and still ran a cracker to pull 5l clear of **Realtra**, with **Patience Alexander** among the also-rans.

27 Irish Thoroughbred Marketing Gimcrack Stakes (Group 2) (6f)
York August 23 (Good)
1 **Muhaarar** 2-9-0   Paul Hanagan
2 **Jungle Cat** 2-9-0   Silvestre De Sousa
3 **Ahlan Emarati** 2-9-0   Jamie Spencer
7/1, 9/2, 14/1. nse, ½l. 9 ran. 1m 10.52s (Charles Hills).

Placed behind Ivawood in the July Stakes, **Muhaarar** and **Jungle Cat** took advantage of that one's absence to fight out the finish of a much weaker Group 2 than many others run during the season, with Muhaarar just reversing the Newmarket placings. Down in trip having failed to stay 7f at Ascot, Muhaarar got up close home to deny Jungle Cat, with **Ahlan Emarati** also running another solid race in third just ahead of **Glenalmond** as that quartet pulled 2¼l clear of the below-par **Accepted** and **Beacon**.

28 Julia Graves Roses Stakes (Listed Race) (5f)
York August 23 (Good)
1 **Mind Of Madness** 2-9-0   Jamie Spencer
2 **Moonraker** 2-9-0   Ryan Moore
3 **Al Fareej** 2-8-9   Jim Crowley
4/1, 2/1F, 14/1. nse, nk. 10 ran. 58.58s (David Brown)

Mind Of Madness and **Moonraker** were both found out in a higher grade but proved quality sprinters at this level and were a cut above their rivals on this significant drop in class, with Mind Of Madness produced late to get up on the line. **Al Fareej** was the only horse to run them close, enjoying quicker ground than when well beaten in a couple of other races.

29 Whiteley Clinic Prestige Stakes (Group 3) (Fillies) (7f)
Goodwood August 23 (Good)
1 **Malabar** 2-9-0   Richard Hughes
2 **Bonnie Grey** 2-9-0   Oisin Murphy
3 **Zifena** 2-9-0   John Fahy
13/8F, 20/1, 11/1. 1l, ¾l. 8 ran. 1m 26.98s (Mick Channon)

A very easy win for **Malabar**, who was still on the bridle inside the final furlong before quickly putting the race to bed and went on to prove herself a very smart filly at the top level. However, those behind were a moderate bunch as runner-up **Bonnie Grey** and the fourth, **Astrelle**, were both thrashed in the May Hill next time, although the latter at least went close in a desperately weak Oh So Sharp Stakes.

30 Darley Prix Morny (Group 1) (6f) Deauville (FR) August 24 (Very Soft)

1 **The Wow Signal** 2-9-0   Frankie Dettori
2 **Hootenanny** 2-9-0   L R Goncalves
3 **Ervedya** 2-8-10   Christophe Soumillon
9/4J, 3/1, 9/4J. ½l, 1l. 9 ran. 1m 11.93s
(John Quinn).

Another good win for **The Wow Signal** as he saw off fellow Royal Ascot winner **Hootenanny**, though he didn't have to improve on his Coventry Stakes form to grind out a narrow victory. The Wow Signal benefited from the lack of any other British or Irish challengers in a race that always tends to come too early for the best French two-year-olds – the French have won just three of the last 17 runnings – and the very testing conditions that helped him to outstay the speedier Hootenanny. Subsequent Prix Marcel Boussac runner-up **Ervedya** ran a fine race in third ahead of **Goken** over a seemingly inadequate trip, with that quartet 3l clear of the rest.

31 Galileo European Breeders Fund Futurity Stakes (Group 2) (7f) Curragh (IRE) August 24 (Good To Firm)

1 **Gleneagles** 2-9-3   Joseph O'Brien
2 **Vert De Grece** 2-9-3   Shane Foley
3 **Hall Of Fame** 2-9-3   Kevin Manning
8/13F, 8/1, 7/1. ¾l, 3½l. 5 ran. 1m 26.32s
(A P O'Brien).

Few fireworks this time but another solid performance from **Gleneagles**, who won far more comfortably than the winning margin suggests over a subsequent Group 1 winner in **Vert De Grece**. Gleneagles soon put the race to bed when quickening clear and was idling as Vert De Grece stayed on well in second, underlined by the fact that he went on to beat **Hall Of Fame** by further in the National Stakes.

32 Debutante Stakes (Group 2) (Fillies) (7f) Curragh (IRE) August 24 (Good To Firm)

1 **Raydara** 2-9-0   Shane Foley
2 **Lucida** 2-9-0   Kevin Manning
3 **Toogoodtobetrue** 2-9-0 Seamie Heffernan
11/1, 3/1J, 11/1. ½l, 1¾l. 9 ran. 1m 25.68s
(M Halford).

A terrific win from **Raydara**, who was much improved for a change in tactics from her previous fourth to Jack Naylor. Held up in rear having made the running that day, Raydara produced a powerful late burst to cut down **Lucida**, comfortably reversing form with the fifth, **Qualify**, to underline her progress, and the subsequent efforts of the runner-up suggest should could have made an impact at Group 1 level had connections not preferred to put her away. **Toogoodtobetrue** also ran a good race in third ahead of **Jeanne Girl**, while **I Am Beautiful** and **Beach Belle** couldn't get clear runs behind.

33 Irish Stallion Farms EBF Ripon Champion Two-Year-Old Trophy (Listed Race) (6f) Ripon August 25 (Good)

1 **Izzthatright** 2-9-3   Tony Hamilton
2 **Bossy Guest** 2-9-3   Charles Bishop
3 **Explosive Lady** 2-8-12   Ben Curtis
9/2, 9/4J, 9/4J. ½l, nk. 7 ran. 1m 12.57s
(Richard Fahey).

A good battle between three useful horses won by the sharply progressive **Izzthatright**, who had gone up 19lb for the second of two nursery wins at Catterick and gamely made all from the solid yardstick **Bossy Guest**. **Explosive Lady** was a close third and looked unlucky not to win a sales race at the Curragh next time and that trio pulled clear of **Prince Bonnaire** and **Dark Reckoning**, whose Group 3 win at Ayr franked the form again even though it clearly flattered her.

MALABAR: easy winner at Goodwood

34 EBF Stallions Stonehenge Stakes (Listed Race) (1m)
Salisbury August 29 (Good)
1 **Elm Park** 2-9-1   David Probert
2 **Groor** 2-9-1   Martin Harley
3 **Mister Universe** 2-9-1   Dane O'Neill
15/8F, 33/1, 7/1. 3l, nk. 5 ran. 1m 44.37s
(Andrew Balding).

A terrific race on paper with Racing Post Trophy winner **Elm Park** and Fillies' Mile third **Winters Moon** in the field, but the latter was well below her best in fourth and that meant Elm Park wasn't extended to run out a clearcut winner. Indeed, the bare form was moderate with runner-up **Groor** coming into the race rated just 79 and two defeats when favourite in Listed races in France showed too much had been made of his performance.

35 European Wealth Solario Stakes (Group 3) (7f16y)
Sandown August 30 (Good To Soft)
1 **Aktabantay** 2-9-1   Ryan Moore
2 **Future Empire** 2-9-1   James Doyle
3 **Lexington Times** 2-9-1   Pat Dobbs
9/4, 5/4F, 16/1. shd, nk. 5 ran. 1m 29.84s
(Hugo Palmer).

A thrilling contest as less than ½l covered four of the five runners, though that told of a lack of quality among them with **Aktabantay** able to come out on top despite not being at his best. Aktabantay had the strongest form credentials despite being beaten 4½l by Estidhkaar in the Superlative Stakes and saw his superiority over the fourth, **Cock Of The North**, diminished, yet he still just proved good enough to pip **Future Empire** as the pair reeled in the unfortunate **Lexington Times** on the line.

36 Flame Of Tara European Breeders Fund Stakes (Listed Race) (Fillies) (1m)
Curragh (IRE) August 31 (Good)
1 **Jack Naylor** 2-9-5   F M Berry
2 **Legatissimo** 2-9-0   Wayne Lordan
3 **Together Forever** 2-9-0   Joseph O'Brien
2/1, 11/8F, 3/1. ¾l, 1¼l. 7 ran. 1m 39.15s
(Mrs John Harrington).

A terrific effort from **Jack Naylor** to defy a 5lb penalty, albeit with her main rival, **Together Forever**, yet to show the level that would see her land the Fillies' Mile later in the year. Jack Naylor, staying on strongly on this step up to a mile, wore down the front-running Together Forever, who would benefit from slightly more restrained tactics, with **Legatissimo** also coming past her for second. **Steip**

Amach was entitled to progress after a fine debut in fourth, though Together Forever still managed to extend her superiority over her when winning a Listed race at the Curragh shortly before her Fillies' Mile win to underline her improvement even before that big breakthrough.

37 Nestle Supporting Irish Autism Action Round Tower Stakes (Group 3) (6f)
Curragh (IRE) August 31 (Good To Yielding)
1 **Cappella Sansevero** 2-9-3   Andrea Atzeni
2 **Rapid Applause** 2-9-3   Fergal Lynch
3 **War Envoy** 2-9-3   Joseph O'Brien
6/4F, 9/2, 5/2. ¾l, ¾l. 7 ran. 1m 13.49s
(G M Lyons).

A decent race for the grade fought out between two horses who had run Dick Whittington close previously and **Cappella Sansevero** confirmed the form of those races by seeing off **Rapid Applause** with a smart turn of foot. **War Envoy** was a fair third.

38 Country Gentlemen's Association Dick Poole Fillies' Stakes (Group 3) (6f)
Salisbury September 4 (Good)
1 **New Providence** 2-9-0   Jim Crowley
2 **Marsh Hawk** 2-9-0   Richard Hughes
3 **Stroll Patrol** 2-9-0   Oisin Murphy
4/1, 11/8F, 9/1. shd, 1¼l. 13 ran. 1m 13.43s
(Hugo Palmer).

Newly upgraded to Group 3 level, this race just about lived up to its billing despite arguably the two best fillies failing to run to form, most notably **Marsh Hawk**, who found the trip just too sharp as she tackled 6f for the only time and was touched off by **New Providence**. New Providence had been steadily progressive but had her limitations exposed when third in the Rockfel, in which **Stroll Patrol** was only fifth, while subsequent Cornwallis winner **Royal Razalma** didn't see out the extra furlong in fifth.

39 totescoop6 "The Millionaire Maker" Sirenia Stakes (Group 3) (6f)
Kempton (AW) September 6 (Standard)
1 **Burnt Sugar** 2-9-1   Gerald Mosse
2 **Maftool** 2-9-1   Paul Hanagan
3 **Home Of The Brave** 2-9-1   Kevin Manning
12/1, 5/2, 11/10F. 2¼l, ¾l. 10 ran. 1m 11.79s
(Richard Hannon).

An excellent performance from **Burnt Sugar**, who had looked well short of Pattern level in four previous runs but showed a terrific turn of foot to win well. The form behind also

DISASTER! George Baker hits the deck with the Flying Childers at his mercy

worked out very well at first glance with runner-up **Maftool** and the fifth, **Accipiter**, going on to win good races, though that may prove slightly flattering with Maftool's Group 3 success coming in a much weaker contest and Accipiter failing to stay the trip. **Home Of The Brave**, having been lit up by an early bump and pulled hard, ran a big race as he was still only headed in the final furlong, while **Fanciful Angel** was fourth.

40 Polypipe Flying Childers Stakes (Group 2) (5f)
Doncaster September 12 (Good)
1 **Beacon** 2-9-1   William Buick
2 **Astrophysics** 2-9-1   Graham Lee
3 **Accepted** 2-9-1   Wayne Lordan
8/1, 50/1, 15/2. hd, ½l. 14 ran. 58.36s (Richard Hannon).

A dramatic finish as **Cotai Glory**, on the brink of what would have been a sensational triumph, unseated his rider when well clear in the final furlong, gifting victory to the fortunate **Beacon**. The Molecomb winner had shown blistering speed to leave a hugely competitive field well strung out when disaster struck as he hung badly right, causing his saddle to slip. Beacon was left to pick up the pieces, staying on strongly to run down **Astrophysics** and **Accepted** as he reversed Molecomb form with **Fast Act** in fourth. Unbeaten Irish filly **Ainippe** was next with Roses Stakes one-two **Moonraker** and **Mind Of Madness** behind, while **Bronze Maquette** found the ground too quick and **Ahlan Emarati** failed to cope with the return to 5f.

41 John Smith's Extra Smooth May Hill Stakes (Group 2) (Fillies) (1m)
Doncaster September 12 (Good)
1 **Agnes Stewart** 2-9-0   Billy Lee
2 **Muraaqaba** 2-9-0   Paul Hanagan
3 **Shagah** 2-9-0   Frankie Dettori
11/4, 13/8F, 12/1. 1¼l, nk. 8 ran. 1m 37.20s (Edward Lynam).

The first sign of Ireland's strength in the juvenile fillies' division dominating the rest of Europe as **Agnes Stewart**, later part of an Irish one-two in the Fillies' Mile to go with their Marcel Boussac and Rockfel wins, showed a terrific turn of foot to cut down a worthy opponent in **Muraaqaba**. **Alonsoa**, who was next in the market, was all wrong as she finished a distant last, but **Bonnie Grey** and **Astrelle** were also beaten upwards of 6½l seemingly without excuses despite being much closer when making the frame in other Pattern races, adding further gloss to the form, which suggests that **Shagah** and **Supreme Occasion** remain capable of much better than they showed subsequently.

42 Weatherbys Stallion Book Flying Scotsman Stakes (Listed Race) (7f)
Doncaster September 12 (Good)
1 **Nafaqa** 2-9-0   Paul Hanagan
2 **Toocoolforschool** 2-9-0   Ben Curtis
3 **Peacock** 2-9-0   Ryan Moore
8/1, 11/4, 20/1. ½l, nk. 7 ran. 1m 23.38s (B W Hills).

An impressive victory from **Nafaqa**, who was considerably better than the bare form as he looked very green when asked to assert, jinking right and hesitating close home. Nafaqa still managed to beat **Toocoolforschool**, with **Peacock** and **White Lake**, who was sent off odds-on after running away with the Convivial Maiden at York, close behind.

43 At The Races Champagne Stakes (Group 2) (7f)

Doncaster September 13 (Good)

1 **Estidhkaar** 2-9-3   Paul Hanagan
2 **War Envoy** 2-9-0   Ryan Moore
3 **Aces** 2-9-0   Oisin Murphy
10/11F, 11/1, 18/1. 1¼l, nk. 6 ran. 1m 24.18s
(Richard Hannon).

A fair Group 2 even with **Belardo** below his best, yet **Estidhkaar** was still good enough to comfortably defy a 3lb penalty. It took a while for Estidhkaar to get on top as a muddling gallop led to all six runners being in contention at the furlong pole, but he took command in the final furlong by pulling away from **War Envoy**, who finally revealed his true potential by relishing the step up to 7f. **Aces** was an excellent third on only his second run ahead of Belardo, who raced far too keenly in the early stages, while **Room Key** was comfortably seen off in fifth with only the non-staying **Glenalmond** behind him.

44 John Deere Juvenile Turf Stakes (Group 3) (1m)

Leopardstown (IRE) September 13 (Good To Firm)

1 **John F Kennedy** 2-9-3   Joseph O'Brien
2 **Tombelaine** 2-9-3   Pat Smullen
3 **Faithful Creek** 2-9-3   F M Berry
4/7F, 4/1, 20/1. 3¼l, 2¼l. 7 ran. 1m 38.44s
(A P O'Brien).

A big statement from **John F Kennedy**, who saw off solid yardstick **Tombelaine** with the minimum of fuss, easing well clear. Tombelaine, subsequently beaten in similar fashion by Ol' Man River in the Tyros, albeit beaten just as cosily, and ran to that form on a line through **East India**, who had been second to Tyros third Convergence subsequently and would have been beaten by a similar distance had he not been eased when beaten in the final furlong.

45 Goffs Vincent O'Brien National Stakes (Group 1) (7f)

Curragh (IRE) September 14 (Good To Firm)

1 **Gleneagles** 2-9-3   Joseph O'Brien
2 **Toscanini** 2-9-3   Shane Foley
3 **Dutch Connection** 2-9-3   George Baker
1/3F, 7/1, 9/2. 1½l, 1l. 5 ran. 1m 25.29s
(A P O'Brien).

TOOCOOLFORSCHOOL (left): only horse to cope with desperate conditions

A disappointing lack of opposition to **Gleneagles** given the prize, though he still had to pull out all the stops to battle past the unfortunate **Toscanini**, who had been second to Richard Pankhurst and Dick Whittington previously and bumped into another real star. Taking time to wear down the runner-up, Gleneagles still picked up well and was going away at the line as the first two pulled clear of Acomb winner **Dutch Connection** and **Hall Of Fame**.

46 Moyglare Stud Stakes (Group 1) (Fillies) (7f)
Curragh (IRE) September 14 (Good To Firm)
1 **Cursory Glance** 2-9-0   Andrea Atzeni
2 **Lucida** 2-9-0   Kevin Manning
3 **Found** 2-9-0   Joseph O'Brien
11/8F, 6/1, 7/2. nk, ½l. 10 ran. 1m 24.80s
(Roger Varian).

A competitive and classy renewal even in the absence of leading Irish fillies Raydara, Jack Naylor and Agnes Stewart, with **Cursory Glance** running out a narrow winner to justify favouritism. Always expected to improve for the extra furlong, Cursory Glance dug deep in the final 50 yards to hold off the late thrust of **Lucida**, whose proximity suggested Raydara might well have come on top, especially as she ran exactly to her Debutante form on a line through **Qualify** in sixth, though Cursory Glance had appeared to be idling after hitting the front earlier than ideal. **Found** ran a stormer in third on only her second run having looked green when asked to challenge, pointing to the improvement she would show at Longchamp later, while **Malabar** finished fast to overhaul **Osaila** as that quintet pulled 2¼l clear of some solid yardsticks, led by Qualify with the likes of **Beach Belle**, **Jeanne Girl** and **I Am Beautiful** behind.

47 EBF Stallions Harry Rosebery Stakes (Listed Race) (5f)
Ayr September 19 (Good)
1 **Accipiter** 2-8-12   Ashley Morgan
2 **Mind Of Madness** 2-9-6   Jamie Spencer
3 **Squats** 2-9-3   Joe Fanning
25/1, 4/1, 3/1F. hd, shd. 14 ran. 58.28s
(Chris Wall).

Suited by 5f on fast ground, **Accipiter** proved herself much better than on three previous attempts at this sort of level with conditions in her favour, though she was still flattered to come out on top in a blanket finish with plenty of hard-luck stories behind. Among them was **Mind Of Madness**, who found room just in time to storm home in a fast-finishing second as he made a bold bid to defy a penalty, while **Fendale** never got a run in fifth.

48 Dubai Duty Free Mill Reef Stakes (Group 2) (6f8y)
Newbury September 20 (Soft)
1 **Toocoolforschool** 2-9-1   S De Sousa
2 **Growl** 2-9-1   Jimmy Fortune
3 **Kibaar** 2-9-1   Dane O'Neill
4/1, 11/1, 16/1. 7l, ½l. 6 ran. 1m 14.35s
(K R Burke).

A demolition job from **Toocoolforschool**, but that probably said more about his rivals' inability to cope with desperate ground. Toocoolforschool made all the running and was never seriously challenged as he roared clear of **Growl**, but that one was beaten further on similar ground behind Code Red in a weak Listed race at Doncaster next time and the likes of **Strath Burn**, **Jungle Cat** and **Baitha Alga** showed nothing at all.

49 William Hill Firth Of Clyde Stakes (Group 3) (Fillies) (6f)
Ayr September 20 (Good To Firm)
1 **Dark Reckoning** 2-9-0   Graham Lee
2 **Parsley** 2-9-0   James Doyle
3 **Ainippe** 2-9-0   Colin Keane
25/1, 9/1, 3/1F. shd, 2¼l. 13 ran. 1m 11.01s
(Ann Duffield).

There wasn't much depth to this race, but the principals were utterly dominant with **Parsley** and **Ainippe** perhaps unlucky not to beat **Dark Reckoning**. Parsley, relishing the good to firm ground, led for much of the way, but Dark Reckoning was aided by a quicker strip on the stands rail and got up close home, while Ainippe couldn't find room at a key stage before finishing powerfully in third. **Royal Razalma** quickened into the lead but then faded in the final furlong to finish fourth, pointing to her victory when dropped in trip in the Cornwallis.

50 Somerville Tattersall Stakes (Group 3) (7f)
Newmarket September 25 (Good)
1 **Maftool** 2-9-0   Richard Hughes
2 **Markaz** 2-9-0   Dane O'Neill
3 **Mubtaghaa** 2-9-0   Paul Hanagan
7/2, 16/1, 3/1F. 2½l, 2½l. 8 ran. 1m 23.34s
(Saeed bin Suroor).

Maftool had finished second in this grade at Kempton and wasn't stretched to go one better against fairly moderate opposition. **Markaz** had looked short of this level previously and **Mubtaghaa**, despite winning a valuable sales race at York, was found out for the second time in Pattern grade in third.

51 Shadwell Rockfel Stakes (Group 2) (Fillies) (7f)

Newmarket September 26 (Good)

1 **Lucida** 2-9-0   Kevin Manning
2 **Fadhayyil** 2-9-0   Paul Hanagan
3 **New Providence** 2-9-0   Jim Crowley
EvensF, 10/1, 5/1. 1l, 2l. 9 ran. 1m 22.82s
(J S Bolger).

Lucida stood out on the strength of finishing second in the two best juvenile fillies' races in Ireland and did well to come out on top despite not being at her best. Lucida took a while to pick up as she appeared to become unbalanced, but once able to quicken she soon reeled in **Fadhayyil** and won going away. Fadhayyil also did herself no favours by running green in front as the pair were much better than **New Providence**, who still confirmed Salisbury form with **Stroll Patrol**, with **Tigrilla** splitting the pair.

52 Connolly's Red Mills Cheveley Park Stakes (Group 1) (Fillies) (6f)

Newmarket September 27 (Good To Firm)

1 **Tiggy Wiggy** 2-9-0   Richard Hughes
2 **Anthem Alexander** 2-9-0   Pat Smullen
3 **High Celebrity** 2-9-0   Maxime Guyon
6/4F, 5/1, 9/4. ¾l, 1¼l. 9 ran. 1m 11.40s
(Richard Hannon).

Another wonderful performance from **Tiggy Wiggy**, who showed she could beat **Anthem Alexander** on level terms even on a stiffer track than York. Tiggy Wiggy was sent straight to the front, but Anthem Alexander sat close to her throughout and still couldn't find enough in the closing stages as Tiggy Wiggy quickened again and stayed on strongly. French raider **High Celebrity** ran a fine race in third, comprehensively reversing previous form with the outclassed **Arabian Queen** in sixth, while maiden winners **Terror** and **Tendu**, separated by a short-head, also ran well in pulling 4½l clear of that filly, with the quality of the race epitomised by the fact that Terror was sent off just 1-5 when winning a Listed race over course and distance next time.

53 Juddmonte Royal Lodge Stakes (Group 2) (1m)

Newmarket September 27 (Good To Firm)

1 **Elm Park** 2-9-0   Andrea Atzeni
2 **Nafaqa** 2-9-0   Paul Hanagan
3 **Salateen** 2-9-0   Jamie Spencer
11/4, 5/4F, 15/2. 1l, 4l. 6 ran. 1m 37.10s
(Andrew Balding).

Another step up the ladder for **Elm Park**, who was given by far his toughest test since being turned over on his defeat but was just too strong for **Nafaqa**. The pair both struggled to keep tabs on long-time leader **Salateen** initially, with Elm Park not helped by taking a false step, but both showed abundant stamina to pull 4l clear of the third despite not heading him until 100 yards from the line.

54 Juddmonte Beresford Stakes (Group 2) (1m)

Curragh (IRE) September 28 (Good To Firm)

1 **Ol' Man River** 2-9-3   Joseph O'Brien
2 **Clonard Street** 2-9-3   F M Berry
3 **Battle Of Marathon** 2-9-3   S Heffernan
1/2F, 20/1, 25/1. 2¾l, ¾l. 6 ran. 1m 39.38s
(A P O'Brien).

Another stroll for a hugely exciting Ballydoyle juvenile as **Ol' Man River** won with a performance that ties in very closely to stablemate John F Kennedy. Ol' Man River showed a smart turn of foot and comfortably beat **Clonard Street**, who saw off **Battle Of Marathon** and the back-to-form **Convergence** for second. **Tombelaine** would have been beaten by an almost identical distance to when second to John F Kennedy at Leopardstown had he not been squeezed out when dropping to fifth in the final furlong.

55 C.L. & M.F. Weld Park Stakes (Group 3) (Fillies) (7f)

Curragh (IRE) September 28 (Good To Firm)

1 **Qualify** 2-9-0   Joseph O'Brien
2 **Lola Beaux** 2-9-0   F M Berry
3 **Stellar Glow** 2-9-0   Kevin Manning
9/4, 11/2, 10/11F. 3l, shd. 6 ran. 1m 22.65s
(A P O'Brien).

Qualify had run well in several top contests and benefited from a drop in grade as she proved much too good for her rivals. Held up in a change of tactics, Qualify quickened clear of **Lola Beaux** and **Stellar Glow**, who was beaten at odds-on for the second time in a weaker race at Leopardstown next time.

56 £500,000 Tattersalls Millions 2YO Trophy (7f)

Newmarket October 4 (Good To Firm)

1 **Secret Brief** 2-9-3   Joe Fanning
2 **Outlaw Country** 2-9-3   Pat Smullen
3 **Bossy Guest** 2-9-3   James Doyle
9/2F, 8/1, 7/1. ¾l, nk. 15 ran. 1m 23.21s
(Mark Johnston).

A big sales double for **Secret Brief**, who had won over 6f at the track previously but saw out the extra furlong strongly to see off

OL' MAN RIVER: Beresford win ties in closely with John F Kennedy's form

maiden winner **Outlaw Country**. Two-Year-Old Trophy runner-up **Bossy Guest** was close behind Secret Brief in both races to set the level of the form around Listed level, seemingly confirmed by Secret Brief's subsequent flop in the Dewhurst.

57 £300,000 Tattersalls Millions 2YO Fillies' Trophy (7f)
Newmarket October 4 (Good To Firm)
1	**Osaila** 2-9-0	Frankie Dettori
2	**Lacing** 2-9-0	Ryan Moore
3	**Very Special** 2-9-0	James Doyle

4/5F, 7/1, 9/4. 1½l, ¾l. 9 ran. 1m 23.53s (Richard Hannon).

Class came to the fore as Moyglare fifth **Osaila** bagged this valuable prize, though she was pushed hard to confirm the 25lb she had in hand on official marks with **Lacing**, who had won a sales race at the track over 6f on her previous outing and confirmed herself a smart filly by running a blinder in second. **Very Special** also ran well in third, staying on strongly having become unbalanced, as that trio pulled 7l clear of the rest.

58 TriConnex Oh So Sharp Stakes (Group 3) (Fillies) (7f)
Newmarket October 4 (Good)
1	**Local Time** 2-9-0	James Doyle
2	**Astrelle** 2-9-0	Paolo Sirigu
3	**Prize Exhibit** 2-9-0	Jamie Spencer

7/4F, 14/1, 5/1. nk, hd. 8 ran. 1m 25.26s (Saeed bin Suroor).

A desperately weak race for the grade but a promising winner in **Local Time**, who underlined the point in Dubai over the winter. Best over further, Local Time just about coped with a drop in trip, taking a while to hit top gear but finally assuming command close home. **Astrelle** and **Prize Exhibit** filled the places having been exposed in similar races, though the latter certainly improved for a step up in trip, while **Shagah** was a disappointing fourth as she seemed to lose her action in the Dip.

59 totepool Two-Year-Old Trophy (Listed Race) (6f)
Redcar October 4 (Good)
1	**Limato** 2-8-12	Graham Lee
2	**Mattmu** 2-8-3	Duran Fentiman
3	**Wet Sail** 2-9-0	Frederik Tylicki

6/5F, 7/1, 14/1. 1½l, 1¼l. 23 ran. 1m 10.66s (Henry Candy).

An unsurprisingly strong Listed race given the huge prize-money yet **Limato** made a mockery of his opposition as he won without ever coming off the bridle, producing arguably the outstanding two-year-old performance of the season. Always cantering close to a strong enough gallop for the field to be

COMMEMORATIVE: impressed in the Autumn Stakes at Newmarket

left well strung out, Limato eased clear in the final furlong in a manner that suggested he would definitely have had a big say at Group 1 level. **Mattmu** was receiving 9lb in second yet proved good enough to comfortably land another Listed race at York just seven days later and a Group 2 at Maisons-Laffitte after that, while the smart **Wet Sail** was third and pulled 2¾l clear of a chasing pack that included Group 2 fourths **Fox Trotter** and **Realtra** plus Listed winners **Bronze Maquette** and **Mind Of Madness** among the first nine.

60 Qatar Prix Jean-Luc Lagardere (Grand Criterium) (Group 1) (7f)
Longchamp (FR) October 5 (Good)
3 **Gleneagles** 2-9-0   Joseph O'Brien
1 **Full Mast** 2-9-0   Thierry Thulliez
2 **Territories** 2-9-0   Maxime Guyon
9/4, 11/2, 14/1. ½l, snk. 9 ran. 1m 20.11s
(Mme C Head-Maarek).

Something of a travesty as **Gleneagles** was demoted to third behind **Full Mast** and **Territories** despite being clearly the best horse in the race and causing only minimal interference to the placed horses. Gleneagles paid for his habit of idling in front as he was all out to hold on and edged to his right having shown his class and looked set to come clear when quickening to the front, meaning the rest were flattered to finish so close in a bunch finish that saw less than 3l cover the first seven. They included **Burnt Sugar**,

War Envoy and **Aktabantay**, but **The Wow Signal** was well below his best and subsequently scoped badly.

61 Total Prix Marcel Boussac (Group 1) (Fillies) (1m)
Longchamp (FR) October 5 (Good)
1 **Found** 2-8-11   Ryan Moore
2 **Ervedya** 2-8-11   Christophe Soumillon
3 **Jack Naylor** 2-8-11   F M Berry
9/4F, 3/1, 6/1. 2½l, 1½l. 12 ran. 1m 37.45s
(A P O'Brien).

Found benefited from the experience of her fine effort in the Moyglare as well as an extra furlong as she ran out an ultimately clearcut winner over leading French filly **Ervedya**. Found quickened clear in terrific fashion in the final half-furlong as Ervedya still stuck on well in second, looking better over this much longer trip than when third in the Prix Morny. **Jack Naylor** finished a good third to add substance to the form, though **Malabar** would certainly have got into the places had she not been left with too much to do as she again finished strongly in fourth.

62 Irish Stallion Farms European Breeders Fund Star Appeal Stakes (Listed Race) (7f)
Dundalk (AW) (IRE) October 10 (Standard)
1 **Smuggler's Cove** 2-9-3   Joseph O'Brien
2 **Orcia** 2-8-12   Shane Foley
3 **Fields Of May** 2-8-12   Kevin Manning
7/4, 12/1, 15/2. 7l, 2l. 6 ran. 1m 23.88s
(A P O'Brien).

A demolition job from **Smuggler's Cove**, who powered clear in the final quarter-mile in hugely impressive fashion. However, with favourite **Bertie Le Belge** disappointing, the opposition wasn't up to much as the third, **Fields Of May**, seemed to run up to her official mark of just 85 to set the level and the jury remains out on Smuggler's Cove after his somewhat tame third in the Dewhurst.

63 Betfred Goals Galore Autumn Stakes (Group 3) (1m)
Newmarket October 11 (Good)
1 **Commemorative** 2-9-1   James Doyle
2 **Restorer** 2-9-1   Martin Dwyer
3 **Future Empire** 2-9-1   Richard Hughes
10/1, 33/1, 11/4F. 1l, 1½l. 9 ran. 1m 37.91s
(Charles Hills).

An impressive all-the-way win from **Commemorative**, who galloped his rivals into submission in terrific fashion. Commemorative gradually wound up the tempo in front and soon had the rest of the field in trouble, particularly Solario runner-up **Future Empire**, who was bred to appreciate the extra furlong and duly finished strongly yet had been outpaced earlier to confirm the winner's quality. **Restorer** was a revelation in second as he split that pair ahead of **Strong Chemistry** and subsequent Listed runner-up **Order Of St George**, who was unlucky not to finish closer having been badly hampered.

64 coral.co.uk Rockingham Stakes (Listed Race) (6f)
York October 11 (Good To Soft)
1 **Mattmu** 2-9-1   David Allan
2 **Bond's Girl** 2-8-10   Patrick Mathers
3 **Fanciful Angel** 2-9-1   Colm O'Donoghue
2/1F, 11/4, 5/1. 2¼l, 2l. 7 ran. 1m 14.43s
(Tim Easterby).

An easy win for **Mattmu**, who confirmed the quality of his second to Limato seven days earlier by making all the running before adding his Maisons-Laffitte success. Doncaster sales race winner **Bond's Girl** was a solid second as that pair pulled clear of the disappointing **Fanciful Angel**.

65 Dubai Dewhurst Stakes (Group 1) (7f)
Newmarket October 17 (Soft)
1 **Belardo** 2-9-1   Andrea Atzeni
2 **Kodi Bear** 2-9-1   Adam Kirby
3 **Smuggler's Cove** 2-9-1   Joseph O'Brien
10/1, 7/1, 7/2. 2l, 2½l. 6 ran. 1m 27.31s
(Roger Varian).

A weak renewal with just six runners, of whom the favourite suffered a serious injury as the two outsiders dominated, but **Belardo** was at least an impressive winner, coming from last to first. Settling much better in a first-time hood than when fourth in the Champagne Stakes, which seemed far more central to his improvement than a return to soft ground (he had won a moderate Listed race in August on good to soft), Belardo was able to demonstrate his stunning turn of foot as he burst past **Kodi Bear**, who had made much of the running and ran a stormer in second, finishing well clear of the rest. **Smuggler's Cove** could never land a blow in third, while **Estidhkaar** suffered a hairline fracture in his one of the hocks, which resulted in him hanging right throughout. It perhaps doesn't bode well for the form that he was still beaten only 5l with the outclassed **Maftool** and **Secret Brief** behind him.

66 vision.ae Middle Park Stakes (Group 1) (6f)
Newmarket October 17 (Soft)
1 **Charming Thought** 2-9-0   William Buick
2 **Ivawood** 2-9-0   Richard Hughes
3 **Muhaarar** 2-9-0   Paul Hanagan
22/1, 1/2F, 8/1. nse, 1¼l. 6 ran. 1m 13.01s
(Charlie Appleby).

A major upset as **Charming Thought**, who had won his last two races but was taking a massive step up in class, turned over red-hot favourite **Ivawood**. Ivawood certainly wasn't at his best as the soft ground blunted his turn of foot – he was entitled to finish much further in front of **Muhaarar** on a line through Jungle Cat – but it was still a fine effort from Charming Thought to run him down in the final furlong. Muhaarar and **Cappella Sansevero** both seemed to have their limitations exposed but still finished in front of the disappointing **Kool Kompany**.

67 Dubai Fillies' Mile (Group 1) (1m)
Newmarket October 17 (Soft)
1 **Together Forever** 2-9-0   Joseph O'Brien
2 **Agnes Stewart** 2-9-0   Billy Lee
3 **Winters Moon** 2-9-0   James Doyle
7/1, 5/1, 20/1. ½l, nse. 7 ran. 1m 41.01s
(A P O'Brien).

Together Forever was clearly progressive but had never looked up to landing a Group 1 and probably dropped lucky in a moderate renewal that saw her get the run of the race. In the form of her life after easily winning a Listed race at the Curragh five days earlier, Together Forever sat close to a steady gallop set by **Marsh Hawk** and was committed early before holding off stronger finishers in **Agnes Stewart**, who could have done with a stiffer test, and **Winters Moon**, who ran a stormer despite a troubled passage. Marsh Hawk could only stick on for fourth ahead of the below-par **Lucida**, who may not have coped with the soft ground.

68 Dubai Cornwallis Stakes (Group 3) (5f)
Newmarket October 17 (Soft)
1 **Royal Razalma** 2-8-12   Richard Kingscote
2 **Strath Burn** 2-9-1   Jamie Spencer
3 **Volatile** 2-9-1   Andrea Atzeni
16/1, 9/2C, 15/2. 1½l, nk. 12 ran. 1m 0.55s
(Jonathan Portman).

A surprising but worthy winner in **Royal Razalma**, who left her previous form behind as she relished the soft ground and drop to 5f, staying on just too strongly for the back-to-form favourite **Strath Burn** and Swedish raider **Volatile**. **Squats** was unlucky not to be in the places as he was hampered close home and that quartet were far superior to the rest, though several of them were unsuited by the conditions such as **Al Fareej**, **Accipiter**, **Moonraker** and **Fendale**.

69 totepool EBF Stallions Silver Tankard Stakes (Listed Race) (1m4y)

Pontefract October 20 (Soft)
1 **Prince Gagarin** 2-9-3   Adam Kirby
2 **Teofilo's Princess** 2-8-12   Franny Norton
3 **My Reward** 2-9-3   George Baker
4/1C, 14/1, 4/1C. 2¼l, ½l. 8 ran. 1m 52.58s
(Ed Dunlop).

A good performance from **Prince Gagarin**, who had been unlucky when going wrong in the Acomb and running into a handicap blot in a nursery but showed his true colours by comfortably beating a fair field for the grade. **Teofilo's Princess** was a surprise second ahead of Kempton novice winner **My Reward**, while **Carry On Deryck** stayed on well into fourth yet was beaten just as far as he had been by Nafaqa at Doncaster previously.

70 Racing Post Trophy (Group 1) (1m)

Doncaster October 25 (Soft)
1 **Elm Park** 2-9-1   Andrea Atzeni
2 **Aloft** 2-9-1   William Buick
3 **Celestial Path** 2-9-1   Luke Morris
13/8F, 10/1, 6/1. 2¾l, ½l. 8 ran. 1m 43.82s
(Andrew Balding).

While this didn't look a particularly strong renewal on paper, **Elm Park** could hardly have been more impressive as he made all the running and drew clear of a couple of promising types in **Aloft** and **Celestial Path** with the rest of the field well strung out. Aloft had landed just a maiden previously and Celestial Path hadn't achieved much more in landing a desperately weak Listed race at Haydock, but both seemed to run good races to fill the places having travelled strongly and they were 5l clear of **Jacobean** with a further 6l back to the rest. **Restorer** and **Cock Of The North** were among the also-rans.

71 Worthington's Whizz Kidz Stakes (registered as the Horris Hill Stakes) (Group 3) (7f)

Newbury October 25 (Soft)
1 **Smaih** 2-9-0   Frankie Dettori
2 **Fox Trotter** 2-9-0   Jimmy Fortune
3 **King Of Normandy** 2-9-0   Pat Dobbs
7/1, 11/2, 12/1. 1l, 1¼l. 6 ran. 1m 32.45s
(Richard Hannon).

Smaih had been well beaten on his previous attempts at a similar level, but his best run

SHAGAH (left): hung right to cost herself victory against Russian Punch

had come on very soft ground at Deauville and he coped best with tough conditions to land a poor contest for the grade. Smaih was ridden prominently and comfortably held off **Fox Trotter**, who was keen early, while favourite **Lexington Times** was below his best in fourth.

72 Al Basti Equiworld Celebration Stakes (registered as the Radley Stakes) (Listed Race) (Fillies) (7f)
Newbury October 25 (Soft)
1 **Russian Punch** 2-9-0   Graham Lee
2 **Shagah** 2-9-0   Frankie Dettori
3 **Sweet Dream** 2-9-0   Richard Kingscote
9/1, 7/2J, 11/1. nk, 3¼l. 8 ran. 1m 31.81s
(James Given).

The Oh So Sharp form was turned on its head as **Russian Punch** beat **Shagah** and **Astrelle**, who had both finished in front of her that day, but both those fillies had excuses in what is likely to prove a moderate contest. Russian Punch coped well with the testing conditions to produce her best performance, but Shagah would surely have beaten her but for hanging across the track in the closing stages and Astrelle lost her chance when her rider lost an iron before halfway, doing well to come fourth.

73 Killavullan Stakes (Group 3) (7f) Leopardstown (IRE) October 25
(Yielding To Soft)
1 **Steip Amach** 2-9-0   Kevin Manning
2 **Royal Navy Ship** 2-9-3   Seamie Heffernan
3 **Cocoon** 2-9-0   Ana O'Brien
12/1, 1/6F, 10/1. ¾l, 2½l. 4 ran. 1m 32.96s
(J S Bolger).

More evidence of the strength of Ireland's juvenile fillies as **Steip Amach**, who had run fine races behind Jack Naylor and Together Forever on her first two starts, turned over red-hot favourite **Royal Navy Ship**. Steip Amach came from last to first and stayed on strongly, comprehensively reversing previous form with Cocoon.

74 thetote.com Eyrefield Stakes (Listed Race) (1m1f)
Leopardstown (IRE) October 26 (Yielding)
1 **Parish Boy** 2-9-3   Kevin Manning
2 **Order Of St George** 2-9-3   S Heffernan
3 **Zafilani** 2-9-3   Pat Smullen
7/2, 7/4F, 7/2. ½l, 2¼l. 9 ran. 1m 54.38s
(J S Bolger).

Order Of St George was well fancied to improve on his unlucky Autumn Stakes fifth yet still bumped into one too good as **Parish Boy** confirmed the form of their previous

meeting in a maiden. Parish Boy missed the break and was keen early, but he still managed to come with a powerful winning run as the first two were far superior to the rest.

75 Criterium International (Group 1) (1m)
Saint-Cloud (FR) October 30 (Soft)
1 **Vert De Grece** 2-9-0   Umberto Rispoli
2 **Johnny Barnes** 2-9-0   William Buick
3 **Sherlock** 2-9-0   A Starke
7/2, 10/1, 25/1. 4l, ¾l. 9 ran. 1m 43.16s
(Roger Varian).

Sent to Roger Varian having been bought following his previous second to Gleneagles, **Vert De Grece** paid a handsome compliment to that horse as he led a British one-two. Vert De Grece drew clear of a tightly packed bunch in which less than 2l covered the next seven, with **Johnny Barnes** taking second from German raider **Sherlock**, while 6-5 favouite **Alea Iacta** was only fifth.

76 EBF Stallions Montrose Fillies' Stakes (Listed Race) (1m)
Newmarket November 1 (Good To Soft)
1 **Irish Rookie** 2-9-0   Fergus Sweeney
2 **Lady Of Dubai** 2-9-0   Tom Queally
3 **Kodiva** 2-9-0   Martin Harley
10/1, 15/8F, 25/1. ½l, 1l. 8 ran. 1m 39.69s
(Martyn Meade).

A desperately weak Listed race, with no filly rated higher than 87 taking part and a lack of early pace meaning the field finished in a bit of a heap, but **Irish Rookie** at least showed a good turn of foot to come out on top. Irish Rookie quickened past favourite **Lady Of Dubai**, who may have been harder to peg back granted a truer test.

77 Criterium de Saint-Cloud (Group 1) (1m2f)
Saint-Cloud (FR) November 8 (Heavy)
1 **Epicuris** 2-9-0   Thierry Thulliez
2 **Palang** 2-9-0   Cristian Demuro
3 **Big Blue** 2-9-0   Mickael Barzalona
10/11F, 14/1, 11/2. 2½l, hd. 6 ran. 2m 17.41s
(Mme C Head-Maarek).

A real test of stamina and **Epicuris** showed that quality in abundance, as well as a touch of class, as he made all and was driven to a comfortable win over German raider **Palang**. The form may not be particularly strong for the top level, though, as he didn't have to improve much on his previous Group 3 win over **Big Blue** and **Capo Maximo** while Beresford Stakes runner-up **Clonard Street**, the sole challenger from Britain or Ireland, failed to get home.

Two-year-old index

All horses placed or commented on in our two-year-old review section, with race numbers

Accepted 27, 40
Accipiter 24, 39, 47, 68
Aces 43
Adaay 12
Agnes Stewart 16, 41, 67
Ahlan Emarati 4, 7, 20, 27, 40
Ainippe 40, 49
Aktabantay 11, 35, 60
Al Fareej 24, 28, 68
Alea Iacta 75
Aloft 70
Alonsoa 22, 41
Angelic Lord 1, 9
Anthem Alexander 3, 26, 52
Arabian Queen 10, 22, 52
Astrelle 29, 41, 58, 72
Astrophysics 40
Baitha Alga 4, 48
Basateen 25
Battle Of Marathon 54
Beach Belle 23, 32, 46
Beacon 19, 27, 40
Belardo 9, 43, 65
Bertie Le Belge 62
Big Blue 77
Bond's Girl 13, 64
Bonnie Grey 29, 41
Bossy Guest 33, 56
Bronze Maquette 24, 40, 59
Burnt Sugar 39, 60
Calypso Beat 22
Capo Maximo 77
Cappella Sansevero 1, 7, 23, 37, 66
Carry On Deryck 69
Celestial Path 70
Charming Thought 66
Clonard Street 54, 77
Cock Of The North 11, 35, 70
Cocoon 73
Commemorative 63
Convergence 15, 54
Cotai Glory 2, 12, 19, 40
Cursory Glance 5, 26, 46
Dark Reckoning 33, 49
Dick Whittington 6, 14, 23
Disegno 18
Dutch Connection 25, 45
East India 44
Elm Park 34, 53, 70
Epicuris 77
Ervedya 30, 61
Estidhkaar 11, 43, 65
Explosive Lady 17, 33

Fadhayyil 51
Faithful Creek 44
Fanciful Angel 39, 64
Fast Act 13, 19, 40
Fendale 47, 68
Fields Of May 62
Found 46, 61
Fox Trotter 21, 59, 71
Full Mast 60
Future Empire 35, 63
Glenalmond 27, 43
Gleneagles 15, 31, 45, 60
Goken 30
Groor 34
Growl 48
Hall Of Fame 31, 45
Haxby 13
High Celebrity 10, 52
Highland Reel 20
Home Of The Brave 39
Hootenanny 2, 30
I Am Beautiful 8, 23, 32, 46
Irish Rookie 76
Ivawood 9, 21, 66
Izzthatright 33
Jack Naylor 16, 36, 61
Jacobean 70
Jamaica 25
Jeanne Girl 8, 32, 46
John F Kennedy 44
Johnny Barnes 75
Jungle Cat 1, 9, 21, 27, 48
Kibaar 48
King Of Normandy 71
Kodi Bear 1, 18, 65
Kodiva 30
Kool Kompany 1, 7, 23, 66
Lacing 57
Lady Of Dubai 76
Legatissimo 36
Lexington Times 35, 71
Limato 12, 59
Local Time 58
Lola Beaux 55
Louie De Palma 21
Lucida 32, 46, 51, 67
Maftool 39, 50, 65
Malabar 5, 29, 46, 61
Markaz 50
Marsh Hawk 38, 67
Mattmu 59, 64
Mind Of Madness 4, 28, 40, 47, 59
Mister Universe 34

WAR ENVOY (second right): didn't live up to lofty expectations following this maiden win in April but at least did better when stepped up in trip

Moonraker	21, 28, 40, 68
Mubtaghaa	2, 50
Muhaarar	9, 18, 27, 66
Muraaqaba	17, 22, 41
Muthmir	19
My Reward	69
Nafaqa	6, 42, 53
New Providence	38, 51
Newsletter	3, 14
Ol' Man River	54
Orcia	62
Order Of St George	63, 74
Osaila	5, 17, 46, 57
Outlaw Country	56
Palang	77
Parish Boy	74
Parsley	10, 24, 49
Patience Alexander	5, 26
Peacock	42
Prince Bonnaire	33
Prince Gagarin	69
Prize Exhibit	58
Qualify	16, 32, 46, 55
Quinta Verde	8
Rapid Applause	14, 37
Raydara	16, 32
Realtra	26, 59
Restorer	63, 70
Richard Pankhurst	6
Room Key	20, 43
Royal Navy Ship	73
Royal Razalma	38, 49, 68
Russian Punch	72
Salateen	53
Secret Brief	56, 65
Shagah	41, 58, 72
Sherlock	75
Smaih	71
Smuggler's Cove	62, 65
Spanish Pipedream	3
Squats	47, 68
Steip Amach	36, 73
Stellar Glow	55
Strath Burn	48, 68
Stroll Patrol	22, 38, 51
Strong Chemistry	63
Supreme Occasion	41
Sweet Dream	72
Tendu	52
Teofilo's Princess	69
Territories	60
Terror	52
The Wow Signal	1, 30, 60
Tiggy Wiggy	3, 13, 26, 52
Tigrilla	51
Together Forever	36, 67
Tombelaine	15, 44, 54
Tongue Twista	10
Toocoolforschool	25, 42, 48
Toogoodtobetrue	32
Toscanini	6, 14, 45
Tupi	20
Union Rose	2
Vert De Grece	31, 75
Very Special	57
Volatile	68
War Envoy	1, 7, 37, 43, 60
Wet Sail	59
White Lake	42
Winters Moon	22, 34, 67
Zafilani	74

Trainer Statistics

Mark Johnston

Johnston's consistency is remarkable and last year was his fifth double-century out of six. Our stats show punters should pay particular attention when he sends one to Goodwood or Newmarket.

By month – 2014

	Overall			Two-year-olds			Three-year-olds			Older horses		
	W-R	%	£1	W-R	%	£1	W-R	%	£1	W-R	%	£1
January	16-45	36	+6.61	0-0	-	+0.00	9-19	47	+14.78	7-26	27	-8.17
February	9-49	18	-16.27	0-0	-	+0.00	5-26	19	-8.38	4-23	17	-7.90
March	21-72	29	+1.84	0-0	-	+0.00	12-36	33	-5.76	9-36	25	+7.60
April	19-127	15	-42.45	1-7	14	-0.50	9-63	14	-20.26	9-57	16	-21.69
May	19-166	11	-26.55	3-21	14	+5.10	11-91	12	-5.65	5-54	9	-26.00
June	32-192	17	+5.71	13-40	33	+32.13	14-99	14	-7.92	5-53	9	-18.50
July	40-203	20	+25.44	7-53	13	-27.89	26-116	22	+5.34	7-34	21	+48.00
August	21-177	12	-70.38	7-49	14	-16.33	14-101	14	-27.04	0-27	-	-27.00
September	25-165	15	-40.78	9-64	14	-42.77	14-85	16	-3.34	2-16	13	+5.33
October	3-102	3	-90.00	1-43	2	-37.50	2-44	5	-37.50	0-15	-	-15.00
November	1-38	3	-32.00	1-23	4	-17.00	0-14	-	-14.00	0-1	-	-1.00
December	1-8	13	-4.25	1-3	33	+0.75	0-4	-	-4.00	0-1	-	-1.00

By month – 2013

	Overall			Two-year-olds			Three-year-olds			Older horses		
	W-R	%	£1	W-R	%	£1	W-R	%	£1	W-R	%	£1
January	4-35	11	-5.25	0-0	-	+0.00	3-25	12	-2.25	1-10	10	-3.00
February	7-36	19	-0.14	0-0	-	+0.00	3-28	11	-7.67	4-8	50	+7.53
March	10-59	17	-20.95	0-2	-	-2.00	10-43	23	-4.95	0-14	-	-14.00
April	22-111	20	-7.72	5-12	42	+0.80	13-72	18	-13.27	4-27	15	+4.75
May	23-172	13	-74.82	4-32	13	-16.75	16-99	16	-29.82	3-41	7	-28.25
June	28-207	14	-49.61	5-52	10	-31.42	17-103	17	-6.02	6-52	12	-12.17
July	41-231	18	-10.22	6-52	12	-15.65	24-125	19	-39.45	11-54	20	+44.88
August	32-226	14	-69.38	6-68	9	-50.14	19-117	16	-15.34	7-41	17	-3.90
September	25-204	12	-66.67	12-75	16	-0.88	10-102	10	-56.62	3-27	11	-9.17
October	10-182	5	-68.71	3-84	4	-64.86	6-77	8	-49.86	1-21	5	+46.00
November	4-55	7	-34.58	2-26	8	-22.08	2-22	9	-5.50	0-7	-	-7.00
December	10-39	26	+11.83	2-12	17	-5.75	5-21	24	+6.08	3-6	50	+11.50

By month – 2012

	Overall			Two-year-olds			Three-year-olds			Older horses		
	W-R	%	£1	W-R	%	£1	W-R	%	£1	W-R	%	£1
January	14-45	31	+19.16	0-0	-	+0.00	9-25	36	+12.88	5-20	25	+6.29
February	14-49	29	-6.04	0-0	-	+0.00	8-29	28	-10.04	6-20	30	+4.00
March	19-71	27	+1.03	0-1	-	-1.00	14-42	33	+10.33	5-28	18	-8.31
April	20-91	22	-11.70	4-5	80	+13.76	12-63	19	-17.19	4-23	17	-8.27
May	18-163	11	-17.63	4-26	15	-6.38	9-104	9	-6.88	5-33	15	-4.38
June	17-178	10	-58.69	3-31	10	-19.00	11-108	10	-24.30	3-39	8	-15.39
July	19-160	12	-29.51	3-32	9	-19.63	14-106	13	-17.88	2-22	9	+8.00
August	42-193	22	+23.93	10-51	20	-4.84	28-121	23	+28.10	4-21	19	+0.68
September	33-189	17	+3.57	8-54	15	-5.22	23-110	21	+20.28	2-25	8	-11.50
October	15-153	10	-45.50	6-70	9	-47.38	7-70	10	-21.13	2-13	15	+23.00
November	2-35	6	-23.50	1-17	6	-11.00	0-11	-	-11.00	1-7	14	-1.50
December	2-17	12	-4.00	2-12	17	+1.00	0-1	-	-1.00	0-4	-	-4.00

By race type – 2014

	Overall			Two-year-olds			Three-year-olds			Older horses		
	W-R	%	£1	W-R	%	£1	W-R	%	£1	W-R	%	£1
Handicap	146-919	16	-140.43	9-68	13	-28.17	96-549	17	-62.61	41-302	14	-49.66
Group 1,2,3	3-40	8	-23.25	1-20	5	-12.00	2-16	13	-7.25	0-4	-	-4.00
Maiden	45-295	15	-101.22	28-182	15	-57.85	13-99	13	-38.87	4-14	29	-4.50

By race type – 2013

	Overall			Two-year-olds			Three-year-olds			Older horses		
	W-R	%	£1	W-R	%	£1	W-R	%	£1	W-R	%	£1
Handicap	129-1023	13	-275.05	8-118	7	-85.26	84-624	13	-215.70	37-281	13	+25.92
Group 1,2,3	3-28	11	-8.25	0-8	-	-8.00	0-11	-	-11.00	3-9	33	+10.75
Maiden	66-409	16	-92.97	31-238	13	-95.64	34-165	21	+0.67	1-6	17	+2.00

By race type – 2012

	Overall			Two-year-olds			Three-year-olds			Older horses		
	W-R	%	£1	W-R	%	£1	W-R	%	£1	W-R	%	£1
Handicap	139-921	15	-79.02	11-85	13	-28.63	97-606	16	-35.36	31-230	13	-15.04
Group 1,2,3	3-28	11	-5.75	2-15	13	-1.25	1-11	9	-2.50	0-2	-	-2.00
Maiden	55-315	17	-93.57	21-172	12	-61.60	30-131	23	-33.96	4-12	33	+2.00

By jockey – 2014

	Overall			Two-year-olds			Three-year-olds			Older horses		
	W-R	%	£1	W-R	%	£1	W-R	%	£1	W-R	%	£1
Joe Fanning	110-601	18	-62.24	21-132	16	-40.39	60-300	20	-9.83	29-169	17	-12.02
Franny Norton	26-254	10	-117.42	8-69	12	-43.88	11-134	8	-62.38	7-51	14	-11.17
S De Sousa	18-125	14	-41.87	1-21	5	-15.50	13-74	18	-17.98	4-30	13	-8.39
Dane O'Neill	11-27	41	+37.00	5-13	38	+15.00	6-12	50	+24.00	0-2	-	-2.00
Adrian Nicholls	9-54	17	-1.35	4-16	25	+6.90	4-25	16	-6.25	1-13	8	-2.00
M J M Murphy	9-74	12	-22.07	1-6	17	+7.00	4-38	11	-18.32	4-30	13	-10.75
Adam Kirby	5-26	19	-14.60	0-1	-	-1.00	5-14	36	-2.60	0-11	-	-11.00
Paul Mulrennan	4-6	67	+14.25	1-1	100	+2.75	3-5	60	+11.50	0-0	-	+0.00
Paul Hanagan	4-24	17	-1.50	1-12	8	-5.00	3-12	25	+3.50	0-0	-	+0.00
R Ffrench	4-31	13	+4.88	0-7	-	-7.00	4-19	21	+16.88	0-5	-	-5.00
Graham Lee	2-7	29	-0.90	1-4	25	-1.90	1-2	50	+2.00	0-1	-	-1.00
Jack Garritty	1-1	100	+3.00	0-0	-	+0.00	0-0	-	+0.00	1-1	100	+3.00

By jockey – 2013

	Overall			Two-year-olds			Three-year-olds			Older horses		
	W-R	%	£1	W-R	%	£1	W-R	%	£1	W-R	%	£1
Joe Fanning	93-639	15	-161.29	20-162	12	-45.66	55-343	16	-103.16	18-134	13	-12.48
Franny Norton	40-244	16	-53.36	6-47	13	-28.45	24-142	17	-30.89	10-55	18	+5.98
S De Sousa	27-156	17	+25.65	7-44	16	-22.48	15-92	16	-32.87	5-20	25	+81.00
Adam Kirby	11-34	32	+25.00	2-12	17	-3.00	4-12	33	+6.50	5-10	50	+21.50
Liam Jones	10-80	13	-13.26	1-25	4	-22.50	8-44	18	+15.91	1-11	9	-6.67
Neil Callan	7-42	17	-10.88	4-15	27	-7.38	3-22	14	+1.50	0-5	-	-5.00
Adrian Nicholls	7-51	14	-12.42	2-20	10	-7.50	4-26	15	-4.25	1-5	20	-0.67
Paul Hanagan	3-27	11	-7.63	1-13	8	+0.00	2-12	17	-5.63	0-2	-	-2.00
Gerald Mosse	2-5	40	+5.38	1-2	50	+0.38	1-1	100	+7.00	0-2	-	-2.00

By jockey – 2012

	Overall			Two-year-olds			Three-year-olds			Older horses		
	W-R	%	£1	W-R	%	£1	W-R	%	£1	W-R	%	£1
Joe Fanning	103-579	18	-44.99	17-132	13	-42.31	61-322	19	-30.47	25-125	20	+27.79
S De Sousa	41-238	17	-27.87	10-60	17	-19.11	28-145	19	+12.64	3-33	9	-21.40
Franny Norton	20-120	17	+23.32	4-31	13	-5.00	14-70	20	+23.82	2-19	11	+4.50
Kieren Fallon	11-60	18	-5.63	5-19	26	-1.38	5-29	17	-3.25	1-12	8	-1.00
Mirco Demuro	8-50	16	-4.38	3-8	38	-0.38	5-32	16	+6.00	0-10	-	-10.00
Neil Callan	6-34	18	-2.00	0-5	-	-5.00	6-21	29	+11.00	0-8	-	-8.00
Frederik Tylicki	3-14	21	+1.50	0-1	-	-1.00	2-9	22	+3.50	1-4	25	-1.00
Martin Lane	3-18	17	+21.00	0-3	-	-3.00	3-14	21	+25.00	0-1	-	-1.00
M J M Murphy	3-18	17	-11.33	0-1	-	-1.00	1-14	7	-11.00	2-3	67	+0.68

By course – 2011-2014

	Overall			Two-year-olds			Three-year-olds			Older horses		
	W-R	%	£1	W-R	%	£1	W-R	%	£1	W-R	%	£1
Ascot	18-241	7	-71.84	1-42	2	-38.25	12-130	9	-64.59	5-69	7	+31.00
Ayr	14-134	10	-85.23	5-50	10	-36.67	8-57	14	-25.90	1-27	4	-22.67
Bath	15-56	27	+28.33	4-14	29	-0.42	9-36	25	+28.75	2-6	33	+0.00
Beverley	57-224	25	+40.90	11-56	20	-16.01	36-127	28	+46.01	10-41	24	+10.90
Brighton	11-57	19	+3.48	2-16	13	-12.11	7-35	20	+7.58	2-6	33	+8.00
Carlisle	12-96	13	-15.17	4-26	15	+7.33	6-45	13	-9.50	2-25	8	-13.00
Catterick	26-108	24	+23.15	6-40	15	-22.50	18-52	35	+51.65	2-16	13	-6.00
Chepstow	6-30	20	+4.25	0-7	-	-7.00	6-21	29	+13.25	0-2	-	-2.00
Chester	36-229	16	+38.70	9-46	20	-10.13	17-125	14	+15.83	10-58	17	+33.00
Doncaster	13-175	7	-88.50	4-55	7	-28.00	8-83	10	-27.00	1-37	3	-33.50
Epsom	13-131	10	-58.75	3-24	13	-12.75	6-64	9	-33.00	4-43	9	-13.00
Ffos Las	3-23	13	-6.88	2-9	22	-2.88	0-9	-	-9.00	1-5	20	+5.00
Folkestone	3-10	30	-0.59	0-0	-	+0.00	3-10	30	-0.59	0-0	-	+0.00
Goodwood	27-197	14	+23.62	9-52	17	-7.26	11-91	12	+9.00	7-54	13	+21.88
Hamilton	48-200	24	+11.38	9-42	21	+4.98	32-122	26	+1.03	7-36	19	+5.38
Haydock	24-228	11	-50.55	2-56	4	-49.13	19-115	17	+34.58	3-57	5	-36.00
Kempton (AW)	40-337	12	-123.59	7-76	9	-47.50	24-187	13	-58.84	9-74	12	-17.25
Leicester	13-122	11	-42.58	7-47	15	+8.00	3-52	6	-41.46	3-23	13	-9.13
Lingfield	3-27	11	-7.27	1-7	14	-5.27	1-14	7	-3.00	1-6	17	+1.00
Lingfield (AW)	59-359	16	-102.11	5-42	12	-6.50	42-227	18	-54.75	12-90	13	-40.86
Musselburgh	38-208	18	+5.56	11-47	23	+24.40	22-113	19	-8.84	5-48	10	-10.00
Newbury	10-76	13	-17.75	5-22	23	-0.13	1-38	3	-30.50	4-16	25	+12.88
Newcastle	11-101	11	-41.38	4-36	11	-12.25	7-41	17	-5.13	0-24	-	-24.00
Newmarket	25-200	13	+25.71	7-62	11	-36.93	13-94	14	-19.12	5-44	11	+81.75
Newmarket (J)	29-185	16	+17.58	4-41	10	-24.10	21-113	19	+39.68	4-31	13	+2.00
Nottingham	9-120	8	-75.79	4-48	8	-24.79	5-60	8	-39.00	0-12	-	-12.00
Pontefract	25-167	15	-56.22	2-40	5	-34.00	20-98	20	-7.82	3-29	10	-14.40
Redcar	9-76	12	-32.68	1-28	4	-26.71	7-31	23	+0.03	1-17	6	-6.00
Ripon	18-158	11	-72.15	1-28	4	-19.50	15-90	17	-18.71	2-40	5	-33.94
Salisbury	1-22	5	-16.50	1-7	14	-1.50	0-13	-	-13.00	0-2	-	-2.00
Sandown	7-86	8	-45.50	1-18	6	-14.00	6-52	12	-15.50	0-16	-	-16.00
S'thwell (AW)	57-233	24	-13.16	10-45	22	-20.58	29-120	24	+7.13	18-68	26	+0.29
Thirsk	7-91	8	-51.10	2-22	9	-16.60	3-46	7	-19.50	2-23	9	-15.00
Warwick	5-36	14	-18.46	3-10	30	+0.71	1-20	5	-15.00	1-6	17	-4.17
Windsor	4-41	10	-15.75	1-5	20	+4.00	2-24	8	-15.75	1-12	8	-4.00
Wolves (AW)	96-475	20	-66.66	7-86	8	-66.79	57-282	20	-55.71	32-107	30	+55.85
Yarmouth	16-99	16	+1.80	6-31	19	+16.98	7-52	13	-19.51	3-16	19	+4.33
York	9-198	5	-147.40	5-65	8	-40.90	2-67	3	-53.50	2-66	3	-53.00

Ten-year summary

	Wins	Runs	%	Win prize-money	Total prize-money	£1
2014	207	1344	15	£1,985,940.54	£2,992,111.82	-283.07
2013	216	1557	14	£1,826,629.78	£2,743,581.49	-396.21
2012	215	1344	16	£1,545,130.29	£2,284,275.76	-148.88
2011	179	1311	14	£927,711.46	£1,550,631.62	-270.93
2010	211	1458	14	£1,657,512.68	£2,419,718.15	-377.04
2009	216	1227	18	£1,747,013.96	£2,843,943.25	-139.14
2008	164	1145	14	£1,345,669.48	£2,070,937.14	-200.11
2007	161	998	16	£1,188,791.46	£1,651,628.48	-122.33
2006	158	1005	16	£1,245,722.50	£1,868,197.71	-87.83
2005	141	885	16	£1,118,373.15	£1,864,674.04	-80.25

BOW CREEK: one of several Mark Johnston horses now with Godolphin

Richard Hannon

The handover from father to son went seamlessly for the Hannon yard last year – a fifth straight double-century and the trainers' title.

*Stats relate to Richard Hannon Snr or both men combined

By month – 2014

	Overall			Two-year-olds			Three-year-olds			Older horses		
	W-R	%	£1	W-R	%	£1	W-R	%	£1	W-R	%	£1
January	2-19	11	-12.00	0-0	-	+0.00	2-15	13	-8.00	0-4	-	-4.00
February	0-6	-	-6.00	0-0	-	+0.00	0-5	-	-5.00	0-1	-	-1.00
March	5-18	28	-2.64	1-2	50	-0.39	4-10	40	+3.75	0-6	-	-6.00
April	18-98	18	-7.51	5-16	31	+2.54	10-67	15	-13.05	3-15	20	+3.00
May	31-180	17	+40.64	16-48	33	+18.77	13-105	12	+43.75	2-27	7	-21.88
June	39-218	18	-36.14	21-83	25	-16.50	14-108	13	-23.44	4-27	15	+3.80
July	28-213	13	-118.97	18-105	17	-53.09	9-87	10	-47.51	1-21	5	-18.38
August	32-234	14	-79.77	24-125	19	-24.12	6-84	7	-38.25	2-25	8	-17.40
September	27-183	15	-47.65	18-115	16	-22.35	7-54	13	-19.04	2-14	14	-6.25
October	15-151	10	-64.25	11-100	11	-41.50	3-38	8	-13.00	1-13	8	-9.75
November	2-48	4	-34.50	0-27	-	-27.00	0-12	-	-12.00	2-9	22	+4.50
December	7-36	19	+2.38	5-17	29	+2.88	2-10	20	+8.50	0-9	-	-9.00

By month – 2013*

	Overall			Two-year-olds			Three-year-olds			Older horses		
	W-R	%	£1	W-R	%	£1	W-R	%	£1	W-R	%	£1
January	0-5	-	-5.00	0-0	-	+0.00	0-3	-	-3.00	0-2	-	-2.00
February	3-9	33	+35.25	0-0	-	+0.00	2-5	40	+24.25	1-4	25	+11.00
March	7-29	24	+3.29	0-0	-	+0.00	7-21	33	+11.29	0-8	-	-8.00
April	24-111	22	-34.42	2-13	15	-9.90	19-72	26	-9.52	3-26	12	-15.00
May	38-200	19	-53.77	23-71	32	+4.66	12-104	12	-54.68	3-25	12	-3.75
June	37-221	17	-81.39	23-93	25	-2.90	12-102	12	-60.74	2-26	8	-17.75
July	38-186	20	-18.93	21-94	22	-4.53	13-69	19	-19.65	4-23	17	+5.25
August	30-226	13	-48.55	20-137	15	-46.63	7-70	10	-25.42	3-19	16	+23.50
September	29-188	15	-23.68	21-129	16	-33.43	6-44	14	+9.75	2-15	13	+0.00
October	23-163	14	-48.13	20-112	18	-16.13	2-35	6	-24.00	1-16	6	-8.00
November	3-49	6	-25.00	2-35	6	-15.50	1-10	10	-5.50	0-4	-	-4.00
December	3-25	12	-6.00	3-17	18	+2.00	0-7	-	-7.00	0-1	-	-1.00

By month – 2012*

	Overall			Two-year-olds			Three-year-olds			Older horses		
	W-R	%	£1	W-R	%	£1	W-R	%	£1	W-R	%	£1
January	1-10	10	-8.17	0-0	-	+0.00	1-9	11	-7.17	0-1	-	-1.00
February	2-10	20	+0.00	0-0	-	+0.00	1-6	17	+2.00	1-4	25	-2.00
March	3-21	14	-12.50	0-1	-	-1.00	3-15	20	-6.50	0-5	-	-5.00
April	12-75	16	+22.33	2-11	18	-5.93	8-57	14	+25.75	2-7	29	+2.50
May	32-174	18	+27.62	12-46	26	+11.05	17-107	16	+21.58	3-21	14	-5.00
June	31-202	15	-55.51	19-90	21	-21.09	10-97	10	-31.75	2-15	13	-2.67
July	31-179	17	-2.35	22-92	24	+16.02	9-70	13	-1.38	0-17	-	-17.00
August	36-256	14	-54.75	26-148	18	+3.09	10-96	10	-45.84	0-12	-	-12.00
September	37-209	18	-27.19	27-134	20	-20.52	9-64	14	-12.67	1-11	9	+6.00
October	24-164	15	-27.25	14-107	13	-36.25	7-47	15	-7.00	3-10	30	+16.00
November	5-47	11	-23.88	5-34	15	-10.88	0-13	-	-13.00	0-0	-	+0.00
December	4-20	20	-4.25	2-14	14	-5.75	2-6	33	+1.50	0-0	-	+0.00

By race type – 2014

	Overall			Two-year-olds			Three-year-olds			Older horses		
	W-R	%	£1	W-R	%	£1	W-R	%	£1	W-R	%	£1
Handicap	66-604	11	-225.55	19-119	16	-15.84	38-394	10	-164.46	9-91	10	-45.25
Group 1,2,3	17-122	14	-12.17	11-46	24	+11.31	2-35	6	+8.00	4-41	10	-31.48
Maiden	84-475	18	-155.71	65-382	17	-134.13	19-91	21	-19.58	0-2	-	-2.00

By race type – 2013*

	Overall			Two-year-olds			Three-year-olds			Older horses		
	W-R	%	£1	W-R	%	£1	W-R	%	£1	W-R	%	£1
Handicap	72-606	12	-168.24	20-142	14	-45.58	42-341	12	-107.54	10-123	8	-15.13
Group 1,2,3	16-102	16	-19.21	5-46	11	-9.25	9-38	24	+0.29	2-18	11	-10.25
Maiden	98-489	20	-63.37	83-409	20	-36.99	14-79	18	-32.37	1-1	100	+6.00

By race type – 2012*

	Overall			Two-year-olds			Three-year-olds			Older horses		
	W-R	%	£1	W-R	%	£1	W-R	%	£1	W-R	%	£1
Handicap	80-574	14	+8.19	22-132	17	+9.60	50-371	15	+18.08	8-71	11	-19.50
Group 1,2,3	13-91	14	-4.88	7-44	16	-21.72	4-27	15	+15.50	2-20	10	+1.33
Maiden	88-503	17	-97.38	72-391	18	-38.08	15-111	14	-60.29	1-1	100	+1.00

By jockey – 2014

	Overall			Two-year-olds			Three-year-olds			Older horses		
	W-R	%	£1	W-R	%	£1	W-R	%	£1	W-R	%	£1
R Hughes	80-433	18	-93.07	53-205	26	-15.01	23-166	14	-28.71	4-62	6	-49.35
Sean Levey	24-213	11	-104.30	13-101	13	-56.52	8-88	9	-38.15	3-24	13	-9.63
Pat Dobbs	19-162	12	-16.93	9-80	11	-31.76	8-64	13	+10.58	2-18	11	+4.25
Frankie Dettori	17-65	26	+7.86	12-48	25	+2.78	4-16	25	+3.70	1-1	100	+1.38
Ryan Moore	12-76	16	-35.33	3-24	13	-16.73	6-37	16	-19.60	3-15	20	+1.00
Paul Hanagan	11-37	30	-9.32	7-18	39	-1.30	4-19	21	-8.03	0-0	-	+0.00
Cam Hardie	10-138	7	-91.26	5-44	11	-28.26	2-79	3	-63.50	3-15	20	+0.50
Kieran O'Neill	7-64	11	-21.09	1-23	4	-14.00	6-36	17	-2.09	0-5	-	-5.00
James Doyle	5-10	50	+30.00	5-8	63	+32.00	0-1	-	-1.00	0-1	-	-1.00
Gary Mahon	3-14	21	+19.50	0-1	-	-1.00	3-11	27	+22.50	0-2	-	-2.00
Jimmy Fortune	3-21	14	-10.25	1-9	11	-6.75	1-7	14	-4.00	1-5	20	+0.50
Gerald Mosse	1-1	100	+12.00	1-1	100	+12.00	0-0	-	+0.00	0-0	-	+0.00

By jockey – 2013*

	Overall			Two-year-olds			Three-year-olds			Older horses		
	W-R	%	£1	W-R	%	£1	W-R	%	£1	W-R	%	£1
R Hughes	127-530	24	-63.68	67-251	27	-29.92	47-204	23	-32.50	13-75	17	-1.25
Pat Dobbs	30-198	15	-61.41	19-118	16	-37.04	11-65	17	-9.36	0-15	-	-15.00
Sean Levey	23-191	12	-40.44	13-95	14	-14.67	8-74	11	-20.27	2-22	9	-5.50
Ryan Moore	16-89	18	-21.79	10-45	22	-8.83	6-35	17	-3.96	0-9	-	-9.00
Dane O'Neill	9-50	18	+9.13	6-29	21	+14.00	3-21	14	-4.88	0-0	-	+0.00
W Twist-Davies	8-85	9	-13.00	2-19	11	-10.75	3-44	7	-31.25	3-22	14	+29.00
Paul Hanagan	5-35	14	-10.07	5-21	24	+3.93	0-14	-	-14.00	0-0	-	+0.00
Kieran O'Neill	5-72	7	-30.75	3-37	8	-23.75	2-30	7	-2.00	0-5	-	-5.00
Jim Crowley	3-9	33	+22.73	3-7	43	+24.73	0-1	-	-1.00	0-1	-	-1.00

By jockey – 2012*

	Overall			Two-year-olds			Three-year-olds			Older horses		
	W-R	%	£1	W-R	%	£1	W-R	%	£1	W-R	%	£1
R Hughes	103-485	21	-40.02	62-237	26	-26.30	37-205	18	+4.45	4-43	9	-18.17
Pat Dobbs	32-234	14	+16.41	18-117	15	+0.08	13-102	13	+25.33	1-15	7	-9.00
Ryan Moore	21-123	17	-5.64	10-64	16	-6.43	9-49	18	-1.72	2-10	20	+2.50
Sean Levey	20-152	13	-29.63	9-71	13	-39.88	7-68	10	+0.75	4-13	31	+9.50
Kieran O'Neill	8-116	7	-83.38	2-45	4	-36.75	6-63	10	-38.63	0-8	-	-8.00
Dane O'Neill	7-37	19	+0.56	6-22	27	+13.73	1-14	7	-12.17	0-1	-	-1.00
Paul Hanagan	5-22	23	-0.67	5-20	25	+1.33	0-2	-	-2.00	0-0	-	+0.00
W Twist-Davies	5-46	11	-5.00	2-19	11	-2.50	3-23	13	+1.50	0-4	-	-4.00
Tadhg O'Shea	3-7	43	-2.04	3-7	43	-2.04	0-0	-	+0.00	0-0	-	+0.00

By course – 2014

	Overall			Two-year-olds			Three-year-olds			Older horses		
	W-R	%	£1	W-R	%	£1	W-R	%	£1	W-R	%	£1
Ascot	6-89	7	-58.70	4-26	15	-0.75	0-36	-	-36.00	2-27	7	-21.95
Ayr	1-5	20	+2.00	1-5	20	+2.00	0-0	-	+0.00	0-0	-	+0.00
Bath	5-32	16	-19.97	4-17	24	-8.97	1-15	7	-11.00	0-0	-	+0.00
Brighton	9-31	29	-9.24	8-19	42	+0.26	1-12	8	-9.50	0-0	-	+0.00
Carlisle	0-1	-	-1.00	0-0	-	+0.00	0-1	-	-1.00	0-0	-	+0.00
Chepstow	7-26	27	-6.02	4-11	36	-3.27	2-13	15	-6.25	1-2	50	+3.50
Chester	4-20	20	-3.61	4-10	40	+6.39	0-9	-	-9.00	0-1	-	-1.00
Doncaster	10-66	15	-7.75	4-37	11	-22.35	5-22	23	+17.60	1-7	14	-3.00
Epsom	5-20	25	-2.79	2-7	29	-1.63	3-11	27	+0.83	0-2	-	-2.00
Ffos Las	3-6	50	+9.50	2-4	50	+3.50	1-1	100	+7.00	0-1	-	-1.00
Goodwood	11-108	10	-40.63	5-42	12	-26.23	4-45	9	+1.75	2-21	10	-16.15
Haydock	4-36	11	-21.63	1-13	8	-8.50	1-16	6	-12.50	2-7	29	-0.63
Kempton (AW)	14-158	9	-86.09	7-79	9	-48.72	5-64	8	-36.38	2-15	13	-1.00
Leicester	5-33	15	-13.00	3-17	18	-3.50	2-14	14	-7.50	0-2	-	-2.00
Lingfield	5-22	23	+5.25	4-11	36	+9.25	1-10	10	-3.00	0-1	-	-1.00
Lingfield (AW)	18-85	21	-16.68	8-28	29	-2.88	9-42	21	-4.80	1-15	7	-9.00
Newbury	13-117	11	-56.05	7-59	12	-22.18	5-49	10	-27.25	1-9	11	-6.63
Newmarket	14-78	18	+50.91	6-28	21	-9.46	8-35	23	+75.38	0-15	-	-15.00
Newmarket (J)	15-100	15	-7.75	11-56	20	+10.75	4-40	10	-14.50	0-4	-	-4.00
Nottingham	5-35	14	-6.67	3-15	20	+6.50	1-18	6	-16.67	1-2	50	+3.50
Pontefract	0-4	-	-4.00	0-3	-	-3.00	0-0	-	+0.00	0-1	-	-1.00
Redcar	0-1	-	-1.00	0-1	-	-1.00	0-0	-	+0.00	0-0	-	+0.00
Ripon	0-5	-	-5.00	0-2	-	-2.00	0-1	-	-1.00	0-2	-	-2.00
Salisbury	13-88	15	-13.97	10-44	23	-6.97	2-39	5	-21.00	1-5	20	+14.00
Sandown	10-65	15	-9.66	6-25	24	+6.39	3-31	10	-13.04	1-9	11	-3.00
S'thwell (AW)	1-1	100	+4.50	0-0	-	+0.00	1-1	100	+4.50	0-0	-	+0.00
Thirsk	1-2	50	+0.38	0-0	-	+0.00	1-2	50	+0.38	0-0	-	+0.00
Warwick	1-8	13	-6.20	1-3	33	-1.20	0-5	-	-5.00	0-0	-	+0.00
Windsor	13-98	13	-53.85	9-40	23	-24.85	3-43	7	-20.00	1-15	7	-9.00
Wolves (AW)	8-31	26	+5.50	4-16	25	+8.75	4-11	36	+0.75	0-4	-	-4.00
Yarmouth	2-5	40	+0.91	0-3	-	-3.00	1-1	100	+0.91	1-1	100	+3.00
York	3-28	11	+5.88	1-17	6	-14.13	2-8	25	+23.00	0-3	-	-3.00

Trainer interviews start on page 6

Ten-year summary*

	Wins	Runs	%	Win prize-money	Total prize-money	£1
2014	206	1404	15	£2,729,648.95	£4,749,469.60	-366.41
2013	235	1412	17	£3,137,720.00	£4,532,464.69	-306.32
2012	218	1367	16	£1,767,369.39	£2,821,469.49	-165.90
2011	218	1408	15	£2,283,589.58	£3,726,396.80	-46.12
2010	210	1341	16	£2,054,058.90	£3,218,574.92	-203.61
2009	188	1371	14	£1,751,642.04	£2,814,384.49	-193.61
2008	189	1406	13	£1,884,767.33	£2,982,090.39	-283.60
2007	148	1075	14	£1,192,346.67	£2,083,975.15	-178.24
2006	127	1067	12	£1,043,024.26	£1,753,310.04	-261.41
2005	145	1261	11	£1,209,719.79	£2,030,928.02	-282.57

NIGHT OF THUNDER: an instant Classic winner for Richard Hannon (right)

Richard Fahey

Fahey obliterated his best tally of winners last year, managing 192 to pass the 165 of 2009. There was just one Group winner in Britain, but Garswood's French Group 1 win was another big highlight.

By month – 2014

	Overall			Two-year-olds			Three-year-olds			Older horses		
	W-R	%	£1	W-R	%	£1	W-R	%	£1	W-R	%	£1
January	8-46	17	+10.30	0-0	-	+0.00	2-14	14	-10.20	6-32	19	+20.50
February	3-23	13	-15.00	0-0	-	+0.00	2-11	18	-5.88	1-12	8	-9.13
March	4-34	12	-3.75	0-0	-	+0.00	1-14	7	-10.75	3-20	15	+7.00
April	16-120	13	-16.77	4-18	22	-4.27	6-53	11	-24.75	6-49	12	+12.25
May	27-205	13	-42.00	10-48	21	-7.28	11-80	13	+4.78	6-77	8	-39.50
June	32-218	15	+40.43	8-61	13	-3.27	14-84	17	+36.83	10-73	14	+6.88
July	20-187	11	-56.34	8-77	10	-32.59	8-62	13	-14.25	4-48	8	-9.50
August	34-206	17	-13.92	12-77	16	-13.63	11-60	18	+0.88	11-69	16	-1.17
September	16-208	8	-77.25	11-94	12	-13.50	2-44	5	-29.25	3-70	4	-34.50
October	19-160	12	+11.21	8-64	13	-3.13	6-38	16	+28.00	5-58	9	-13.67
November	11-57	19	+7.85	5-21	24	-2.40	2-14	14	+2.50	4-22	18	+7.75
December	2-38	5	+36.00	2-13	15	+61.00	0-8	-	-8.00	0-17	-	-17.00

By month – 2013

	Overall			Two-year-olds			Three-year-olds			Older horses		
	W-R	%	£1	W-R	%	£1	W-R	%	£1	W-R	%	£1
January	5-26	19	-1.80	0-0	-	+0.00	2-5	40	+2.86	3-21	14	-4.67
February	3-19	16	-12.00	0-0	-	+0.00	2-9	22	-6.00	1-10	10	-6.00
March	9-51	18	-1.96	0-3	-	-3.00	2-14	14	-8.71	7-34	21	+9.75
April	20-118	17	+14.02	1-12	8	-8.25	11-50	22	+13.88	8-56	14	+8.40
May	22-169	13	-33.64	10-36	28	-1.00	6-61	10	-29.75	6-72	8	-2.89
June	15-183	8	-87.43	8-53	15	-22.93	1-58	2	-48.00	6-72	8	-16.50
July	22-168	13	-36.68	12-62	19	+12.19	5-41	12	-15.63	5-65	8	-33.25
August	31-175	18	-17.56	11-64	17	-31.43	8-47	17	+21.00	12-64	19	-7.13
September	16-170	9	-13.25	6-60	10	+3.25	4-52	8	-29.50	6-58	10	+13.00
October	18-123	15	+19.21	7-41	17	-17.29	8-38	21	+59.50	3-44	7	-23.00
November	3-45	7	-25.80	1-11	9	-8.90	1-11	9	-8.90	1-23	4	-8.00
December	0-40	-	-40.00	0-13	-	-13.00	0-9	-	-9.00	0-18	-	-18.00

By month – 2012

	Overall			Two-year-olds			Three-year-olds			Older horses		
	W-R	%	£1	W-R	%	£1	W-R	%	£1	W-R	%	£1
January	6-40	15	+8.00	0-0	-	+0.00	1-12	8	-6.00	5-28	18	+14.00
February	1-31	3	-24.00	0-0	-	+0.00	0-11	-	-11.00	1-20	5	-13.00
March	4-28	14	+13.00	1-1	100	+5.00	1-7	14	-3.00	2-20	10	+11.00
April	9-87	10	-14.83	1-5	20	+7.00	3-32	9	-10.33	5-50	10	-11.50
May	18-168	11	-75.22	4-25	16	-10.47	9-61	15	-14.75	5-82	6	-50.00
June	15-175	9	-24.88	5-34	15	+32.13	5-52	10	-4.50	5-89	6	-54.50
July	29-177	16	-25.27	12-55	22	+9.80	9-51	18	-12.13	8-71	11	-22.94
August	26-187	14	+48.67	10-70	14	+43.04	10-54	19	-3.13	6-63	10	+8.75
September	15-182	8	-93.00	8-69	12	-26.25	3-52	6	-29.00	4-61	7	-37.75
October	12-127	9	-55.13	6-49	12	-19.63	2-30	7	-17.00	4-48	8	-18.50
November	4-49	8	-28.00	0-10	-	-10.00	3-14	21	-3.00	1-25	4	-15.00
December	3-43	7	-22.00	1-13	8	-6.00	0-18	-	-18.00	2-12	17	+2.00

By race type – 2014

	Overall			Two-year-olds			Three-year-olds			Older horses		
	W-R	%	£1	W-R	%	£1	W-R	%	£1	W-R	%	£1
Handicap	130-991	13	-7.28	21-115	18	+33.88	54-376	14	+17.51	55-500	11	-58.67
Group 1,2,3	1-30	3	-25.50	0-9	-	-9.00	1-7	14	-2.50	0-14	-	-14.00
Maiden	42-371	11	-98.80	34-284	12	-55.96	8-82	10	-37.84	0-5	-	-5.00

By race type – 2013

	Overall			Two-year-olds			Three-year-olds			Older horses		
	W-R	%	£1	W-R	%	£1	W-R	%	£1	W-R	%	£1
Handicap	97-860	11	-100.73	15-81	19	+38.63	36-319	11	-40.38	46-460	10	-98.98
Group 1,2,3	5-38	13	+4.25	2-12	17	-3.00	1-7	14	-3.75	2-19	11	+11.00
Maiden	44-264	17	-90.87	30-211	14	-100.86	11-46	24	-3.63	3-7	43	+13.62

By race type – 2012

	Overall			Two-year-olds			Three-year-olds			Older horses		
	W-R	%	£1	W-R	%	£1	W-R	%	£1	W-R	%	£1
Handicap	76-855	9	-256.29	9-93	10	-1.38	32-294	11	-94.92	35-468	7	-160.00
Group 1,2,3	3-42	7	-7.50	0-8	-	-8.00	1-9	11	+0.00	2-25	8	+0.50
Maiden	37-249	15	+14.69	29-181	16	+41.10	8-63	13	-21.42	0-5	-	-5.00

By jockey – 2014

	Overall			Two-year-olds			Three-year-olds			Older horses		
	W-R	%	£1	W-R	%	£1	W-R	%	£1	W-R	%	£1
Tony Hamilton	56-408	14	-121.06	25-183	14	-74.38	20-131	15	-26.55	11-94	12	-20.13
G Chaloner	36-259	14	-9.79	7-69	10	-9.63	10-82	12	-33.38	19-108	18	+33.21
Paul Hanagan	21-94	22	+48.05	10-29	34	+20.55	5-28	18	+3.25	6-37	16	+24.25
Jack Garritty	18-105	17	+30.56	8-36	22	+13.23	8-35	23	+39.50	2-34	6	-22.17
David Nolan	16-125	13	+28.43	5-33	15	+48.60	3-35	9	-20.92	8-57	14	+0.75
Patrick Mathers	8-83	10	+18.50	4-29	14	+18.50	3-33	9	+4.00	1-21	5	-4.00
Samantha Bell	6-99	6	-36.17	0-14	-	-14.00	2-23	9	-11.67	4-62	6	-10.50
Graham Lee	4-13	31	+19.25	0-3	-	-3.00	3-6	50	+15.25	1-4	25	+7.00
Ryan Moore	4-60	7	-48.94	2-21	10	-17.44	1-15	7	-11.25	1-24	4	-20.25
Jamie Spencer	3-25	12	-10.45	0-1	-	-1.00	1-9	11	-7.20	2-15	13	-2.25
Frederik Tylicki	2-5	40	+13.50	1-2	50	+1.50	1-2	50	+13.00	0-1	-	-1.00
Adam Kirby	2-6	33	-1.13	1-3	33	-1.00	1-3	33	-0.13	0-0	-	+0.00

By jockey – 2013

	Overall			Two-year-olds			Three-year-olds			Older horses		
	W-R	%	£1	W-R	%	£1	W-R	%	£1	W-R	%	£1
Tony Hamilton	49-408	12	-154.94	25-149	17	-64.14	11-132	8	-65.86	13-127	10	-24.94
Paul Hanagan	20-164	12	-26.00	6-35	17	-5.25	7-47	15	-15.50	7-82	9	-5.25
G Chaloner	18-132	14	-5.84	3-12	25	+7.91	4-37	11	-11.25	11-83	13	-2.50
Lee Topliss	17-109	16	-41.98	8-37	22	-9.59	5-33	15	-2.75	4-39	10	-29.64
Samantha Bell	9-70	13	-2.17	2-12	17	-0.67	4-22	18	+13.00	3-36	8	-14.50
Ryan Moore	8-21	38	+25.50	3-10	30	+0.25	4-8	50	+21.25	1-3	33	+4.00
Barry McHugh	8-92	9	-21.17	0-24	-	-24.00	4-27	15	+15.00	4-41	10	-12.17
Jamie Spencer	7-27	26	+20.25	0-1	-	-1.00	4-10	40	+10.50	3-16	19	+10.75
Frederik Tylicki	4-26	15	+3.50	0-5	-	-5.00	3-10	30	+15.00	1-11	9	-6.50

By jockey – 2012

	Overall			Two-year-olds			Three-year-olds			Older horses		
	W-R	%	£1	W-R	%	£1	W-R	%	£1	W-R	%	£1
Tony Hamilton	47-383	12	-85.71	24-142	17	-2.96	13-93	14	-24.58	10-148	7	-58.17
Paul Hanagan	31-209	15	-3.38	11-41	27	+8.25	5-59	8	-24.63	15-109	14	+13.00
Frederik Tylicki	17-94	18	-1.95	3-22	14	-12.42	9-32	28	+17.13	5-40	13	-6.65
Laura Barry	9-52	17	+19.25	1-3	33	+31.00	5-20	25	+1.75	3-29	10	-13.50
Lee Topliss	8-100	8	-56.75	3-22	14	-8.25	5-27	19	+2.50	0-51	-	-51.00
Barry McHugh	6-79	8	-23.50	2-18	11	-6.00	3-38	8	-15.50	1-23	4	-2.00
David Nolan	4-52	8	+16.00	1-18	6	+33.00	2-13	15	-2.00	1-21	5	-15.00
Patrick Mathers	4-60	7	-30.50	1-22	5	-10.00	1-26	4	-21.50	2-12	17	+1.00
Shane B Kelly	4-82	5	-61.50	0-9	-	-9.00	0-23	-	-23.00	4-50	8	-29.50

By course – 2011-2014

	Overall			Two-year-olds			Three-year-olds			Older horses		
	W-R	%	£1	W-R	%	£1	W-R	%	£1	W-R	%	£1
Ascot	4-119	3	-84.00	1-19	5	-13.00	2-35	6	-16.00	1-65	2	-55.00
Ayr	33-306	11	-57.84	10-77	13	+9.03	8-81	10	-24.00	15-148	10	-42.88
Bath	0-4	-	-4.00	0-0	-	+0.00	0-1	-	-1.00	0-3	-	-3.00
Beverley	31-229	14	-63.88	15-88	17	-4.47	9-83	11	-46.42	7-58	12	-13.00
Carlisle	14-143	10	-37.79	6-54	11	+0.88	3-47	6	-29.67	5-42	12	-9.00
Catterick	24-127	19	-20.80	15-51	29	+5.66	5-37	14	-5.67	4-39	10	-20.79
Chepstow	0-4	-	-4.00	0-2	-	-2.00	0-2	-	-2.00	0-0	-	+0.00
Chester	40-295	14	-75.26	13-62	21	-4.76	10-103	10	-43.25	17-130	13	-27.25
Doncaster	37-345	11	-19.54	9-90	10	-14.00	6-90	7	-39.13	22-165	13	+33.58
Epsom	10-63	16	+11.50	3-10	30	+3.50	2-15	13	-5.50	5-38	13	+13.50
Goodwood	7-121	6	-45.75	2-28	7	-5.50	3-28	11	-3.75	2-65	3	-36.50
Hamilton	24-168	14	-55.43	6-45	13	-10.88	9-59	15	-18.38	9-64	14	-26.17
Haydock	29-264	11	-54.13	7-70	10	-25.00	18-88	20	+46.00	4-106	4	-75.13
Kempton (AW)	6-130	5	-88.00	1-24	4	-18.00	1-40	3	-39.00	4-66	6	-31.00
Leicester	12-77	16	+63.63	4-28	14	+48.50	3-27	11	-1.38	5-22	23	+16.50
Lingfield (AW)	15-149	10	-11.41	2-18	11	-8.63	2-50	4	-40.64	11-81	14	+37.85
Musselburgh	40-174	23	+78.54	11-48	23	-12.40	17-65	26	+79.16	12-61	20	+11.78
Newbury	7-70	10	-23.00	3-26	12	-10.50	1-19	5	-11.00	3-25	12	-1.50
Newcastle	32-199	16	+2.83	16-63	25	-7.43	5-50	10	+2.60	11-86	13	+7.67
Newmarket	13-122	11	-28.70	2-28	7	-16.20	7-49	14	+8.50	4-45	9	-21.00
Newmarket (J)	16-117	14	-0.38	3-34	9	-20.25	5-40	13	-16.38	8-43	19	+36.25
Nottingham	12-94	13	-23.13	6-24	25	+2.63	5-45	11	-13.75	1-25	4	-12.00
Pontefract	32-175	18	+35.60	12-46	26	+50.60	12-65	18	-5.50	8-64	13	-9.50
Redcar	26-159	16	-24.14	12-74	16	-23.22	8-45	18	-0.75	6-40	15	-0.17
Ripon	28-206	14	-35.82	11-61	18	+2.20	10-66	15	-11.17	7-79	9	-26.85
Salisbury	0-3	-	-3.00	0-2	-	-2.00	0-1	-	-1.00	0-0	-	+0.00
Sandown	2-30	7	-23.25	0-8	-	-8.00	0-10	-	-10.00	2-12	17	-5.25
S'thwell (AW)	24-164	14	-58.30	7-38	18	-5.49	6-51	11	-31.01	11-75	14	-21.80
Thirsk	27-189	14	-22.34	10-65	15	-27.59	9-59	15	+7.75	8-65	12	-2.50
Warwick	4-29	14	-6.83	2-12	17	-6.33	2-9	22	+7.50	0-8	-	-8.00
Windsor	5-21	24	+21.00	1-5	20	+12.00	1-7	14	+5.00	3-9	33	+4.00
Wolves (AW)	53-459	12	-80.47	12-116	10	+3.93	15-119	12	-49.23	26-224	12	-35.17
Yarmouth	9-35	26	+9.43	2-9	22	-2.94	5-17	29	+13.13	2-9	22	-0.75
York	35-532	7	-193.01	13-157	8	-49.34	7-104	7	-37.00	15-271	6	-106.67

Ten-year summary

	Wins	Runs	%	Win prize-money	Total prize-money	£1
2014	192	1502	13	£1,882,767.02	£2,882,652.01	-119.24
2013	164	1287	13	£1,588,826.54	£2,455,584.17	-236.90
2012	142	1294	11	£1,213,826.13	£1,982,267.62	-294.66
2011	151	1224	12	£980,328.63	£1,650,127.14	-260.88
2010	181	1356	13	£1,325,389.94	£2,075,925.44	-273.54
2009	165	1106	15	£1,123,057.39	£1,657,128.68	+25.22
2008	113	971	12	£753,492.30	£1,247,043.13	-285.77
2007	85	926	9	£643,994.08	£1,132,827.97	-327.77
2006	87	734	12	£677,880.08	£1,098,407.35	-98.05
2005	79	768	10	£487,562.61	£802,151.94	-131.29

ANGEL GABRIAL: wins the Northumberland Plate for Richard Fahey last year

John Gosden

It was a phenomenal year for Gosden, who couldn't quite land the trainers' title but passed £4m in prize-money thanks to a best ever tally of 132 winners. His maiden runners have shown a profit for two straight years.

By month – 2014

	Overall			Two-year-olds			Three-year-olds			Older horses		
	W-R	%	£1	W-R	%	£1	W-R	%	£1	W-R	%	£1
January	2-11	18	-5.05	0-0	-	+0.00	2-10	20	-4.05	0-1	-	-1.00
February	1-8	13	-4.50	0-0	-	+0.00	1-7	14	-3.50	0-1	-	-1.00
March	2-12	17	-1.50	0-0	-	+0.00	2-8	25	+2.50	0-4	-	-4.00
April	20-64	31	+7.20	1-1	100	+10.00	17-56	30	-1.38	2-7	29%	-1.42
May	12-81	15	+8.52	0-5	-	-5.00	7-59	12	+1.45	5-17	29%	+12.07
June	16-80	20	-9.54	1-4	25	+7.00	12-63	19	-18.29	3-13	23%	+1.75
July	12-70	17	-23.83	1-13	8	-11.09	10-49	20	-13.74	1-8	13%	+1.00
August	19-65	29	+23.05	3-16	19	-5.25	12-40	30	+9.50	4-9	44%	+18.80
September	17-73	23	+33.67	9-32	28	+19.67	6-30	20	+8.50	2-11	18%	+5.50
October	11-76	14	-38.77	7-44	16	-22.52	4-25	16	-9.25	0-7	-	-7.00
November	8-41	20	-13.14	5-31	16	-10.19	3-8	38	-0.95	0-2	-	-2.00
December	12-32	38	-0.73	10-25	40	+3.13	2-7	29	-3.86	0-0	-	+0.00

By month – 2013

	Overall			Two-year-olds			Three-year-olds			Older horses		
	W-R	%	£1	W-R	%	£1	W-R	%	£1	W-R	%	£1
January	4-15	27	-4.91	0-0	-	+0.00	3-10	30	-2.53	1-5	20	-2.38
February	2-4	50	-0.45	0-0	-	+0.00	2-4	50	-0.45	0-0	-	+0.00
March	2-14	14	-9.63	0-0	-	+0.00	2-11	18	-6.63	0-3	-	-3.00
April	5-31	16	-11.75	0-0	-	+0.00	5-29	17	-9.75	0-2	-	-2.00
May	12-65	18	+7.92	0-3	-	-3.00	8-40	20	+16.25	4-22	18	-5.33
June	12-62	19	-6.30	2-9	22	-3.64	8-36	22	+6.08	2-17	12	-8.75
July	14-63	22	-14.87	1-17	6	-10.00	9-30	30	+1.08	4-16	25	-5.95
August	22-73	30	+28.92	8-20	40	+10.80	11-37	30	+24.24	3-16	19	-6.13
September	10-66	15	-3.30	3-25	12	+4.88	4-29	14	-12.05	3-12	25	+3.88
October	12-68	18	-0.25	4-35	11	-8.75	6-25	24	+4.75	2-8	25	+3.75
November	3-40	8	-34.69	1-25	4	-23.60	1-8	13	-6.00	1-7	14	-5.09
December	10-24	42	+24.48	9-18	50	+24.48	0-4	-	-4.00	1-2	50	+4.00

By month – 2012

	Overall			Two-year-olds			Three-year-olds			Older horses		
	W-R	%	£1	W-R	%	£1	W-R	%	£1	W-R	%	£1
January	5-13	38	+11.81	0-0	-	+0.00	4-8	50	+13.69	1-5	20	-1.88
February	4-8	50	+6.75	0-0	-	+0.00	2-6	33	+3.50	2-2	100	+3.25
March	5-23	22	-9.78	0-0	-	+0.00	1-16	6	-11.00	4-7	57	+1.22
April	11-65	17	-14.96	0-0	-	+0.00	6-45	13	-25.63	5-20	25	+10.67
May	15-92	16	-50.64	0-0	-	+0.00	10-62	16	-40.91	5-30	17	-9.73
June	22-108	20	+25.05	3-16	19	+0.63	10-59	17	-23.08	9-33	27	+47.50
July	8-58	14	-24.50	2-10	20	+2.50	3-34	9	-23.50	3-14	21	-3.50
August	10-76	13	-27.13	4-25	16	-7.13	6-37	16	-6.00	0-14	-	-14.00
September	14-66	21	+1.85	6-23	26	+7.22	5-30	17	-14.20	3-13	23	+8.83
October	17-84	20	+18.82	6-31	19	+2.49	9-40	23	+1.33	2-13	15	+15.00
November	5-19	26	+11.00	1-9	11	-5.50	4-7	57	+19.50	0-3	-	-3.00
December	3-17	18	-8.92	2-13	15	-6.75	1-4	25	-2.17	0-0	-	+0.00

By race type – 2014

	Overall			Two-year-olds			Three-year-olds			Older horses		
	W-R	%	£1	W-R	%	£1	W-R	%	£1	W-R	%	£1
Handicap	30-173	17	-33.96	4-15	27	-0.50	21-136	15	-50.29	5-22	23	+16.83
Group 1,2,3	13-63	21	+14.50	0-3	-	-3.00	8-34	24	+5.00	5-26	19	+12.50
Maiden	73-296	25	+14.44	28-140	20	-17.95	43-150	29	+31.59	2-6	33	+0.80

By race type – 2013

	Overall			Two-year-olds			Three-year-olds			Older horses		
	W-R	%	£1	W-R	%	£1	W-R	%	£1	W-R	%	£1
Handicap	37-159	23	-16.89	1-8	13	-1.50	25-105	24	-13.48	11-46	24	-1.91
Group 1,2,3	9-58	16	-8.46	1-5	20	-3.71	3-18	17	+10.25	5-35	14	-15.00
Maiden	52-241	22	+27.11	26-131	20	+4.38	26-107	24	+25.73	0-3	-	-3.00

By race type – 2012

	Overall			Two-year-olds			Three-year-olds			Older horses		
	W-R	%	£1	W-R	%	£1	W-R	%	£1	W-R	%	£1
Handicap	33-202	16	-48.59	1-9	11	-5.25	14-111	13	-44.00	18-82	22	+0.66
Group 1,2,3	13-85	15	-5.29	1-7	14	-4.25	6-39	15	-2.38	6-39	15	+1.33
Maiden	54-268	20	-55.55	19-101	19	+5.41	31-159	19	-62.19	4-8	50	+1.23

By jockey – 2014

	Overall			Two-year-olds			Three-year-olds			Older horses		
	W-R	%	£1	W-R	%	£1	W-R	%	£1	W-R	%	£1
William Buick	56-291	19	-55.62	9-61	15	-20.47	36-182	20%	-46.45	11-48	23	+11.30
Robert Havlin	29-148	20	-27.21	14-60	23	+1.69	15-80	19%	-20.89	0-8	-	-8.00
Paul Hanagan	15-38	39	+14.50	3-8	38	-0.48	12-25	48%	+19.98	0-5	-	-5.00
Nicky Mackay	13-53	25	+6.03	4-16	25	-2.50	7-32	22%	-12.47	2-5	40	+21.00
James Doyle	8-27	30	-5.91	2-7	29	-1.50	5-13	38%	+0.75	1-7	14	-5.17
Dane O'Neill	5-20	25	+12.00	4-10	40	+14.00	1-10	10%	-2.00	0-0	-	+0.00
Frankie Dettori	3-12	25	-1.43	1-2	50	+2.00	0-5	-	-5.00	2-5	40	+1.57
Ted Durcan	1-1	100	+40.00	0-0	-	+0.00	1-1	100%	+40.00	0-0	-	+0.00
Graham Lee	1-3	33	+6.00	0-0	-	+0.00	0-1	-	-1.00	1-2	50	+7.00
Steve Drowne	1-10	10	-3.00	0-5	-	-5.00	1-5	20%	+2.00	0-0	-	+0.00
Kieren Fallon	0-1	-	-1.00	0-0	-	+0.00	0-1	-	-1.00	0-0	-	+0.00
Martin Dwyer	0-1	-	-1.00	0-0	-	+0.00	0-1	-	-1.00	0-0	-	+0.00

By jockey – 2013

	Overall			Two-year-olds			Three-year-olds			Older horses		
	W-R	%	£1	W-R	%	£1	W-R	%	£1	W-R	%	£1
William Buick	54-265	20	-28.70	9-65	14	-24.44	33-139	24	+14.57	12-61	20	-18.83
Robert Havlin	35-134	26	+1.69	14-54	26	-1.43	16-58	28	+0.22	5-22	23	+2.91
Nicky Mackay	4-52	8	-16.70	1-17	6	-2.00	2-27	7	-7.75	1-8	13	-6.95
Ryan Moore	3-7	43	+1.83	1-1	100	+2.75	1-3	33	-1.17	1-3	33	+0.25
Paul Hanagan	3-27	11	-6.75	1-6	17	+3.00	1-17	6	-14.75	1-4	25	+5.00
Martin Dwyer	2-2	100	+28.33	0-0	-	+0.00	2-2	100	+28.33	0-0	-	+0.00
Dane O'Neill	2-9	22	+13.50	1-2	50	+19.00	1-4	25	-2.50	0-3	-	-3.00
Franny Norton	1-1	100	+0.80	0-0	-	+0.00	1-1	100	+0.80	0-0	-	+0.00
Joe Fanning	1-1	100	+1.63	0-0	-	+0.00	0-0	-	+0.00	1-1	100	+1.63

By jockey – 2012

	Overall			Two-year-olds			Three-year-olds			Older horses		
	W-R	%	£1	W-R	%	£1	W-R	%	£1	W-R	%	£1
William Buick	68-309	22	+12.44	13-60	22	+1.01	33-155	21	-41.84	22-94	23	+53.27
Nicky Mackay	16-86	19	-20.80	1-13	8	-9.50	12-60	20	-5.55	3-13	23	-5.75
Robert Havlin	14-111	13	-47.00	5-24	21	+3.42	7-73	10	-49.42	2-14	14	-1.00
Paul Hanagan	11-43	26	-0.70	4-10	40	+1.53	3-20	15	-3.93	4-13	31	+1.70
Ryan Moore	2-6	33	-3.40	0-0	-	+0.00	1-3	33	-1.80	1-3	33	-1.60
Dane O'Neill	1-1	100	+16.00	1-1	100	+16.00	0-0	-	+0.00	0-0	-	+0.00
Jim Crowley	1-1	100	+2.75	0-0	-	+0.00	0-0	-	+0.00	1-1	100	+2.75
Martin Dwyer	1-1	100	+5.00	0-0	-	+0.00	1-1	100	+5.00	0-0	-	+0.00
Luke Morris	1-2	50	-0.56	0-0	-	+0.00	1-1	100	+0.44	0-1	-	-1.00

By course – 2011-2014

	Overall			Two-year-olds			Three-year-olds			Older horses		
	W-R	%	£1	W-R	%	£1	W-R	%	£1	W-R	%	£1
Ascot	28-158	18	+45.57	3-14	21	+14.75	12-80	15	-12.95	13-64	20	+43.78
Ayr	0-1	-	-1.00	0-1	-	-1.00	0-0	-	+0.00	0-0	-	+0.00
Bath	2-10	20	-1.50	0-1	-	-1.00	2-8	25	+0.50	0-1	-	-1.00
Brighton	1-5	20	-3.83	1-2	50	-0.83	0-3	-	-3.00	0-0	-	+0.00
Carlisle	0-2	-	-2.00	0-1	-	-1.00	0-0	-	+0.00	0-1	-	-1.00
Catterick	1-2	50	+0.75	1-1	100	+1.75	0-1	-	-1.00	0-0	-	+0.00
Chepstow	2-4	50	-0.70	1-1	100	+0.80	1-3	33	-1.50	0-0	-	+0.00
Chester	7-32	22	-8.92	1-2	50	+0.88	6-22	27	-1.79	0-8	-	-8.00
Doncaster	24-135	18	-25.12	4-27	15	-12.74	16-77	21	-8.88	4-31	13	-3.50
Epsom	8-44	18	-12.92	2-3	67	+3.00	3-24	13	-10.50	3-17	18	-5.42
Ffos Las	0-1	-	-1.00	0-1	-	-1.00	0-0	-	+0.00	0-0	-	+0.00
Folkestone	1-3	33	-1.00	1-1	100	+1.00	0-2	-	-2.00	0-0	-	+0.00
Goodwood	18-100	18	+13.26	4-24	17	+0.08	9-46	20	+8.10	5-30	17	+5.07
Hamilton	1-1	100	+0.14	0-0	-	+0.00	1-1	100	+0.14	0-0	-	+0.00
Haydock	24-77	31	+46.94	5-17	29	+3.90	11-35	31	+5.37	8-25	32	+37.67
Kempton (AW)	61-304	20	-45.05	20-117	17	-2.78	36-159	23	-34.50	5-28	17	-7.77
Leicester	9-43	21	-13.32	2-18	11	-10.09	7-24	29	-2.23	0-1	-	-1.00
Lingfield	4-20	20	-3.00	2-7	29	-0.50	2-12	17	-1.50	0-1	-	-1.00
Lingfield (AW)	47-215	22	-7.96	10-64	16	-14.55	32-131	24	+6.14	5-20	27	+0.45
Musselburgh	1-2	50	-0.17	0-0	-	+0.00	1-2	50	-0.17	0-0	-	+0.00
Newbury	30-138	22	+39.04	7-27	26	+13.50	20-88	23	+26.54	3-23	13	-1.00
Newcastle	6-29	21	-3.97	2-10	20	+2.00	4-13	31	+0.03	0-6	-	-6.00
Newmarket	31-203	15	-5.39	9-64	14	+12.11	14-104	13	-46.12	8-35	23	+28.62
Newmarket (J)	34-200	17	+27.31	9-68	13	-12.25	18-105	17	-1.06	7-27	26	+40.63
Nottingham	10-63	16	-21.60	2-18	11	-12.13	7-38	18	-6.23	1-7	14	-3.25
Pontefract	4-21	19	-5.50	0-2	-	-2.00	3-11	27	+1.75	1-8	13	-5.25
Redcar	1-6	17	-4.50	1-3	33	-1.50	0-2	-	-2.00	0-1	-	-1.00
Ripon	0-4	-	-4.00	0-0	-	+0.00	0-4	-	-4.00	0-0	-	+0.00
Salisbury	6-38	16	-18.47	1-9	11	-4.50	2-23	9	-19.72	3-6	50	+5.75
Sandown	21-128	16	-32.51	6-28	21	+1.79	8-75	11	-37.50	7-25	28	+3.21
S'thwell (AW)	7-20	35	-4.55	2-3	67	+2.44	3-13	23	-7.45	2-4	50	+0.46
Thirsk	1-4	25	-1.63	1-1	100	+1.38	0-3	-	-3.00	0-0	-	+0.00
Warwick	0-3	-	-3.00	0-1	-	-1.00	0-0	-	+0.00	0-2	-	-2.00
Windsor	11-67	16	-20.35	1-8	13	-5.75	9-47	19	-6.10	1-12	8	-8.50
Wolves (AW)	37-110	34	+0.83	14-39	36	+9.49	19-63	30	-8.71	4-8	50	+0.05
Yarmouth	12-68	18	-37.36	3-24	13	-16.65	6-36	17	-19.76	3-8	38	-0.95
York	10-64	16	-7.88	0-4	-	-4.00	5-30	17	-1.63	5-30	17	-2.25

Ten-year summary

	Wins	Runs	%	Win prize-money	Total prize-money	£1
2014	132	613	22	£2,876,012.06	£4,241,990.89	-24.63
2013	108	525	21	£1,263,914.58	£2,033,077.64	-24.83
2012	119	629	19	£2,150,284.26	£3,739,407.23	-60.64
2011	99	553	18	£1,828,265.33	£2,529,369.21	-14.31
2010	105	518	20	£1,101,277.72	£1,714,237.43	-28.71
2009	88	516	17	£1,447,841.46	£2,308,709.36	-97.55
2008	95	498	19	£1,843,697.13	£2,596,896.00	+19.30
2007	68	401	17	£1,055,409.41	£1,644,331.67	-75.22
2006	56	299	19	£605,236.89	£848,468.86	-21.24
2005	91	486	19	£1,064,566.17	£1,487,571.10	+95.30

EAGLE TOP: next in line after John Gosden had three Group 1 winners retired?

Andrew Balding

Balding has been getting progressively stronger for many years and last season was a real breakthrough with a first century. The emphasis was on quality as it was achieved with an 18% strike-rate from fewer runners.

By month – 2014

	Overall			Two-year-olds			Three-year-olds			Older horses		
	W-R	%	£1	W-R	%	£1	W-R	%	£1	W-R	%	£1
January	2-14	14	-9.81	0-0	-	+0.00	2-4	50	+0.19	0-10	-	-10.00
February	4-18	22	-8.40	0-0	-	+0.00	4-10	40	-0.40	0-8	-	-8.00
March	11-32	34	-5.47	0-0	-	+0.00	9-21	43	-0.72	2-11	18	-4.75
April	10-53	19	+3.95	0-0	-	+0.00	6-35	17	+8.10	4-18	22	-4.15
May	15-83	18	-23.88	0-2	-	-2.00	7-47	15	-23.13	8-34	24	+1.25
June	8-78	10	-30.25	0-5	-	-5.00	5-43	12	-8.25	3-30	10	-17.00
July	11-63	17	+24.25	2-7	29	+4.50	5-33	15	+11.50	4-23	17	+8.25
August	12-78	15	+2.50	3-15	20	-7.38	7-36	19	+18.88	2-27	7	-9.00
September	12-86	14	-17.13	4-22	18	-6.75	7-45	16	+5.75	1-19	5	-16.13
October	16-87	18	+30.42	5-26	19	+11.09	6-38	16	-0.17	5-23	22	+19.50
November	6-36	17	-13.23	2-12	17	-6.89	2-12	17	-4.09	2-12	17	-2.25
December	12-31	39	+11.42	1-7	14	+6.00	9-16	56	+7.42	2-8	25	-2.00

By month – 2013

	Overall			Two-year-olds			Three-year-olds			Older horses		
	W-R	%	£1	W-R	%	£1	W-R	%	£1	W-R	%	£1
January	4-28	14	-4.75	0-0	-	+0.00	1-11	9	-8.25	3-17	18	+3.50
February	2-13	15	+0.50	0-0	-	+0.00	1-4	25	+2.50	1-9	11	-2.00
March	5-21	24	-2.84	0-0	-	+0.00	3-12	25	-4.45	2-9	22	+1.62
April	7-57	12	+5.30	0-0	-	+0.00	6-37	16	+21.30	1-20	5	-16.00
May	9-92	10	-29.97	0-4	-	-4.00	7-46	15	-17.97	2-42	5	-8.00
June	16-101	16	+14.80	1-7	14	-2.50	5-48	10	-6.20	10-46	22	+23.50
July	8-84	10	-43.25	1-10	10	-6.50	5-44	11	-12.00	2-30	7	-24.75
August	14-90	16	-14.63	3-18	17	-3.64	4-38	11	-17.25	7-34	21	+6.25
September	15-96	16	-7.38	4-34	12	-23.53	5-35	14	-7.06	6-27	22	+23.21
October	13-86	15	+39.20	7-38	18	+27.57	2-28	7	-21.25	4-20	20	+32.88
November	3-29	10	+38.00	2-10	20	+31.00	0-7	-	-7.00	1-12	8	+14.00
December	3-16	19	-8.33	2-6	33	-2.08	1-2	50	+1.75	0-8	-	-8.00

By month – 2012

	Overall			Two-year-olds			Three-year-olds			Older horses		
	W-R	%	£1	W-R	%	£1	W-R	%	£1	W-R	%	£1
January	1-13	8	-11.82	0-0	-	+0.00	0-4	-	-4.00	1-9	11	-7.82
February	0-5	-	-5.00	0-0	-	+0.00	0-2	-	-2.00	0-3	-	-3.00
March	2-13	15	-8.55	0-0	-	+0.00	0-7	-	-7.00	2-6	33	-1.55
April	6-54	11	-16.13	0-0	-	+0.00	5-37	14	-1.88	1-17	6	-14.25
May	15-96	16	-0.71	0-7	-	-7.00	9-58	16	-10.21	6-31	19	+16.50
June	10-98	10	-58.60	2-9	22	+2.25	5-58	9	-43.97	3-31	10	-16.88
July	11-89	12	-9.50	1-15	7	-11.25	8-50	16	+10.25	2-24	8	-8.50
August	20-122	16	+49.15	4-39	10	-14.00	8-46	17	+50.40	8-37	22	+12.75
September	13-88	15	-28.53	5-29	17	-6.90	6-33	18	-0.25	2-26	8	-21.39
October	7-70	10	-29.25	1-31	3	-25.50	5-28	18	+3.50	1-11	9	-7.25
November	3-37	8	-29.35	2-18	11	-14.10	0-10	-	-10.00	1-9	11	-5.25
December	5-27	19	-7.25	3-14	21	-2.25	2-10	20	-2.00	0-3	-	-3.00

By race type – 2014

	Overall			Two-year-olds			Three-year-olds			Older horses		
	W-R	%	£1	W-R	%	£1	W-R	%	£1	W-R	%	£1
Handicap	73-380	19	+10.83	3-12	25	+0.75	45-207	22	+40.73	25-161	16	-30.65
Group 1,2,3	4-35	11	-14.13	2-4	50	+2.38	0-6	-	-6.00	2-25	8	-10.50
Maiden	30-172	17	-37.05	10-73	14	-9.17	20-98	20	-26.88	0-1	-	-1.00

By race type – 2013

	Overall			Two-year-olds			Three-year-olds			Older horses		
	W-R	%	£1	W-R	%	£1	W-R	%	£1	W-R	%	£1
Handicap	58-422	14	-15.58	1-12	8	-10.33	25-190	13	-33.83	32-220	15	+28.58
Group 1,2,3	1-27	4	-1.00	0-2	-	-2.00	0-8	-	-8.00	1-17	6	+9.00
Maiden	28-193	15	+4.37	15-99	15	+31.89	12-89	13	-24.14	1-5	20	-3.39

By race type – 2012

	Overall			Two-year-olds			Three-year-olds			Older horses		
	W-R	%	£1	W-R	%	£1	W-R	%	£1	W-R	%	£1
Handicap	43-375	11	-102.33	1-29	3	-25.00	26-199	13	-36.83	16-147	11	-40.50
Group 1,2,3	4-38	11	-20.25	0-3	-	-3.00	1-10	10	-6.00	3-25	12	-11.25
Maiden	34-215	16	-5.59	16-113	14	-37.25	16-98	16	+33.27	2-4	50	-1.62

By jockey – 2014

	Overall			Two-year-olds			Three-year-olds			Older horses		
	W-R	%	£1	W-R	%	£1	W-R	%	£1	W-R	%	£1
David Probert	59-278	21	-11.84	7-47	15	-17.58	43-163	26	+30.49	9-68	13	-24.75
Oisin Murphy	26-132	20	+17.35	2-17	12	-7.50	11-61	18	+4.75	13-54	24	+20.10
Liam Keniry	6-46	13	+5.25	2-10	20	+19.50	2-20	10	-7.25	2-16	13	-7.00
Jimmy Fortune	5-22	23	+3.12	2-4	50	+2.12	1-5	20	+3.00	2-13	15	-2.00
Jim Crowley	5-26	19	+11.98	0-3	-	-3.00	4-20	20	+8.98	1-3	33	+6.00
Thomas Brown	4-33	12	-16.38	1-5	20	+2.00	1-12	8	-8.00	2-16	13	-10.38
Andrea Atzeni	3-4	75	+4.04	3-4	75	+4.04	0-0	-	+0.00	0-0	-	+0.00
Rob Hornby	3-20	15	+11.50	0-0	-	+0.00	2-8	25	+18.00	1-12	8	-6.50
Mr H Hunt	2-8	25	+3.00	0-0	-	+0.00	1-4	25	+2.00	1-4	25	+1.00
Jack Garritty	2-9	22	-5.29	0-0	-	+0.00	2-5	40	-1.29	0-4	-	-4.00
Sam Hitchcott	1-1	100	+3.50	0-0	-	+0.00	1-1	100	+3.50	0-0	-	+0.00
Jamie Spencer	1-8	13	-4.75	0-0	-	+0.00	0-6	-	-6.00	1-2	50	+1.25

By jockey – 2013

	Overall			Two-year-olds			Three-year-olds			Older horses		
	W-R	%	£1	W-R	%	£1	W-R	%	£1	W-R	%	£1
David Probert	33-227	15	+62.51	10-60	17	+25.06	15-99	15	+2.95	8-68	12	+34.50
Thomas Brown	14-68	21	+24.27	3-13	23	+2.41	6-30	20	+12.50	5-25	20	+9.37
Oisin Murphy	12-41	29	+39.71	0-4	-	-4.00	4-18	22	-1.00	8-19	42	+44.71
Liam Keniry	10-84	12	-39.41	1-16	6	-14.39	5-41	12	-22.15	4-27	15	-2.88
Jimmy Fortune	7-91	8	-40.20	0-9	-	-9.00	1-40	3	-38.20	6-42	14	+7.00
Jamie Spencer	5-24	21	-5.33	2-8	25	-3.33	2-8	25	+2.00	1-8	13	-4.00
Cathy Gannon	4-20	20	+5.50	0-0	-	+0.00	3-14	21	+7.75	1-6	17	-2.25
Ryan Moore	3-11	27	-4.49	2-4	50	+1.07	1-5	20	-3.56	0-2	-	-2.00
Jack Garritty	2-11	18	-2.75	0-0	-	+0.00	0-3	-	-3.00	2-8	25	+0.25

By jockey – 2012

	Overall			Two-year-olds			Three-year-olds			Older horses		
	W-R	%	£1	W-R	%	£1	W-R	%	£1	W-R	%	£1
David Probert	42-259	16	+28.10	7-51	14	-16.95	24-140	17	+49.42	11-68	16	-4.37
Jimmy Fortune	21-225	9	-119.09	4-58	7	-37.00	8-94	9	-50.70	9-73	12	-31.39
Liam Keniry	8-65	12	-26.90	3-19	16	-6.15	5-37	14	-11.75	0-9	-	-9.00
Franny Norton	4-7	57	+16.25	1-2	50	+3.50	3-5	60	+12.75	0-0	-	+0.00
Thomas Brown	4-18	22	+1.75	1-4	25	+0.00	2-8	25	+4.00	1-6	17	-2.25
Richard Mullen	3-5	60	+15.50	0-0	-	+0.00	2-2	100	+12.00	1-3	33	+3.50
Jamie Spencer	3-16	19	-7.28	2-10	20	-4.15	1-5	20	-2.13	0-1	-	-1.00
Daniel Muscutt	2-27	7	-16.00	0-1	-	-1.00	1-16	6	-10.00	1-10	10	-5.00
Cristian Demuro	1-1	100	+5.50	0-0	-	+0.00	0-0	-	+0.00	1-1	100	+5.50

By course – 2011-2014

	Overall			Two-year-olds			Three-year-olds			Older horses		
	W-R	%	£1	W-R	%	£1	W-R	%	£1	W-R	%	£1
Ascot	10-169	6	-94.92	0-17	-	-17.00	3-56	5	-31.75	7-96	7	-46.17
Ayr	2-7	29	+15.62	0-1	-	-1.00	0-1	-	-1.00	2-5	40	+17.61
Bath	15-76	20	-7.95	2-9	22	+1.25	9-49	18	-6.45	4-18	22	-2.75
Beverley	0-2	-	-2.00	0-1	-	-1.00	0-1	-	-1.00	0-0	-	+0.00
Brighton	7-44	16	-2.88	2-8	25	+0.62	4-23	17	+3.50	1-13	8	-7.00
Carlisle	1-8	13	-5.25	1-1	100	+1.75	0-4	-	-4.00	0-3	-	-3.00
Chepstow	19-75	25	+9.61	2-8	25	+6.50	11-49	22	-6.76	6-18	33	+9.87
Chester	24-103	23	+34.13	2-15	13	+3.25	17-52	33	+32.88	5-36	14	-2.00
Doncaster	13-72	18	+54.25	4-8	50	+32.13	4-22	18	+2.25	5-42	12	+19.88
Epsom	15-106	14	-15.59	6-22	27	+4.66	3-41	7	-11.75	6-43	14	-8.50
Ffos Las	5-23	22	+11.58	1-7	14	-3.00	2-10	20	+13.00	2-6	33	+1.58
Folkestone	1-8	13	-4.25	0-1	-	-1.00	1-5	20	-1.25	0-2	-	-2.00
Goodwood	13-135	10	-33.00	3-34	9	-18.25	4-47	9	-17.25	6-54	11	+2.50
Hamilton	0-6	-	-6.00	0-0	-	+0.00	0-4	-	-4.00	0-2	-	-2.00
Haydock	9-58	16	-6.43	0-9	-	-9.00	4-19	21	+6.44	5-30	17	-3.88
Kempton (AW)	53-387	14	-56.75	6-76	8	-56.54	32-191	17	+25.72	15-120	12	-25.94
Leicester	5-46	11	-6.93	1-11	9	-9.43	3-27	11	-10.50	1-8	13	+13.00
Lingfield	4-24	17	-14.93	0-5	-	-5.00	2-11	18	-7.18	2-8	25	-2.75
Lingfield (AW)	38-225	17	-25.01	9-36	25	+49.72	19-119	16	-42.66	10-70	15	-32.07
Musselburgh	1-4	25	+0.50	0-0	-	+0.00	1-4	25	+0.50	0-0	-	+0.00
Newbury	10-120	8	-47.14	4-44	9	+2.25	6-47	13	-20.39	0-29	-	-29.00
Newcastle	0-3	-	-3.00	0-0	-	+0.00	0-0	-	+0.00	0-3	-	-3.00
Newmarket	16-153	10	+2.88	3-45	7	-19.75	6-49	12	+5.38	7-59	12	+17.25
Newmarket (J)	10-101	10	-30.00	1-24	4	-15.50	2-40	5	-24.25	7-37	19	+9.75
Nottingham	5-43	12	-6.25	1-17	6	-11.00	4-19	21	+11.75	0-7	-	-7.00
Pontefract	2-15	13	+0.50	1-3	33	+1.50	0-7	-	-7.00	1-5	20	+6.00
Redcar	0-2	-	-2.00	0-1	-	-1.00	0-1	-	-1.00	0-0	-	+0.00
Ripon	0-1	-	-1.00	0-0	-	+0.00	0-0	-	+0.00	0-1	-	-1.00
Salisbury	17-126	13	-32.45	4-38	11	-13.88	5-49	10	-15.20	8-39	21	-3.38
Sandown	24-137	18	+37.94	4-30	13	-0.56	12-68	18	+17.50	8-39	21	+21.00
S'thwell (AW)	10-30	33	+7.45	2-4	50	+12.50	8-18	44	+2.95	0-8	-	-8.00
Thirsk	0-2	-	-2.00	0-1	-	-1.00	0-1	-	-1.00	0-0	-	+0.00
Warwick	3-26	12	-15.25	0-7	-	-7.00	2-14	14	-6.50	1-5	20	-1.75
Windsor	27-108	25	+48.34	8-21	38	+20.47	13-59	22	+26.46	6-28	21	+1.42
Wolves (AW)	16-118	14	-28.84	2-23	9	-20.29	11-64	17	-1.15	3-31	10	-7.40
Yarmouth	2-16	13	-6.75	0-4	-	-4.00	1-7	14	-1.50	1-5	20	-1.25
York	5-53	9	-33.22	1-5	20	+0.50	2-17	12	-11.33	2-31	6	-22.39

Ten-year summary

	Wins	Runs	%	Win prize-money	Total prize-money	£1
2014	119	659	18	£1,335,198.23	£2,035,497.26	-35.60
2013	99	713	14	£873,940.78	£1,356,742.43	-13.36
2012	93	712	13	£779,847.73	£1,365,377.42	-155.54
2011	70	543	13	£620,393.39	£971,676.62	-59.07
2010	78	511	15	£707,996.22	£1,116,809.38	-11.81
2009	68	498	14	£460,056.19	£783,172.54	-38.44
2008	67	436	15	£510,631.82	£865,416.84	+12.56
2007	39	410	10	£525,039.35	£711,375.94	-114.90
2006	48	467	10	£357,958.81	£563,634.99	-160.67
2005	40	507	8	£212,863.31	£389,047.11	-128.11

HERE COMES WHEN (left): a seriously progressive horse for Andrew Balding

William Haggas

It's four years in a row that Haggas has improved his annual tally, peaking at 113 winners. Interesting the betting market still underrates him – he's the only trainer in our top ten who returned a level-stakes profit last year.

By month – 2014

	Overall			Two-year-olds			Three-year-olds			Older horses		
	W-R	%	£1	W-R	%	£1	W-R	%	£1	W-R	%	£1
January	2-10	20	-5.50	0-0	-	+0.00	2-6	33	-1.50	0-4	-	-4.00
February	0-3	-	-3.00	0-0	-	+0.00	0-1	-	-1.00	0-2	-	-2.00
March	2-4	50	+2.75	0-0	-	+0.00	1-1	100	+1.25	1-3	33	+1.50
April	10-29	34	+12.91	0-1	-	-1.00	9-24	38	+15.16	1-4	25	-1.25
May	16-66	24	-2.01	1-11	9	-7.00	14-45	31	+10.49	1-10	10	-5.50
June	24-83	29	+18.29	6-16	38	+5.86	16-50	32	+17.68	2-17	12	-5.25
July	17-65	26	+19.57	3-16	19	-7.33	11-40	28	+13.40	3-9	33	+13.50
August	19-74	26	+33.96	6-20	30	+16.36	9-40	23	+9.09	4-14	29	+8.50
September	15-78	19	+5.97	7-45	16	+3.25	7-27	26	+4.72	1-6	17	-2.00
October	6-78	8	-43.38	2-46	4	-31.50	2-24	8	-17.88	2-8	25	+6.00
November	2-19	11	-11.50	1-9	11	-6.50	0-6	-	-6.00	1-4	25	+1.00
December	0-11	-	-11.00	0-6	-	-6.00	0-4	-	-4.00	0-1	-	-1.00

By month – 2013

	Overall			Two-year-olds			Three-year-olds			Older horses		
	W-R	%	£1	W-R	%	£1	W-R	%	£1	W-R	%	£1
January	2-6	33	+1.50	0-0	-	+0.00	0-4	-	-4.00	2-2	100	+5.50
February	2-7	29	+1.50	0-0	-	+0.00	1-5	20	+1.00	1-2	50	+0.50
March	0-3	-	-3.00	0-0	-	+0.00	0-1	-	-1.00	0-2	-	-2.00
April	10-26	38	+16.38	1-1	100	+2.75	6-20	30	+7.13	3-5	60	+6.50
May	7-58	12	-31.12	1-8	13	+0.00	3-29	10	-21.99	3-21	14	-9.13
June	16-80	20	-34.31	3-14	21	-9.45	12-47	26	-9.36	1-19	5	-15.50
July	19-81	23	-7.13	5-19	26	-4.27	9-43	21	-19.30	5-19	26	+16.44
August	18-77	23	+0.34	4-22	18	-2.13	9-40	23	-17.03	5-15	33	+19.50
September	11-68	16	+1.50	7-31	23	+19.50	3-24	13	-15.00	1-13	8	-3.00
October	10-58	17	+24.46	5-36	14	+25.50	2-13	15	-4.00	3-9	33	+2.96
November	10-22	45	+27.36	2-9	22	+1.36	6-8	75	+19.25	2-5	40	+6.75
December	2-17	12	-9.75	2-12	17	-4.75	0-3	-	-3.00	0-2	-	-2.00

By month – 2012

	Overall			Two-year-olds			Three-year-olds			Older horses		
	W-R	%	£1	W-R	%	£1	W-R	%	£1	W-R	%	£1
January	0-0	-	+0.00	0-0	-	+0.00	0-0	-	+0.00	0-0	-	+0.00
February	0-0	-	+0.00	0-0	-	+0.00	0-0	-	+0.00	0-0	-	+0.00
March	1-4	25	-2.33	0-0	-	+0.00	0-0	-	+0.00	1-4	25	-2.33
April	5-23	22	+3.50	0-0	-	+0.00	4-20	20	+4.00	1-3	33	-0.50
May	18-58	31	+20.85	1-2	50	+1.75	13-45	29	+17.69	4-11	36	+1.41
June	13-70	19	-11.77	2-8	25	+0.25	10-54	19	-10.02	1-8	13	-2.00
July	8-51	16	-23.79	1-8	13	-3.50	7-36	19	-13.29	0-7	-	-7.00
August	12-71	17	-21.08	4-27	15	-12.00	7-34	21	-1.95	1-10	10	-7.13
September	10-72	14	-20.44	3-26	12	-6.50	4-32	13	-17.63	3-14	21	+3.70
October	12-70	17	-0.93	10-38	26	+23.19	2-24	8	-16.13	0-8	-	-8.00
November	3-21	14	-9.37	0-7	-	-7.00	2-11	18	-5.37	1-3	33	+3.00
December	1-8	13	+0.00	0-5	-	-5.00	1-3	33	+5.00	0-0	-	+0.00

By race type – 2014

	Overall			Two-year-olds			Three-year-olds			Older horses		
	W-R	%	£1	W-R	%	£1	W-R	%	£1	W-R	%	£1
Handicap	51-211	24	+9.22	5-28	18	-13.14	35-137	26	+5.35	11-46	24	+17.00
Group 1,2,3	1-38	3	-23.00	0-8	-	-8.00	0-16	-	-16.00	1-14	7	+1.00
Maiden	46-199	23	+4.11	18-118	15	-14.31	27-77	35	+20.91	1-4	25	-2.50

By race type – 2013

	Overall			Two-year-olds			Three-year-olds			Older horses		
	W-R	%	£1	W-R	%	£1	W-R	%	£1	W-R	%	£1
Handicap	47-204	23	+22.06	3-19	16	-3.39	25-108	23	-16.01	19-77	25	+41.46
Group 1,2,3	4-32	13	-16.56	1-8	13	-2.00	0-7	-	-7.00	3-17	18	-7.56
Maiden	48-200	24	+23.53	22-101	22	+42.78	24-96	25	-23.25	2-3	67	+4.00

By race type – 2012

	Overall			Two-year-olds			Three-year-olds			Older horses		
	W-R	%	£1	W-R	%	£1	W-R	%	£1	W-R	%	£1
Handicap	31-174	18	-8.87	2-18	11	+9.00	18-112	16	-20.53	11-44	25	+2.65
Group 1,2,3	3-33	9	-20.00	2-9	22	+1.50	0-13	-	-13.00	1-11	9	-8.50
Maiden	45-192	23	+2.79	16-84	19	-11.41	29-108	27	+14.20	0-0	-	+0.00

By jockey – 2014

	Overall			Two-year-olds			Three-year-olds			Older horses		
	W-R	%	£1	W-R	%	£1	W-R	%	£1	W-R	%	£1
Ryan Moore	15-68	22	-11.48	2-19	11	-14.02	11-34	32	+6.79	2-15	13	-4.25
Paul Hanagan	14-55	25	+15.03	2-14	14	-8.17	9-32	28	+4.20	3-9	33	+19.00
Seb Sanders	12-41	29	-0.59	2-11	18	-7.39	8-19	42	+9.30	2-11	18	-2.50
Liam Jones	11-67	16	+5.10	4-28	14	+1.25	7-38	18	+4.85	0-1	-	-1.00
G Gibbons	7-19	37	+9.64	3-10	30	+1.94	3-8	38	+5.95	1-1	100	+1.75
Si De Sousa	7-23	30	+9.15	2-8	25	+8.75	5-14	36	+1.40	0-1	-	-1.00
Nathan Alison	6-19	32	+13.96	0-2	-	-2.00	6-15	40	+17.96	0-2	-	-2.00
Andrea Atzeni	6-21	29	+21.16	3-9	33	+8.25	3-11	27	+13.91	0-1	-	-1.00
Graham Lee	6-22	27	-0.76	2-10	20	-4.09	1-8	13	-3.67	3-4	75	+7.00
Dane O'Neill	5-14	36	-3.66	2-4	50	+0.61	3-7	43	-1.27	0-3	-	-3.00
Joe Fanning	4-30	13	+8.25	2-17	12	+13.00	2-12	17	-3.75	0-1	-	-1.00
Richard Hughes	3-11	27	+3.00	2-5	40	+1.00	1-6	17	+2.00	0-0	-	+0.00

By jockey – 2013

	Overall			Two-year-olds			Three-year-olds			Older horses		
	W-R	%	£1	W-R	%	£1	W-R	%	£1	W-R	%	£1
Liam Jones	15-70	21	-4.13	6-33	18	-3.50	9-32	28	+4.38	0-5	-	-5.00
Paul Hanagan	14-57	25	-16.36	3-12	25	-5.63	7-28	25	-6.68	4-17	24	-4.06
Ryan Moore	10-47	21	-5.82	3-18	17	-0.50	6-21	29	-1.65	1-8	13	-3.67
Seb Sanders	9-19	47	+28.63	2-10	20	+5.50	2-3	67	+3.38	5-6	83	+19.75
Richard Hughes	6-23	26	-6.46	1-2	50	+1.50	3-12	25	-5.33	2-9	22	-2.63
Graham Lee	5-31	16	-12.09	2-9	22	-5.59	3-15	20	+0.50	0-7	-	-7.00
S De Sousa	4-10	40	+19.83	1-2	50	+19.00	3-8	38	+0.83	0-0	-	+0.00
Frankie Dettori	4-12	33	+0.87	1-1	100	+0.62	2-6	33	+1.75	1-5	20	-1.50
Joe Fanning	4-15	27	+15.74	2-9	22	+15.36	2-5	40	+1.38	0-1	-	-1.00

By jockey – 2012

	Overall			Two-year-olds			Three-year-olds			Older horses		
	W-R	%	£1	W-R	%	£1	W-R	%	£1	W-R	%	£1
Liam Jones	13-77	17	-2.29	4-22	18	+16.00	8-47	17	-23.29	1-8	13	+5.00
Paul Hanagan	10-32	31	-4.14	1-12	8	-5.50	8-18	44	+0.74	1-2	50	+0.63
Ryan Moore	8-31	26	-12.38	0-4	-	-4.00	6-14	43	-1.63	2-13	15	-6.75
A Beschizza	5-26	19	+7.50	1-7	14	-2.00	3-14	21	+7.50	1-5	20	+2.00
Eddie Ahern	5-29	17	-7.36	1-8	13	-5.50	3-14	21	-7.86	1-7	14	+6.00
Kieren Fallon	5-32	16	-14.75	0-9	-	-9.00	3-16	19	-5.50	2-7	29	-0.25
Johnny Murtagh	4-14	29	+27.00	1-5	20	+3.50	3-7	43	+25.50	0-2	-	-2.00
Richard Hills	4-27	15	-18.42	2-10	20	-3.97	2-11	18	-8.45	0-6	-	-6.00
Tadhg O'Shea	3-14	21	+6.55	2-3	67	+13.80	1-10	10	-6.25	0-1	-	-1.00

By course – 2011-2014

	Overall			Two-year-olds			Three-year-olds			Older horses		
	W-R	%	£1	W-R	%	£1	W-R	%	£1	W-R	%	£1
Ascot	11-135	8	-79.38	1-22	5	-18.75	8-62	13	-18.63	2-51	4	-42.00
Ayr	2-12	17	+1.00	2-7	29	+6.00	0-2	-	-2.00	0-3	-	-3.00
Bath	7-23	30	-1.64	2-5	40	+1.25	4-17	24	-6.39	1-1	100	+3.50
Beverley	7-26	27	-5.78	2-8	25	+0.00	5-17	29	-4.78	0-1	-	-1.00
Brighton	4-19	21	-1.92	2-11	18	+1.00	2-8	25	-2.92	0-0	-	+0.00
Carlisle	4-8	50	+2.95	1-3	33	+0.75	3-5	60	+2.20	0-0	-	+0.00
Catterick	2-6	33	-2.18	1-4	25	-2.56	1-2	50	+0.38	0-0	-	+0.00
Chepstow	5-15	33	+2.45	0-3	-	-3.00	4-11	36	+2.45	1-1	100	+3.00
Chester	10-39	26	-10.48	5-8	63	+6.42	4-25	16	-15.89	1-6	17	-1.00
Doncaster	13-76	17	-15.01	2-19	11	-2.25	6-38	16	-24.76	5-19	26	+12.00
Epsom	3-29	10	+12.50	0-5	-	-5.00	2-17	12	+19.00	1-7	14	-1.50
Ffos Las	2-8	25	-4.14	1-2	50	-0.39	1-5	20	-2.75	0-1	-	-1.00
Folkestone	0-5	-	-5.00	0-1	-	-1.00	0-4	-	-4.00	0-0	-	+0.00
Goodwood	11-54	20	+5.71	2-9	22	+2.50	5-25	20	-10.79	4-20	20	+14.00
Hamilton	4-9	44	+0.85	0-0	-	+0.00	2-7	29	-4.27	2-2	100	+5.13
Haydock	19-57	33	+27.20	7-14	50	+21.38	9-25	36	+6.32	3-18	17	-0.50
Kempton (AW)	19-137	14	-26.49	4-43	9	-19.50	11-70	16	-10.65	4-24	17	+3.66
Leicester	8-37	22	+8.70	3-18	17	+12.50	5-17	29	-1.80	0-2	-	-2.00
Lingfield	8-28	29	+0.22	3-12	25	-0.70	5-14	36	+2.92	0-2	-	-2.00
Lingfield (AW)	29-114	25	-13.85	4-41	10	-25.75	17-54	30	-0.26	8-19	42	+12.17
Musselburgh	4-11	36	+4.86	2-3	67	+0.52	2-6	33	+6.33	0-2	-	-2.00
Newbury	20-101	20	+3.13	3-33	9	-5.90	12-50	24	+11.83	5-18	28	-2.80
Newcastle	10-29	34	-0.27	1-4	25	-2.80	9-19	47	+8.53	0-6	-	-6.00
Newmarket	16-153	10	-12.15	8-65	12	+30.50	7-66	11	-28.15	1-22	5	-14.50
Newmarket (J)	15-120	13	-63.39	3-28	11	-14.75	12-74	16	-30.64	0-18	-	-18.00
Nottingham	6-45	13	-19.69	1-16	6	-14.64	3-25	12	-12.80	2-4	50	+7.75
Pontefract	12-41	29	-0.41	3-13	23	-4.97	9-24	38	+8.56	0-4	-	-4.00
Redcar	5-18	28	+0.28	0-5	-	-5.00	4-10	40	+3.28	1-3	33	+2.00
Ripon	12-37	32	-5.54	3-10	30	-2.19	7-25	28	-5.60	2-2	100	+2.25
Salisbury	5-30	17	-7.75	1-7	14	+1.00	3-20	15	-10.75	1-3	33	+2.00
Sandown	11-55	20	+6.63	0-10	-	-10.00	8-30	27	+9.13	3-15	20	+7.50
S'thwell (AW)	4-18	22	-8.94	1-3	33	-1.64	3-14	21	-6.30	0-1	-	-1.00
Thirsk	5-23	22	+15.67	2-6	33	+8.25	3-14	21	+10.42	0-3	-	-3.00
Warwick	5-23	22	+14.42	3-12	25	+21.25	2-10	20	-5.83	0-1	-	-1.00
Windsor	13-47	28	-4.88	3-12	25	-1.77	6-26	23	-5.86	4-9	44	+2.75
Wolves (AW)	14-101	14	-59.48	2-29	7	-24.42	11-65	17	-31.82	1-7	14	-3.25
Yarmouth	29-94	31	+31.75	8-35	23	+10.25	18-48	38	+8.62	3-11	27	+12.88
York	26-116	22	+51.85	6-29	21	+11.07	9-42	21	+22.75	11-45	24	+18.03

Ten-year summary

	Wins	Runs	%	Win prize-money	Total prize-money	£1
2014	113	520	22	£1,478,038.78	£2,281,869.22	+17.06
2013	107	503	21	£1,133,364.77	£1,896,067.18	-12.27
2012	83	448	19	£748,501.35	£1,257,840.26	-65.35
2011	76	423	18	£848,955.18	£1,228,089.25	-96.35
2010	59	361	16	£942,548.43	£1,181,417.91	-91.16
2009	69	346	20	£793,312.00	£1,320,567.05	-53.39
2008	86	425	20	£793,358.07	£1,056,524.73	+93.92
2007	66	376	18	£546,929.84	£763,916.97	+34.50
2006	59	334	18	£531,546.78	£771,050.59	+2.90
2005	53	355	15	£313,641.55	£543,899.79	-77.88

MUTHMIR: William Haggas has a hugely exciting sprinter on his hands

David O'Meara

O'Meara has been the success story of the training ranks in recent seasons with a stunningly rapid rise.

The winners dropped last year, despite a second ton, but four Group winners were his first since 2012.

By month – 2014

	Overall			Two-year-olds			Three-year-olds			Older horses		
	W-R	%	£1	W-R	%	£1	W-R	%	£1	W-R	%	£1
January	3-20	15	-8.25	0-0	-	+0.00	0-3	-	-3.00	3-17	18	-5.25
February	3-20	15	+1.75	0-0	-	+0.00	0-7	-	-7.00	3-13	23	+8.75
March	3-27	11	-12.25	0-0	-	+0.00	1-8	13	-1.00	2-19	11	-11.25
April	11-56	20	+10.38	0-0	-	+0.00	4-18	22	-4.00	7-38	18	+14.38
May	15-108	14	-18.40	0-5	-	-5.00	6-28	21	-11.23	9-75	12	-2.17
June	19-119	16	+7.92	0-8	-	-8.00	5-29	17	-2.80	14-82	17	+18.73
July	11-110	10	-43.17	1-16	6	-8.00	2-25	8	-16.67	8-69	12	-18.50
August	21-117	18	-6.50	4-21	19	-4.25	5-37	14	-7.50	12-59	20	+5.25
September	16-102	16	+24.86	3-17	18	-3.40	4-29	14	+1.23	9-56	16	+27.03
October	3-84	4	-56.00	0-12	-	-12.00	1-21	5	-12.00	2-51	4	-32.00
November	4-36	11	+7.50	1-6	17	-1.50	0-5	-	-5.00	3-25	12	+14.00
December	3-31	10	-10.00	0-7	-	-7.00	2-10	20	+5.50	1-14	7	-8.50

By month – 2013

	Overall			Two-year-olds			Three-year-olds			Older horses		
	W-R	%	£1	W-R	%	£1	W-R	%	£1	W-R	%	£1
January	11-24	46	+6.50	0-0	-	+0.00	3-5	60	+1.80	8-19	42	+4.70
February	2-16	13	-10.50	0-0	-	+0.00	1-4	25	-1.25	1-12	8	-9.25
March	6-27	22	-11.42	0-0	-	+0.00	1-8	13	-6.00	5-19	26	-5.42
April	11-62	18	-9.85	0-0	-	+0.00	1-16	6	-8.00	10-46	22	-1.85
May	20-118	17	-8.57	2-9	22	+14.00	7-32	22	+0.56	11-77	14	-23.13
June	19-127	15	-28.15	0-12	-	-12.00	7-27	26	+1.07	12-88	14	-17.22
July	20-125	16	-45.40	3-20	15	-8.50	6-31	19	-11.90	11-74	15	-25.00
August	21-126	17	+46.19	3-16	19	+2.75	6-32	19	-4.02	12-78	15	+47.46
September	12-114	11	-16.25	1-19	5	-13.50	2-24	8	-9.00	9-71	13	+6.25
October	4-75	5	-44.09	2-12	17	+11.00	0-15	-	-15.00	2-48	4	-40.09
November	6-46	13	+7.00	0-3	-	-3.00	3-21	14	+6.50	3-22	14	+3.50
December	4-45	9	-6.75	1-8	13	+9.00	1-19	5	-16.25	2-18	11	+0.50

By month – 2012

	Overall			Two-year-olds			Three-year-olds			Older horses		
	W-R	%	£1	W-R	%	£1	W-R	%	£1	W-R	%	£1
January	2-10	20	+4.13	0-0	-	+0.00	0-0	-	+0.00	2-10	20	+4.13
February	1-8	13	-6.33	0-0	-	+0.00	0-0	-	+0.00	1-8	13	-6.33
March	2-8	25	+1.57	0-0	-	+0.00	0-0	-	+0.00	2-8	25	+1.57
April	5-41	12	+1.00	0-0	-	+0.00	0-9	-	-9.00	5-32	16	+10.00
May	7-64	11	-28.75	1-8	13	-5.13	2-10	20	-4.13	4-46	9	-19.50
June	13-94	14	-23.67	0-13	-	-13.00	4-16	25	+5.33	9-65	14	-16.00
July	12-76	16	+21.93	1-11	9	-2.50	1-15	7	-11.25	10-50	20	+35.68
August	14-93	15	+18.25	1-12	8	-5.00	7-23	30	+16.75	6-58	10	+6.50
September	7-68	10	+17.38	1-8	13	+18.00	2-13	15	+4.88	4-47	9	-5.50
October	2-43	5	-30.50	0-5	-	-5.00	1-7	14	-1.50	1-31	3	-24.00
November	1-21	5	-19.43	1-2	50	-0.43	0-6	-	-6.00	0-13	-	-13.00
December	3-16	19	+10.00	1-3	33	-1.75	2-6	33	+18.75	0-7	-	-7.00

By race type – 2014

	Overall			Two-year-olds			Three-year-olds			Older horses		
	W-R	%	£1	W-R	%	£1	W-R	%	£1	W-R	%	£1
Handicap	84-625	13	-63.48	3-24	13	-9.00	20-156	13	-42.54	61-445	14	-11.94
Group 1,2,3	4-22	18	+39.00	0-1	-	-1.00	1-6	17	+6.00	3-15	20	+34.00
Maiden	14-103	14	-45.68	4-53	8	-32.90	8-36	22	-7.03	2-14	14	-5.75

By race type – 2013

	Overall			Two-year-olds			Three-year-olds			Older horses		
	W-R	%	£1	W-R	%	£1	W-R	%	£1	W-R	%	£1
Handicap	100-664	15	-46.93	5-29	17	+12.00	26-162	16	-36.66	69-473	15	-22.26
Group 1,2,3	0-22	-	-22.00	0-2	-	-2.00	0-3	-	-3.00	0-17	-	-17.00
Maiden	10-106	9	-42.94	7-51	14	+6.75	1-46	2	-44.43	2-9	22	-5.26

By race type – 2012

	Overall			Two-year-olds			Three-year-olds			Older horses		
	W-R	%	£1	W-R	%	£1	W-R	%	£1	W-R	%	£1
Handicap	49-422	12	-64.94	1-9	11	-2.00	15-85	18	-8.04	33-328	10	-54.90
Group 1,2,3	2-8	25	+9.00	0-0	-	+0.00	0-0	-	+0.00	2-8	25	+9.00
Maiden	7-65	11	+0.50	4-41	10	-2.38	3-17	18	+9.88	0-7	-	-7.00

By jockey – 2014

	Overall			Two-year-olds			Three-year-olds			Older horses		
	W-R	%	£1	W-R	%	£1	W-R	%	£1	W-R	%	£1
Daniel Tudhope	65-398	16	-65.84	4-35	11	-11.90	18-108	17	-35.70	43-255	17	-18.24
Sam James	20-177	11	-21.17	5-33	15	-13.25	6-51	12	-10.50	9-93	10	+2.58
David Nolan	9-65	14	-4.50	0-6	-	-6.00	2-14	14	-2.00	7-45	16	+3.50
Josh Doyle	4-43	9	-9.00	0-1	-	-1.00	1-12	8	-3.50	3-30	10	-4.50
S De Sousa	3-12	25	+38.00	0-0	-	+0.00	0-3	-	-3.00	3-9	33	+41.00
Julie Burke	2-37	5	-17.50	0-5	-	-5.00	0-18	-	-18.00	2-14	14	+5.50
James Doyle	1-1	100	+10.00	0-0	-	+0.00	0-0	-	+0.00	1-1	100	+10.00
Oisin Murphy	1-2	50	+15.00	0-0	-	+0.00	1-1	100	+16.00	0-1	-	-1.00
Pat Dobbs	1-2	50	+3.00	0-1	-	-1.00	0-0	-	+0.00	1-1	100	+4.00
Jack Garritty	1-3	33	+12.00	0-1	-	-1.00	0-0	-	+0.00	1-2	50	+13.00
Jamie Spencer	1-4	25	+5.00	0-0	-	+0.00	0-0	-	+0.00	1-4	25	+5.00
Luke Morris	1-5	20	+5.00	0-1	-	-1.00	0-0	-	+0.00	1-4	25	+6.00

By jockey – 2013

	Overall			Two-year-olds			Three-year-olds			Older horses		
	W-R	%	£1	W-R	%	£1	W-R	%	£1	W-R	%	£1
Daniel Tudhope	74-404	18	-41.58	7-39	18	+7.25	20-99	20	-14.50	47-266	18	-34.34
David Nolan	18-110	16	+24.06	2-15	13	+13.00	4-32	13	-17.02	12-63	19	+28.08
David Bergin	12-109	11	-29.62	0-7	-	-7.00	6-29	21	-6.70	6-73	8	-15.92
G Gibbons	11-52	21	-0.36	0-5	-	-5.00	1-15	7	-12.38	10-32	31	+17.02
Julie Burke	4-40	10	+1.50	3-18	17	+6.50	1-14	7	+3.00	0-8	-	-8.00
M O'Connell	3-7	43	+6.00	0-0	-	+0.00	1-1	100	+2.75	2-6	33	+3.25
S De Sousa	3-7	43	+9.50	0-0	-	+0.00	2-2	100	+11.50	1-5	20	-2.00
Graham Lee	2-12	17	-4.40	0-1	-	-1.00	1-2	50	+0.10	1-9	11	-3.50
S H James	2-13	15	+2.75	0-3	-	-3.00	1-4	25	-1.25	1-6	17	+7.00

By jockey – 2012

	Overall			Two-year-olds			Three-year-olds			Older horses		
	W-R	%	£1	W-R	%	£1	W-R	%	£1	W-R	%	£1
Daniel Tudhope	45-258	17	+85.82	3-28	11	+9.38	9-38	24	+2.75	33-192	17	+73.70
David Bergin	9-72	13	-11.82	0-6	-	-6.00	6-22	27	+20.58	3-44	7	-26.40
Kieren Fallon	3-13	23	+3.17	0-2	-	-2.00	0-2	-	-2.00	3-9	33	+7.17
Tom Eaves	3-21	14	-7.92	1-2	50	-0.75	1-5	20	+2.50	1-14	7	-9.67
G Gibbons	2-23	9	-12.25	1-4	25	+3.00	1-2	50	+1.75	0-17	-	-17.00
Ryan Powell	1-1	100	+10.00	0-0	-	+0.00	0-0	-	+0.00	1-1	100	+10.00
Paul Mulrennan	1-3	33	+0.75	0-0	-	+0.00	0-1	-	-1.00	1-2	50	+1.75
Robert Winston	1-6	17	-2.75	0-0	-	+0.00	1-5	20	-1.75	0-1	-	-1.00
David Nolan	1-10	10	+5.00	0-1	-	-1.00	0-2	-	-2.00	1-7	14	+8.00

By course – 2011-2014

	Overall			Two-year-olds			Three-year-olds			Older horses		
	W-R	%	£1	W-R	%	£1	W-R	%	£1	W-R	%	£1
Ascot	5-72	7	+1.00	0-2	-	-2.00	1-9	11	-4.50	4-61	7	+7.50
Ayr	17-82	21	+19.00	1-11	9	+6.00	3-11	27	+0.63	13-60	22	+12.38
Beverley	22-137	16	-0.13	0-27	-	-27.00	8-50	16	-2.82	14-60	23	+29.68
Carlisle	8-66	12	-18.38	2-12	17	-5.88	2-16	13	-2.50	4-38	11	-10.00
Catterick	23-163	14	-59.70	2-21	10	-8.50	9-46	20	-13.41	12-96	13	-37.79
Chester	3-43	7	-19.50	0-5	-	-5.00	0-4	-	-4.00	3-34	9	-10.50
Doncaster	11-173	6	-65.00	0-9	-	-9.00	1-22	5	-15.00	10-142	7	-41.00
Epsom	2-14	14	-8.15	0-0	-	+0.00	1-4	25	-1.90	1-10	10	-6.25
Goodwood	0-20	-	-20.00	0-1	-	-1.00	0-4	-	-4.00	0-15	-	-15.00
Hamilton	10-60	17	-9.88	1-10	10	+1.00	3-23	13	-12.50	6-27	22	+1.63
Haydock	19-135	14	+9.13	0-9	-	-9.00	2-16	13	-0.50	17-110	15	+18.63
Kempton (AW)	3-27	11	+9.00	1-1	100	+3.50	0-8	-	-8.00	2-18	11	+13.50
Leicester	6-25	24	+0.05	0-2	-	-2.00	2-8	25	+3.25	4-15	27	-1.20
Lingfield	1-2	50	+6.00	0-0	-	+0.00	0-1	-	-1.00	1-1	100	+7.00
Lingfield (AW)	2-15	13	-9.70	0-1	-	-1.00	2-6	33	-0.70	0-8	-	-8.00
Musselburgh	18-94	19	-5.59	0-16	-	-16.00	5-22	23	-0.75	13-56	23	+11.16
Newbury	0-8	-	-8.00	0-0	-	+0.00	0-2	-	-2.00	0-6	-	-6.00
Newcastle	18-144	13	-29.84	6-20	30	+6.10	7-50	14	-14.94	5-74	7	-21.00
Newmarket	3-39	8	-12.00	0-1	-	-1.00	0-3	-	-3.00	3-35	9	-8.00
Newmarket (J)	3-18	17	-3.88	0-1	-	-1.00	1-4	25	+2.50	2-13	15	-5.38
Nottingham	3-38	8	-17.25	0-3	-	-3.00	1-10	10	-2.00	2-25	8	-12.25
Pontefract	10-92	11	-22.25	0-10	-	-10.00	0-16	-	-16.00	10-66	15	+3.75
Redcar	28-176	16	+6.79	5-39	13	-2.13	8-53	15	-3.17	15-84	18	+12.08
Ripon	34-185	18	+15.40	3-29	10	-14.50	10-43	23	-6.02	21-113	19	+35.92
Salisbury	0-1	-	-1.00	0-0	-	+0.00	0-0	-	+0.00	0-1	-	-1.00
Sandown	4-20	20	-1.25	0-0	-	+0.00	1-8	13	-3.50	3-12	25	+2.25
S'thwell (AW)	28-199	14	-77.59	2-22	9	-3.43	8-57	14	-31.55	18-120	15	-42.61
Thirsk	21-153	14	-10.47	5-18	28	+30.50	3-39	8	-24.54	13-96	14	-16.43
Warwick	0-1	-	-1.00	0-0	-	+0.00	0-0	-	+0.00	0-1	-	-1.00
Windsor	1-2	50	+7.00	0-0	-	+0.00	0-1	-	-1.00	1-1	100	+8.00
Wolves (AW)	35-262	13	-60.50	1-29	3	-27.75	9-85	11	-11.75	25-148	17	-21.00
Yarmouth	0-1	-	-1.00	0-0	-	+0.00	0-0	-	+0.00	0-1	-	-1.00
York	28-249	11	-28.75	1-17	6	-13.00	9-43	21	+11.50	18-189	10	-27.25

Five-year summary

	Wins	Runs	%	Win prize-money	Total prize-money	£1
2014	112	830	13	£1,257,328.64	£1,772,806.65	-102.16
2013	136	905	15	£777,659.87	£1,159,386.21	-121.29
2012	69	542	13	£517,175.66	£709,691.68	-34.43
2011	48	423	11	£297,865.68	£479,370.95	-149.06
2010	25	153	16	£87,754.32	£122,742.04	-29.60

LOUIS THE PIOUS: pulled off a big handicap double for David O'Meara

Charlie Appleby

Appleby has slotted in at Godolphin's Moulton Paddocks having taken over midway through 2013. His focus is primarily on the two-year-olds and Charming Thought showed he is already making his mark.

By month – 2014

	Overall			Two-year-olds			Three-year-olds			Older horses		
	W-R	%	£1	W-R	%	£1	W-R	%	£1	W-R	%	£1
January	0-0	-	+0.00	0-0	-	+0.00	0-0	-	+0.00	0-0	-	+0.00
February	0-0	-	+0.00	0-0	-	+0.00	0-0	-	+0.00	0-0	-	+0.00
March	0-0	-	+0.00	0-0	-	+0.00	0-0	-	+0.00	0-0	-	+0.00
April	4-28	14	-13.38	0-3	-	-3.00	3-21	14	-8.58	1-4	25	-1.80
May	10-73	14	-33.22	4-19	21	-0.84	4-33	12	-21.38	2-21	10	-11.00
June	11-82	13	-27.94	5-28	18	-16.57	4-37	11	-14.88	2-17	12	+3.50
July	13-78	17	-14.18	4-29	14	-8.47	8-34	24	+6.03	1-15	7	-11.75
August	11-80	14	-32.26	9-44	20	-7.26	2-26	8	-15.00	0-10	-	-10.00
September	20-85	24	-8.90	15-50	30	+1.10	4-26	15	-5.00	1-9	11	-5.00
October	9-59	15	+4.82	5-35	14	+7.99	3-15	20	+0.83	1-9	11	-4.00
November	13-35	37	+8.81	6-23	26	+3.88	6-9	67	+4.93	1-3	33	+0.00
December	11-29	38	+3.12	3-14	21	-8.30	8-15	53	+11.42	0-0	-	+0.00

By month – 2013

	Overall			Two-year-olds			Three-year-olds			Older horses		
	W-R	%	£1	W-R	%	£1	W-R	%	£1	W-R	%	£1
January	0-0	-	+0.00	0-0	-	+0.00	0-0	-	+0.00	0-0	-	+0.00
February	0-0	-	+0.00	0-0	-	+0.00	0-0	-	+0.00	0-0	-	+0.00
March	0-0	-	+0.00	0-0	-	+0.00	0-0	-	+0.00	0-0	-	+0.00
April	0-0	-	+0.00	0-0	-	+0.00	0-0	-	+0.00	0-0	-	+0.00
May	0-0	-	+0.00	0-0	-	+0.00	0-0	-	+0.00	0-0	-	+0.00
June	0-0	-	+0.00	0-0	-	+0.00	0-0	-	+0.00	0-0	-	+0.00
July	2-11	18	-1.00	0-4	-	-4.00	2-5	40	+5.00	0-2	-	-2.00
August	22-106	21	-5.41	14-55	25	+0.48	5-40	13	-18.38	3-11	27	+12.50
September	17-97	18	-21.23	11-55	20	-5.22	6-32	19	-6.01	0-10	-	-10.00
October	12-70	17	+7.50	7-46	15	+1.75	5-17	29	+12.75	0-7	-	-7.00
November	7-20	35	+3.06	5-13	38	+0.56	2-3	67	+6.50	0-4	-	-4.00
December	0-0	-	+0.00	0-0	-	+0.00	0-0	-	+0.00	0-0	-	+0.00

By race type – 2014

	Overall			Two-year-olds			Three-year-olds			Older horses		
	W-R	%	£1	W-R	%	£1	W-R	%	£1	W-R	%	£1
Handicap	41-192	21	-15.56	9-32	28	-5.52	29-117	25	+18.71	3-43	7	-28.75
Group 1,2,3	2-37	5	-6.50	1-7	14	+16.00	0-11	-	-11.00	1-19	5	-11.50
Maiden	44-249	18	-58.53	32-179	18	-30.90	10-66	15	-38.83	2-4	50	+11.20

By race type – 2013

	Overall			Two-year-olds			Three-year-olds			Older horses		
	W-R	%	£1	W-R	%	£1	W-R	%	£1	W-R	%	£1
Handicap	18-89	20	-2.13	6-29	21	-3.13	10-45	22	+2.49	2-15	13	-1.50
Group 1,2,3	3-27	11	-8.88	1-12	8	-9.38	1-7	14	-1.50	1-8	13	+2.00
Maiden	28-148	19	-4.69	20-111	18	-0.56	8-37	22	-4.14	0-0	-	+0.00

By jockey – 2014

	Overall			Two-year-olds			Three-year-olds			Older horses		
	W-R	%	£1	W-R	%	£1	W-R	%	£1	W-R	%	£1
Adam Kirby	34-102	33	+35.77	14-47	30	+16.73	15-38	39	+14.28	5-17	29	+4.75
William Buick	28-123	23	-12.15	17-54	31	+7.14	11-48	23	+1.71	0-21	-	-21.00
S De Sousa	8-50	16	-6.84	6-23	26	+8.91	2-22	9	-10.75	0-5	-	-5.00
M Barzalona	8-53	15	-15.51	2-9	22	+4.00	4-31	13	-15.71	2-13	15	-3.80
Phillip Makin	5-8	63	+6.35	2-5	40	+0.50	2-2	100	+2.85	1-1	100	+3.00
Shane Gray	4-7	57	+11.25	1-2	50	+0.75	3-5	60	+10.50	0-0	-	+0.00
Cam Hardie	4-19	21	-2.59	3-14	21	-6.59	1-4	25	+5.00	0-1	-	-1.00
Martin Lane	4-72	6	-36.50	2-34	6	-16.50	1-29	3	-24.00	1-9	11	+4.00
Richard Hughes	2-10	20	-4.67	1-2	50	-0.67	1-4	25	+0.00	0-4	-	-4.00
Kevin Stott	1-3	33	+0.50	0-2	-	-2.00	1-1	100	+2.50	0-0	-	+0.00
Kieran Shoemark	1-4	25	-1.50	1-4	25	-1.50	0-0	-	+0.00	0-0	-	+0.00
Paul Hanagan	1-7	14	-3.75	1-2	50	+1.25	0-2	-	-2.00	0-3	-	-3.00

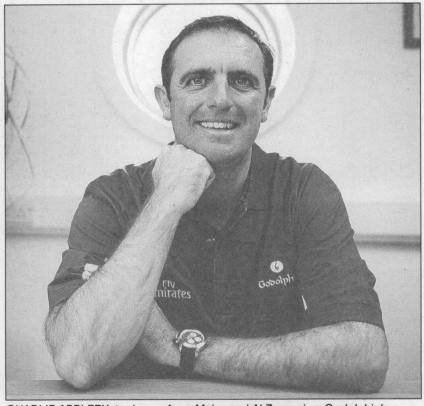

CHARLIE APPLEBY: took over from Mahmood Al Zarooni as Godolphin's second trainer at Moulton Paddocks following the 2013 doping scandal

By jockey – 2013

	Overall			Two-year-olds			Three-year-olds			Older horses		
	W-R	%	£1	W-R	%	£1	W-R	%	£1	W-R	%	£1
M Barzalona	32-140	23	-18.57	20-81	25	-6.93	11-45	24	-4.64	1-14	7%	-7.00
S De Sousa	16-49	33	+31.92	11-29	38	+17.42	4-12	33	+12.50	1-8	13%	+2.00
Martin Lane	4-18	22	+10.25	3-13	23	+8.25	1-5	20	+2.00	0-0	-	+0.00
Ahmed Ajtebi	3-44	7	-29.88	1-21	5	-18.38	2-18	11	-6.50	0-5	-	-5.00
Joao Moreira	1-1	100	+5.50	0-0	-	+0.00	0-0	-	+0.00	1-1	100%	+5.50
Robert Havlin	1-2	50	+5.00	0-0	-	+0.00	1-2	50	+5.00	0-0	-	+0.00
Frederik Tylicki	1-3	33	+3.50	0-1	-	-1.00	1-2	50	+4.50	0-0	-	+0.00
William Buick	1-4	25	-2.80	1-1	100	+0.20	0-1	-	-1.00	0-2	-	-2.00
Kieren Fallon	1-7	14	+14.00	1-7	14	+14.00	0-0	-	+0.00	0-0	-	+0.00

By course – 2013-2014

	Overall			Two-year-olds			Three-year-olds			Older horses		
	W-R	%	£1	W-R	%	£1	W-R	%	£1	W-R	%	£1
Ascot	4-41	10	-14.50	1-9	11	-2.50	2-16	13	-2.50	1-16	6	-9.50
Bath	1-11	9	-8.13	0-2	-	-2.00	1-7	14	-4.13	0-2	-	+0.00
Beverley	1-8	13	-5.38	1-7	14	-4.38	0-1	-	-1.00	0-0	-	+0.00
Brighton	2-14	14	-10.44	1-10	10	-8.27	1-4	25	-2.17	0-0	-	+0.00
Catterick	1-2	50	+2.00	0-1	-	-1.00	1-1	100	+3.00	0-0	-	+0.00
Chepstow	0-1	-	-1.00	0-1	-	-1.00	0-0	-	+0.00	0-0	-	+0.00
Chester	0-3	-	-3.00	0-2	-	-2.00	0-1	-	-1.00	0-0	-	+0.00
Doncaster	6-43	14	-11.58	3-18	17	-8.07	3-14	21	+7.50	0-11	-	-11.00
Epsom	2-10	20	+2.00	1-5	20	-0.50	0-4	-	-4.00	1-1	100	+6.50
Ffos Las	1-8	13	-6.00	1-4	25	-2.00	0-4	-	-4.00	0-0	-	+0.00
Goodwood	5-30	17	+9.75	1-11	9	-7.75	2-11	18	+9.50	2-8	25	+8.00
Hamilton	0-1	-	-1.00	0-0	-	+0.00	0-1	-	-1.00	0-0	-	+0.00
Haydock	5-38	13	-18.97	4-22	18	-9.47	1-9	11	-2.50	0-7	-	-7.00
Kempton (AW)	38-153	25	+35.19	23-89	26	+31.74	14-57	25	+8.24	1-7	14	-4.80
Leicester	6-27	22	-12.32	5-17	29	-5.20	1-8	13	-5.13	0-2	-	-2.00
Lingfield	3-14	21	-3.14	3-10	30	+0.86	0-2	-	-2.00	0-2	-	-2.00
Lingfield (AW)	22-71	31	+13.22	5-21	24	-6.64	12-36	33	+14.86	5-14	36	+5.00
Newbury	2-26	8	-13.50	1-4	25	-0.50	1-13	8	-4.00	0-9	-	-9.00
Newcastle	0-6	-	-6.00	0-3	-	-3.00	0-3	-	-3.00	0-0	-	+0.00
Newmarket	14-63	22	+40.73	9-32	28	+47.98	3-19	16	-5.25	2-12	17	-2.00
Newmarket (J)	14-81	17	-11.22	9-40	23	+3.78	4-30	13	-11.00	1-11	9	-4.00
Nottingham	3-23	13	-14.13	2-13	15	-7.63	1-8	13	-4.50	0-2	-	-2.00
Pontefract	5-15	33	+0.08	3-8	38	-0.25	1-5	20	-1.75	1-2	50	+2.00
Redcar	1-14	7	-10.75	1-7	14	-3.75	0-5	-	-5.00	0-2	-	-2.00
Ripon	0-1	-	-1.00	0-0	-	+0.00	0-1	-	-1.00	0-0	-	+0.00
Salisbury	2-16	13	-10.00	1-9	11	-6.25	0-3	-	-3.00	1-4	25	-0.75
Sandown	5-22	23	-7.30	4-10	40	+1.58	1-8	13	-4.88	0-4	-	-4.00
S'thwell (AW)	0-2	-	-2.00	0-0	-	+0.00	0-1	-	-1.00	0-1	-	-1.00
Thirsk	1-12	8	-9.13	1-10	10	-7.13	0-1	-	-1.00	0-1	-	-1.00
Warwick	0-2	-	-2.00	0-0	-	+0.00	0-2	-	-2.00	0-0	-	+0.00
Windsor	2-16	13	-10.93	0-1	-	-1.00	2-11	18	-5.93	0-4	-	-4.00
Wolves (AW)	25-83	30	-24.95	7-36	19	-18.82	17-44	39	-5.13	1-3	33	-1.00
Yarmouth	2-19	11	-16.50	1-13	8	-11.75	1-5	20	-3.75	0-1	-	-1.00
York	2-15	13	+2.50	0-3	-	-3.00	1-6	17	+1.50	1-6	17	+4.00

Two-year summary

	Wins	Runs	%	Win prize-money	Total prize-money	£1
2014	102	549	19	£924,235.69	£1,493,782.48	-113.14
2013	60	304	20	£693,520.24	£970,334.52	-17.07

CHARMING THOUGHT: a first Group 1 winner for Charlie Appleby

Saeed bin Suroor

A quieter year for Bin Suroor after the trouble at Godolphin in 2013 saw his best strike-rate since 2009. Fifteen of his 21 Group winners in the last three years have come from older horses.

By month – 2014

	Overall			Two-year-olds			Three-year-olds			Older horses		
	W-R	%	£1	W-R	%	£1	W-R	%	£1	W-R	%	£1
January	0-0	-	+0.00	0-0	-	+0.00	0-0	-	+0.00	0-0	-	+0.00
February	0-0	-	+0.00	0-0	-	+0.00	0-0	-	+0.00	0-0	-	+0.00
March	0-1	-	-1.00	0-0	-	+0.00	0-0	-	+0.00	0-1	-	-1.00
April	6-16	38	+1.75	0-0	-	+0.00	6-14	43	+3.75	0-2	-	-2.00
May	8-37	22	+13.28	1-3	33	+6.00	4-17	24	+4.45	3-17	18	+2.83
June	5-45	11	-26.63	0-4	-	-4.00	4-22	18	-7.63	1-19	5	-15.00
July	14-70	20	-9.58	3-16	19	-5.75	5-28	18	-3.75	6-26	23	-0.08
August	12-67	18	-18.24	5-22	23	-6.24	5-21	24	+4.50	2-24	8	-16.50
September	18-62	29	+15.28	7-26	27	-0.82	7-18	39	+18.63	4-18	22	-2.52
October	23-76	30	+11.02	11-33	33	+3.14	7-31	23	+1.08	5-12	42	+6.80
November	4-22	18	-8.38	1-12	8	-8.50	2-8	25	-3.38	1-2	50	+3.50
December	3-9	33	-3.25	2-8	25	-3.75	1-1	100	+0.50	0-0	-	+0.00

By month – 2013

	Overall			Two-year-olds			Three-year-olds			Older horses		
	W-R	%	£1	W-R	%	£1	W-R	%	£1	W-R	%	£1
January	0-0	-	+0.00	0-0	-	+0.00	0-0	-	+0.00	0-0	-	+0.00
February	0-0	-	+0.00	0-0	-	+0.00	0-0	-	+0.00	0-0	-	+0.00
March	0-0	-	+0.00	0-0	-	+0.00	0-0	-	+0.00	0-0	-	+0.00
April	0-9	-	-9.00	0-0	-	+0.00	0-7	-	-7.00	0-2	-	-2.00
May	9-28	32	+8.98	1-3	33	-0.75	1-9	11	-4.50	7-16	44	+14.23
June	23-117	20	-6.13	7-37	19	-4.42	10-48	21	-17.72	6-32	19	+16.00
July	32-122	26	+5.14	13-34	38	+14.04	16-54	30	+17.92	3-34	9	-26.82
August	16-85	19	-23.33	6-19	32	+2.28	4-33	12	-21.67	6-33	18	-3.95
September	12-72	17	+5.10	2-13	15	-8.28	7-34	21	+22.88	3-25	12	-9.50
October	9-72	13	-35.08	2-20	10	-13.50	4-32	13	-15.33	3-20	15	-6.25
November	5-18	28	+0.14	3-10	30	+4.50	2-8	25	-4.36	0-0	-	+0.00
December	0-0	-	+0.00	0-0	-	+0.00	0-0	-	+0.00	0-0	-	+0.00

By month – 2012

	Overall			Two-year-olds			Three-year-olds			Older horses		
	W-R	%	£1	W-R	%	£1	W-R	%	£1	W-R	%	£1
January	0-0	-	+0.00	0-0	-	+0.00	0-0	-	+0.00	0-0	-	+0.00
February	0-0	-	+0.00	0-0	-	+0.00	0-0	-	+0.00	0-0	-	+0.00
March	0-2	-	-2.00	0-0	-	+0.00	0-0	-	+0.00	0-2	-	-2.00
April	2-13	15	-4.17	0-0	-	+0.00	1-10	10	-5.67	1-3	33	+1.50
May	10-51	20	-14.03	0-3	-	-3.00	5-22	23	-1.67	5-26	19	-9.37
June	7-54	13	-10.25	3-5	60	+15.00	3-26	12	-9.25	1-23	4	-16.00
July	15-46	33	+5.44	1-3	33	+0.00	10-23	43	+9.57	4-20	20	-4.13
August	10-77	13	-31.13	1-12	8	-6.00	7-41	17	-18.13	2-24	8	-7.00
September	15-85	18	+20.28	6-21	29	+18.03	4-35	11	+1.75	5-29	17	+0.50
October	17-63	27	-2.02	9-27	33	-0.84	7-20	35	+11.33	1-16	6	-12.50
November	9-45	20	-5.13	4-14	29	+7.50	4-16	25	-4.13	1-15	7	-8.50
December	0-0	-	+0.00	0-0	-	+0.00	0-0	-	+0.00	0-0	-	+0.00

By race type – 2014

	Overall			Two-year-olds			Three-year-olds			Older horses		
	W-R	%	£1	W-R	%	£1	W-R	%	£1	W-R	%	£1
Handicap	36-167	22	-1.00	6-16	38	+6.75	21-93	23	+5.63	9-58	16	-13.38
Group 1,2,3	7-48	15	-9.92	2-10	20	-2.75	0-9	-	-9.00	5-29	17	+1.83
Maiden	34-135	25	-2.68	17-84	20	-21.63	16-47	34	+21.78	1-4	25	-2.83

By race type – 2013

	Overall			Two-year-olds			Three-year-olds			Older horses		
	W-R	%	£1	W-R	%	£1	W-R	%	£1	W-R	%	£1
Handicap	30-189	16	-19.63	1-4	25	-1.38	18-100	18	-1.16	11-85	13	-17.10
Group 1,2,3	9-68	13	-22.07	2-12	17	-6.15	1-15	7	-10.00	6-41	15	-5.92
Maiden	48-197	24	-20.98	26-104	25	+5.52	22-93	24	-26.51	0-0	-	+0.00

By race type – 2012

	Overall			Two-year-olds			Three-year-olds			Older horses		
	W-R	%	£1	W-R	%	£1	W-R	%	£1	W-R	%	£1
Handicap	35-207	17	-29.58	5-10	50	+9.63	24-131	18	-13.46	6-66	9	-25.75
Group 1,2,3	5-46	11	-20.00	1-4	25	+1.50	0-0	-	+0.00	4-42	10	-21.50
Maiden	34-124	27	+20.34	17-65	26	+20.07	17-59	29	+0.27	0-0	-	+0.00

By jockey – 2014

	Overall			Two-year-olds			Three-year-olds			Older horses		
	W-R	%	£1	W-R	%	£1	W-R	%	£1	W-R	%	£1
S De Sousa	16-63	25	+16.53	1-2	50	-0.09	12-36	33	+18.88	3-25	12	-2.25
Kieren Fallon	16-81	20	-17.05	1-6	17	+3.00	8-34	24	-0.80	7-41	17	-19.25
Frederik Tylicki	14-47	30	+9.71	5-23	22	-7.30	5-15	33	+0.71	4-9	44	+16.30
Richard Hughes	8-20	40	+8.66	4-6	67	+8.75	3-8	38	+4.00	1-6	17	-4.09
James Doyle	6-25	24	-5.21	4-18	22	-4.71	1-3	33	-1.00	1-4	25	+0.50
Kevin Stott	5-14	36	+8.50	1-5	20	-1.00	3-8	38	+5.00	1-1	100	+4.50
Harry Bentley	5-28	18	-1.25	3-14	21	+2.00	2-10	20	+0.75	0-4	-	-4.00
Dane O'Neill	4-19	21	+2.75	0-6	-	-6.00	2-9	22	+5.50	2-4	50	+3.25
Ryan Moore	3-5	60	+0.55	2-3	67	+0.35	0-0	-	+0.00	1-2	50	+0.20
A Rawlinson	2-2	100	+2.25	2-2	100	+2.25	0-0	-	+0.00	0-0	-	+0.00
Kieran Shoemark	2-3	67	+7.00	2-2	100	+8.00	0-1	-	-1.00	0-0	-	+0.00
Graham Lee	2-6	33	-2.50	1-2	50	+0.00	1-1	100	+0.50	0-3	-	-3.00

By jockey – 2013

	Overall			Two-year-olds			Three-year-olds			Older horses		
	W-R	%	£1	W-R	%	£1	W-R	%	£1	W-R	%	£1
S De Sousa	45-224	20	-43.57	15-56	27	+0.66	15-92	16	-45.24	15-76	20	+1.02
M Barzalona	25-110	23	-24.17	12-35	34	+8.10	11-52	21	-16.57	2-23	9	-15.70
Harry Bentley	6-21	29	+13.75	1-4	25	+5.00	4-11	36	+6.75	1-6	17	+2.00
Dane O'Neill	4-15	27	+6.75	2-3	67	+2.75	1-10	10	-3.00	1-2	50	+7.00
Paul Hanagan	4-16	25	-4.61	0-2	-	-2.00	2-7	29	-2.71	2-7	29	+0.10
Adam Kirby	3-5	60	+7.00	1-2	50	+4.00	1-1	100	+2.50	1-2	50	+0.50
William Buick	3-10	30	-0.38	2-6	33	+0.38	1-3	33	+0.25	0-1	-	-1.00
Ahmed Ajtebi	3-13	23	+32.00	0-1	-	-1.00	3-8	38	+37.00	0-4	-	-4.00
Kieren Fallon	3-26	12	-5.25	0-7	-	-7.00	0-6	-	-6.00	3-13	23	+7.75

By jockey – 2012

	Overall			Two-year-olds			Three-year-olds			Older horses		
	W-R	%	£1	W-R	%	£1	W-R	%	£1	W-R	%	£1
Frankie Dettori	29-148	20	-27.59	5-28	18	-12.72	12-54	22	-11.76	12-66	18	-3.12
S De Sousa	28-130	22	-19.90	9-25	36	+2.03	16-63	25	+9.69	3-42	7	-31.63
M Barzalona	12-72	17	+16.00	4-13	31	+28.00	5-36	14	-7.00	3-23	13	-5.00
Harry Bentley	3-9	33	+8.25	0-1	-	-1.00	3-6	50	+11.25	0-2	-	-2.00
Ted Durcan	3-18	17	-7.00	1-3	33	+2.50	2-10	20	-4.50	0-5	-	-5.00
Frederik Tylicki	2-4	50	+5.88	1-2	50	+5.00	1-2	50	+0.88	0-0	-	+0.00
William Buick	2-6	33	+5.50	1-2	50	+2.50	0-2	-	-2.00	1-2	50	+5.00
Pat Cosgrave	1-1	100	+1.75	0-0	-	+0.00	1-1	100	+1.75	0-0	-	+0.00
Ian Mongan	1-2	50	+5.50	1-1	100	+6.50	0-0	-	+0.00	0-1	-	-1.00

By course – 2011-2014

	Overall			Two-year-olds			Three-year-olds			Older horses		
	W-R	%	£1	W-R	%	£1	W-R	%	£1	W-R	%	£1
Ascot	13-110	12	-16.88	3-15	20	-4.97	6-26	23	+30.33	4-69	6	-42.25
Ayr	1-5	20	-1.25	0-0	-	+0.00	0-0	-	+0.00	1-5	20	-1.25
Bath	5-11	45	+3.67	3-6	50	+0.92	2-5	40	+2.75	0-0	-	+0.00
Beverley	1-4	25	-2.75	0-0	-	+0.00	1-4	25	-2.75	0-0	-	+0.00
Brighton	7-15	47	+27.83	2-6	33	+23.25	5-9	56	+4.58	0-0	-	+0.00
Catterick	1-1	100	+4.00	0-0	-	+0.00	1-1	100	+4.00	0-0	-	+0.00
Chepstow	0-6	-	-6.00	0-2	-	-2.00	0-3	-	-3.00	0-1	-	-1.00
Chester	2-24	8	-18.38	1-6	17	-3.63	1-6	17	-2.75	0-12	-	-12.00
Doncaster	19-101	19	-24.32	6-22	27	+1.72	6-38	16	-11.88	7-41	17	-14.17
Epsom	6-37	16	-11.47	1-7	14	-4.75	1-14	7	-11.50	4-16	25	+4.78
Ffos Las	0-2	-	-2.00	0-0	-	+0.00	0-2	-	-2.00	0-0	-	+0.00
Folkestone	1-9	11	-7.56	1-3	33	-1.56	0-6	-	-6.00	0-0	-	+0.00
Goodwood	6-82	7	-42.30	1-7	14	-4.80	1-24	4	-13.00	4-51	8	-24.50
Hamilton	1-8	13	-5.00	0-0	-	+0.00	1-5	20	-2.00	0-3	-	-3.00
Haydock	8-62	13	-30.38	4-14	29	+0.62	2-15	13	-6.00	2-33	6	-25.00
Kempton (AW)	57-214	27	+57.49	22-68	32	+8.96	23-103	23	+26.03	12-43	28	+22.50
Leicester	6-27	22	-13.88	3-12	25	-2.85	2-14	14	-11.33	1-1	100	+0.30
Lingfield	2-16	13	-10.75	1-7	14	-4.75	1-8	13	-5.00	0-1	-	-1.00
Lingfield (AW)	25-80	31	+10.29	10-28	36	+6.60	13-44	30	+2.85	2-8	25	+0.83
Musselburgh	2-5	40	+3.00	1-2	50	+2.00	1-2	50	+2.00	0-1	-	-1.00
Newbury	15-66	23	-0.51	2-10	20	-1.00	3-21	14	-10.88	10-35	29	+11.37
Newcastle	4-27	15	+9.00	2-8	25	+9.00	1-11	9	-5.00	1-8	13	-14.00
Newmarket	18-125	14	-16.50	5-35	14	-13.00	9-49	18	+13.50	4-41	10	-17.00
Newmarket (J)	30-137	22	-3.52	13-50	26	+6.52	12-44	27	+5.41	5-43	12	-15.45
Nottingham	14-63	22	-14.20	5-23	22	-10.20	8-33	24	-4.00	1-7	14	+0.00
Pontefract	7-32	22	-10.72	1-5	20	-3.09	4-17	24	-2.42	2-10	20	-5.20
Redcar	2-24	8	-13.00	2-12	17	-1.00	0-6	-	-6.00	0-6	-	-6.00
Ripon	2-16	13	-5.25	1-4	25	+3.00	1-9	11	-5.25	0-3	-	-3.00
Salisbury	8-44	18	+2.78	2-10	20	-4.56	4-23	17	-5.67	2-11	18	+13.00
Sandown	10-76	13	-40.07	2-12	17	-2.50	4-31	13	-14.75	4-33	12	-22.82
S'thwell (AW)	2-12	17	-5.50	0-3	-	-3.00	2-9	22	-2.50	0-0	-	+0.00
Thirsk	5-20	25	-8.76	0-5	-	-5.00	2-9	22	-4.43	3-6	50	+0.67
Warwick	5-19	26	+2.75	2-7	29	-0.25	0-6	-	-6.00	3-6	50	+9.00
Windsor	10-37	27	+14.80	1-3	33	+4.50	5-18	28	+0.30	4-16	25	+10.00
Wolves (AW)	31-93	33	+2.38	12-30	40	+6.91	17-55	31	-2.41	2-8	25	-2.13
Yarmouth	6-37	16	-2.84	3-19	16	+3.50	3-11	27	+0.66	0-7	-	-7.00
York	10-92	11	-40.85	1-8	13	-3.00	0-18	-	-18.00	9-66	14	-19.85

Ten-year summary

	Wins	Runs	%	Win prize-money	Total prize-money	£1
2014	93	405	23	£957,720.87	£1,575,124.75	-25.73
2013	106	523	20	£1,934,401.24	£2,665,780.91	-54.19
2012	85	436	19	£1,020,127.41	£1,817,649.48	-42.99
2011	58	375	15	£494,862.68	£921,445.34	-100.23
2010	90	400	23	£1,383,089.08	£2,064,698.09	-42.77
2009	148	530	28	£1,743,062.05	£2,765,249.72	+17.66
2008	58	313	19	£758,691.92	£1,268,209.97	-56.42
2007	72	285	25	£1,225,192.68	£1,680,865.13	-20.61
2006	70	247	28	£935,405.65	£1,610,204.02	+13.15
2005	78	407	19	£901,450.30	£1,522,250.25	-52.73

CAVALRYMAN: a legend for Saeed bin Suroor who will be much missed

Michael Appleby

Appleby's career has been transformed by a spell as head lad to Andrew Balding before he took up training on his own again in 2010. Having had a best tally of just three prior to that, last year he sent out 89 winners.

By month – 2014

	Overall			Two-year-olds			Three-year-olds			Older horses		
	W-R	%	£1	W-R	%	£1	W-R	%	£1	W-R	%	£1
January	11-56	20	-8.34	0-0	-	+0.00	0-1	-	-1.00	11-55	20	-7.34
February	6-31	19	+4.50	0-0	-	+0.00	0-0	-	+0.00	6-31	19	+4.50
March	8-36	22	+13.33	0-0	-	+0.00	1-2	50	+7.00	7-34	21	+6.33
April	8-47	17	+1.35	0-4	-	-4.00	4-10	40	+21.00	4-33	12	-15.65
May	3-46	7	-15.00	1-3	33	+3.00	0-8	-	-8.00	2-35	6	-10.00
June	10-42	24	+13.13	0-2	-	-2.00	3-14	21	-1.75	7-26	27	+16.88
July	5-39	13	-9.50	0-1	-	-1.00	1-12	8	-6.00	4-26	15	-2.50
August	6-42	14	-15.50	0-4	-	-4.00	1-8	13	-1.50	5-30	17	-10.00
September	6-45	13	+4.83	0-7	-	-7.00	0-9	-	-9.00	6-29	21	+20.83
October	9-70	13	+21.25	1-8	13	+9.00	1-10	10	-4.00	7-52	13	+16.25
November	8-58	14	-20.44	0-6	-	-6.00	2-12	17	-4.17	6-40	15	-10.28
December	9-53	17	-24.84	0-3	-	-3.00	3-18	17	-9.59	6-32	19	-12.25

By month – 2013

	Overall			Two-year-olds			Three-year-olds			Older horses		
	W-R	%	£1	W-R	%	£1	W-R	%	£1	W-R	%	£1
January	1-29	3	-25.50	0-0	-	+0.00	0-3	-	-3.00	1-26	4	-22.50
February	8-27	30	+9.46	0-0	-	+0.00	1-5	20	-2.25	7-22	32	+11.71
March	4-36	11	-15.70	0-1	-	-1.00	1-4	25	+2.00	3-31	10	-16.70
April	4-37	11	-12.77	1-1	100	+4.00	1-9	11	+4.00	2-27	7	-20.77
May	7-41	17	-3.75	0-3	-	-3.00	2-10	20	+2.00	5-28	18	-2.75
June	3-33	9	-3.75	0-1	-	-1.00	0-4	-	-4.00	3-28	11	+1.25
July	3-36	8	-9.50	0-1	-	-1.00	1-9	11	-2.50	2-26	8	-6.00
August	4-47	9	-15.75	0-1	-	-1.00	0-11	-	-11.00	4-35	11	-3.75
September	4-37	11	+13.00	0-4	-	-4.00	0-5	-	-5.00	4-28	14	+22.00
October	4-38	11	-3.00	2-4	50	+10.25	0-9	-	-9.00	2-25	8	-4.25
November	8-40	20	-3.17	1-2	50	+2.50	3-9	33	+0.08	4-29	14	-5.75
December	11-42	26	+13.00	1-4	25	+2.00	1-9	11	-4.00	9-29	31	+15.00

By month – 2012

	Overall			Two-year-olds			Three-year-olds			Older horses		
	W-R	%	£1	W-R	%	£1	W-R	%	£1	W-R	%	£1
January	2-32	6	-13.50	0-0	-	+0.00	0-7	-	-7.00	2-25	8	-6.50
February	3-25	12	+15.50	0-0	-	+0.00	0-7	-	-7.00	3-18	17	+22.50
March	2-23	9	-14.75	0-0	-	+0.00	0-7	-	-7.00	2-16	13	-7.75
April	1-18	6	-15.75	0-0	-	+0.00	0-7	-	-7.00	1-11	9	-8.75
May	1-13	8	-9.50	0-0	-	+0.00	0-6	-	-6.00	1-7	14	-3.50
June	6-31	19	+34.00	0-0	-	+0.00	5-13	38	+33.00	1-18	6	+1.00
July	6-27	22	+26.00	0-1	-	-1.00	0-9	-	-9.00	6-17	35	+36.00
August	2-37	5	-25.25	0-1	-	-1.00	0-14	-	-14.00	2-22	9	-10.25
September	2-24	8	-1.00	0-0	-	+0.00	2-6	33	+17.00	0-18	-	-18.00
October	7-44	16	+40.00	0-1	-	-1.00	2-19	11	+13.00	5-24	21	+28.00
November	3-24	13	+12.50	0-0	-	+0.00	1-6	17	+3.00	2-18	11	+9.50
December	5-34	15	+6.50	0-1	-	-1.00	2-11	18	+9.00	3-22	14	-1.50

By race type – 2014

	Overall			Two-year-olds			Three-year-olds			Older horses		
	W-R	%	£1	W-R	%	£1	W-R	%	£1	W-R	%	£1
Handicap	81-472	17	+0.65	0-6	-	-6.00	15-81	19	+2.74	66-385	17	+3.91
Group 1,2,3	1-4	25	-0.75	0-1	-	-1.00	1-2	50	+1.25	0-1	-	-1.00
Maiden	3-48	6	-14.00	2-28	7	-5.00	0-14	-	-14.00	1-6	17	+5.00

By race type – 2013

	Overall			Two-year-olds			Three-year-olds			Older horses		
	W-R	%	£1	W-R	%	£1	W-R	%	£1	W-R	%	£1
Handicap	54-359	15	-26.26	2-5	40	+5.50	9-57	16	-4.50	43-297	14	-27.26
Group 1,2,3	0-2	-	-2.00	0-1	-	-1.00	0-0	-	+0.00	0-1	-	-1.00
Maiden	5-56	9	-13.92	3-13	23	+6.25	1-26	4	-24.17	1-17	6	+4.00

By race type – 2012

	Overall			Two-year-olds			Three-year-olds			Older horses		
	W-R	%	£1	W-R	%	£1	W-R	%	£1	W-R	%	£1
Handicap	35-257	14	+88.50	0-1	-	-1.00	11-78	14	+31.00	24-178	13	+58.50
Group 1,2,3	0-0	-	+0.00	0-0	-	+0.00	0-0	-	+0.00	0-0	-	+0.00
Maiden	0-48	-	-48.00	0-3	-	-3.00	0-27	-	-27.00	0-18	-	-18.00

By jockey – 2014

	Overall			Two-year-olds			Three-year-olds			Older horses		
	W-R	%	£1	W-R	%	£1	W-R	%	£1	W-R	%	£1
Andrew Mullen	46-289	16	+7.78	0-18	-	-18.00	7-44	16	+6.25	39-227	17	+19.53
A Rawlinson	21-128	16	-24.82	0-6	-	-6.00	6-26	23	+2.58	15-96	16	-21.40
Hayley Turner	4-17	24	+3.63	0-0	-	+0.00	0-5	-	-5.00	4-12	33	+8.63
Luke Morris	4-19	21	-7.97	0-1	-	-1.00	3-5	60	+3.16	1-13	8	-10.13
Tom Queally	3-8	38	+0.18	0-0	-	+0.00	0-0	-	+0.00	3-8	38	+0.18
Ryan Tate	3-17	18	+15.88	0-0	-	+0.00	0-3	-	-3.00	3-14	21	+18.88
Dane O'Neill	1-2	50	+6.00	0-0	-	+0.00	0-0	-	+0.00	1-2	50	+6.00
Liam Jones	1-2	50	+1.75	0-0	-	+0.00	0-0	-	+0.00	1-2	50	+1.75
Cam Hardie	1-4	25	+13.00	1-2	50	+15.00	0-0	-	+0.00	0-2	-	-2.00
Gary Mahon	1-5	20	-0.67	0-0	-	+0.00	0-1	-	-1.00	1-4	25	+0.33
Jason Hart	1-5	20	+4.00	0-1	-	-1.00	0-0	-	+0.00	1-4	25	+5.00
S De Sousa	1-6	17	-0.50	0-2	-	-2.00	0-1	-	-1.00	1-3	33	+2.50

By jockey – 2013

	Overall			Two-year-olds			Three-year-olds			Older horses		
	W-R	%	£1	W-R	%	£1	W-R	%	£1	W-R	%	£1
Andrew Mullen	40-295	14	-15.47	3-14	21	+8.00	7-63	11	-18.75	30-218	14	-4.72
A Rawlinson	3-7	43	+17.00	0-0	-	+0.00	0-0	-	+0.00	3-7	43	+17.00
Tom Queally	3-13	23	+5.00	0-0	-	+0.00	0-2	-	-2.00	3-11	27	+7.00
Luke Morris	3-21	14	-7.00	1-2	50	+2.50	1-4	25	+2.00	1-15	7	-11.50
George Buckell	2-2	100	+5.00	0-0	-	+0.00	0-0	-	+0.00	2-2	100	+5.00
Conor Harrison	1-1	100	+0.80	0-0	-	+0.00	0-0	-	+0.00	1-1	100	+0.80
Paul Hanagan	1-1	100	+2.25	1-1	100	+2.25	0-0	-	+0.00	0-0	-	+0.00
S De Sousa	1-2	50	-0.17	0-0	-	+0.00	1-2	50	-0.17	0-0	-	+0.00
Charles Bishop	1-3	33	-1.09	0-0	-	+0.00	0-0	-	+0.00	1-3	33	-1.09

By jockey – 2012

	Overall			Two-year-olds			Three-year-olds			Older horses		
	W-R	%	£1	W-R	%	£1	W-R	%	£1	W-R	%	£1
Dominic Fox	7-36	19	+52.00	0-0	-	+0.00	5-26	19	+38.00	2-10	20	+14.00
Luke Morris	7-56	13	-19.00	0-1	-	-1.00	2-11	18	-0.50	5-44	11	-17.50
Tom Queally	4-16	25	+37.50	0-1	-	-1.00	1-4	25	+5.50	3-11	27	+33.00
Jack Duern	4-32	13	+14.50	0-0	-	+0.00	0-8	-	-8.00	4-24	17	+22.50
Andrew Mullen	4-35	11	-3.50	0-1	-	-1.00	2-15	13	+5.00	2-19	11	-7.50
S De Sousa	3-4	75	+20.50	0-0	-	+0.00	0-0	-	+0.00	3-4	75	+20.50
Darryll Holland	1-1	100	+5.50	0-0	-	+0.00	0-0	-	+0.00	1-1	100	+5.50
James Doyle	1-1	100	+14.00	0-0	-	+0.00	1-1	100	+14.00	0-0	-	+0.00
Darren Egan	1-3	33	+1.00	0-0	-	+0.00	0-2	-	-2.00	1-1	100	+3.00

By course – 2011-2014

	Overall			Two-year-olds			Three-year-olds			Older horses		
	W-R	%	£1	W-R	%	£1	W-R	%	£1	W-R	%	£1
Ascot	0-16	-	-16.00	0-1	-	-1.00	0-2	-	-2.00	0-13	-	-13.00
Ayr	0-5	-	-5.00	0-0	-	+0.00	0-1	-	-1.00	0-4	-	-4.00
Bath	3-11	27	+14.10	0-0	-	+0.00	2-4	50	+19.00	1-7	14	-4.90
Beverley	3-27	11	-5.50	0-6	-	-6.00	2-6	33	+11.00	1-15	7	-10.50
Brighton	1-15	7	-7.50	0-0	-	+0.00	0-4	-	-4.00	1-11	9	-3.50
Carlisle	0-6	-	-6.00	0-0	-	+0.00	0-2	-	-2.00	0-4	-	-4.00
Catterick	5-27	19	+21.75	1-1	100	+5.00	1-8	13	+5.00	3-18	17	+11.75
Chepstow	0-14	-	-14.00	0-1	-	-1.00	0-2	-	-2.00	0-11	-	-11.00
Chester	4-18	22	+24.50	1-3	33	+23.00	0-2	-	-2.00	3-13	23	+3.50
Doncaster	5-63	8	+3.00	0-5	-	-5.00	0-8	-	-8.00	5-50	10	+16.00
Ffos Las	0-3	-	-3.00	0-0	-	+0.00	0-2	-	-2.00	0-1	-	-1.00
Goodwood	2-17	12	-5.50	0-1	-	-1.00	1-5	20	+1.00	1-11	9	-5.50
Hamilton	0-2	-	-2.00	0-1	-	-1.00	0-0	-	+0.00	0-1	-	-1.00
Haydock	3-26	12	-1.50	0-3	-	-3.00	0-8	-	-8.00	3-15	20	+9.50
Kempton (AW)	10-106	9	-8.29	1-4	25	+13.00	2-23	9	+2.33	7-79	9	-23.63
Leicester	4-56	7	-31.25	1-5	20	-1.75	1-19	5	-12.50	2-32	6	-17.00
Lingfield	1-1	100	+14.00	0-0	-	+0.00	1-1	100	+14.00	0-0	-	+0.00
Lingfield (AW)	8-65	12	-4.00	0-0	-	+0.00	1-7	14	+6.00	7-58	12	-10.00
Musselburgh	1-7	14	+4.00	0-0	-	+0.00	0-1	-	-1.00	1-6	17	+5.00
Newbury	0-8	-	-8.00	0-2	-	-2.00	0-2	-	-2.00	0-4	-	-4.00
Newcastle	2-17	12	-8.25	0-2	-	-2.00	1-2	50	+1.25	1-13	8	-7.50
Newmarket	5-20	25	+19.75	0-3	-	-3.00	1-3	33	+4.00	4-14	29	+18.75
Newmarket (J)	1-10	10	-3.50	0-1	-	-1.00	1-1	100	+5.50	0-8	-	-8.00
Nottingham	20-96	21	+77.13	1-6	17	+15.00	7-32	22	+27.50	12-58	21	+34.63
Pontefract	6-56	11	-29.17	1-7	14	-2.00	0-12	-	-12.00	5-37	14	-15.17
Redcar	1-10	10	+1.00	1-1	100	+10.00	0-1	-	-1.00	0-8	-	-8.00
Ripon	3-12	25	+7.50	0-1	-	-1.00	0-2	-	-2.00	3-9	33	+10.50
Salisbury	0-3	-	-3.00	0-0	-	+0.00	0-1	-	-1.00	0-2	-	-2.00
Sandown	0-6	-	-6.00	0-1	-	-1.00	0-1	-	-1.00	0-4	-	-4.00
S'thwell (AW)	64-323	20	-3.16	1-17	6	-11.00	9-69	14	-31.09	54-237	23	+38.93
Thirsk	0-18	-	-18.00	0-0	-	+0.00	0-5	-	-5.00	0-13	-	-13.00
Warwick	3-22	14	+20.00	0-2	-	-2.00	1-6	17	+0.00	2-14	14	+22.00
Windsor	1-7	14	-1.50	0-0	-	+0.00	0-3	-	-3.00	1-4	25	+1.50
Wolves (AW)	42-382	11	-114.79	1-15	7	-10.50	7-80	8	-47.67	34-287	12	-56.63
Yarmouth	6-42	14	+27.38	0-2	-	-2.00	0-10	-	-10.00	6-30	20	+39.38
York	2-23	9	+6.00	0-4	-	-4.00	0-7	-	-7.00	2-12	17	+17.00

Ten-year summary

	Wins	Runs	%	Win prize-money	Total prize-money	£1
2014	89	565	16	£472,340.26	£693,483.17	-35.23
2013	61	443	14	£230,740.42	£334,736.66	-57.43
2012	40	332	12	£164,239.25	£230,342.98	+54.75
2011	15	195	8	£43,764.24	£66,322.53	-31.90
2010	3	29	10	£9,973.04	£16,335.47	+106.00
2009	0	0	-	£0.00	£0.00	+0.00
2008	0	22	-	£0.00	£737.64	-22.00
2007	1	47	2	£2,914.65	£5,185.23	-39.00
2006	1	82	1	£2,266.95	£5,171.50	-77.00
2005	3	70	4	£7,108.42	£10,628.53	-45.50

DEMORA: top sprinter was Michael Appleby's biggest money-spinner last year

Top trainers by winners (Turf)

	All runs			First time out			Horses		
Won	Ran	%	Trainer	Won	Ran	%	Won	Ran	%
168	1283	13	**Richard Fahey**	29	279	10	131	279	47
165	1129	15	**Richard Hannon**	39	303	13	141	303	47
137	1001	14	**Mark Johnston**	40	212	19	115	212	54
94	673	14	**David O'Meara**	15	134	11	67	134	50
92	419	22	**William Haggas**	30	138	22	73	138	53
86	423	20	**John Gosden**	43	195	22	100	195	51
72	433	17	**Andrew Balding**	20	144	14	68	144	47
67	612	11	**Mick Channon**	12	105	11	57	105	54
62	363	17	**Sir Michael Stoute**	10	134	7	57	134	43
61	366	17	**Roger Varian**	20	139	14	60	139	43
57	285	20	**Saeed bin Suroor**	24	135	18	61	135	45
57	494	12	**Kevin Ryan**	12	125	10	54	125	43
52	373	14	**Charlie Appleby**	18	171	11	68	171	40
48	264	18	**Luca Cumani**	6	76	8	37	76	49
48	410	12	**Charles Hills**	13	150	9	51	150	34
48	312	15	**Ralph Beckett**	22	117	19	58	117	50
48	334	14	**K R Burke**	8	84	10	46	84	55
47	728	6	**Tim Easterby**	4	124	3	41	124	33
47	469	10	**Brian Ellison**	9	125	7	43	125	34
45	450	10	**Jim Goldie**	2	58	3	27	58	47
44	301	15	**Clive Cox**	9	82	11	40	82	49
43	324	13	**Marco Botti**	13	151	9	59	151	39
42	411	10	**Keith Dalgleish**	9	84	11	38	84	45
40	290	14	**David Simcock**	17	95	18	49	95	52
40	306	13	**David Barron**	7	73	10	34	73	47
39	320	12	**Tom Dascombe**	13	97	13	43	97	44
38	218	17	**Roger Charlton**	12	79	15	36	79	46
37	280	13	**Michael Dods**	10	58	17	24	58	41
37	314	12	**David Evans**	7	97	7	46	97	47
36	259	14	**Michael Appleby**	13	104	13	48	104	46
36	213	17	**Alan Swinbank**	7	41	17	24	41	59
35	366	10	**Ruth Carr**	4	47	9	25	47	53
31	214	14	**Henry Candy**	8	55	15	27	55	49
31	250	12	**Brian Meehan**	9	82	11	32	82	39
31	268	12	**John Quinn**	10	73	14	24	73	33
28	200	14	**William Muir**	6	49	12	24	49	49
28	218	13	**George Baker**	2	63	3	26	63	41
28	150	19	**Gary Moore**	9	77	12	30	77	39
27	229	12	**Paul Midgley**	2	35	6	18	35	51
27	371	7	**Michael Easterby**	3	78	4	22	78	28
26	289	9	**David Nicholls**	3	46	7	25	46	54
26	254	10	**Michael Bell**	7	83	8	32	83	39
25	164	15	**Shaun Harris**	2	39	5	20	39	51
24	119	20	**Sir Mark Prescott Bt**	10	57	18	22	57	39
23	187	12	**Sylvester Kirk**	2	50	4	20	50	40
22	176	13	**Robert Cowell**	7	58	12	23	58	40
22	211	10	**Bryan Smart**	2	57	4	18	57	32

Top trainers by prize-money (Turf)

Total prizemoney	Trainer	Win prizemoney	Wins	Class 1-3			Class 4-6		
				Won	Ran	%	Won	Ran	%
£4,462,370	Richard Hannon	£2,535,180	165	59	488	12	106	641	17
£3,979,665	John Gosden	£2,704,927	86	43	198	22	43	225	19
£2,882,212	A P O'Brien	£2,025,979	11	10	80	13	1	1	100
£2,645,329	Richard Fahey	£1,707,242	168	50	522	10	118	761	16
£2,580,079	Mark Johnston	£1,689,965	137	45	435	10	92	566	16
£2,155,996	Roger Varian	£1,314,905	61	21	142	15	40	224	18
£2,123,316	Sir Michael Stoute	£1,229,227	62	31	175	18	31	188	16
£2,017,703	William Haggas	£1,255,332	92	37	220	17	55	199	28
£1,677,681	Andrew Balding	£1,104,181	72	33	216	15	39	217	18
£1,619,183	David O'Meara	£1,155,769	94	40	315	13	54	358	15
£1,260,173	Saeed bin Suroor	£731,458	57	29	174	17	28	111	25
£1,219,176	Edward Lynam	£1,083,161	7	7	15	47	0	0	-
£1,141,728	Marco Botti	£613,018	43	19	158	12	24	166	14
£1,130,308	Charlie Appleby	£626,174	52	16	168	10	36	205	18
£1,112,904	Kevin Ryan	£541,224	57	18	185	10	39	309	13
£1,052,555	Luca Cumani	£580,123	48	24	140	17	24	124	19
£1,027,172	Lady Cecil	£937,437	11	7	39	18	4	56	7
£1,023,955	David Simcock	£768,700	40	17	151	11	23	139	17
£904,473	Mick Channon	£494,576	67	19	159	12	48	453	11
£874,171	Roger Charlton	£371,127	38	12	75	16	26	143	18
£823,368	Charles Hills	£507,337	48	16	144	11	32	266	12
£700,984	Tim Easterby	£319,181	47	11	183	6	36	545	7
£688,062	F Head	£632,345	1	1	3	33	0	0	-
£687,190	Ralph Beckett	£395,956	48	11	96	11	37	216	17
£631,948	Clive Cox	£303,659	44	7	88	8	37	213	17
£599,623	Brian Ellison	£377,878	47	11	151	7	36	318	11
£591,304	K R Burke	£327,342	48	10	112	9	38	222	17
£565,311	D K Weld	£306,234	3	3	8	38	0	0	-
£518,098	A Fabre	£320,341	3	3	11	27	0	0	-
£508,740	Henry Candy	£357,274	31	10	60	17	21	154	14
£505,218	Tom Dascombe	£304,653	39	14	128	11	25	192	13
£461,880	David Barron	£297,177	40	15	166	9	25	140	18
£440,448	Michael Dods	£293,059	37	9	73	12	28	207	14
£429,156	Ed Dunlop	£209,892	17	3	94	3	14	141	10
£410,781	Robert Cowell	£238,434	22	9	80	11	13	96	14
£399,768	Michael Appleby	£286,138	36	8	70	11	28	189	15
£399,491	Peter Chapple-Hyam	£133,720	16	3	54	6	13	93	14
£394,244	Marcus Tregoning	£333,025	18	3	39	8	15	89	17
£380,800	Brian Meehan	£225,402	31	8	84	10	23	166	14
£371,638	Clive Brittain	£261,180	10	2	53	4	8	74	11
£364,160	Jim Goldie	£205,452	45	4	70	6	41	380	11
£360,678	Hugo Palmer	£199,308	18	7	60	12	11	55	20
£349,601	John Quinn	£227,964	31	7	79	9	24	189	13
£346,589	William Muir	£122,664	28	3	30	10	25	170	15
£313,136	Dean Ivory	£67,320	10	2	47	4	8	54	15
£309,776	Hughie Morrison	£180,579	21	5	53	9	16	118	14
£294,239	Ruth Carr	£176,397	35	7	78	9	28	288	10

Top trainers by winners (AW)

Won	All runs Ran	%	Trainer	Won	First time out Ran	%	Won	Horses Ran	%
70	343	20	**Mark Johnston**	40	212	19	115	212	54
53	306	17	**Michael Appleby**	13	104	13	48	104	46
50	176	28	**Charlie Appleby**	18	171	11	68	171	40
47	226	21	**Andrew Balding**	20	144	14	68	144	47
46	190	24	**John Gosden**	43	195	22	100	195	51
41	275	15	**Richard Hannon**	39	303	13	141	303	47
38	184	21	**David Simcock**	17	95	18	49	95	52
38	338	11	**Tony Carroll**	4	86	5	31	86	36
37	255	15	**Marco Botti**	13	151	9	59	151	39
36	120	30	**Saeed bin Suroor**	24	135	18	61	135	45
32	141	23	**Ralph Beckett**	22	117	19	58	117	50
29	368	8	**David Evans**	7	97	7	46	97	47
26	171	15	**Jamie Osborne**	5	60	8	27	60	45
25	131	19	**Keith Dalgleish**	9	84	11	38	84	45
24	219	11	**Richard Fahey**	29	279	10	131	279	47
24	123	20	**James Fanshawe**	4	62	6	31	62	50
23	167	14	**Tom Dascombe**	13	97	13	43	97	44
23	142	16	**Hughie Morrison**	5	61	8	26	61	43
22	137	16	**Ian Williams**	5	57	9	20	57	35
21	101	21	**William Haggas**	30	138	22	73	138	53
21	130	16	**James Tate**	10	80	13	30	80	38
21	140	15	**Kevin Ryan**	12	125	10	54	125	43
20	76	26	**Jeremy Noseda**	6	49	12	22	49	45
20	131	15	**Charles Hills**	13	150	9	51	150	34
20	129	16	**Alan Bailey**	3	27	11	14	27	52
20	221	9	**Derek Shaw**	5	49	10	17	49	35
20	184	11	**Lee Carter**	4	41	10	16	41	39
19	107	18	**K R Burke**	8	84	10	46	84	55
19	143	13	**Paul Cole**	2	60	3	21	60	35
19	156	12	**Scott Dixon**	4	42	10	20	42	48
19	89	21	**Ed Walker**	7	58	12	26	58	45
19	203	9	**J R Jenkins**	3	43	7	22	43	51
19	98	19	**Sir Michael Stoute**	10	134	7	57	134	43
18	157	11	**David O'Meara**	15	134	11	67	134	50
18	84	21	**Clive Cox**	9	82	11	40	82	49
18	111	16	**Michael Bell**	7	83	8	32	83	39
17	152	11	**Simon Dow**	3	28	11	11	28	39
17	105	16	**Roger Varian**	20	139	14	60	139	43
17	90	19	**Chris Wall**	2	43	5	23	43	53
17	106	16	**Stuart Williams**	7	57	12	23	57	40
17	166	10	**Daniel Mark Loughnane**	2	29	7	13	29	45
16	148	11	**Gary Moore**	9	77	12	30	77	39
15	86	17	**Amanda Perrett**	5	47	11	20	47	43
15	111	14	**Robert Cowell**	7	58	12	23	58	40
15	121	12	**James Given**	5	42	12	14	42	33
15	131	11	**Andrew Hollinshead**	0	33	-	11	33	33
15	118	13	**Sir Mark Prescott Bt**	10	57	18	22	57	39

Top trainers by prize-money (AW)

Total prizemoney	Trainer	Win prizemoney	Wins	Class 1-3 Won	Class 1-3 Ran	Class 1-3 %	Class 4-6 Won	Class 4-6 Ran	Class 4-6 %
£438,366	Marco Botti	£246,895	37	13	88	15	24	167	14
£412,033	Mark Johnston	£295,976	70	6	63	10	64	280	23
£363,474	Charlie Appleby	£298,062	50	15	33	45	35	143	24
£357,816	Andrew Balding	£231,018	47	9	41	22	38	184	21
£314,952	Saeed bin Suroor	£226,263	36	12	27	44	24	93	26
£293,715	Michael Appleby	£186,202	53	4	37	11	47	263	18
£287,099	Richard Hannon	£194,469	41	6	48	13	35	227	15
£271,391	David Simcock	£204,844	38	7	37	19	31	146	21
£264,166	William Haggas	£222,706	21	6	19	32	15	82	18
£262,326	John Gosden	£171,085	46	4	15	27	42	175	24
£257,625	Jeremy Noseda	£232,273	20	4	10	40	16	66	24
£237,323	Richard Fahey	£175,525	24	3	26	12	21	193	11
£188,011	Tom Dascombe	£102,979	23	6	37	16	17	130	13
£169,101	Roger Charlton	£140,096	14	2	11	18	12	66	18
£167,968	David Evans	£88,625	29	2	25	8	27	339	8
£165,798	Tony Carroll	£98,909	38	2	17	12	33	294	11
£157,026	Seamus Durack	£148,125	9	4	7	57	5	37	14
£153,623	David O'Meara	£101,560	18	5	34	15	13	122	11
£152,172	Ralph Beckett	£118,095	32	1	16	6	31	125	25
£145,753	Phil McEntee	£130,285	12	2	8	25	10	104	10
£145,624	Keith Dalgleish	£107,069	25	2	26	8	23	104	22
£145,048	James Fanshawe	£101,462	24	4	17	24	20	106	19
£135,021	Ed Vaughan	£96,427	13	2	9	22	11	59	19
£132,069	K R Burke	£70,753	19	2	22	9	16	84	19
£130,699	William Knight	£49,439	12	2	20	10	10	88	11
£126,925	Charles Hills	£67,291	20	1	9	11	19	122	16
£119,708	James Tate	£62,611	21	0	11	-	21	119	18
£118,735	Alan Bailey	£84,923	20	3	37	8	17	92	18
£116,665	Amanda Perrett	£68,462	15	4	15	27	11	71	15
£113,231	Simon Dow	£66,518	17	2	21	10	15	128	12
£111,434	Paul Cole	£71,259	19	2	20	10	17	123	14
£108,940	Scott Dixon	£79,462	19	2	17	12	17	137	12
£108,926	Hughie Morrison	£70,512	23	0	8	-	23	134	17
£104,962	Jamie Osborne	£71,741	26	0	9	-	26	162	16
£103,233	Ed Walker	£80,684	19	2	8	25	17	81	21
£96,223	Roger Varian	£59,946	17	1	9	11	16	96	17
£94,205	Robert Cowell	£49,916	15	1	20	5	14	91	15
£92,700	Roger Teal	£68,714	10	1	9	11	9	69	13
£92,279	J R Jenkins	£48,873	19	0	4	-	17	194	9
£91,764	Dean Ivory	£68,020	13	2	18	11	11	130	8
£91,445	Clive Cox	£74,255	18	3	5	60	15	79	19
£88,478	Sir Michael Stoute	£64,004	19	2	6	33	17	92	18
£86,694	William Muir	£65,724	12	2	6	33	10	85	12
£84,579	David Barron	£49,445	7	1	22	5	6	24	25
£84,061	James Given	£53,596	15	1	15	7	13	105	12
£83,195	Chris Wall	£59,463	17	0	6	-	17	84	20
£82,994	Derek Shaw	£49,368	20	0	9	-	20	205	10

Top jockeys (Turf)

Won	Ran	%	Jockey	Best Trainer	Won	Ran
132	744	18	**Richard Hughes**	Richard Hannon	80	433
128	649	20	**Ryan Moore**	Sir Michael Stoute	41	197
126	816	15	**Graham Lee**	Jim Goldie	20	155
98	699	14	**Joe Fanning**	Mark Johnston	110	601
93	539	17	**Andrea Atzeni**	Roger Varian	29	156
93	497	19	**Paul Hanagan**	Richard Fahey	21	94
93	621	15	**Paul Mulrennan**	Michael Dods	21	99
90	539	17	**William Buick**	John Gosden	56	291
84	547	15	**Daniel Tudhope**	David O'Meara	65	398
78	514	15	**Adam Kirby**	Charlie Appleby	34	102
77	483	16	**James Doyle**	Roger Charlton	22	112
70	490	14	**Silvestre De Sousa**	Mark Johnston	18	125
68	579	12	**Luke Morris**	Sir Mark Prescott Bt	32	170
67	360	19	**George Baker**	Ed Walker	15	47
61	447	14	**Jim Crowley**	Ralph Beckett	27	135
61	466	13	**Graham Gibbons**	David Barron	32	200
59	492	12	**David Probert**	Andrew Balding	59	278
56	452	12	**Oisin Murphy**	Andrew Balding	26	132
52	404	13	**Kieren Fallon**	Saeed bin Suroor	16	81
52	445	12	**Tony Hamilton**	Richard Fahey	56	408
51	474	11	**David Allan**	Tim Easterby	25	263
49	414	12	**Phillip Makin**	John Quinn	14	114
48	358	13	**Richard Kingscote**	Tom Dascombe	43	291
48	401	12	**Dane O'Neill**	Henry Candy	13	78
48	559	9	**P J McDonald**	Ann Duffield	10	129
46	377	12	**Robert Winston**	Charles Hills	9	48
45	408	11	**Jamie Spencer**	Kevin Ryan	9	91
44	306	14	**Frederik Tylicki**	Saeed bin Suroor	14	47
43	421	10	**Jason Hart**	Eric Alston	11	107
42	284	15	**Martin Harley**	Marco Botti	35	193
42	318	13	**George Chaloner**	Richard Fahey	36	259
41	395	10	**Franny Norton**	Mark Johnston	26	254
41	300	14	**Martin Dwyer**	William Muir	25	155
40	384	10	**Cam Hardie**	Richard Hannon	10	138
40	578	7	**Tom Eaves**	Keith Dalgleish	35	283
37	378	10	**Connor Beasley**	Michael Dods	14	143
36	286	13	**Pat Dobbs**	Richard Hannon	19	162
35	318	11	**Ben Curtis**	Alan Swinbank	19	125
34	281	12	**Fergus Sweeney**	Henry Candy	10	83
33	313	11	**Sean Levey**	Richard Hannon	24	213
32	272	12	**Joey Haynes**	K R Burke	21	130
30	227	13	**David Nolan**	Richard Fahey	16	125
30	279	11	**Jack Garritty**	Richard Fahey	18	105
30	172	17	**Ryan Tate**	Clive Cox	28	125
29	179	16	**Charles Bishop**	Mick Channon	32	156
28	307	9	**Jimmy Fortune**	Hughie Morrison	6	50
28	422	7	**James Sullivan**	Ruth Carr	25	246
28	351	8	**William Twiston-Davies**	Mick Channon	20	219

Top jockeys (AW)

Won	Ran	%	Jockey	Best Trainer	Won	Ran
121	945	13	**Luke Morris**	Sir Mark Prescott Bt	32	170
114	686	17	**Adam Kirby**	Charlie Appleby	34	102
95	466	20	**George Baker**	Ed Walker	15	47
70	478	15	**Joe Fanning**	Mark Johnston	110	601
54	426	13	**Jim Crowley**	Ralph Beckett	27	135
54	384	14	**Tom Queally**	Michael Bell	8	80
48	375	13	**David Probert**	Andrew Balding	59	278
45	498	9	**Liam Keniry**	Neil Mulholland	9	27
44	200	22	**James Doyle**	Roger Charlton	22	112
40	363	11	**Shane Kelly**	James Fanshawe	10	68
39	337	12	**Robert Havlin**	John Gosden	29	148
39	228	17	**Richard Kingscote**	Tom Dascombe	43	291
38	257	15	**Robert Winston**	Charles Hills	9	48
37	295	13	**Martin Harley**	Marco Botti	35	193
35	153	23	**William Buick**	John Gosden	56	291
34	126	27	**Ryan Moore**	Sir Michael Stoute	41	197
34	197	17	**Richard Hughes**	Richard Hannon	80	433
33	224	15	**Frederik Tylicki**	Saeed bin Suroor	14	47
33	255	13	**Graham Lee**	Jim Goldie	20	155
32	184	17	**Silvestre De Sousa**	Mark Johnston	18	125
32	165	19	**Andrea Atzeni**	Roger Varian	29	156
30	265	11	**Chris Catlin**	Rae Guest	13	83
29	157	18	**Jamie Spencer**	Kevin Ryan	9	91
27	193	14	**Andrew Mullen**	Michael Appleby	46	289
26	119	22	**Daniel Tudhope**	David O'Meara	65	398
26	274	9	**Tom Eaves**	Keith Dalgleish	35	283
24	362	7	**William Carson**	John Bridger	19	152
24	192	13	**Martin Lane**	David Simcock	13	75
24	129	19	**Ted Durcan**	Chris Wall	15	88
24	130	18	**Connor Beasley**	Michael Dods	14	143
23	306	8	**Hayley Turner**	Conor Dore	8	85
23	210	11	**Pat Cosgrave**	George Baker	21	159
23	266	9	**Stevie Donohoe**	Ian Williams	11	100
22	157	14	**Robert Tart**	Geoffrey Oldroyd	6	27
22	271	8	**Liam Jones**	William Haggas	11	67
22	115	19	**Alistair Rawlinson**	Michael Appleby	21	128
21	170	12	**Sean Levey**	Richard Hannon	24	213
21	158	13	**Dale Swift**	Brian Ellison	15	117
21	177	12	**Ben Curtis**	Alan Swinbank	19	125
20	181	11	**Oisin Murphy**	Andrew Balding	26	132
20	174	11	**Martin Dwyer**	William Muir	25	155
20	275	7	**Fergus Sweeney**	Henry Candy	10	83
19	204	9	**Cam Hardie**	Richard Hannon	10	138
18	169	11	**Graham Gibbons**	David Barron	32	200
18	140	13	**Eoin Walsh**	Tony Newcombe	4	14
16	133	12	**Louis Steward**	Michael Bell	10	59
14	87	16	**Paul Hanagan**	Richard Fahey	21	94
14	95	15	**Dane O'Neill**	Henry Candy	13	78

Est. 1909
RACING & FOOTBALL OUTLOOK

Group 1 records

Year	Winner	Age (if appropriate)	Trainer	Jockey	SP	draw/ran

2,000 Guineas (1m) Newmarket

Year	Winner	Trainer	Jockey	SP	draw/ran
2005	Footstepsinthesand	A O'Brien	K Fallon	13-2	3/19
2006	George Washington	A O'Brien	K Fallon	6-4f	9/14
2007	Cockney Rebel	G Huffer	O Peslier	25-1	8/24
2008	Henrythenavigator	A O'Brien	J Murtagh	11-1	6/15
2009	Sea The Stars	J Oxx	M Kinane	8-1	15/15
2010	Makfi	M Delzangles	C-P Lemaire	33-1	5/19
2011	Frankel	Sir H Cecil	T Queally	1-2f	1/13
2012	Camelot	A O'Brien	J O'Brien	15-8f	12/18
2013	Dawn Approach	J Bolger	K Manning	11-8f	6/13
2014	Night Of Thunder	R Hannon	K Fallon	40-1	3/14

THIS HAS increasingly become a specialist miler's race rather than a stepping stone to the Derby despite the recent success of Camelot and Sea The Stars – prior to the latter there had been a 20-year wait for a horse to do the double. Most winners had proved themselves at two, with 14 of the last 23 winners having won a Group race, including nine at the highest level. The Dewhurst tends to be a far better guide than the Racing Post Trophy, with Camelot the first to complete that double since High Top in 1973. Favourites had a desperate record until three of the last four winners hit back for punters. Only three winners have come via a domestic trial since Mystiko in 1991 and in fact there have been just four British-trained winners in 12 years.

1,000 Guineas (1m) Newmarket

Year	Winner	Trainer	Jockey	SP	draw/ran
2005	Virginia Waters	A O'Brien	K Fallon	12-1	20/20
2006	Speciosa	Mrs P Sly	M Fenton	10-1	11/13
2007	Finsceal Beo	J Bolger	K Manning	5-4f	14/21
2008	Natagora	P Bary	C Lemaire	11-4f	3/15
2009	Ghanaati	B Hills	R Hills	20-1	7/14
2010	Special Duty	C Head-Maarek	S Pasquier	9-2f	18/17
2011	Blue Bunting	M Al Zarooni	L Dettori	16-1	16/18
2012	Homecoming Queen	A O'Brien	R Moore	25-1	16/17
2013	Sky Lantern	R Hannon Sr	R Hughes	9-1	7/15
2014	Miss France	A Fabre	M Guyon	7-1	4/17

COURSE FORM is the key factor in this race and is likely to become even more vital with the Fillies' Mile run at Newmarket for the first time in 2011. The Rockfel is the key trial, throwing up five of the last 13 winners with Finsceal Beo, Lahan and Speciosa all doing the double, while Special Duty, Natagora, Attraction and Russian Rhythm had been first or second in the Cheveley Park, Speciosa won the Nell Gwyn, in which Sky Lantern was second, Miss France landed the Oh So Sharp Stakes and Blue Bunting won a Listed race over course and distance the previous October. Punters have hit back in recent years with three of the last eight favourites obliging, but still ten of the last 17 winners have been priced in double figures. French fillies have a fair record, with seven winners since 1993, and Miss France was the first not to have Group 1 form as a juvenile.

Lockinge Stakes (1m) Newbury

2005	**Rakti**	6	M Jarvis	P Robinson	7-4f	5/8
2006	**Soviet Song**	6	J Fanshawe	J Spencer	7-2f	10/10
2007	**Red Evie**	4	M Bell	J Spencer	8-1	7/8
2008	**Creachadoir**	4	S bin Suroor	L Dettori	3-1f	7/11
2009	**Virtual**	4	J Gosden	J Fortune	6-1	10/11
2010	**Paco Boy**	5	R Hannon Sr	R Hughes	8-11f	3/9
2011	**Canford Cliffs**	4	R Hannon Sr	R Hughes	4-5f	4/7
2012	**Frankel**	4	Sir H Cecil	T Queally	2-7f	6/6
2013	**Farhh**	5	S bin Suroor	S de Sousa	10-3	5/12
2014	**Olympic Glory**	4	R Hannon	F Dettori	11-8f	3/8

IT'S ESSENTIAL to look for horses who have already shown themselves to be Group 1 milers as 16 of the last 20 winners had won at the top level over the trip and three of the exceptions had been second. Consequently it has been straightforward to identify the winner as nine of the last 12 favourites have obliged and two of the exceptions were second in the market. Four-year-olds have by far the strongest record, accounting for 19 of the last 28 winners, and fillies can also do well with three winners in the last 11 years. The Sandown Mile is a popular prep race yet Paco Boy is the only horse to ever do the double with 20 others failing.

Coronation Cup (1m4f) Epsom

2005	**Yeats**	4	A O'Brien	K Fallon	5-1	9/7
2006	**Shirocco**	5	A Fabre	C Soumillon	8-11f	5/6
2007	**Scorpion**	5	A O'Brien	M Kinane	8-1	2/7
2008	**Soldier Of Fortune**	4	A O'Brien	J Murtagh	9-4	7/11
2009	**Ask**	6	Sir M Stoute	R Moore	5-1	8/8
2010	**Fame And Glory**	4	A O'Brien	J Murtagh	5-6f	8/9
2011	**St Nicholas Abbey**	4	A O'Brien	R Moore	Evsf	1/5
2012	**St Nicholas Abbey**	5	A O'Brien	J O'Brien	8-11f	4/6
2013	**St Nicholas Abbey**	6	A O'Brien	J O'Brien	3-10f	3/5
2014	**Cirrus Des Aigles**	8	C Barande-Barbe	C Soumillon	10-11f	7/7

AIDAN O'BRIEN has a sensational record in this race with seven of the last ten winners, led by St Nicholas Abbey's hat-trick. That horse was favourite on every occasion, as were Fame And Glory and Cirrus Des Aigles either side of him, which represents a major shift after just two market leaders had obliged in the previous 12 years. Perhaps punters have learned not to be seduced by youngsters, with just four of the last 12 runnings being won by four-year-olds.

The Oaks (1m4f) Epsom

2005	**Eswarah**	M Jarvis	R Hills	11-4jf	2/12
2006	**Alexandrova**	A O'Brien	K Fallon	9-4f	1/10
2007	**Light Shift**	H Cecil	T Durcan	13-2	11/14
2008	**Look Here**	R Beckett	S Sanders	33-1	13/16
2009	**Sariska**	M Bell	J Spencer	9-4f	5/10
2010	**Snow Fairy**	E Dunlop	R Moore	9-1	15/15
2011	**Dancing Rain**	W Haggas	J Murtagh	20-1	7/13
2012	**Was**	A O'Brien	S Heffernan	20-1	10/12
2013	**Talent**	R Beckett	R Hughes	20-1	3/11
2014	**Taghrooda**	J Gosden	P Hanagan	5-1	9/17

GUARANTEED STAMINA is more important than proven top-class form for this race, which can make things tricky for punters with four of the last seven winners priced at least 20-1. None of the last eight winners had been tried in a Group 1, yet six of them had triumphed over at least 1m2f and you have to go back to Casual Look in 2003 to find the last winner who hadn't raced beyond a mile. It therefore follows that the 1,000 Guineas has become a weaker guide with none of the five fillies to run in the race having placed at Epsom since Kazzia's 2002 double finishing better than fourth, although none of the trials stands above any other and too much is often made of the Musidora winner with Sariska the only one to double up since Reams Of Verse in 1997.

The Derby (1m4f) Epsom

2005	**Motivator**	M Bell	J Murtagh	3-1f	5/13
2006	**Sir Percy**	M Tregoning	M Dwyer	6-1	10/18
2007	**Authorized**	P Chapple-Hyam	L Dettori	5-4f	14/17

OLYMPIC GLORY (left): the 16th Lockinge winner in the last 20 years who had already won a Group 1 over the trip and a ninth winning favourite out of 12

AL KAZEEM (right): among four Tattersalls Gold Cup winners to follow up in the Prince of Wales's Stakes among the last six to have tried

2008	**New Approach**	J Bolger	K Manning	5-1	3/16
2009	**Sea The Stars**	J Oxx	M Kinane	11-4	4/12
2010	**Workforce**	Sir M Stoute	R Moore	6-1	8/12
2011	**Pour Moi**	A Fabre	M Barzalona	4-1	7/13
2012	**Camelot**	A O'Brien	J O'Brien	8-13f	5/9
2013	**Ruler Of The World**	A O'Brien	R Moore	7-1	10/12
2014	**Australia**	A O'Brien	J O'Brien	11-8f	12/16

MANY HIGH-CLASS colts are beaten here due to lack of stamina and it's important to have a top-class staying sire (ten of the last 12 winners had a sire with a stamina index of at least 1m1f) plus more stamina on the dam's side. Australia, Camelot and Sea The Stars all came via the 2,000 Guineas, but they all had middle-distance pedigrees and 12 of the last 18 winners warmed up in one of the recognised trials with four Dante winners (Benny The Dip, North Light, Motivator and Authorized) and a runner-up (Workforce), three Leopardstown winners (Sinndar, Galileo and High Chaparral), three Chester winners (Oath, Kris Kin and Ruler Of The World) and one Lingfield winner (High-Rise). This is a race for fancied runners from the first four in the betting – 20-1 hero High-Rise in 1998 is the biggest-priced winner in 39 years.

Queen Anne Stakes (1m) Royal Ascot

2005	**Valixir**	4	A Fabre	C Soumillon	4-1	1/10*
2006	**Ad Valorem**	4	A O'Brien	K Fallon	13-2	6/7
2007	**Ramonti**	5	S bin Suroor	L Dettori	5-1	7/8

2008	Haradasun	5	A O'Brien	J Murtagh	5-1	2/11
2009	Paco Boy	4	R Hannon Sr	R Hughes	10-3	7/9
2010	Goldikova	5	F Head	O Peslier	11-8f	10/10
2011	Canford Cliffs	4	R Hannon Sr	R Hughes	11-8	6/7
2012	Frankel	4	Sir H Cecil	T Queally	1-10f	8/11
2013	Declaration Of War	4	A O'Brien	J O'Brien	15-2	6/13
2014	Toronado	4	R Hannon	R Hughes	4-5f	8/10

Note – all Royal Ascot races were run at York in 2005

FOUR-YEAR-OLDS once considered Classic contenders fit the bill and this age group has taken 21 of the last 26 runnings. No horse older than five has triumphed since 1976 with Goldikova among some top-class ones to fail when defending her crown in 2010, having become the only female winner in 40 years when successful the year before. Six of the last eight winners ran in the Lockinge at Newbury, which is obviously the key trial, though Canford Cliffs and Frankel are the only horses to have won both races since Medicean in 2001. Toronado was the first horse to ever win the race first time out.

St James's Palace Stakes (1m) Royal Ascot

2005	Shamardal	S bin Suroor	K McEvoy	7-4f	2/8*
2006	Araafa	J Noseda	A Munro	2-1f	10/11
2007	Excellent Art	A O'Brien	J Spencer	8-1	8/8
2008	Henrythenavigator	A O'Brien	J Murtagh	4-7f	3/8
2009	Mastercraftsman	A O'Brien	J Murtagh	5-6f	3/10
2010	Canford Cliffs	R Hannon Sr	R Hughes	11-4j	4/9
2011	Frankel	Sir H Cecil	T Queally	3-10f	5/9
2012	Most Improved	B Meehan	K Fallon	9-1	15/16
2013	Dawn Approach	J Bolger	K Manning	5-4f	5/9
2014	Kingman	J Gosden	J Doyle	8-11f	7/7

GUINEAS FORM holds the key to this prize and eight of the last ten winners had come out on top in one of the Classics. The Curragh tends to be the best guide as five Irish 2,000 Guineas winners have followed up in that time compared to three from Newmarket and one from Longchamp (Henrythenavigator had won at Newmarket and the Curragh) and it's also bearing in mind that Frankel was the first Newmarket to win without a run in between since Bolkonski in 1975. Most Improved was the first winner to have skipped the Classics altogether since Dr Fong in 1998 and Shavian in 1990 was the last winner not to have previously run in a Group 1 at all.

Prince of Wales's Stakes (1m2f) Royal Ascot

2005	Azamour	4	J Oxx	M Kinane	11-8f	3/8*
2006	Ouija Board	5	E Dunlop	O Peslier	8-1	3/7
2007	Manduro	5	A Fabre	S Pasquier	15-8f	3/6
2008	Duke Of Marmalade	4	A O'Brien	J Murtagh	Evsf	1/12
2009	Vision D'Etat	4	E Libaud	O Peslier	4-1	2/8
2010	Byword	4	A Fabre	M Guyon	5-2f	5/12
2011	Rewilding	4	M Al Zarooni	L Dettori	17-2	6/7
2012	So You Think	6	A O'Brien	J O'Brien	4-5f	7/11
2013	Al Kazeem	5	R Charlton	J Doyle	11-4	9/11
2014	The Fugue	5	J Gosden	W Buick	11-2	7/8

A RACE that has altered hugely since gaining Group 1 status in 2000, when Dubai

Millennium provided one of the outstanding moments in Royal Ascot history. The race now attracts a field of international quality and ten of the last 15 winners had one of their previous two starts outside Britain whereas traditional trials like the Brigadier Gerard Stakes and the Gordon Richards Stakes tend to lack sufficient quality. The most telling pointer is the Tattersalls Gold Cup as four of the last six horses to attempt it managed to complete the double. Thirteen of the last 14 winners had already triumphed at Group 1 level and ten of those over the big-race trip of 1m2f.

Gold Cup (2m4f) Royal Ascot

2005	**Westerner**	6	E Lellouche	O Peslier	7-4f	4/17*
2006	**Yeats**	5	A O'Brien	K Fallon	7-1	5/12
2007	**Yeats**	6	A O'Brien	M Kinane	8-13f	13/14
2008	**Yeats**	7	A O'Brien	J Murtagh	11-8f	7/10
2009	**Yeats**	8	A O'Brien	J Murtagh	6-4f	4/9
2010	**Rite Of Passage**	6	D Weld	P Smullen	20-1	1/12
2011	**Fame And Glory**	5	A O'Brien	J Spencer	11-8f	3/15
2012	**Colour Vision**	4	S Bin Suroor	L Dettori	6-1	5/9
2013	**Estimate**	4	Sir M Stoute	R Moore	7-2f	5/14
2014	**Leading Light**	4	A O'Brien	J O'Brien	10-11f	14/13

THREE-QUARTERS of a mile longer than any other British Group 1, this race understandably attracts plenty of real specialists, with Royal Rebel, Kayf Tara, Drum Taps and Sadeem all dual winners since 1988 before Yeats became the first ever four-time winner in 2009. His trainer Aidan O'Brien remains the trainer to follow as he also won with Fame And Glory in 2011 and Leading Light last year, as well as having been just touched off with Age Of Aquarius in 2010, and O'Brien's last five winners all started their year in the Vintage Crop Stakes at Navan. Four-year-olds have won the last three renewals, but any winner older than four has to have proved themselves at the top level already as the last eight had previously won a Group 1. Thirteen of the last 15 winners had been successful over at least 2m and the best of the domestic trials is Sandown's Henry II Stakes, the route taken by eight of the 13 winners prior to Yeats's reign, both placed horses in 2009 and the runner-up in 2012.

Coronation Stakes (1m) Royal Ascot

2005	**Maids Causeway**	B Hills	M Hills	9-2	9/10*
2006	**Nannina**	J Gosden	J Fortune	6-1jf	3/15
2007	**Indian Ink**	R Hannon Sr	R Hughes	8-1	12/13
2008	**Lush Lashes**	J Bolger	K Manning	5-1	9/11
2009	**Ghanaati**	B Hills	R Hills	2-1f	5/10
2010	**Lillie Langtry**	A O'Brien	J Murtagh	7-2f	3/13
2011	**Immortal Verse**	R Collet	G Mosse	8-1	11/12
2012	**Fallen For You**	J Gosden	W Buick	12-1	11/10
2013	**Sky Lantern**	R Hannon Sr	R Hughes	9-2jf	16/17
2014	**Rizeena**	C Brittain	R Moore	11-2	7/12

A CHAMPIONSHIP race for three-year-old fillies. The 1,000 Guineas at Newmarket is much the best guide as four of the last 12 winners – Sky Lantern, Ghanaati, Attraction and Russian Rhythm – had also come out on top on the Rowley Mile and three others achieved a top-seven finish there. It's generally best to have been off the track since then, though, as just two of the last 22 winners ran in the Newmarket Classic and the Irish 1,000 Guineas at the Curragh, which often counts against many in the field. Equally any horse who has been stepped up in trip can be opposed as Lush Lashes is the only winner in the last 23 years to have raced over further.

Diamond Jubilee Stakes (6f) Royal Ascot

2004	Fayr Jag	4	T Easterby	W Supple	12-1	6/14
2005	Cape of Good Hope	7	D Oughton	M Kinane	6-1	2/15*
2006	Les Arcs	6	T Pitt	J Egan	33-1	15/18
2007	Soldier's Tale	6	J Noseda	J Murtagh	9-1	11/21
2008	Kingsgate Native	3	J Best	S Sanders	33-1	15/17
2009	Art Connoisseur	3	M Bell	T Queally	20-1	11/14
2010	Starspangledbanner	4	A O'Brien	J Murtagh	13-2j	21/24
2011	Society Rock	4	J Fanshawe	P Cosgrave	25-1	3/16
2012	Black Caviar	5	P Moody	L Nolen	1-6f	15/14
2013	Lethal Force	4	C Cox	A Kirby	11-1	15/18
2014	Slade Power	5	E Lynam	W Lordan	7-2f	4/14

A RACE whose profile has been steadily on the rise and reached fever pitch with its inauguration into the Global Sprint Challenge alongside the King's Stand Stakes, attracting the best sprinters from around the world, most notably the legendary Black Caviar in 2012. Its essence hasn't changed, though, as Black Caviar is the only winner trained outside Britain and Ireland since Cape Of Good Hope in 2005 and in that time several fancied foreign raiders – Takeover Target (twice), J J The Jet Plane, Sacred Kingdom and Star Witness – have been beaten at 4-1 or shorter. In contrast course form remains critical because, of the last 15 winners at Ascot, eight had already been successful at the course and nine had managed a top-four finish at Royal Ascot. The race throws up more than its share of shocks, with four winners priced 20-1 or bigger in the last seven years, and two of those are among a host of unfancied three-year-olds to run well from very few representatives including five places at 40-1 or bigger since 2003.

Coral-Eclipse (1m2f) Sandown

2005	Oratorio	3	A O'Brien	K Fallon	12-1	7/7
2006	David Junior	4	B Meehan	J Spencer	9-4	8/9
2007	Notnowcato	5	Sir M Stoute	R Moore	7-1	8/8
2008	Mount Nelson	4	A O'Brien	J Murtagh	7-2	8/8
2009	Sea The Stars	3	J Oxx	M Kinane	4-7f	6/10
2010	Twice Over	5	H Cecil	T Queally	13-8f	1/5
2011	So You Think	5	A O'Brien	S Heffernan	4-6f	3/5
2012	Nathaniel	4	J Gosden	W Buick	7-2	4/9
2013	Al Kazeem	5	R Charlton	J Doyle	15-8f	2/7
2014	Mukhadram	5	W Haggas	P Hanagan	14-1	10/9

TRADITIONALLY THE first clash of the generations, but in recent times it has suffered from a lack of three-year-old representation. The great Sea The Stars won for the Classic generation in 2009, but the previous four Derby winners to take their chance – Authorized, Motivator, Benny The Dip and Erhaab – were all beaten, which may have put off connections of the top three-year-olds. That said, three-year-old winners tend to be milers stepping up in trip anyway as the last ten had all run in a Guineas. Fillies are to be avoided – Pebbles, in 1985, is the only filly to succeed since the 19th century, since when Bosra Sham and Ouija Board were beaten favourites. Royal Ascot form is the key, particularly the Prince of Wales's Stakes, although Al Kazeem was the first to do the double since Mtoto 26 years earlier with many horses beaten at Ascot, most recently

Mukhadram, So You Think, Twice Over and David Junior, improving on that form.

July Cup (6f) Newmarket

2005	Pastoral Pursuits	4	H Morrison	J Egan	22-1	10/19
2006	Les Arcs	6	T Pitt	J Egan	10-1	1/15
2007	Sakhee's Secret	3	H Morrison	S Drowne	9-2	3/18
2008	Marchand d'Or	5	F Head	D Bonilla	5-2f	5/13
2009	Fleeting Spirit	4	J Noseda	T Queally	12-1	5/13
2010	Starspangledbanner	4	A O'Brien	J Murtagh	2-1f	4/14
2011	Dream Ahead	3	D Simcock	H Turner	7-1	2/16
2012	Mayson	4	R Fahey	P Hanagan	20-1	11/12
2013	Lethal Force	4	C Cox	A Kirby	9-2	4/11
2014	Slade Power	5	E Lynam	W Lordan	7-4f	13/13

FOUR OF the last nine winners were following up victories in the Diamond Jubilee Stakes over the same trip at Royal Ascot, but surprisingly it pays to ignore Group 1 form in other races as eight of the other ten winners since 2001 were scoring for the first time at the top level. This is a race in which stars are often born with 38 of the 47 winners being aged three or four. Often that's because horses are dropping into sprints having been tried over further as stamina is an important asset on this stiff uphill finish, as greats like Ajdal and Soviet Song showed many years ago with Dream Ahead the latest to have had his previous run over a mile.

King George VI and Queen Elizabeth Stakes (1m4f) Ascot

2005	Azamour	4	J Oxx	M Kinane	5-2f	12/12*
2006	Hurricane Run	4	A Fabre	C Soumillon	5-6f	3/6
2007	Dylan Thomas	4	A O'Brien	J Murtagh	5-4f	3/7
2008	Duke Of Marmalade	4	A O'Brien	J Murtagh	4-6f	5/8
2009	Conduit	4	Sir M Stoute	R Moore	13-8f	8/9
2010	Harbinger	4	Sir M Stoute	O Peslier	4-1	1/6
2011	Nathaniel	3	J Gosden	W Buick	11-2	3/5
2012	Danedream	4	P Schiergen	A Starke	9-1	4/10
2013	Novellist	4	A Wohler	J Murtagh	13-2	3/8
2014	Taghrooda	3	J Gosden	P Hanagan	7-2	7/8

*Run at Newbury

THIS RACE has suffered from a lack of three-year-old representation in recent years, but Taghrooda bucked the pattern last year when becoming only the fourth horse of her age to come out on top since the mighty Lammtarra in 1995, with Nathaniel, Alamshar and Galileo being the others. Taghrooda was an even bigger trends-buster in another way as she became the first British-trained three-year-old filly to win any Group 1 over this trip against older males in the worldwide history of the sport, although German four-year-old Danedream had at least led the way for the fillies just two years earlier. It generally pays to look for an older horse proven at the top level and the trip because since Belmez in 1990 just three winners hadn't previously landed a Group 1 and just four hadn't been first or second in a Group 1 over 1m4f. The Coronation Cup is a poor guide, though, with only Opera House and Daylami doing the double in the last 40 years.

Sussex Stakes (1m) Goodwood

2005	Proclamation	3	J Noseda	M Kinane	3-1	6/12
2006	Court Masterpiece	6	E Dunlop	E Dunlop	15-2	3/7

SLADE POWER (left): the fourth horse in nine years to win the Diamond Jubilee Stakes and the July Cup, though other Group 1 form is a poor guide

2007	**Ramonti**	5	Sir M Stoute	L Dettori	9-2	1/8
2008	**Henrythenavigator**	3	A O'Brien	J Murtagh	4-11f	4/6
2009	**Rip Van Winkle**	3	A O'Brien	J Murtagh	6-4f	7/8
2010	**Canford Cliffs**	3	R Hannon Sr	R Hughes	4-6f	7/7
2011	**Frankel**	3	Sir H Cecil	T Queally	8-13f	3/4
2012	**Frankel**	4	Sir H Cecil	T Queally	1-20f	3/4
2013	**Toronado**	3	R Hannon Sr	R Hughes	11-4	7/7
2014	**Kingman**	3	J Gosden	J Doyle	2-5f	4/4

THIS IS a great race for glamorous three-year-olds as that age group has provided 28 of the 40 winners since it was opened to all ages in 1975. Eight of the last 11 triumphant three-year-olds were favourites and ten of the last 12 had been first or second in the St James's Palace Stakes, which is the key trial. Six of the last eight successful older horses had contested the Queen Anne Stakes, with placed horses doing as well as the winner.

Nassau Stakes (1m1f192yds) Goodwood

2005	**Alexander Goldrun**	4	J Bolger	K Manning	13-8f	3/11
2006	**Ouija Board**	5	E Dunlop	L Dettori	Evensf	1/7
2007	**Peeping Fawn**	3	A O'Brien	J Murtagh	2-1f	5/8
2008	**Halfway To Heaven**	3	A O'Brien	J Murtagh	5-1	6/9
2009	**Midday**	3	H Cecil	T Queally	11-2	10/10
2010	**Midday**	4	H Cecil	T Queally	15-8f	6/7
2011	**Midday**	5	Sir H Cecil	T Queally	6-4f	6/6
2012	**The Fugue**	3	J Gosden	R Hughes	11-4	7/8
2013	**Winsili**	3	J Gosden	W Buick	20-1	15/14
2014	**Sultanina**	4	J Gosden	W Buick	11-2	2/6

THIS IS a fantastic race for punters as 19 of the last 21 winners emerged from the top three in the market including 12 favourites. The key is to side with a top-class three-year-old as the Classic generation have provided 30 of the 40 winners since the race was opened to older fillies in 1975, despite Midday's best efforts in racking up a hat-trick. Preferably they should be dropping down in trip rather than stepping up as only Halfway To Heaven is the only winner to have had her previous run over a mile since 2004, during which time The Fugue, Midday and Peeping Fawn all improved on placed efforts in the Oaks.

Juddmonte International Stakes (1m2f85yds) York

2005	Electrocutionist	4	V Valiani	M Kinane	9-2	5/7
2006	Notnowcato	4	Sir M Stoute	R Moore	8-1	5/7
2007	Authorized	3	P Chapple-Hyam	L Dettori	6-4f	1/7
2008	Duke Of Marmalade	4	A O'Brien	J Murtagh	4-6f	4/9*
2009	Sea The Stars	3	J Oxx	M Kinane	1-4f	3/4
2010	Rip Van Winkle	4	A O'Brien	J Murtagh	7-4f	7/9
2011	Twice Over	6	Sir H Cecil	I Mongan	11-2	4/5
2012	Frankel	4	Sir H Cecil	T Queally	1-10f	7/9
2013	Declaration Of War	4	A O'Brien	J O'Brien	7-1	2/6
2014	Australia	3	A O'Brien	J O'Brien	8-13f	6/6

Note – this race and following two York races all run at Newmarket in 2008

FAMOUS FOR its many upsets since Brigadier Gerard suffered his only defeat to Roberto in 1972, the race has turned in punters' favour in recent times with no winner returned bigger than 8-1 since Ezzoud in 1993 and six of the last eight favourites winning. Older horses have dominated the three-year-olds with just five younger horses triumphing since 1984, all of whom were recent Group 1 winners with the last three being Derby

NOTNOWCATO (left): the biggest-priced Juddmonte winner since 1993 at 8-1

winners. The key trial is the Coral-Eclipse, which has provided nine of the last 18 winners, including six who did the double.

Yorkshire Oaks (1m3f195yds) York

2005	**Punctilious**	4	S bin Suroor	K McEvoy	13-2	5/11
2006	**Alexandrova**	3	A O'Brien	M Kinane	4-9f	4/6
2007	**Peeping Fawn**	3	A O'Brien	J Murtagh	4-9f	8/8
2008	**Lush Lashes**	3	J Bolger	K Manning	Evsf	2/6*
2009	**Dar Re Mi**	4	J Gosden	J Fortune	11-2	4/6
2010	**Midday**	4	H Cecil	T Queally	11-4	6/8
2011	**Blue Bunting**	3	M Al Zarooni	L Dettori	11-4f	6/8
2012	**Shareta**	4	A de Royer-Dupre	C Lemaire	2-1	7/6
2013	**The Fugue**	4	J Gosden	W Buick	2-1f	6/7
2014	**Tapestry**	3	A O'Brien	R Moore	8-1	6/7

ALWAYS A top-class race, this has been won by the Classic generation ten times in the last 16 years, although older horses have a superior strike-rate with fewer representatives. However, the last four Oaks heroines to run – Taghrooda, Was, Snow Fairy and Sariska – were all beaten, three of them when favourite, and the last Epsom winner to follow up, Alexandrova, had significantly won the Irish Oaks in between because that has been a better guide. The five-year-old Super Tassa was the ultimate trend-buster in 2001 – the first Italian winner in Britain for 41 years and consequently sent off at 25-1.

Nunthorpe Stakes (5f) York

2005	**La Cucaracha**	4	B Hills	M Hills	7-1	8/16
2006	**Reverence**	5	E Ahern	K Darley	5-1	6/14
2007	**Kingsgate Native**	2	J Best	J Quinn	12-1	13/16
2008	**Borderlescott**	6	R Bastiman	P Cosgrave	12-1	12/14
2009	**Borderlescott**	7	R Bastiman	N Callan	9-1	2/16
2010	**Sole Power**	3	E Lynam	W Lordan	100-1	11/12
2011	**Margot Did**	3	M Bell	H Turner	20-1	11/15
2012	**Ortensia**	7	P Messara	W Buick	7-2jf	8/19
2013	**Jwala**	4	R Cowell	S Drowne	40-1	8/17
2014	**Sole Power**	7	E Lynam	R Hughes	11-4f	10/13

THIS HAS become a real race for upsets, none bigger than Sole Power at 100-1 in 2010, and there have also been 20-1 and 40-1 winners since then. The main reason is that the race is rarely won by a proven top-level sprinter, with eight of the last 13 winners never having previously landed a Group race, let alone a Group 1 race. It's therefore little wonder that progressive younger horses have tended to hold sway, although all six winners older than five since 1945 have come in the last 17 years.

Sprint Cup (6f) Haydock

2005	**Goodricke**	3	D Loder	J Spencer	14-1	4/17
2006	**Reverence**	5	E Alston	K Darley	5-1	6/14
2007	**Red Clubs**	4	B Hills	M Hills	33-1	4/18
2008	**African Rose**	3	Mme C Head	S Pasquier	7-2f	12/15
2009	**Regal Parade**	5	D Nicholls	A Nicholls	14-1	13/14
2010	**Markab**	7	H Candy	P Cosgrave	12-1	14/13
2011	**Dream Ahead**	3	D Simcock	W Buick	4-1f	9/16

2012	Society Rock	5	J Fanshawe	K Fallon	10-1	3/13
2013	Gordon Lord Byron	5	T Hogan	J Murtagh	7-2	2/13
2014	G Force	3	D O'Meara	D Tudhope	11-1	10/17

THIS CAN often be run on ground with plenty of give, so there have been a string of upsets as midsummer form proves misleading, with nine of the last 13 winners returned in double figures including 33-1 Red Clubs in 2007. Dream Ahead was the first July Cup winner to follow up at Haydock since Ajdal in 1987, with Lethal Force, Starspangledbanner and Fleeting Spirit the latest to be beaten favourites in the last five years, and he was only the second winning jolly since Godolphin hotpot Diktat in 1999.

St Leger (1m6f132yds) Doncaster

2005	Scorpion	A O'Brien	L Dettori	10-11f	2/6
2006	Sixties Icon	J Noseda	L Dettori	11-8f	11/11*
2007	Lucarno	J Gosden	J Fortune	11-8f	11/11
2008	Conduit	Sir M Stoute	L Dettori	8-1	5/14
2009	Mastery	S bin Suroor	T Durcan	14-1	7/8
2010	Arctic Cosmos	J Gosden	W Buick	12-1	8/10
2011	Masked Marvel	J Gosden	W Buick	15-2	3/9
2012	Encke	M Al Zarooni	M Barzalona	25-1	1/9
2013	Leading Light	A O'Brien	J O'Brien	7-2f	7/11
2014	Kingston Hill	R Varian	A Atzeni	9-4f	4/12

*Run at York

KINGSTON HILL'S victory last year could be just the shot in the arm this race required as there has been a long trend of class horses increasingly being kept to shorter trips, which was only likely to increase after Camelot's shock defeat in 2012. Indeed, Kingston Hill was the first winner in more than 25 years to have had his prep run over just 1m2f, though during that time only Leading Light warmed up beyond the Leger distance. Sixteen of the last 18 winners had previously landed a Group race so it's rare for a real dark horse to emerge, though their progress tends to have been steady rather than spectacular – four of the seven winners to come via the Derby since 1997 finished outside the places at Epsom and three of the eight to have warmed up in the Great Voltigeur in that time were beaten there. In the same period Gordon Stakes winners have had more success, with four doing the double, though none since Conduit in 2008.

Prix de l'Arc de Triomphe (1m4f) Longchamp

2005	Hurricane Run	3	A Fabre	K Fallon	11-4	6/15
2006	Rail Link	3	A Fabre	S Pasquier	8-1	4/8
2007	Dylan Thomas	4	A O'Brien	K Fallon	11-2	6/12
2008	Zarkava	3	A de Royer-Dupre	C Soumillon	13-8f	1/16
2009	Sea The Stars	3	J Oxx	M Kinane	4-6f	6/19
2010	Workforce	3	Sir M Stoute	R Moore	6-1	8/19
2011	Danedream	3	P Schiergen	A Starke	20-1	2/16
2012	Solemia	4	C Laffon-Parias	O Peslier	33-1	6/18
2013	Treve	3	C Head-Maarek	T Jarnet	9-2	15/17
2014	Treve	4	C Head-Maarek	T Jarnet	11-1	3/20

THIS RACE has restored its status as the premier middle-distance championship of Europe, with top-class 1m4f horses now trained specifically for the race from the summer. They also come from all over the world to run in it, with Japan producing three of the last four runners-up and Danedream winning for Germany. However, the French remain dominant overall with the victories of Treve and Solemia in the last three years restoring the status quo after a three-year blank and taking their tally to 17 of the last 25 winners. Interestingly, though, it's the fillies who have been doing it for them in recent times rather than the colts. The girls have won five of the last seven renewals and the last French colt to triumph was Rail Link in 2006 – it would have been hard to believe back then that, having provided the Arc winner in ten years out of 12, the Prix Niel would endure an eight-year blank. Furthermore, no French colt older than three has won since Subotica in 1992, which was the last time the Prix Foy provided the winner. British-trained horses are really struggling with Workforce their only winner since Marienbard in 2002.

Queen Elizabeth II Stakes (1m) Ascot

2005	Starcraft	3	L Cumani	C Lemaire	7-2	5/6
2006	George Washington	3	A O'Brien	K Fallon	13-8f	2/8
2007	Ramonti	5	S bin Suroor	L Dettori	5-1	1/7
2008	Raven's Pass	3	J Gosden	J Fortune	3-1	7/7
2009	Rip Van Winkle	3	A O'Brien	J Murtagh	8-13f	4/4
2010	Poet's Voice	3	S Bin Suroor	L Dettori	9-2	7/8
2011	Frankel	3	Sir H Cecil	T Queally	4-11f	2/8
2012	Excelebration	4	A O'Brien	J O'Brien	10-11f	6/8
2013	Olympic Glory	3	R Hannon Sr	R Hughes	11-2	7/12
2014	Charm Spirit	3	F Head	O Peslier	5-1	7/11

KNOWN AS the mile championship of Europe, and one in which the Classic generation has held sway with 21 of the last 30 winners. That has made the St James's Palace Stakes the key trial as seven of the last 14 winning three-year-olds ran there, although Frankel was the first to do the double since Bahri in 1995, while Frankel and George Washington followed up 2,000 Guineas victories. Ten of the last 12 winners had already won a Group 1 and the last five older winners all contested a Group 1 at Royal Ascot. Milligram was the last winning filly or mare in 1987.

Champion Stakes (1m2f) Ascot

2005	David Junior	3	B Meehan	J Spencer	25-1	3/15
2006	Pride	6	A de Royer-Dupre	C Lemaire	7-2	7/8
2007	Literato	3	J-C Rouget	C Lemaire	7-2	8/12
2008	New Approach	3	J Bolger	K Manning	6-5f	2/11
2009	Twice Over	4	H Cecil	T Queally	14-1	6/14
2010	Twice Over	5	H Cecil	T Queally	7-2	4/10
2011	Cirrus Des Aigles	5	C Barande-Barbe	C Soumillon	12-1	1/12
2012	Frankel	4	Sir H Cecil	T Queally	2-11f	6/8
2013	Farhh	5	S Bin Suroor	S de Sousa	11-4	5/10
2014	Noble Mission	5	Lady Cecil	J Doyle	7-1	5/9

Run at Newmarket until 2011.

THE SUBJECT of a big-money makeover when switched to Ascot in 2011. Older horses have increasingly come to the fore, accounting for each of the last six winners including four five-year-olds, although three-year-olds still have the edge overall with 23 of the last 40 winners including 17 since 1980. Twelve of those 17 had won a Classic with Guineas form more influential than the Epsom races – New Approach became the first Classic-winning three-year-old over 1m4f to cope with the drop in trip since Time Charter in 1982, while Frankel's win in 2012 also came a year after his 2,000 Guineas victory. This has been the best British Group 1 for French horses, with three winners in the last nine years extending a long tradition of success.

Big handicap records

Lincoln (1m) Doncaster

Year	Winner	Age	Weight	Trainer	Jockey	SP	Draw/ran
2005	**Stream Of Gold**	4	9-0	Sir M Stoute	R Winston	5-1f	13/22
2006	**Blythe Knight**	6	8-10	J Quinn	G Gibbons	22-1	9/30*
2007	**Very Wise**	5	8-11	W Haggas	J Fanning	9-1	16/20
2008	**Smokey Oakey**	4	8-9	M Tompkins	J Quinn	10-1	12/21
2009	**Expresso Star**	4	8-12	J Gosden	J Fortune	10-3f	9/20
2010	**Penitent**	4	9-2	W Haggas	J Murtagh	3-1f	1/21
2011	**Sweet Lightning**	6	9-4	M Dods	J Murtagh	16-1	16/21**
2012	**Brae Hill**	6	9-1	R Fahey	T Hamilton	25-1	12/22
2013	**Levitate**	5	8-7	J Quinn	D Egan (3)	20-1	3/22
2014	**Ocean Tempest**	5	9-3	J Ryan	A Kirby	20-1	3/17

*Run at Redcar   **Run at Newcastle*

THIS ALWAYS used to be regarded as something of a lottery and the last four winners, none of whom was shorter than 16-1, suggest a return to those days after a run of success for punters, crowned when Expresso Star and Penitent landed nationwide gambles. Those four were also aged five or six, bucking a trend that had seen four-year-olds win six of the previous eight runnings. The ongoing shift at this time has been the rating required to get a run becoming higher and higher, so past trends about siding with a progressive horse on a low weight have been rendered obsolete, although a big weight is still a drawback with no winner carrying more than 9st 4lb since Babodana in 2004. The draw is inevitably a factor with just one of the last 11 winners at Doncaster coming from a stall higher than 16. Look for trainers who have won the race recently as John Quinn, William Haggas and Mark Tompkins are all dual winners in the last 11 years.

Royal Hunt Cup (1m) Royal Ascot

2005	**New Seeker**	5	9-0	C Cox	P Robinson	11-1	6/22*
2006	**Cesare**	5	8-8	J Fanshawe	J Spencer	14-1	28/30
2007	**Royal Oath**	4	9-0	J Gosden	J Fortune	9-1	13/26
2008	**Mr Aviator**	4	9-5	R Hannon Sr	R Hughes	25-1	26/29
2009	**Forgotten Voice**	4	9-1	J Noseda	J Murtagh	4-1f	25/25
2010	**Invisible Man**	4	8-9	S Bin Suroor	L Dettori	28-1	7/29
2011	**Julienas**	4	8-8	W Swinburn	E Ahern	12-1	24/28
2012	**Prince Of Johanne**	6	9-3	T Tate	J Fahy	16-1	33/30
2013	**Belgian Bill**	5	8-11	G Baker	J Doyle	33-1	6/28
2014	**Field Of Dream**	7	9-1	J Osborne	A Kirby	20-1	33/28

Royal Hunt Cup and the Wokingham run at York in 2005

A GREAT betting race in which there are few pointers and plots are thick on the ground, so most winners go off at a decent price – Forgotten Voice in 2009 was the first winning favourite since Yeast 13 years earlier. A common mistake is to side with a lightly raced improver because experience is in fact a vital commodity – 15 of the last 17 winners had run at least eight times, which is more than many of the beaten favourites. As with most big handicaps, weight trends have changed markedly with fewer runners getting in below the 9st barrier, but five of the last six still carried no more than 9st 1lb. A high draw is generally essential, with Belgian Bill only the second to defy a single-figure berth at Ascot since Surprise Encounter in 2001.

Wokingham (6f) Royal Ascot

2005	**Iffraaj**	4	9-6	M Jarvis	P Robinson	9-4f	12/17
2006	**Baltic King**	6	9-10	H Morrison	J Fortune	10-1	23/28
2007	**Dark Missile**	4	8-6	A Balding	W Buick	22-1	2/26
2008	**Big Timer**	4	9-2	Miss L Perrett	T Eaves	20-1	1/27
2009	**High Standing**	4	8-12	W Haggas	R Moore	6-1	4/26
2010	**Laddies Poker Two**	5	8-11	J Noseda	J Murtagh	9-2f	26/27
2011	**Deacon Blues**	4	8-13	J Fanshawe	J Murtagh	15-2	11/25
2012	**Dandy Boy**	6	9-8	D Marnane	P Dobbs	33-1	15/28
2013	**York Glory**	5	9-2	K Ryan	J Spencer	14-1	22/26
2014	**Baccarat**	5	9-5	R Fahey	G Chaloner (3)	9-1	27/28

THE DRAW bias in the Hunt Cup has often completely changed by this race, with lower numbers having the edge, although the opposite is true in years when the Hunt Cup has been won from a low berth so fresher ground is clearly the key. So too fresh horses as nine of the last 13 winners had raced no more than twice that year, which is remarkable for a sprint handicap in June. Class horses have been increasingly successful since the

OCEAN TEMPEST (left): just below the 9st 4lb threshold in the Lincoln

HEAVEN'S GUEST (left): the fifth successive Bunbury Cup winner gaining a first victory of the season yet still classy enough to be allotted 9st 1lb or more

turn of the century, with ten of the last 17 winners carrying at least 9st 2lb to victory and four winning favourites in 14 years. Eleven of the last 13 winners had won over the big-race trip and the two exceptions had won over further, so stamina is clearly important, and a key trial is the Victoria Cup over an extra furlong at the same track in May. Nine of the last 22 winners ran in that race or the 6f handicap at Newmarket's Guineas meeting.

Northumberland Plate (2m) Newcastle

2005	**Sergeant Cecil**	6	8-8	D Millman	A Munro	14-1	7/20
2006	**Toldo**	4	8-2	G Moore	N de Souza	33-1	16/20
2007	**Juniper Girl**	4	8-11	M Bell	L Morris	5-1f	13/20
2008	**Arc Bleu**	7	8-2	A Martin	A Nicholls	14-1	6/18
2009	**Som Tala**	6	8-8	M Channon	T Culhane	16-1	4/17
2010	**Overturn**	6	8-7	D McCain	E Ahern	14-1	21/19
2011	**Tominator**	4	8-8	R Hollinshead	P Pickard (3)	25-1	14/19
2012	**Ile De Re**	6	9-3	D McCain	J Crowley	5-2f	9/16
2013	**Tominator**	6	9-10	J O'Neill	G Lee	8-1	4/18
2014	**Angel Gabrial**	5	9-1	R Fahey	G Chaloner (3)	4-1f	1/19

WITH SO much of the season revolving around Royal Ascot and Newcastle's biggest day of the summer generally coming just a week later, this provides a good opportunity for horses laid out for the race rather than coming here as an afterthought. Just two of the last 12 winners had run at Royal Ascot despite several fancied runners, including four beaten favourites, coming from the royal meeting. Older horses have increasingly come to the fore, with five of the last seven winners aged at least six and two eight-year-olds among the previous eight to triumph. The first bend comes shortly after the start, so those drawn high can be disadvantaged, with ten of the last 16 winners drawn seven or lower, and Overturn used controversial tactics to overcome that in 2010. The Chester

Cup is traditionally a strong guide and that has been reinforced recently with Ile De Re doing the double before Tominator and Angel Gabrial stepped up on placed efforts at Chester.

Bunbury Cup (7f) Newmarket

2005	Mine	7	9-9	J Bethell	T Quinn	16-1	13/18
2006	Mine	8	9-10	J Bethell	M Kinane	10-1	6/19
2007	Giganticus	4	8-8	B Hills	P Robinson	16-1	16/18
2008	Little White Lie	4	9-0	J Jenkins	D Holland	14-1	1/18
2009	Plum Pudding	6	9-10	R Hannon Sr	R Moore	12-1	15/19
2010	St Moritz	4	9-1	M Johnston	L Dettori	4-1f	4/19
2011	Brae Hill	5	9-1	R Fahey	B McHugh	11-1	2/20
2012	Bonnie Brae	5	9-9	D Elsworth	R Moore	13-2	12/15
2013	Field Of Dream	6	9-7	J Osborne	A Kirby	14-1	20/19
2014	Heaven's Guest	4	9-3	R Fahey	T Hamilton	12-1	9/13

IT'S REMARKABLE how many times this race is won by a horse carrying a big weight. Mine, a three-time winner between 2002 and 2006, twice defied a burden of at least 9st 9lb and has been emulated by Bonnie Brae and Plum Pudding since then. Despite that only one of the last 22 winners had won more than once that year – 14 hadn't won at all, including each of the last five – so the key is clearly to find a horse slipping down the weights but classy enough to still be near the top of the handicap. This is run over a specialist trip and each of the last 12 winners had already won a handicap over the distance.

John Smith's Cup (1m2f85yds) York

2005	Mullins Bay	4	9-7	A O'Brien	K Fallon	4-1f	19/20
2006	Fairmile	4	9-1	W Swinburn	A Kirby (3)	6-1j	9/20
2007	Charlie Tokyo	4	8-12	R Fahey	J Moriarty (3)	11-1	4/17
2008	Flying Clarets	5	8-12	R Fahey	F Tylicki (7)	12-1	12/16
2009	Sirvino	4	8-8	T Brown	N Brown (3)	16-1	16/18
2010	Wigmore Hall	3	8-5	M Bell	M Lane (3)	5-1	13/19
2011	Green Destiny	4	8-13	W Haggas	A Beschizza (3)	6-1	17-19
2012	King's Warrior	5	8-9	P Chapple-Hyam	R Havlin	33-1	19/18
2013	Danchai	4	8-11	W Haggas	A Atzeni	10-1	16/19
2014	Farraaj	5	9-11	R Varian	A Atzeni	6-1	22/16

YOUTH SEEMS to be the key to this race, with only three winners aged five – and none older – since Vintage Premium in 2002 despite three-year-olds struggling desperately to get a run. Indeed, subsequent Grade 1 winner Wigmore Hall was the only runner from that age group when coming out on top in 2010 and none have made the field since. Like the Northumberland Plate, this is another handicap in which missing Royal Ascot is vital, in keeping with nine of the last 12 winners, whereas 11 of the last 12 beaten favourites registered a top-four finish at the royal meeting. This is run on one of the best Saturdays of the summer and, with many top jockeys engaged elsewhere, it provides an opportunity for some younger riders as six of the last nine winners were partnered by an apprentice.

Stewards' Cup (6f) Goodwood

2005	Gift Horse	5	9-7	D Nicholls	K Fallon	9-2	9/27
2006	Borderlescott	4	9-5	R Bastiman	R Ffrench	10-1	10/27
2007	Zidane	5	9-1	J Fanshawe	J Spencer	6-1f	17/27

2008	Conquest	4	8-9	W Haggas	D O'Neill	40-1	13/26
2009	Genki	5	9-1	R Charlton	S Drowne	14-1	17/26
2010	Evens And Odds	6	9-1	D Nicholls	B Cray (5)	20-1	11/28
2011	Hoof It	4	10-0	M Easterby	K Fallon	13-2jf	18/27
2012	Hawkeyethenoo	6	9-9	J Goldie	G Lee	9-1	4/27
2013	Rex Imperator	4	9-4	W Haggas	N Callan	12-1	26/27
2014	Intrinsic	4	8-11	R Cowell	R Hughes	6-1	22/24

THIS IS a major betting heat with a strong ante-post market and the betting has become a good guide as seven winners at single-figure odds in 12 years, plus three more not a lot bigger, is a fine record given the size of the field. This is a race for established sprint handicappers with 14 of the last 18 winners coming via the Wokingham, though none of them had won at Royal Ascot and all but one had another run in between. Plenty of top-class sprinters drop into handicap company for this race, but the weight tends to stop them as Crews Hill in 1981 was the last winner to have prepped in a Group race and only Hoof It and Hawkeyethenoo have carried more than 9st 7lb to victory since Petong in 1984.

Ebor (1m6f) York

2005	Sergeant Cecil	6	8-12	B Millman	A Munro	11-1	18/20
2006	Mudawin	5	8-4	J Chapple-Hyam	J Egan	100-1	13/22
2007	Purple Moon	4	9-4	L Cumani	J Spencer	7-2f	14/19
2008	All The Good	5	9-0	S bin Suroor	D O'Neill	25-1	7/20
2009	Sesenta	5	8-8	W Mullins	G Carroll (5)	25-1	16/19
2010	Dirar	5	9-1	G Elliott	J Spencer	14-1	22/20
2011	Moyenne Corniche	6	8-13	B Ellison	D Swift (3)	25-1	10/20
2012	Willing Foe	5	9-2	S Bin Suroor	L Dettori	12-1	16/19
2013	Tiger Cliff	4	9-0	Lady Cecil	T Queally	5-1	18/14
2014	Mutual Regard	5	9-9	J Murtagh	L Steward (5)	20-1	16/19

Run at Newbury as the Newburgh Handicap in 2008

ONE OF the oldest and most famous handicaps, first run in 1847, again has an extremely strong ante-post market and was moved to a Saturday in 2011 to boost its profile further. Sea Pigeon brought the house down when lumping top-weight home in 1979, but low weights are massively favoured and just three winners have carried more than 9st 2lb since 1998 – and only Mutual Regard more than 9st 4lb – despite the weights becoming more and more condensed. Watch out for three-year-olds as they had a tremendous record around the turn of the century and have simply found it increasingly tough to get a run since then, with two of the three to run since 2006, Honolulu and Changingoftheguard, finishing honourable seconds. Indeed, progressive horses are always preferred with just two winners older than five since Sea Pigeon and eight of the last 12 having raced no more than nine times on the Flat.

Ayr Gold Cup (6f) Ayr

2005	Presto Shinko	4	9-2	R Hannon Sr	S Sanders	12-1	2/27
2006	Fonthill Road	6	9-2	R Fahey	P Hanagan	16-1	6/28
2007	Advanced	4	9-9	K Ryan	J Spencer	20-1	22/28
2008	Regal Parade	4	8-10	D Nicholls	W Carson (5)	18-1	20/27
2009	Jimmy Styles	5	9-2	C Cox	L Dettori	14-1	15/26
2010	Redford	5	9-2	D Nicholls	L Dettori	14-1	17/26
2011	Our Jonathan	4	9-6	K Ryan	F Norton	11-1	12/26

MUTUAL REGARD: defied the Ebor trends with his weight-carrying heroics

2012	Captain Ramius	6	9-0	K Ryan	P Smullen	16-1	8/26
2013	Highland Colori	5	9-4	A Balding	O Murphy (5)	20-1	19/26
2014	Louis The Pious	6	9-4	D O'Meara	J Doyle	10-1	19/27

A HISTORIC race first run in 1804, but punters are still struggling to get to grips with it – Louis The Poius was the most fancied winner of the last 13 years at 10-1. There seems little clue from the draw in recent runnings, but the effect can be gleaned from the consolation races – the Bronze Cup was run for the first time in 2009 and now precedes the big one, along with the Silver Cup. Be wary of recent winning form as that can mean too much weight, with just two of the last 12 winners having triumphed more than once that year and just four of those 12 having landed any of their previous four outings. Kevin Ryan has won three of the last eight renewals, including two of the last four, to take over from David Nicholls as the trainer to follow.

Cambridgeshire (1m1f) Newmarket

2005	Blue Monday	4	9-3	R Charlton	S Drowne	5-1f	3/30
2006	Formal Decree	3	8-9	G Swinbank	J Spencer	9-1	17/33
2007	Pipedreamer	3	8-12	J Gosden	J Fortune	5-1f	24/34
2008	Tazeez	4	9-2	J Gosden	R Hills	25-1	8/28
2009	Supaseus	6	9-1	H Morrison	T Block	16-1	7/32
2010	Credit Swap	5	8-7	M Wigham	J Crowley	14-1	3/35
2011	Prince Of Johanne	5	8-12	T Tate	J Fahy (3)	40-1	31/32
2012	Bronze Angel	3	8-8	M Tregoning	W Buick	9-1	21/33
2013	Educate	4	9-9	I Mohammed	J Murtagh	8-1f	4/33
2014	Bronze Angel	5	8-13	M Tregoning	L Steward (5)	14-1	11/31

THE FIRST leg of the Autumn Double. Because of its unusual distance and its straight course, this has thrown up a number of specialists down the years, with dual winner Bronze Angel being the most obvious recent example, so consider horses who have run well in the race before. Many of the runners are milers racing over an extra furlong, but stronger stayers often come to the fore and the only winners in the last 13 years without a previous win over at least 1m2f are Credit Swap and Bronze Angel. Handicap experience is vital, with ten of the last 12 winners having previously beaten a field of at least 13. Big weights spell trouble as Educate is the only horse to carry more than 9st 3lb to victory since Beauchamp Pilot in 2002. The heritage handicap at Newbury in September was the key trial, throwing up four out of seven winners from 2004 to 2010, but the Cambridgeshire's date switch means there's now just a week between them.

Cesarewitch (2m2f) Newmarket

2005	Sergeant Cecil	6	9-8	B Millman	A Munro	10-1	7/34
2006	Detroit City	4	9-1	P Hobbs	J Spencer	9-2f	4/32
2007	Leg Spinner	6	8-11	A Martin	J Murtagh	14-1	11/33
2008	Caracciola	11	9-6	N Henderson	E Ahern	50-1	22/32
2009	Darley Sun	3	8-6	D Simcock	A Atzeni (3)	9-2f	8/32
2010	Aaim To Prosper	7	8-2	B Meehan	L-P Beuzelin (3)	16-1	3/32
2011	Never Can Tell	4	8-11	J Osborne	L Dettori	25-1	36/33
2012	Aaim To Prosper	8	9-10	B Meehan	K Fallon	66-1	1/34
2013	Scatter Dice	4	8-8	M Johnston	S de Sousa	66-1	18/33
2014	Big Easy	7	8-7	P Hobbs	T Queally	66-1	2/33

THE SECOND leg of the Autumn Double. This is another race in which a long sweeping bend makes the draw far more important than you would think from the trip with Caracciola and Never Can Tell the only winners drawn higher than 18 since Turnpole in 1997. Generally punters are too swayed by a young improver as Darley Sun is one of only two winning three-year-olds in 22 years and he was the only favourite to win in the last eight years during a spell that has seen winners returned twice at 66-1 and once at 50-1. One of the big-priced winners, Aaim To Prosper, reinforced the significance of previous form in the race as he followed up his victory two years earlier. Scatter Dice is the only winner since Old Red in 1995 not to have been previously successful over at least 2m, which includes several hurdlers as just four of the last 19 runnings didn't have a recognised hurdler in the first two. The Northumberland Plate is the best trial having thrown up nine of the last 21 winners.

November Handicap (1m4f) Doncaster

2005	Come On Jonny	3	8-0	R Beckett	N de Souza	14-1	18/21
2006	Group Captain	4	9-5	R Charlton	R Hughes	10-1	20/20
2007	Malt Or Mash	3	8-10	R Hannon Sr	R Moore	5-1	13/21
2008	Tropical Strait	5	8-13	D Arbuthnot	M Dwyer	20-1	22/21
2009	Charm School	4	8-12	J Gosden	J Fortune	17-2	14/23
2010	Times Up	4	8-13	J Dunlop	D O'Neill	14-1	9/22
2011	Zuider Zee	4	8-13	J Gosden	R Havlin	8-1	20/23
2012	Art Scholar	5	8-7	M Appleby	F Norton	20-1	9/23
2013	Conduct	6	9-2	W Haggas	S Sanders	8-1	21/23
2014	Open Eagle	5	8-12	D O'Meara	D Tudhope	15-2f	18/23

THE LAST big betting heat of the season and one that has changed in recent years due to the lack of three-year-olds able to get a run. When Malt Or Mash won in 2007 that age group had won 14 of the last 24 renewals, and three-year-olds still have to be feared – bear in mind that four of the last eight to come out on top had been unraced as a juvenile and were therefore late developers. However, the last three winners were five or six, a massive change given just five of the previous 32 had been older than four. A big weight remains a major drawback as seven of the last eight winners carried less than 9st. Ten of the last 15 winners were returned at double-figure odds and favourites have a desperate record, with Open Eagle the first to oblige since Snow Princess in 1995.

Big-Race Dates, Fixtures and Track Facts

Fixtures

Key - Flat, **Jumps**

March

28	Saturday	........Doncaster, **Stratford**, Chelmsford City, **Uttoxeter**, Kempton
29	Sunday	.... Doncaster, **Ascot**
30	Monday	.... **Warwick, Chepstow, Kempton**
31	Tuesday	.... **Huntingdon, Exeter**, Southwell

April

1	Wednesday	.... **Towcester**, Chelmsford City, Kempton, **Wincanton**
2	Thursday	......................................**Ludlow, Taunton**, Wolverhampton
3	Friday	....Musselburgh, Lingfield
4	Saturday	.... **Carlisle**, Kempton, **Haydock, Newton Abbot**
5	Sunday	.... Musselburgh, **Plumpton, Sedgefield**
6	Monday	.... Redcar, **Fakenham, Chepstow, Huntingdon, Plumpton**,
		.... **Market Rasen**, Wolverhampton
7	Tuesday	.... Pontefract, Chelmsford City, Lingfield
8	Wednesday	............................Catterick, Nottingham, Kempton, Lingfield
9	Thursday	...........................**Aintree**, Southwell, Chelmsford City, **Taunton**
10	Friday	..........................**Aintree**, Leicester, **Fontwell**, Wolverhampton
11	Saturday	..........**Aintree**, Wolverhampton, **Chepstow**, Newcastle, Lingfield
12	Sunday	.... **Market Rasen, Ffos Las**
13	Monday	.... **Kelso**, Windsor, Redcar
14	Tuesday	.... **Carlisle**, Southwell, **Exeter**
15	Wednesday	........................Beverley, **Cheltenham**, Kempton, Newmarket
16	Thursday	.........Ripon, **Cheltenham**, Chelmsford City, Newmarket
17	Friday	............................**Ayr, Southwell**, Bath, **Fontwell**, Newbury
18	Saturday	...... **Ayr, Bangor**, Newbury, Thirsk, Nottingham, Wolverhampton
19	Sunday	....**Stratford, Wincanton**
20	Monday	.... **Hexham, Kempton**, Pontefract, **Newton Abbot**, Windsor
21	Tuesday	...................**Ludlow**, Brighton, Wolverhampton, **Exeter**, Kempton
22	Wednesday	.....................Catterick, Epsom, **Perth, Ffos Las, Taunton**
23	Thursday	................................Beverley, Southwell, Bath, **Perth, Warwick**
24	Friday	..........................Doncaster, **Chepstow, Perth, Plumpton**, Sandown
25	Saturday	........Doncaster, Leicester, **Sandown**, Haydock, Wolverhampton,
		....Ripon
26	Sunday	.... Wetherby, Chelmsford City
27	Monday	......................Ayr, Southwell, Kempton, Wolverhampton, Windsor
28	Tuesday	.... Newcastle, Nottingham, Brighton, Wolverhampton,
		....Chelmsford City
29	Wednesday	......Pontefract, **Cheltenham**, Ascot, Wolverhampton, Lingfield
30	Thursday	..........Redcar, **Towcester**, Lingfield, **Sedgefield, Newton Abbot**

May

1	Friday	.... Musselburgh, **Bangor**, Chepstow, **Fontwell**, Lingfield
2	Saturday	............Doncaster, Newmarket, Goodwood, **Hexham, Uttoxeter**,
		....Thirsk

| 3 | Sunday | Hamilton, Newmarket, Salisbury |

3 Sunday... Hamilton, Newmarket, Salisbury
4 Monday................................Beverley, **Warwick**, Bath, **Kempton**, Windsor
5 Tuesday.......................Catterick, **Fakenham**, Brighton, **Sedgefield**, **Exeter**
6 Wednesday..............**Kelso**, Chester, Brighton, **Uttoxeter**, Chelmsford City
7 Thursday......... **Carlisle**, Chester, Ascot, **Newton Abbot**, **Worcester**, **Wincanton**
8 Friday...........Ripon, Chester, Ascot, **Market Rasen**, Lingfield, Nottingham
9 Saturday ....Haydock (Mixed), Nottingham, Ascot, **Hexham**, **Warwick**,
....Lingfield, Thirsk
10 Sunday.. **Ludlow**, **Plumpton**
11 Monday............................. Doncaster, **Towcester**, Windsor, Musselburgh,
....Wolverhampton
12 Tuesday...................... Beverley, **Southwell**, Chelmsford City, **Sedgefield**,
.... **Wincanton**
13 Wednesday................................... **Perth**, Bath, York, **Kempton**, Newcastle
14 Thursday.............................. **Perth**, Newmarket, **Fontwell**, York, Salisbury
15 Friday....................................**Aintree**, Newmarket, Newbury, Hamilton, York
16 Saturday ...... Doncaster, **Bangor**, Newbury, Thirsk, Newmarket, **Uttoxeter**
17 Sunday.. Ripon, **Market Rasen**, **Stratford**
18 Monday...................... Redcar, Leicester, Windsor, Southwell, **Towcester**
19 Tuesday....................Newcastle, Nottingham, Chelmsford City, Chepstow,
....**Newton Abbot**
20 Wednesday......................... Ayr, **Southwell**, Kempton, **Warwick**, Lingfield
21 Thursday..................... Ayr, Nottingham, Goodwood, **Wetherby**, Sandown
22 Friday.................... Haydock, **Worcester**, Bath, Musselburgh, Goodwood,
....Pontefract
23 Saturday ....Beverley, **Ffos Las**, Catterick, Goodwood, Haydock,
....Salisbury
24 Sunday..**Kelso**, **Uttoxeter**, **Fontwell**
25 Monday................................Carlisle, Leicester, Windsor, **Cartmel**, Redcar
26 Tuesday...................... **Hexham**, **Huntingdon**, Lingfield, Redcar, Leicester
27 Wednesday.............. **Cartmel**, Kempton, Hamilton, **Newton Abbot**, Thirsk
28 Thursday..................Haydock, **Worcester**, Lingfield, **Wetherby**, Sandown
29 Friday ....Catterick, Newmarket, Brighton, Haydock, **Stratford**,
....Newcastle
30 Saturday ....Haydock, Chester, Chepstow, York, Newmarket, **Stratford**
31 Sunday..**Fakenham**, Nottingham

June

1 Monday.......................................Carlisle, Leicester, Lingfield, Windsor
2 Tuesday................................ Ripon, **Southwell**, Brighton, Wolverhampton
3 Wednesday............ Ripon, Nottingham, Chelmsford City, Wolverhampton,
....**Fontwell**
4 Thursday............Hamilton, Wolverhampton, **Ffos Las**, Kempton, Lingfield
5 Friday ....Epsom, Catterick, **Market Rasen**, Bath, Goodwood
6 Saturday .... Epsom, Doncaster, **Worcester**, **Hexham**, Lingfield,
....Musselburgh, Newcastle
7 Sunday... **Perth**, Goodwood
8 Monday.. Ayr, Windsor, Pontefract, Thirsk
9 Tuesday.............................. **Southwell**, **Fontwell**, Lingfield, Salisbury
10 Wednesday....................Beverley, Brighton, Hamilton, Kempton, Haydock
11 Thursday.............. Haydock, Nottingham, Newbury, **Uttoxeter**, **Worcester**

12 Friday .... **Aintree**, Chepstow, York, Goodwood, **Newton Abbot**,
.... Sandown
13 Saturday .... **Hexham**, Chester, Bath, Musselburgh, Leicester, Lingfield,
.... York, Sandown
14 Sunday.. Doncaster, Salisbury
15 Monday................................. Carlisle, Nottingham, Windsor, **Southwell**
16 Tuesday......................... Royal Ascot, Beverley, **Stratford**, Thirsk, Brighton
17 Wednesday...... Royal Ascot, Hamilton, **Uttoxeter**, Ripon, Chelmsford City
18 Thursday...........Royal Ascot, Ripon, Leicester, Chelmsford City, **Ffos Las**,
.... Lingfield
19 Friday .... Royal Ascot, Redcar, **Market Rasen**, Newmarket, Goodwood
20 Saturday ....Royal Ascot, Ayr, Newmarket, Haydock, Lingfield, Redcar
21 Sunday................................... **Hexham**, **Worcester**, Pontefract
22 Monday ....Wetherby, Wolverhampton, Chepstow, Windsor
23 Tuesday.................... Beverley, Leicester, Brighton, **Newton Abbot**
24 Wednesday ....Carlisle, **Worcester**, Bath, Kempton, Salisbury
25 Thursday............ Hamilton, Newmarket, Newbury, Newcastle, Nottingham
26 Friday .... **Cartmel**, Chester, Doncaster, Newmarket, Newcastle,
.... Yarmouth
27 Saturday ....Doncaster, Chester, Lingfield, Newcastle, Newmarket,
.... Windsor
28 Sunday..**Cartmel**, **Uttoxeter**, Windsor
29 Monday .... Musselburgh, Wolverhampton, Windsor, Pontefract
30 Tuesday.................................... Hamilton, **Stratford**, Brighton, Chepstow

July

1   Wednesday.................................**Perth**, **Worcester**, Bath, Thirsk,Kempton
2   Thursday.............................. Haydock, Yarmouth, Epsom, **Perth**, Newbury
3   Friday ....Beverley, **Newton Abbot**, Doncaster, Sandown, Haydock
4   Saturday .... Beverley, Leicester, Sandown, Carlisle, Nottingham, Haydock
5   Sunday...Ayr, **Market Rasen**
6   Monday .... Ayr, **Worcester**, Windsor, Ripon
7   Tuesday......................... Pontefract, Uttoxeter, Brighton, Wolverhampton
8   Wednesday ....Catterick, Yarmouth, Bath, Kempton, Lingfield
9   Thursday.....................Carlisle, Newmarket, Epsom, Doncaster, Newbury
10 Friday .... York, Chester, Ascot, Newmarket, Chepstow
11 Saturday ....Hamilton, Chester, Ascot, York, Newmarket, Salisbury
12 Sunday...**Perth**, **Southwell**, **Stratford**
13 Monday .... Ayr, Wolverhampton, Windsor, Wetherby
14 Tuesday.. Beverley, Yarmouth, Bath, Thirsk
15 Wednesday ....Catterick, **Uttoxeter**, Lingfield, **Worcester**, Sandown
16 Thursday...................... Doncaster, Leicester, Chepstow, Hamilton, Epsom
17 Friday ....Hamilton, Newmarket, Newbury, Haydock, Nottingham,
.... Pontefract
18 Saturday .... **Cartmel**, Chester, Lingfield, Haydock, **Market Rasen**,
.... Newbury, Ripon, Newmarket
19 Sunday.................................Redcar, **Stratford**, **Newton Abbot**
20 Monday....................................... Ayr, Windsor, Beverley, **Cartmel**
21 Tuesday........................ Musselburgh, Chelmsford City, Wetherby, Ffos Las
22 Wednesday ....Catterick, Leicester, Bath, Lingfield, Sandown
23 Thursday............... Doncaster, **Worcester**, Newbury, Yarmouth, Sandown
24 Friday ....Thirsk, Newmarket, Ascot, York, **Uttoxeter**, Chepstow

25	Saturday	Newcastle, Newmarket, Ascot, York, Lingfield, Salisbury
26	Sunday	Carlisle, **Uttoxeter**, Pontefract
27	Monday	Ayr, Southwell, **Newton Abbot**, Windsor
28	Tuesday	Beverley, **Worcester**, Goodwood, **Perth**, Yarmouth
29	Wednesday	**Perth**, Leicester, Goodwood, Redcar, Sandown
30	Thursday	Nottingham, Epsom, **Stratford**, Ffos Las, Goodwood
31	Friday	Musselburgh, **Bangor**, Bath, Thirsk, Newmarket, Goodwood

August

1	Saturday	Doncaster, Newmarket, Goodwood, Hamilton, Lingfield, Thirsk
2	Sunday	Chester, Chepstow, **Market Rasen**
3	Monday	Carlisle, Nottingham, Windsor, Ripon
4	Tuesday	Catterick, Chelmsford City, Ripon, Salisbury
5	Wednesday	Pontefract, Yarmouth, Brighton, Chepstow, Kempton
6	Thursday	Haydock, Southwell, Brighton, Newcastle, Yarmouth, Sandown
7	Friday	Haydock, Newmarket, Brighton, Musselburgh, Lingfield
8	Saturday	Ayr, Newmarket, Ascot, Haydock, Lingfield, Redcar
9	Sunday	Leicester, Windsor
10	Monday	Ayr, Wolverhampton, Windsor, Thirsk
11	Tuesday	Carlisle, Nottingham, Ffos Las, Lingfield
12	Wednesday	Beverley, Bath, Kempton, **Newton Abbot**, Salisbury
13	Thursday	Beverley, Yarmouth, **Fontwell**, Lingfield, Salisbury
14	Friday	Catterick, Newmarket, Newbury, Newcastle, Nottingham
15	Saturday	Doncaster, **Market Rasen**, Lingfield, Ripon, Newmarket, Newbury
16	Sunday	Pontefract, **Southwell**
17	Monday	Thirsk, Chelmsford City, Kempton, Windsor
18	Tuesday	Ripon, Leicester, Chelmsford City, Kempton
19	Wednesday	Carlisle, **Worcester**, Ffos Las, York, Kempton
20	Thursday	Hamilton, **Stratford**, Chepstow, York, Lingfield
21	Friday	York, **Bangor**, Salisbury, Wolverhampton, Sandown
22	Saturday	**Perth**, Chester, Bath, York, Chelmsford City, **Newton Abbot**, Sandown
23	Sunday	**Worcester**, Brighton
24	Monday	Carlisle, Leicester, Brighton, Kempton
25	Tuesday	Yarmouth, Brighton, **Fontwell**, Newbury
26	Wednesday	Catterick, Bath, Musselburgh, Kempton, Lingfield
27	Thursday	Musselburgh, **Southwell**, **Sedgefield**, **Stratford**, Wolverhampton
28	Friday	Hamilton, Newmarket, Ffos Las (Mixed), Newcastle, Goodwood, Thirsk
29	Saturday	Beverley, Newmarket, Goodwood, **Cartmel**, Windsor, Redcar
30	Sunday	Beverley, Yarmouth, Goodwood
31	Monday	**Cartmel**, **Huntingdon**, Chepstow, Newcastle, Epsom, Ripon

September

1	Tuesday	Hamilton, Epsom, Goodwood, **Newton Abbot**
2	Wednesday	**Southwell**, Bath, **Worcester**, Lingfield
3	Thursday	Haydock, Chelmsford City, **Sedgefield**, Salisbury
4	Friday	Haydock, Ascot, Musselburgh, Kempton, Newcastle

GLORIOUS GOODWOOD: the summer showpiece – now officially known as the Qatar Goodwood Festival – runs from July 28 to August 1 this year

5	Saturday	.... Haydock, **Stratford**, Ascot, Thirsk, Wolverhampton, Kempton
6	Sunday	.... York, **Fontwell**
7	Monday	....**Perth**, Brighton, Windsor
8	Tuesday	....**Perth**, Leicester, Redcar, **Worcester**
9	Wednesday	.... Carlisle, **Uttoxeter**, Kempton, Doncaster
10	Thursday	...........................Doncaster, Chelmsford City, Chepstow, Epsom
11	Friday	....Doncaster, Chester, Salisbury, Sandown
12	Saturday	.... Doncaster, Chester, Bath, Musselburgh, Lingfield
13	Sunday	.... Bath, Ffos Las
14	Monday	....**Stratford**, Brighton, Wolverhampton
15	Tuesday	.... Carlisle, Yarmouth, Chepstow, Catterick
16	Wednesday	.... Beverley, Yarmouth, Sandown, **Kelso**
17	Thursday	..................................Ayr, Yarmouth, Chelmsford City, Pontefract
18	Friday	...............................Ayr, Newbury, **Hexham**, **Newton Abbot**
19	Saturday	.................Ayr, Newmarket, Newbury, Catterick, Wolverhampton
20	Sunday	....Hamilton, **Uttoxeter**, **Plumpton**
21	Monday	....Hamilton, Leicester, Kempton
22	Tuesday	..............................Beverley, **Warwick**, Kempton, Lingfield
23	Wednesday	....**Perth**, Goodwood, Redcar, Kempton
24	Thursday	.... **Perth**, Newmarket, Chelmsford City, Pontefract
25	Friday	.... Haydock, Newmarket, Wolverhampton, **Worcester**

26 Saturday .... Haydock, Chester, Chelmsford City, Ripon, **Market Rasen**, ... Newmarket
27 Sunday..Musselburgh, Epsom
28 Monday... Hamilton, Bath, **Newton Abbot**
29 Tuesday................................ Ayr, **Southwell**, **Sedgefield**, Wolverhampton
30 Wednesday........................... Nottingham, **Chepstow**, Kempton, Salisbury

October

1 Thursday...........................Newcastle, **Bangor**, Chelmsford City, **Warwick**
2 Friday ....**Hexham**, Wolverhampton, Ascot, **Fontwell**
3 Saturday .... Redcar, Newmarket, Ascot, Wolverhampton, **Fontwell**
4 Sunday..**Kelso**, **Huntingdon**, **Uttoxeter**
5 Monday...................................Pontefract, **Market Rasen**, Windsor
6 Tuesday .... Catterick, Leicester, Brighton, Kempton
7 Wednesday...........................**Ludlow**, Kempton, Nottingham, **Towcester**
8 Thursday .... Ayr, **Worcester**, Chelmsford City, **Exeter**
9 Friday .... York, Newmarket, **Fakenham**, **Newton Abbot**, Wolverhampton
10 Saturday ....**Hexham**, Newmarket, Chelmsford City, York, **Chepstow**
11 Sunday..**Chepstow**, Goodwood
12 Monday.....................................**Sedgefield**, Salisbury, Windsor
13 Tuesday .... Newcastle, **Huntingdon**, Leicester, Wolverhampton
14 Wednesday.....................**Wetherby**, Nottingham, Kempton, **Worcester**
15 Thursday.......................**Carlisle**, **Uttoxeter**, Brighton, Chelmsford City
16 Friday ....Haydock, **Wincanton**, Redcar, Wolverhampton
17 Saturday .... Catterick, **Market Rasen**, Ascot, **Stratford**, **Ffos Las**, ... Wolverhampton
18 Sunday...Bath, **Kempton**
19 Monday...................................Pontefract, **Plumpton**, Windsor
20 Tuesday................................Wolverhampton, **Exeter**, Yarmouth, Lingfield
21 Wednesday........................... Newmarket, **Fontwell**, **Worcester**, Kempton
22 Thursday....................**Carlisle**, **Ludlow**, Chelmsford City, **Southwell**
23 Friday .... Doncaster, **Cheltenham**, Newbury, Wolverhampton
24 Saturday .... Doncaster, **Cheltenham**, Chelmsford City, **Kelso**, Newbury
25 Sunday...**Aintree**, **Wincanton**
26 Monday...**Ayr**, Leicester, Redcar
27 Tuesday.................... Catterick, **Bangor**, Wolverhampton, Yarmouth
28 Wednesday................**Fakenham**, Chelmsford City, Nottingham, Kempton
29 Thursday.................... **Sedgefield**, **Stratford**, Chelmsford City, Lingfield
30 Friday .... **Wetherby**, Newmarket, **Uttoxeter**, Wolverhampton
31 Saturday .... **Ayr**, Newmarket, **Ascot**, **Wetherby**, Wolverhampton

November

1 Sunday...**Carlisle**, **Huntingdon**
2 Monday ....**Ludlow**, **Kempton**, **Plumpton**
3 Tuesday...................................Redcar, Southwell, **Exeter**, Wolverhampton
4 Wednesday............................. Nottingham, **Chepstow**, **Warwick**, Kempton
5 Thursday........**Musselburgh**, **Market Rasen**, Chelmsford City, **Towcester**
6 Friday .... **Hexham**, Chelmsford City, **Musselburgh**, **Fontwell**
7 Saturday ....**Aintree**, Chelmsford City, Doncaster, **Wincanton**, **Kelso**
8 Sunday...**Ffos Las**, **Sandown**
9 Monday...................................**Carlisle**, **Southwell**, Kempton
10 Tuesday................... **Sedgefield**, **Huntingdon**, **Lingfield**, Wolverhampton

11	Wednesday	**Ayr**, **Bangor**, **Exeter**, Kempton
12	Thursday	**Ludlow**, Chelmsford City, Southwell, **Taunton**
13	Friday	**Newcastle**, **Cheltenham**, Lingfield, Wolverhampton
14	Saturday	**Wetherby**, **Cheltenham**, Lingfield, **Uttoxeter**, Wolverhampton
15	Sunday	**Cheltenham**, **Fontwell**
16	Monday	**Leicester**, **Plumpton**, Wolverhampton
17	Tuesday	**Fakenham**, Lingfield, **Southwell**
18	Wednesday	Hexham, Warwick, Chepstow, Kempton
19	Thursday	**Market Rasen**, Chelmsford City, Lingfield, **Wincanton**
20	Friday	**Haydock**, Wolverhampton, **Ascot**, **Ffos Las**
21	Saturday	**Haydock**, **Huntingdon**, **Ascot**, Wolverhampton, Lingfield
22	Sunday	**Uttoxeter**, **Exeter**
23	Monday	**Ludlow**, Chelmsford City, **Kempton**
24	Tuesday	**Sedgefield**, Southwell, **Lingfield**
25	Wednesday	**Wetherby**, **Fontwell**, Kempton, Lingfield
26	Thursday	Southwell, Chelmsford City, **Newbury**, **Taunton**
27	Friday	**Doncaster**, Wolverhampton, **Newbury**, **Musselburgh**
28	Saturday	**Doncaster**, **Bangor**, **Newbury**, **Newcastle**, Wolverhampton
29	Sunday	**Carlisle**, **Leicester**
30	Monday	Wolverhampton, Kempton, **Plumpton**

December

1	Tuesday	**Southwell**, **Lingfield**, Wolverhampton
2	Wednesday	**Catterick**, **Ludlow**, Kempton, Lingfield
3	Thursday	**Leicester**, Kempton, **Market Rasen**, **Wincanton**
4	Friday	**Sedgefield**, Wolverhampton, **Exeter**, **Sandown**
5	Saturday	**Aintree**, Wolverhampton, **Chepstow**, **Wetherby**, **Sandown**
6	Sunday	**Kelso**, **Huntingdon**
7	Monday	**Musselburgh**, Chelmsford City, Lingfield
8	Tuesday	Southwell, **Fontwell**, **Uttoxeter**
9	Wednesday	**Hexham**, **Leicester**, Kempton, Lingfield
10	Thursday	**Newcastle**, **Warwick**, Chelmsford City, **Taunton**
11	Friday	**Doncaster**, **Bangor**, **Cheltenham**, Wolverhampton
12	Saturday	**Doncaster**, **Cheltenham**, **Lingfield**, Southwell, Wolverhampton
13	Sunday	**Carlisle**, **Southwell**
14	Monday	Wolverhampton, **Ffos Las**, **Plumpton**
15	Tuesday	**Catterick**, Southwell, Kempton
16	Wednesday	**Ludlow**, Kempton, Lingfield, **Newbury**
17	Thursday	Southwell, Chelmsford City, **Towcester**, **Exeter**
18	Friday	Southwell, **Ascot**, **Uttoxeter**, Wolverhampton
19	Saturday	**Haydock**, **Ascot**, **Newcastle**, Lingfield
20	Sunday	**Fakenham**, Lingfield
21	Monday	**Bangor**, Chelmsford City, Wolverhampton
22	Tuesday	**Ayr**, Southwell, **Lingfield**, Wolverhampton
26	Saturday	**Sedgefield**, **Huntingdon**, **Fontwell**, **Wetherby**, **Market Rasen**, **Kempton**, Wolverhampton, **Wincanton**
27	Sunday	**Wetherby**, Southwell, Chelmsford City, **Chepstow**, **Kempton**
28	Monday	**Catterick**, **Leicester**, Lingfield
29	Tuesday	**Doncaster**, Southwell, **Newbury**, **Kelso**
30	Wednesday	**Haydock**, Lingfield, **Taunton**
31	Thursday	**Uttoxeter**, Lingfield, **Warwick**

Big-race dates

March
28 Mar   Doncaster .... Lincoln (Heritage Handicap)

April
3 Apr   Lingfield .... All-Weather Championship Finals
15 Apr   Newmarket .... Nell Gwyn Stakes (Group 3)
16 Apr   Newmarket .... Earl of Sefton Stakes (Group 3)
16 Apr   Newmarket .... Craven Stakes (Group 3)
18 Apr   Newbury .... Fred Darling Stakes (Group 3)
18 Apr   Newbury .... Greenham Stakes (Group 3)
18 Apr   Newbury .... John Porter Stakes (Group 3)
24 Apr   Sandown Park .... Gordon Richards Stakes (Group 3)
24 Apr   Sandown Park .... bet365 Mile (Group 2)
29 Apr   Ascot .... Sagaro Stakes (Group 3)

May
2 May   Newmarket .... 2,000 Guineas (Group 1)
2 May   Newmarket .... Dahlia Stakes (Group 3)
3 May   Newmarket .... 1,000 Guineas (Group 1)
3 May   Newmarket .... Jockey Club Stakes (Group 2)
6 May   Chester .... Chester Cup (Heritage Handicap)
7 May   Chester .... Chester Vase (Group 3)
7 May   Chester .... Huxley Stakes (Group 3)
8 May   Chester .... Ormonde Stakes (Group 3)
8 May   Chester .... Dee Stakes (Group 3)
9 May   Ascot .... Victoria Cup (Heritage Handicap)
9 May   Lingfield Park .... Derby Trial (Group 3)
13 May   York .... Duke of York Stakes (Group 2)
13 May   York .... Musidora Stakes (Group 3)
14 May   York .... Dante Stakes (Group 2)
14 May   York .... Middleton Stakes (Group 3)
15 May   York .... Yorkshire Cup (Group 2)
16 May   Newbury .... Lockinge Stakes (Group 1)
23 May   Haydock Park .... Temple Stakes (Group 2)
28 May   Sandown Park .... Henry II Stakes (Group 2)
28 May   Sandown Park .... Brigadier Gerard Stakes (Group 3)
30 May   Haydock Park .... John of Gaunt Stakes (Group 3)

June
5 Jun   Epsom .... Coronation Cup (Group 1)
5 Jun   Epsom .... Oaks (Group 1)
6 Jun   Epsom .... The Derby (Group 1)
6 Jun   Epsom .... Princess Elizabeth Stakes (Group 3)
6 Jun   Haydock Park .... John Of Gaunt Stakes (Group 3)
16 Jun   Royal Ascot .... King's Stand Stakes (Group 1)
16 Jun   Royal Ascot .... Queen Anne Stakes (Group 1)
16 Jun   Royal Ascot .... St James's Palace Stakes (Group 1)
16 Jun   Royal Ascot .... Coventry Stakes (Group 2)
17 Jun   Royal Ascot .... Prince of \Wales's Stakes (Group 1)
17 Jun   Royal Ascot .... Queen Mary Stakes (Group 2)
17 Jun   Royal Ascot .... Windsor Forest Stakes (Group 2)
17 Jun   Royal Ascot .... Jersey Stakes (Group 3)

17 Jun	Royal Ascot	Royal Hunt Cup (Heritage Handicap)
18 Jun	Royal Ascot	Gold Cup (Group 1)
18 Jun	Royal Ascot	Ribblesdale Stakes (Group 2)
18 Jun	Royal Ascot	Norfolk Stakes (Group 2)
19 Jun	Royal Ascot	Coronation Stakes (Group 1)
19 Jun	Royal Ascot	Three-Year-Old Sprint (Group 1)
19 Jun	Royal Ascot	King Edward VII Stakes (Group 2)
19 Jun	Royal Ascot	Albany Stakes (Group 3)
19 Jun	Royal Ascot	Queen's Vase (Group 3)
20 Jun	Royal Ascot	Golden Jubilee Stakes (Group 1)
20 Jun	Royal Ascot	Hardwicke Stakes (Group 2)
20 Jun	Royal Ascot	Wokingham (Heritage Handicap)
27 Jun	Newcastle	Northumberland Plate (Heritage Handicap)
27 Jun	Newmarket	Criterion Stakes (Group 3)

July

4 Jul	Haydock Park	Lancashire Oaks (Group 2)
4 Jul	Sandown Park	Coral-Eclipse Stakes (Group 1)
9 Jul	Newmarket	Falmouth Stakes (Group 1)
9 Jul	Newmarket	Cherry Hinton Stakes (Group 2)
10 Jul	Newmarket	Princess of Wales's Stakes (Group 2)
10 Jul	Newmarket	July Stakes (Group 2)
10 Jul	York	Summer Stakes (Group 3)
11 Jul	Newmarket	July Cup (Group 1)
11 Jul	Newmarket	Superlative Stakes (Group 2)
11 Jul	Newmarket	Bunbury Cup (Heritage Handicap)
11 Jul	York	John Smith's Cup (Heritage Handicap)
18 Jul	Newbury	Hackwood Stakes (Group 3)
25 Jul	Ascot	King George VI and Queen Elizabeth Stakes (Group 1)
25 Jul	Ascot	Summer Mile (Group 2)
25 Jul	York	York Stakes (Group 2)
28 Jul	Goodwood	Lennox Stakes (Group 2)
28 Jul	Goodwood	Gordon Stakes (Group 3)
28 Jul	Goodwood	Molecomb Stakes (Group 3)
29 Jul	Goodwood	Sussex Stakes (Group 1)
29 Jul	Goodwood	Vintage Stakes (Group 2)
30 Jul	Goodwood	Goodwood Cup (Group 2)
30 Jul	Goodwood	King George Stakes (Group 3)
31 Jul	Goodwood	Richmond Stakes (Group 2)
31 Jul	Goodwood	Oak Tree Stakes (Group 3)

August

1 Aug	Goodwood	Nassau Stakes (Group 1)
1 Aug	Goodwood	Stewards' Cup (Heritage Handicap)
8 Aug	Ascot	Shergar Cup Day
8 Aug	Haydock Park	Rose of Lancaster Stakes (Group 3)
8 Aug	Newmarket	Sweet Solera Stakes (Group 3)
13 Aug	Salisbury	Sovereign Stakes (Group 3)
15 Aug	Newbury	Hungerford Stakes (Group 2)
15 Aug	Newbury	Geoffrey Freer Stakes (Group 3)
19 Aug	York	Juddmonte International (Group 1)
19 Aug	York	Great Voltigeur Stakes (Group 2)
19 Aug	York	Acomb Stakes (Group 3)
20 Aug	York	Yorkshire Oaks (Group 1)
20 Aug	York	Lowther Stakes (Group 2)
21 Aug	York	Gimcrack Stakes (Group 2)

21 Aug	York	Nunthorpe Stakes (Group 1)
22 Aug	York	Lonsdale Cup (Group 2)
22 Aug	York	Ebor (Heritage Handicap)
22 Aug	Sandown Park	Solario Stakes (Group 3)
29 Aug	Goodwood	Celebration Mile (Group 2)
29 Aug	Goodwood	Prestige Stakes (Group 3)
29 Aug	Windsor	Winter Hill Stakes (Group 3)
30 Aug	Goodwood	Supreme Stakes (Group 3)

September

5 Sep	Haydock Park	Sprint Cup (Group 1)
5 Sep	Kempton Park	Sirenia Stakes (Group 3)
5 Sep	Kempton Park	September Stakes (Group 3)
10 Sep	Doncaster	May Hill Stakes (Group 2)
10 Sep	Doncaster	Park Hill Stakes (Group 2)
11 Sep	Doncaster	Doncaster Cup (Group 2)
11 Sep	Doncaster	Flying Childers Stakes (Group 2)
12 Sep	Doncaster	St Leger (Group 1)
12 Sep	Doncaster	Park Stakes (Group 2)
12 Sep	Doncaster	Champagne Stakes (Group 2)
12 Sep	Doncaster	Portland (Heritage Handicap)
19 Sep	Ayr	Firth Of Clyde Stakes (Group 3)
19 Sep	Ayr	Ayr Gold Cup (Heritage Handicap)
19 Sep	Newbury	Mill Reef Stakes (Group 2)
19 Sep	Newbury	World Trophy (Group 3)
19 Sep	Newbury	Arc Trial (Group 3)
24 Sep	Newmarket	Somerville Tattersall Stakes (Group 3)
25 Sep	Newmarket	Rockfel Stakes (Group 2)
25 Sep	Newmarket	Joel Stakes (Group 3)
26 Sep	Newmarket	Middle Park Stakes (Group 1)
26 Sep	Newmarket	Cheveley Park Stakes (Group 1)
26 Sep	Newmarket	Royal Lodge Stakes (Group 2)
26 Sep	Newmarket	Cambridgeshire (Heritage Handicap)

October

3 Oct	Ascot	Cumberland Lodge Stakes (Group 3)
3 Oct	Ascot	Bengough Stakes (Group 3)
3 Oct	Newmarket	Sun Chariot Stakes (Group 1)
3 Oct	Newmarket	Oh So Sharp Stakes (Group 3)
9 Oct	Newmarket	Fillies' Mile (Group 1)
9 Oct	Newmarket	Challenge Stakes (Group 2)
9 Oct	Newmarket	Cornwallis Stakes (Group 3)
10 Oct	Newmarket	Dewhurst Stakes (Group 1)
10 Oct	Newmarket	Autumn Stakes (Group 3)
10 Oct	Newmarket	Darley Stakes (Group 3)
10 Oct	Newmarket	Cesarewitch (Heritage Handicap)
17 Oct	Ascot	Queen Elizabeth II Stakes (Group 1)
17 Oct	Ascot	Champion Stakes (Group 1)
17 Oct	Ascot	Champions Sprint (Group 2)
17 Oct	Ascot	Champions Filly & Mare Stakes (Group 2)
17 Oct	Ascot	Champions Long Distance Cup (Group 3)
24 Oct	Doncaster	Racing Post Trophy (Group 1)
24 Oct	Newbury	Horris Hill Stakes (Group 3)
24 Oct	Newbury	St Simon Stakes (Group 3)

November

| 7 Nov | Doncaster | November (Heritage Handicap) |

Track Facts

WANT TO size up the layout and undulations of the course where your fancy's about to line up? Over the next 30-odd pages, we bring you three-dimensional maps of all Britain's Flat tracks, allowing you to see at a glance the task facing your selection. The maps come to you courtesy of the Racing Post's website (www.racingpost.com).

We've listed the top dozen trainers and jockeys at each course, ranked by strike-rate, with a breakdown of their relevant statistics over the last five years. We've also included addresses, phone numbers, directions and fixture lists for each track, together with Racing Post standard times for all you clock-watchers.

ASCOT..192	LINGFIELD (SAND)....................................211
AYR...193	MUSSELBURGH...212
BATH...194	NEWBURY...213
BEVERLEY 195	NEWCASTLE...214
BRIGHTON 196	NEWMARKET (ROWLEY)..................................215
CARLISLE 197	NEWMARKET (JULY) 216
CATTERICK..198	NOTTINGHAM 218
CHELMSFORD...199	PONTEFRACT..219
CHEPSTOW...200	REDCAR..220
CHESTER..201	RIPON...221
DONCASTER 202	SALISBURY 222
EPSOM..203	SANDOWN...223
FFOS LAS...204	SOUTHWELL...224
GOODWOOD...205	THIRSK 225
HAMILTON 206	WETHERBY 226
HAYDOCK..207	WINDSOR...227
KEMPTON 208	WOLVERHAMPTON.......................................228
LEICESTER..209	YARMOUTH 229
LINGFIELD (TURF) 210	YORK..230

ASCOT

Ascot, Berkshire SL5 7JX
0870 7227 227

How to get there Road: M4 junction 6 or M3 junction 3 on to A332. Rail: Frequent service from Reading or Waterloo

Features RH, stiff climb for final mile on round course

2015 Fixtures April 29, May 8-9, June 16-20, July 10-11, 24-25, August 8, September 4-5, October 2-3, 17

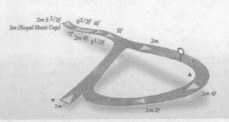

O Winning Post
⌐ Startpoint
▲ Highest Point
▼ Lowest Point
⌐ Open ditch
Water jump
/ Fence

Racing Post standard times

5f	59.5	1m2f	2min5
6f	1min12.4	1m4f	2min28.9
7f	1min25.6	2m	3min22
1m (str)	1min38.8	2m4f	4min20
1m (rnd)	1min39.8	2m5f159yds	4min45

Trainers	Wins-Runs	%	2yo	3yo+	£1 level stks
John Gosden	28-158	18	3-14	25-144	+45.57
Richard Hannon Snr	24-244	10	12-105	12-139	-60.66
Mark Johnston	18-241	7	1-42	17-199	-71.84
Sir Michael Stoute	14-107	13	1-7	13-100	-43.63
A P O'Brien	14-103	14	3-18	11-85	-11.59
Saeed bin Suroor	13-110	12	3-15	10-95	-16.88
William Haggas	11-135	8	1-22	10-113	-79.38
Roger Varian	11-84	13	2-11	9-73	+23.13
Roger Charlton	11-52	21	1-6	10-46	+5.30
Andrew Balding	10-169	6	0-17	10-152	-94.92
Mick Channon	9-141	6	6-62	3-79	-64.09
Clive Cox	9-102	9	4-19	5-83	-34.92
Marco Botti	9-62	15	1-4	8-58	+0.75

Jockeys	Wins-Rides	%	£1 level stks	Best Trainer	W-R
Ryan Moore	37-231	16	-56.17	Sir Michael Stoute	12-73
William Buick	24-174	14	-8.43	John Gosden	19-91
Richard Hughes	22-225	10	-83.83	Richard Hannon Snr	14-87
Jamie Spencer	16-147	11	-29.83	Kevin Ryan	3-12
James Doyle	15-118	13	-16.27	Roger Charlton	5-22
Jimmy Fortune	13-169	8	-85.92	Andrew Balding	3-51
Tom Queally	13-121	11	-10.72	Sir Henry Cecil	4-25
Kieren Fallon	12-145	8	-70.17	Luca Cumani	3-22
Johnny Murtagh	12-65	18	+42.50	James Fanshawe	2-4
Paul Hanagan	10-159	6	-97.25	John Gosden	2-8
Martin Harley	10-122	8	-59.88	Mick Channon	5-56
Adam Kirby	10-106	9	+32.08	Clive Cox	4-39
Frankie Dettori	9-136	7	-81.25	Richard Hannon	3-8

Favourites

2yo	31.8%	-10.47	3yo	39.3%	+49.41	TOTAL	29.6%	-28.94

Whitletts Road Ayr KA8 0JE.
Tel 01292 264 179

AYR

How to get there
Road: south from
Glasgow on A77
or A75, A70, A76.
Rail: Ayr, bus
service from
station on big
race days

Features LH

2015 Fixtures
April 27, May 20-21, June 8, 20, July
5-6, 13, 20, 27, August 8-10,
September 17-19, 29, October 8

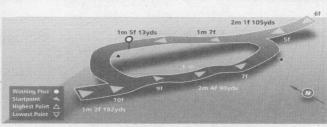

Racing Post standard times

5f	57.7	1m2f192yds	2min17.5
6f	1min10	1m5f13yds	2min47
7f50yds	1min28	1m7f	3min15
1m	1min38	2m1f105yds	3min49
1m1f20yds	1min51	2m4f90yds	4min31
1m2f	2min6		

Trainers	Wins-Runs	%	2yo	3yo+	£1 level stks
Jim Goldie	45-467	10	0-21	45-446	-79.17
Richard Fahey	33-306	11	10-77	23-229	-57.84
Keith Dalgleish	33-261	13	5-54	28-207	-6.08
Linda Perratt	23-273	8	1-4	22-269	+24.75
Michael Dods	20-137	15	3-23	17-114	-9.55
David O'Meara	17-82	21	1-11	16-71	+19.00
Kevin Ryan	16-143	11	9-53	7-90	-22.78
Tim Easterby	16-115	14	5-19	11-96	-14.77
Mark Johnston	14-134	10	5-50	9-84	-85.23
Ruth Carr	11-104	11	0-3	11-101	-43.25
Alistair Whillans	11-89	12	0-1	11-88	-4.27
John Quinn	11-37	30	4-12	7-25	+38.63
David Nicholls	10-108	9	0-4	10-104	-22.78

Jockeys	Wins-Rides	%	£1 level stks	Best Trainer	W-R
Graham Lee	34-247	14	+13.38	Jim Goldie	22-160
Tom Eaves	29-229	13	+1.17	Keith Dalgleish	13-106
Daniel Tudhope	23-153	15	-28.35	David O'Meara	10-51
Joe Fanning	22-147	15	-15.44	Mark Johnston	10-61
Paul Mulrennan	21-113	19	+22.80	Michael Dods	8-33
P J McDonald	20-172	12	-23.75	Alistair Whillans	5-19
Robert Winston	15-86	17	+0.58	Charles Hills	6-15
Jason Hart	14-88	16	-18.44	Shaun Harris	4-9
Paul Hanagan	14-79	18	-22.72	Richard Fahey	6-49
Phillip Makin	13-134	10	-54.13	John Quinn	3-4
Tony Hamilton	11-131	8	-13.84	Richard Fahey	8-98
David Allan	11-92	12	-26.17	Tim Easterby	8-55
James Sullivan	10-118	8	-49.25	Ruth Carr	6-54

Favourites

2yo	39.8% -5.76	3yo	29.5% -12.87	TOTAL	30.3% -57.49

BATH

Lansdown, Bath, Glos BA1 9BU
Tel 01291 622 260

How to get there
Road: M4, Jctn
18, then A46
south.
Rail: Bath Spa,
special bus
service to course
on race days

Features LH
uphill 4f straight

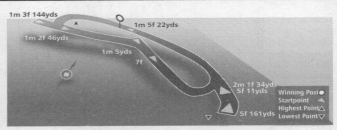

2015 Fixtures April 17, 23, May 4, 13,
22, June 5, 13, 24, July 1, 8, 14, 22,
31, August 12, 22, 26, September 2,
12-13, 28, October 18

Racing Post standard times

5f11yds	1min0.8	1m3f144yds	2min28
5f161yds	1min9.6	1m5f22yds	2min48.5
1m5yds	1min39	2m1f34yds	3min40
1m2f46yds	2min8		

Trainers	Wins-Runs	%	2yo	3yo+	£1 level stks
Mick Channon	24-203	12	10-69	14-134	-65.05
Richard Hannon Snr	24-95	25	14-55	10-40	+29.42
Clive Cox	17-78	22	3-14	14-64	+18.80
Ron Hodges	15-86	17	0-2	15-84	-4.79
Andrew Balding	15-76	20	2-9	13-67	-7.95
Mark Johnston	15-56	27	4-14	11-42	+28.33
David Evans	13-127	10	2-27	11-100	-33.37
Malcolm Saunders	13-106	12	3-22	10-84	+1.25
Ronald Harris	12-218	6	2-41	10-177	-119.38
Sir Mark Prescott Bt	12-36	33	3-11	9-25	-9.79
Tony Carroll	10-96	10	1-7	9-89	-19.75
Jo Hughes	10-75	13	2-27	8-48	-0.38
William Muir	10-66	15	0-10	10-56	-9.88

Jockeys	Wins-Rides	%	£1 level stks	Best Trainer	W-R
Luke Morris	21-187	11	-72.36	Sir Mark Prescott Bt	9-25
Richard Hughes	21-82	26	+7.98	Richard Hannon Snr	6-17
Cathy Gannon	17-144	12	-45.27	Jo Hughes	4-14
Dane O'Neill	17-107	16	-35.74	Malcolm Saunders	2-4
Liam Keniry	16-121	13	+6.43	David Elsworth	3-5
David Probert	15-121	12	-30.00	Andrew Balding	8-28
Pat Dobbs	14-74	19	-26.59	Richard Hannon Snr	6-27
George Baker	13-67	19	-12.30	Gary Moore	2-7
Chris Catlin	12-115	10	-45.25	Bernard Llewellyn	2-3
Sean Levey	12-65	18	+20.61	Ed McMahon	3-10
Martin Dwyer	11-65	17	+0.73	William Muir	3-21
Kieran O'Neill	11-51	22	+13.13	Richard Hannon Snr	5-15
Martin Harley	10-70	14	-15.87	Mick Channon	8-47

Favourites

2yo	40%	-12.22		3yo	31.7%	-55.38	
					TOTAL	33.6%	-73.07

York Road, Beverley, E Yorkshire
HU17 8QZ. Tel 01482 867 488

BEVERLEY

How to get there
Road: Course is
signposted from
the M62. Rail:
Beverley, bus
service to course
on race days

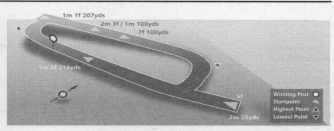

Features RH,
uphill finish

2015 Fixtures
April 15, 23, May 4, 12, 23, June 10,
16, 23, July 3-4, 14, 20, 28, August
12-13, 29-30, September 16, 22

Racing Post standard times

5f	1min1	1m4f16yds	2min34.2
7f100yds	1min30	2m35yds	3min30
1m100yds	1min43	2m3f100yds	4min17
1m1f207yds	2min1.3		

Trainers	Wins-Runs	%	2yo	3yo+	£1 level stks
Mark Johnston	57-224	25	11-56	46-168	+41.40
Richard Fahey	31-229	14	15-88	16-141	-63.88
David O'Meara	22-137	16	0-27	22-110	-0.13
Tim Easterby	19-298	6	3-108	16-190	-162.75
Kevin Ryan	18-142	13	6-48	12-94	-11.42
Michael Easterby	16-177	9	0-35	16-142	-72.13
Paul Midgley	15-146	10	1-22	14-124	-24.88
Brian Ellison	15-100	15	7-25	8-75	+32.00
David Nicholls	14-106	13	0-15	14-91	+24.33
Mel Brittain	13-101	13	1-21	12-80	-21.63
Neville Bycroft	13-90	14	0-0	13-90	+22.88
Bryan Smart	12-92	13	3-34	9-58	+2.15
Ann Duffield	10-90	11	6-48	4-42	+17.27

Jockeys	Wins-Rides	%	£1 level stks	Best Trainer	W-R
Silvestre De Sousa	35-117	30	+54.54	Mark Johnston	15-43
Paul Mulrennan	25-171	15	-18.29	Michael Easterby	3-18
Robert Winston	25-135	19	+21.46	Mel Brittain	7-23
Joe Fanning	23-120	19	-8.89	Mark Johnston	17-74
Graham Gibbons	19-149	13	-11.09	David Barron	5-29
David Allan	15-163	9	-55.08	Tim Easterby	10-111
Daniel Tudhope	15-95	16	-36.65	David O'Meara	10-65
Franny Norton	15-80	19	+15.29	Mark Johnston	10-41
Paul Hanagan	14-98	14	-36.75	Richard Fahey	6-42
Tony Hamilton	13-139	9	-41.21	Richard Fahey	8-84
P J McDonald	13-122	11	-20.04	James Turner	3-4
Tom Eaves	12-152	8	-72.60	Bryan Smart	5-31
Graham Lee	12-72	17	+6.58	Ann Duffield	2-7

Favourites

2yo	38.7% -2.73	3yo	36.1% -5.33	TOTAL 33%	-44.97

BRIGHTON

Freshfield Road, Brighton, E Sussex
BN2 2XZ. Tel 01273 603 580

How to get there
Road:
Signposted from
A23 London
Road and A27.
Rail: Brighton,
bus to course on
race days

Features LH,
undulating, sharp

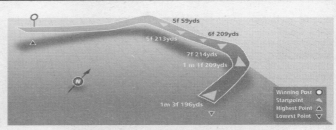

2015 Fixtures April 21, 28, May 5-6,
29, June 2, 10, 16, 23, 30, July 7,
August 5-7, 23-25, September 7, 14,
October 6, 15

Racing Post standard times

5f59yds	1min0.4	7f214yds	1min33
5f213yds	1min8.4	1m1f209yds	1min59.4
6f209yds	1min20.5	1m3f196yds	2min28.8

Trainers	Wins-Runs	%	2yo	3yo+	£1 level stks
Gary Moore	20-131	15	3-13	17-118	-17.05
John Bridger	18-125	14	0-3	18-122	-21.38
David Evans	14-96	15	2-11	12-85	+61.13
David Simcock	14-40	35	5-12	9-28	+13.47
George Baker	13-62	21	0-8	13-54	+95.00
Mick Channon	11-88	13	4-27	7-61	-13.85
Richard Hannon Snr	11-72	15	7-37	4-35	-28.55
Mark Johnston	11-57	19	2-16	9-41	+3.48
Tony Carroll	9-49	18	0-2	9-47	-3.65
Richard Hannon	9-31	29	8-19	1-12	-9.24
Ronald Harris	8-63	13	1-11	7-52	+10.00
Eve Johnson Houghton	8-54	15	1-12	7-42	-12.25
Joseph Tuite	8-43	19	1-4	7-39	+4.50

Jockeys	Wins-Rides	%	£1 level stks	Best Trainer	W-R
Richard Hughes	28-88	32	+10.55	Richard Hannon Snr	6-15
George Baker	23-137	17	-7.24	Gary Moore	10-52
William Carson	16-125	13	-10.75	John Bridger	8-34
Luke Morris	15-109	14	-34.32	Sir Mark Prescott Bt	3-14
Martin Lane	15-92	16	+45.27	David Simcock	6-15
Seb Sanders	14-72	19	-5.15	Rae Guest	2-2
Fergus Sweeney	13-113	12	-16.50	Malcolm Saunders	2-7
Pat Cosgrave	13-82	16	-10.38	George Baker	6-28
Neil Callan	13-73	18	-36.30	James Tate	4-10
Jim Crowley	13-72	18	-19.05	Amanda Perrett	2-4
Cathy Gannon	12-94	13	-21.50	Eve Johnson Houghton	3-17
Chris Catlin	11-85	13	-16.02	Peter Hiatt	3-13
Oisin Murphy	11-65	17	-3.72	Alan McCabe	2-3

Favourites

2yo	50.6% -2.65	3yo	34.5% -32.48	TOTAL	37% -22.79

Durdar Road, Carlisle, Cumbria,
CA2 4TS. Tel 01228 554 700

CARLISLE

How to get there
Road: M6 Jctn
42, follow signs
on Dalston Road.
Rail: Carlisle, 66
bus to course on
race days

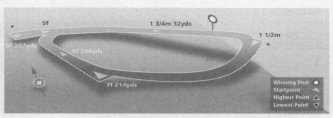

Features RH,
undulating, uphill
finish

2015 Fixtures May 25, June 1, 15,
24, July 4, 9, 26, August 3, 11, 19, 24,
September 9, 15

Racing Post standard times

5f	1min	1m1f61yds	1min55.2
5f193yds	1min12.2	1m3f107yds	2min23.5
6f192yds	1min25.7	1m6f32yds	3min2.5
7f200yds	1min38.5	2m1f52yds	3min46

Trainers	Wins-Runs	%	2yo	3yo+	£1 level stks
Keith Dalgleish	19-133	14	2-29	17-104	+8.46
Tim Easterby	18-151	12	5-51	13-100	+4.25
Richard Fahey	14-143	10	6-54	8-89	-37.79
Mark Johnston	12-96	13	4-26	8-70	-15.17
Brian Ellison	11-68	16	1-5	10-63	-19.13
Kevin Ryan	10-64	16	6-34	4-30	+33.13
David Nicholls	10-44	23	0-3	10-41	+20.50
Michael Easterby	8-78	10	1-13	7-65	+5.50
David O'Meara	8-66	12	2-12	6-54	-18.38
Paul Green	7-46	15	1-10	6-36	+48.00
Michael Dods	6-83	7	1-25	5-58	-18.75
Alan Swinbank	6-72	8	0-7	6-65	-41.00
Bryan Smart	6-56	11	3-26	3-30	+22.83

Jockeys	Wins-Rides	%	£1 level stks	Best Trainer	W-R
Joe Fanning	16-104	15	+18.83	Mark Johnston	9-59
Tom Eaves	14-152	9	-13.42	Keith Dalgleish	7-64
P J McDonald	13-100	13	-12.39	Ann Duffield	4-21
Graham Lee	13-87	15	+4.10	James Tate	2-2
Phillip Makin	11-76	14	+17.74	Keith Dalgleish	2-4
Paul Hanagan	10-48	21	-3.98	Richard Fahey	4-22
Paul Mulrennan	9-88	10	-53.25	Kevin Ryan	2-4
Daniel Tudhope	9-59	15	-7.75	David O'Meara	5-28
Dale Swift	9-42	21	+43.75	Brian Ellison	3-11
Duran Fentiman	8-69	12	+28.88	Tim Easterby	7-42
James Sullivan	7-82	9	+16.08	Michael Easterby	2-17
Graham Gibbons	7-62	11	+10.83	David Barron	2-10
Franny Norton	7-41	17	+10.25	Mark Johnston	2-18

Favourites

2yo	35%	-8.86	3yo	34.2%	-10.84	TOTAL	30%	-43.07

CATTERICK

Catterick Bridge, Richmond, N Yorks
DL10 7PE. Tel 01748 811 478

How to get there
Road: A1, exit 5m
south of Scotch
Corner. Rail:
Darlington or
Northallerton and
bus

Features LH,
undulating, tight

2015 Fixtures
April 8, 22, May 5, 23, 29, June 5, July
8, 15, 22, August 4, 14, 26, September
15, 19, October 6, 17, 27

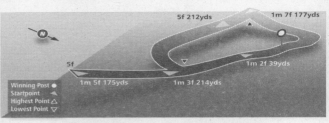

Racing Post standard times

5f	58.3	1m3f214yds	2min33
5f212yds	1min11.3	1m5f175yds	2min57
7f	1min23.3	1m7f177yds	3min23

Trainers	Wins-Runs	%	2yo	3yo+	£1 level stks
Mark Johnston	26-108	24	6-40	20-68	+23.15
Richard Fahey	24-127	19	15-51	9-76	-20.80
David O'Meara	23-163	14	2-21	21-142	-59.70
David Nicholls	21-177	12	5-20	16-157	-51.05
Tim Easterby	19-187	10	5-56	14-131	-58.24
Ruth Carr	15-110	14	0-1	15-109	+10.50
Kevin Ryan	14-79	18	7-33	7-46	+6.24
Brian Ellison	13-70	19	0-4	13-66	+51.00
Michael Easterby	11-127	9	0-31	11-96	-17.50
Paul Midgley	10-133	8	0-19	10-114	-43.88
Ann Duffield	10-94	11	3-45	7-49	-33.79
John Quinn	10-93	11	1-30	9-63	-23.34
Tracy Waggott	9-104	9	0-2	9-102	-13.00

Jockeys	Wins-Rides	%	£1 level stks	Best Trainer	W-R
Daniel Tudhope	27-142	19	+9.26	David O'Meara	17-79
P J McDonald	25-201	12	-24.28	Ruth Carr	5-27
Silvestre De Sousa	21-82	26	+17.20	Mark Johnston	7-17
Joe Fanning	20-105	19	+8.21	Mark Johnston	11-50
Graham Lee	17-117	15	-21.90	Donald McCain	2-4
Graham Gibbons	16-115	14	-1.01	Michael Easterby	4-35
David Allan	14-110	13	-47.99	Tim Easterby	10-80
Paul Mulrennan	14-96	15	-19.77	James Tate	3-6
Tony Hamilton	12-97	12	-37.47	Richard Fahey	11-58
Robert Winston	12-89	13	-19.84	Geoffrey Harker	2-6
Michael O'Connell	11-80	14	-27.50	David Nicholls	2-10
Duran Fentiman	10-135	7	-32.13	Tim Easterby	5-52
Adrian Nicholls	10-101	10	-56.43	David Nicholls	6-80

Favourites

2yo	39.4%	-10.75	3yo	33.8%	-20.98	TOTAL	31.1% -60.20

Great Leighs, CM3 1QP.
Tel 01245 362 412

CHELMSFORD

How to get there
Road: M11 Jctn
8, A120 towards
Chelmsford,
signposted from
A131. Rail:
Chelmsford, bus to
course on racedays

Features LH,
Polytrack, 1m circuit
with wide sweeping bends

2015 Fixtures March 26, April 1, 7, 9, 16,
26, 28, May 6, 12, 19, June 3, 17-18, July
21, August 4, 17-18, 22, September 3,
10, 17, 24, 26, October 1, 8, 10, 15, 22,
24, 28-29, November 5-7, 12, 19, 23, 26,
December 7, 10, 17, 21, 27

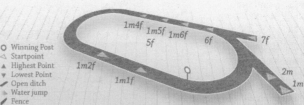

O Winning Post
◁ Startpoint
▲ Highest Point
▼ Lowest Point
⌒ Open ditch
⌒ Water jump
/ Fence

Racing Post standard times

5f	59.6
6f	1min12.3
1m	1min39
1m2f	2min6.5
1m6f	3min0.6
2m	3min28

A NEW ERA: Runners are underway for the first race at the reopened course in January this year, now rebranded as Chelmsford City from Great Leighs

CHEPSTOW

Chepstow, Monmouthshire,
NP16 6BE. Tel 01291 622 260

How to get there
Road: M4 Jct 22 on
west side of Severn
Bridge, A48 north,
A446. Rail: Chep-
stow, bus to course
on race days

Features LH,
undulating

2015 Fixtures May
1, 19, 30, June 12, 22, 30, July 10, 16,
24, August 2, 5, 20, 31, September
10, 15

Racing Post standard times

5f16yds	58.3	1m2f36yds	2min6.5
6f16yds	1min9.8	1m4f23yds	2min34
7f16yds	1min21.5	2m49yds	3min28
1m14yds	1min33.5	2m2f	3min52

Trainers	Wins-Runs	%	2yo	3yo+	£1 level stks
Andrew Balding	19-75	25	2-8	17-67	+9.61
Bernard Llewellyn	16-114	14	0-0	16-114	+16.83
Richard Hannon Snr	15-80	19	10-41	5-39	-24.94
Ronald Harris	14-185	8	4-39	10-146	-58.25
David Evans	13-138	9	2-40	11-98	-21.50
Mick Channon	13-74	18	5-33	8-41	-12.79
Ralph Beckett	11-43	26	1-14	10-29	+13.41
George Baker	11-43	26	1-9	10-34	+54.38
Malcolm Saunders	9-74	12	1-13	8-61	-28.50
John Spearing	9-31	29	0-2	9-29	+5.63
Jonathan Portman	8-72	11	1-13	7-59	-1.50
John O'Shea	8-53	15	0-0	8-53	-8.00
David Simcock	8-32	25	2-6	6-26	-1.15

Jockeys	Wins-Rides	%	£1 level stks	Best Trainer	W-R
David Probert	26-136	19	-0.02	Andrew Balding	13-33
Cathy Gannon	20-129	16	+8.63	John Spearing	6-14
Richard Hughes	18-92	20	-31.56	Richard Hannon Snr	5-18
Martin Lane	12-95	13	+34.10	Bernard Llewellyn	5-38
Pat Dobbs	12-38	32	+4.74	Richard Hannon Snr	7-18
Jim Crowley	11-58	19	-5.25	Ralph Beckett	4-20
Luke Morris	9-117	8	-68.89	Sir Mark Prescott Bt	3-7
Fergus Sweeney	9-85	11	-18.75	David Simcock	2-3
Dane O'Neill	9-74	12	-28.75	Henry Candy	3-10
Chris Catlin	8-69	12	-44.23	Rae Guest	3-7
James Doyle	8-37	22	+29.75	John Spearing	3-3
Adam Kirby	7-52	13	-7.00	Jamie Osborne	2-2
Pat Cosgrave	7-47	15	+24.00	George Baker	6-16

Favourites

2yo	38.5%	-8.11		3yo	39.7%	-8.62	TOTAL 34.4% -35.57

Steam Mill Street, Chester, CH1 2LY
Tel 01244 304 600

CHESTER

How to get there
Road: Inner Ring
Road and A458
Queensferry
Road.
Rail: Chester
General, bus to
city centre

Features LH, flat,
very sharp

2015 Fixtures May 6-8, 30, June 13,
26-27, July 10-11, 18, August 2, 22,
September 11-12, 26

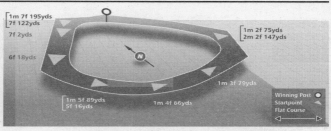

1m 7f 195yds
7f 122yds
7f 2yds
6f 18yds
1m 2f 75yds
2m 2f 147yds
1m 3f 79yds
1m 5f 89yds
5f 16yds
1m 4f 66yds
Winning Post
Startpoint
Flat Course

Racing Post standard times

5f16yds	59.6	1m3f79yds	2min22.7
5f110yds	1min5.6	1m4f66yds	2min34.6
6f18yds	1min13.1	1m5f89yds	2min48
7f2yds	1min24.3	1m7f195yds	3min24
7f122yds	1min31.4	2m2f147yds	4min1
1m2f75yds	2min7.9		

Trainers	Wins-Runs	%	2yo	3yo+	£1 level stks
Richard Fahey	40-295	14	13-62	27-233	-75.26
Mark Johnston	36-229	16	9-46	27-183	+38.70
Andrew Balding	24-103	23	2-15	22-88	+34.13
Tom Dascombe	17-156	11	9-59	8-97	-54.68
Kevin Ryan	12-80	15	3-15	9-65	-12.54
Mick Channon	11-98	11	2-30	9-68	-9.00
A P O'Brien	11-19	58	0-0	11-19	+11.69
David Evans	10-149	7	1-61	9-88	-43.00
William Haggas	10-39	26	5-8	5-31	-10.48
Paul Green	8-56	14	1-11	7-45	-1.75
John Quinn	8-35	23	1-6	7-29	+0.75
Tim Easterby	7-107	7	1-15	6-92	-62.00
Ian Williams	7-53	13	0-1	7-52	+40.50

Jockeys	Wins-Rides	%	£1 level stks	Best Trainer	W-R
Franny Norton	37-228	16	+44.57	Mark Johnston	16-83
Joe Fanning	18-124	15	-10.50	Mark Johnston	11-73
Richard Kingscote	16-116	14	-45.80	Tom Dascombe	12-85
Ryan Moore	16-58	28	+4.93	A P O'Brien	7-11
Paul Hanagan	13-58	22	+15.04	Richard Fahey	7-25
David Probert	12-69	17	-12.00	Andrew Balding	12-46
Tony Hamilton	10-78	13	+1.50	Richard Fahey	7-54
Robert Winston	9-58	16	-5.72	Mark H Tompkins	2-3
Sean Levey	9-56	16	-20.57	Richard Hannon Snr	4-11
Graham Lee	9-44	20	-4.46	James Tate	2-2
Graham Gibbons	8-64	13	-3.50	David Barron	4-16
Martin Harley	8-26	31	+30.13	Mick Channon	5-12
Jamie Spencer	7-61	11	-19.22	Luca Cumani	1-1

Favourites

2yo	45.9%	+5.47		3yo	32.9%	-12.01	
					TOTAL	32.8%	-23.51

DONCASTER

Leger Way, Doncaster
DN2 6BB. Tel 01302 320066/7

How to get there
Road: M18 Jct 3,
A638, A18 to Hull.
Rail: Doncaster
Central

Features LH, flat

2015 Fixtures
March 28-29,
April 24-25, May
2, 11, 16, June 6,
14, 26-27, July 3, 9, 16, 23, August 1,
15, September 9-12, October 23-24,
November 7

Racing Post standard times

5f	57.9	1m (Rnd)	1min36.2
5f140yds	1min6.2	1m2f60yds	2m6
6f	1min10.5	1m4f	2min29
6f110yds	1min17	1m6f132yds	3min3
7f	1min23.3	2m110yds	3min33
1m (Str)	1min36	2m2f	3min52

Trainers	Wins-Runs	%	2yo	3yo+	£1 level stks
Richard Fahey	37-345	11	9-90	28-255	-19.54
John Gosden	24-135	18	4-27	20-108	-25.12
Richard Hannon Snr	24-133	18	17-82	7-51	+3.22
Saeed bin Suroor	19-101	19	6-22	13-79	-24.32
Roger Varian	19-82	23	4-21	15-61	+24.04
Charles Hills	18-128	14	7-44	11-84	+23.97
Luca Cumani	16-82	20	0-11	16-71	-10.13
Tim Easterby	13-277	5	2-55	11-222	-150.75
Mark Johnston	13-175	7	4-55	9-120	-88.50
William Haggas	13-76	17	2-19	11-57	-15.01
Andrew Balding	13-72	18	4-8	9-64	+54.25
Marco Botti	12-93	13	4-21	8-72	-13.50
Michael Bell	12-83	14	5-24	7-59	-34.50

Jockeys	Wins-Rides	%	£1 level stks	Best Trainer	W-R
William Buick	30-152	20	-3.40	John Gosden	12-63
Paul Hanagan	29-216	13	-33.79	Richard Fahey	10-88
Andrea Atzeni	26-129	20	+20.85	Roger Varian	10-34
Jamie Spencer	23-130	18	+23.57	Michael Bell	7-23
Silvestre De Sousa	17-142	12	-44.47	Saeed bin Suroor	8-23
Richard Hughes	17-102	17	-6.79	Richard Hannon Snr	11-49
Daniel Tudhope	16-143	11	+17.50	David O'Meara	8-93
Robert Winston	16-134	12	-0.13	Alan Swinbank	3-11
Ryan Moore	16-93	17	-33.56	Sir Michael Stoute	4-15
Paul Mulrennan	12-151	8	+77.75	Michael Dods	3-32
Dane O'Neill	12-57	21	+33.25	Richard Hannon Snr	3-6
Graham Gibbons	11-147	7	-26.50	David Barron	6-56
Graham Lee	11-137	8	-47.67	Jim Goldie	4-19

Favourites

2yo	38.4% -7.49	3yo	30.5% -40.69	TOTAL	30.1% -81.33

Epsom Downs, Surrey, KT18 5LQ
Tel 01372 726 311

EPSOM

How to get there
Road: M25 Jct 8
(A217) or 9 (A24),
2m south of
Epsom on B290.
Rail: Epsom
and bus, Epsom
Downs or
Tattenham
Corner

Features LH,
undulating

2015 Fixtures April 22, June 5-6, July
2, 9, 16, 30, August 31, September 1,
10, 27

Racing Post standard times

5f	54.9	1m114yds	1min41.8
6f	1min7	1m2f18yds	2min5.3
7f	1min20	1m4f10yds	2min33.6

Trainers	Wins-Runs	%	2yo	3yo+	£1 level stks
Richard Hannon Snr	19-94	20	13-39	6-55	-13.94
Andrew Balding	15-106	14	6-22	9-84	-15.59
Mark Johnston	13-131	10	3-24	10-107	-58.75
Mick Channon	11-82	13	5-31	6-51	-1.30
Richard Fahey	10-63	16	3-10	7-53	+11.50
Ralph Beckett	10-43	23	2-7	8-36	+7.44
David Simcock	10-36	28	1-3	9-33	+17.92
John Gosden	8-44	18	2-3	6-41	-12.92
Roger Varian	7-35	20	0-3	7-32	+0.25
A P O'Brien	7-35	20	0-0	7-35	+3.02
Stuart Williams	6-40	15	0-1	6-39	-5.56
Saeed bin Suroor	6-37	16	1-7	5-30	-11.47
Stuart Kittow	6-27	22	0-1	6-26	+12.25

Jockeys	Wins-Rides	%	£1 level stks	Best Trainer	W-R
Richard Hughes	22-92	24	+10.80	Richard Hannon Snr	10-45
Silvestre De Sousa	13-76	17	-9.18	Mark Johnston	7-43
Neil Callan	13-74	18	+1.00	James Tate	3-8
Ryan Moore	13-71	18	+3.75	Roger Varian	2-2
David Probert	11-67	16	+12.75	Andrew Balding	8-47
Jamie Spencer	10-71	14	-3.50	Ed de Giles	2-3
Kieren Fallon	8-64	13	+2.91	Saeed bin Suroor	2-6
Jim Crowley	8-47	17	+0.63	Ralph Beckett	5-19
James Doyle	7-52	13	-16.00	Roger Charlton	2-7
Adam Kirby	7-32	22	+24.00	Tony Carroll	2-2
William Buick	6-55	11	-28.00	John Gosden	5-32
Tom Queally	6-32	19	+3.44	Sir Henry Cecil	3-8
Luke Morris	6-21	29	+55.75	John Best	2-2

Favourites

2yo	38.5% -11.38	3yo	26.9% -31.26	TOTAL	28.9% -60.65

FFOS LAS

Trimsaran, Carmarthenshire, SA17 4DE
Tel: 01554 811092

How to get there
Road: M4 Jctn 48 and follow the A4138 to Llanelli.
Rail: Llanelli, Kidwelly or Carmarthen

Features LH, flat, galloping

2015 Fixtures
July 21, 30, August 11, 19, 28, September 13

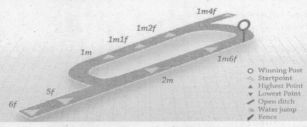

Racing Post standard times

5f	57	1m4f	2min34
6f	1min8.5	1m6f	3min
1m	1min38	2m	3min28.5
1m2f	2min6		

Trainers	Wins-Runs	%	2yo	3yo+	£1 level stks
David Evans	15-108	14	2-25	13-83	+32.33
Ronald Harris	8-68	12	5-21	3-47	-23.50
Mick Channon	7-52	13	3-24	4-28	-22.67
Daniel Mark Loughnane	6-31	19	0-3	6-28	+2.25
Brian Meehan	6-20	30	2-7	4-13	+2.08
Peter Makin	6-17	35	1-3	5-14	+19.17
Bernard Llewellyn	5-54	9	0-0	5-54	-25.00
Rod Millman	5-48	10	2-12	3-36	-22.00
David Simcock	5-34	15	2-9	3-25	-7.25
Richard Price	5-32	16	0-0	5-32	+10.75
William Muir	5-30	17	1-7	4-23	+15.00
Roger Charlton	5-25	20	3-8	2-17	-14.49
Andrew Balding	5-23	22	1-7	4-16	+11.58

Jockeys	Wins-Rides	%	£1 level stks	Best Trainer	W-R
Steve Drowne	12-53	23	+58.78	Peter Makin	5-10
Martin Dwyer	9-34	26	+12.83	William Muir	4-12
Martin Harley	9-28	32	+14.88	Mick Channon	4-10
Declan Bates	8-33	24	+16.54	David Evans	5-19
James Doyle	7-39	18	-14.50	David Evans	2-9
William Twiston-Davies	7-37	19	+11.08	Michael Bell	2-4
David Probert	6-55	11	-2.64	David Evans	2-5
Cathy Gannon	6-48	13	+3.50	David Evans	2-15
Martin Lane	6-45	13	-19.71	Andrew Haynes	1-1
Richard Hughes	6-27	22	+0.08	Richard Hannon	2-2
Chris Catlin	6-21	29	+11.88	David Simcock	1-1
Daniel Muscutt	5-28	18	+0.25	Richard Price	3-10
Paul Hanagan	5-13	38	+5.86	Bill Turner	1-1

Favourites

2yo	42.6%	-6.42		3yo	37%	-13.72		TOTAL	30.4%	-61.16

Chichester, W Sussex,
PO18 0PS. Tel 01243 755 022

GOODWOOD

How to get there
Road: signposted
from A27 south
and A285 north.
Rail: Chichester,
bus to course on
race days

Features RH,
undulating

2015 Fixtures
May 2, 21-23, June 5, 7, 12, 19, July
28-31, August 1, 28-30, September 1,
23, October 11

Racing Post standard times

5f	57	1m3f	2min21
6f	1min9.7	1m4f	2min34
7f	1min24	1m6f	2min58.5
1m	1min36.7	2m	3min21
1m1f	1min51.4	2m4f	4min14
1m1f192yds	2min4		

Trainers	Wins-Runs	%	2yo	3yo+	£1 level stks
Richard Hannon Snr	49-319	15	23-155	26-164	+6.38
Mark Johnston	27-197	14	9-52	18-145	+23.62
Amanda Perrett	19-168	11	2-28	17-140	+1.75
John Gosden	18-100	18	4-24	14-76	+13.26
Sir Michael Stoute	16-89	18	2-10	14-79	-22.67
Jeremy Noseda	14-45	31	3-9	11-36	+54.30
Andrew Balding	13-135	10	3-34	10-101	-33.00
Sir Henry Cecil	12-48	25	0-2	12-46	-7.90
Mick Channon	11-206	5	6-90	5-116	-98.47
Richard Hannon	11-108	10	5-42	6-66	-40.63
William Haggas	11-54	20	2-9	9-45	+5.71
Clive Cox	10-95	11	2-24	8-71	+9.38
Roger Charlton	10-55	18	2-5	8-50	-4.88

Jockeys	Wins-Rides	%	£1 level stks	Best Trainer	W-R
Richard Hughes	63-294	21	+19.85	Richard Hannon Snr	33-157
William Buick	29-163	18	+40.03	John Gosden	12-62
Ryan Moore	24-181	13	-79.60	Sir Michael Stoute	8-50
Pat Dobbs	19-139	14	+52.25	Amanda Perrett	8-37
Kieren Fallon	18-113	16	-6.01	Luca Cumani	3-17
Tom Queally	17-125	14	-23.38	Sir Henry Cecil	10-36
James Doyle	15-116	13	-41.81	Roger Charlton	5-30
George Baker	15-102	15	+13.13	William Haggas	2-3
Joe Fanning	14-100	14	+16.88	Mark Johnston	13-70
Frankie Dettori	14-83	17	-17.18	Mahmood Al Zarooni	4-15
Adam Kirby	12-98	12	-10.04	Clive Cox	4-44
Jim Crowley	10-160	6	-58.00	Amanda Perrett	3-23
Hayley Turner	10-70	14	+6.50	James Fanshawe	3-5

Favourites

2yo	39.1%	+7.47	3yo	28.1%	-34.19	TOTAL 31.7%	-22.82

HAMILTON

Bothwell Road, Hamilton, Lanarkshire
ML3 0DW. Tel 01698 283 806

How to get there
Road: M74 Jct 5,
off the A74. Rail:
Hamilton West

Features RH,
undulating, dip
can become
testing in wet
weather

2015 Fixtures
May 3, 15, 27, June 4, 10, 17, 25,
30, July 11, 16-17, August 1, 20, 28,
September 1, 20-21, 28

Racing Post standard times

5f4yds	58.2	1m3f16yds	2min20
6f5yds	1min10	1m4f17yds	2min33.7
1m65yds	1min45	1m5f9yds	2min47.5
1m1f36yds	1min55.5		

Trainers	Wins-Runs	%	2yo	3yo+	£1 level stks
Mark Johnston	48-200	24	9-42	39-158	+11.38
Keith Dalgleish	33-237	14	6-34	27-203	-42.34
Kevin Ryan	30-127	24	6-42	24-85	+27.95
Richard Fahey	24-168	14	6-45	18-123	-55.43
Alan Swinbank	19-104	18	1-4	18-100	+20.44
Jim Goldie	18-182	10	0-3	18-179	-42.60
David Nicholls	16-82	20	0-3	16-79	+30.00
Alan Berry	15-169	9	1-9	14-160	-5.50
Ann Duffield	15-91	16	3-21	12-70	-9.50
Bryan Smart	14-84	17	7-24	7-60	+74.13
Eric Alston	13-80	16	0-1	13-79	+6.70
David Barron	13-61	21	3-11	10-50	+21.16
Linda Perratt	10-270	4	0-6	10-264	-138.50

Jockeys	Wins-Rides	%	£1 level stks	Best Trainer	W-R
Joe Fanning	41-189	22	-7.30	Mark Johnston	31-114
Graham Lee	21-155	14	-52.05	Jim Goldie	5-57
P J McDonald	18-163	11	-45.04	Ann Duffield	5-31
Tom Eaves	17-229	7	-106.59	Keith Dalgleish	8-81
Phillip Makin	17-131	13	-57.85	Kevin Ryan	6-35
Jason Hart	17-108	16	-0.05	Eric Alston	10-56
Paul Mulrennan	15-126	12	-30.59	Kevin Ryan	3-9
Julie Burke	15-87	17	+1.55	Kevin Ryan	8-19
Paul Hanagan	13-54	24	-4.77	Richard Fahey	8-22
Daniel Tudhope	12-73	16	-10.63	David O'Meara	6-29
Silvestre De Sousa	11-39	28	+13.40	Mark Johnston	7-14
David Allan	9-59	15	-16.17	Alan Swinbank	2-3
Andrew Mullen	9-49	18	+51.58	Alan Swinbank	2-4

Favourites

2yo	41%	-6.61	3yo	41.9%	+8.58	TOTAL	36.4%	-8.13

Newton-Le-Willows, Merseyside
WA12 0HQ. Tel 01942 725 963

HAYDOCK

How to get there
Road: M6 Jct 23,
A49 to Wigan.
Rail: Wigan & 320
bus or Newton-le-
Willows

Features LH, flat,
easy turns, suits
the galloping type

2015 Fixtures
April 25, May 9, 22-23, 28-30, June
10-11, 20, July 2-4, 17-18, August 6-8,
September 3-5, 25-26, October 16

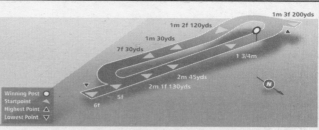

Racing Post standard times

5f	58.5	1m2f95yds	2min9
5f (Inner)	58	1m3f200yds	2min26.5
6f	1min11	1m6f	2min54
6f (Inner)	1min10.3	2m45yds	3min24
7f	1min26	2m1f130yds	3min51
1m	1min38		

Trainers	Wins-Runs	%	2yo	3yo+	£1 level stks
Tom Dascombe	39-193	20	14-77	25-116	+59.11
Richard Fahey	29-264	11	7-70	22-194	-54.13
Roger Varian	25-90	28	6-18	19-72	+26.75
Mark Johnston	24-228	11	2-56	22-172	-50.55
John Gosden	24-77	31	5-17	19-60	+47.44
Kevin Ryan	21-147	14	7-54	14-93	+107.57
David O'Meara	19-135	14	0-9	19-126	+9.13
William Haggas	19-57	33	7-14	12-43	+27.20
Mrs K Burke	16-85	19	4-20	12-65	+23.52
Richard Hannon Snr	14-96	15	12-54	2-42	-36.13
Tim Easterby	11-162	7	2-34	9-128	-68.15
Luca Cumani	11-76	14	0-3	11-73	-3.02
Mick Channon	10-109	9	4-41	6-68	-23.50

Jockeys	Wins-Rides	%	£1 level stks	Best Trainer	W-R
Richard Kingscote	32-174	18	+15.00	Tom Dascombe	28-134
Paul Hanagan	28-148	19	-19.86	Richard Fahey	7-35
Daniel Tudhope	22-130	17	+19.50	David O'Meara	14-71
Joe Fanning	16-144	11	+24.29	Mark Johnston	11-97
Graham Lee	16-120	13	+32.25	Kevin Ryan	4-11
Jamie Spencer	16-118	14	-32.89	Michael Bell	3-14
William Buick	16-71	23	+10.34	John Gosden	9-33
Silvestre De Sousa	15-111	14	-30.18	Mark Johnston	4-34
Tom Queally	14-93	15	-20.42	Sir Henry Cecil	4-11
Ryan Moore	14-79	18	-34.90	Sir Michael Stoute	4-21
Phillip Makin	13-114	11	+28.78	Kevin Ryan	5-49
Franny Norton	13-103	13	-10.25	Mark Johnston	5-34
Paul Mulrennan	13-89	15	+44.17	James Tate	2-3

Favourites

2yo	34.3% -31.15		3yo	40.1% +19.64	TOTAL	32.2% -76.08

KEMPTON

Staines Rd East, Sunbury-On-Thames
TW16 5AQ. Tel 01932 782 292

How to get there
Road: M3 Jct 1,
A308 to Kingston-
on-Thames. Rail:
Kempton Park
from Waterloo

Features RH,
Polytrack, sharp

2015 Fixtures
March 28, April
1, 4, 8, 15, 21, 27, May 20, 27, June 4,
10, 24, July 1, 8, August 5, 12, 17-19,
24, 26, September 4-5, 9, 21-23, 30,
October 6-7, 14, 21, 28, November
4, 9, 11, 18, 25, 30, December 2-3, 9,
15-16

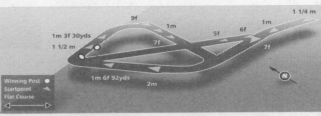

Racing Post standard times

5f	58.8	1m2f	2min4
6f	1min10.6	1m3f	2min17
7f	1min23.7	1m4f	2min30
1m	1min36.6	2m	3min22.5

Trainers	Wins-Runs	%	2yo	3yo+	£1 level stks
Richard Hannon Snr	88-540	16	45-276	43-264	+4.33
Ralph Beckett	62-276	22	27-103	35-173	+71.91
John Gosden	61-304	20	20-117	41-187	-45.05
Saeed bin Suroor	57-214	27	22-68	35-146	+57.49
James Fanshawe	56-251	22	3-32	53-219	+67.13
Andrew Balding	53-387	14	6-76	47-311	-56.75
Tony Carroll	47-538	9	0-14	47-524	-198.97
Gary Moore	47-325	14	9-44	38-281	-93.76
Marco Botti	46-324	14	17-108	29-216	-123.55
Mark Johnston	40-337	12	7-76	33-261	-123.09
Charlie Appleby	38-153	25	23-89	15-64	+35.19
Ronald Harris	32-249	13	3-34	29-215	+17.08
David Simcock	32-222	14	9-58	23-164	-10.46

Jockeys	Wins-Rides	%	£1 level stks	Best Trainer	W-R
Jim Crowley	137-893	15	-23.11	Ralph Beckett	42-172
Adam Kirby	131-865	15	-110.76	Clive Cox	19-86
Luke Morris	124-1093	11	-180.64	Ronald Harris	22-128
George Baker	92-610	15	-18.63	Gary Moore	19-114
Richard Hughes	85-480	18	-78.88	Richard Hannon Snr	43-178
William Buick	76-351	22	-3.14	John Gosden	30-151
Ryan Moore	70-297	24	+9.52	Sir Michael Stoute	18-60
Silvestre De Sousa	63-360	18	-6.68	Mark Johnston	14-79
David Probert	59-498	12	-44.00	Andrew Balding	26-153
James Doyle	52-406	13	-111.19	Sir Michael Stoute	6-15
Jamie Spencer	49-250	20	-17.97	David Simcock	7-24
Martin Harley	48-382	13	-75.54	Marco Botti	18-91
Liam Keniry	46-684	7	-334.87	Sylvester Kirk	7-84

Favourites

2yo	36.5%	-54.75		3yo	36.5%	-63.41	TOTAL 34.2% -176.01

LEICESTER

London Road, Oadby, Leicester,
LE2 4QH. Tel 0116 271 6515

How to get there
Road: M1 Jct 21,
A6, 2m south of
city. Rail:
Leicester, bus

Features RH,
straight mile is
downhill for first
4f, then uphill to
finish

2015 Fixtures April 10, 25, May 18,
25-26, June 1, 13, 18, 23, July 4, 16,
22, 29, August 9, 18, 24, September 8,
21, October 6, 13, 26

Racing Post standard times

5f2yds	59	1m60yds	1min42.5
5f218yds	1min10.5	1m1f218yds	2min4.5
7f9yds	1min23	1m3f183yds	2min29.3
1m8yds	1min41		

Trainers	Wins-Runs	%	2yo	3yo+	£1 level stks
Richard Hannon Snr	25-123	20	16-69	9-54	-5.37
Sir Michael Stoute	15-46	33	6-24	9-22	+0.36
Mark Johnston	13-122	11	7-47	6-75	-42.58
Charles Hills	13-48	27	8-23	5-25	+5.90
Richard Fahey	12-77	16	4-28	8-49	+63.63
Mick Channon	11-81	14	7-40	4-41	-25.65
Luca Cumani	11-42	26	2-16	9-26	-2.65
David Evans	10-114	9	3-44	7-70	-17.43
Roger Varian	10-46	22	1-20	9-26	+12.70
Rae Guest	10-37	27	4-14	6-23	+51.00
John Gosden	9-43	21	2-18	7-25	-13.32
Roger Charlton	9-31	29	2-12	7-19	-5.49
Brian Meehan	8-61	13	5-34	3-27	-31.18

Jockeys	Wins-Rides	%	£1 level stks	Best Trainer	W-R
Ryan Moore	30-96	31	+6.22	Sir Michael Stoute	10-25
Paul Hanagan	25-112	22	+20.66	William Haggas	4-9
Richard Hughes	19-77	25	-5.78	Richard Hannon Snr	11-36
Silvestre De Sousa	17-81	21	+2.69	Mark Johnston	5-28
James Doyle	16-81	20	+50.04	Roger Charlton	4-9
Kieren Fallon	16-69	23	-6.19	Luca Cumani	4-12
Adam Kirby	15-88	17	-16.81	Clive Cox	5-30
Martin Dwyer	11-85	13	-8.25	James Tate	4-6
Andrea Atzeni	11-76	14	+13.35	Roger Varian	4-13
William Buick	11-60	18	-13.36	John Gosden	5-28
Jamie Spencer	10-62	16	-26.28	Paul Cole	2-2
Martin Harley	10-61	16	-1.12	Mick Channon	3-20
Tom Queally	9-99	9	-49.14	Barry Leavy	2-3

Favourites

2yo	44%	+4.18		3yo	44.5%	+25.72		TOTAL 40.2% +21.11

LINGFIELD turf

Racecourse Road, Lingfield
RH7 6PQ. Tel 01342 834 800

How to get there
Road: M25 Jctn 6, south on A22, then B2029. Rail: Lingfield from London Bridge or Victoria

Features LH, undulating

2015 Fixtures
May 8-9, 20, June 4, 6, 9, 13, 20, 27, July 8, 15, 18, 25, August 1, 8, 13, 15, 20, 26, September 2, 12

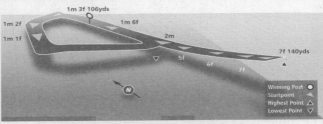

Racing Post standard times

5f	56.9	1m2f	2min6.7
6f	1min9.4	1m3f106yds	2min27
7f	1min21	1m6f	3min
7f140yds	1min28	2m	3min27.5
1m1f	1min53		

Trainers	Wins-Runs	%	2yo	3yo+	£1 level stks
Mick Channon	13-67	19	3-28	10-39	+52.75
Richard Hannon Snr	9-68	13	8-36	1-32	-33.27
J R Jenkins	8-37	22	1-4	7-33	+2.88
Ralph Beckett	8-29	28	1-9	7-20	+8.44
William Haggas	8-28	29	3-12	5-16	+0.22
Roger Varian	8-25	32	1-3	7-22	+10.60
Roger Charlton	8-18	44	3-5	5-13	-0.50
Tony Carroll	7-32	22	0-1	7-31	-2.13
Sir Michael Stoute	7-29	24	1-9	6-20	+5.90
John Bridger	6-67	9	0-5	6-62	-22.50
Gary Moore	6-56	11	2-8	4-48	-11.63
David Simcock	6-29	21	2-6	4-23	-2.00
John Spearing	6-23	26	0-6	6-17	+18.00

Jockeys	Wins-Rides	%	£1 level stks	Best Trainer	W-R
Richard Hughes	19-80	24	+21.15	Richard Hannon Snr	4-22
Luke Morris	11-83	13	-31.45	Paul Cole	2-3
Martin Harley	11-30	37	+30.00	Mick Channon	6-15
Adam Kirby	10-59	17	-9.46	Tony Carroll	2-2
Jim Crowley	10-46	22	-1.35	Ralph Beckett	4-12
George Baker	8-61	13	-13.89	Roger Charlton	2-2
Andrea Atzeni	8-54	15	+11.50	Derek Haydn Jones	2-3
William Buick	8-43	19	-4.64	Jeremy Noseda	2-3
David Probert	8-33	24	+1.48	Andrew Balding	3-7
Dane O'Neill	7-55	13	-19.43	Roger Varian	2-3
James Doyle	7-41	17	-0.71	Roger Charlton	3-6
Ian Mongan	7-39	18	-6.04	Sir Henry Cecil	2-2
Harry Bentley	6-44	14	-16.90	Roger Varian	1-1

Favourites

2yo	50.7%	+18.22	3yo	39.8%	-0.34	TOTAL	38.2%	+0.82

LINGFIELD sand

Features LH,
Polytrack, tight

2015 Fixtures
April 3, 7-8, 11,
29-30, May 1, 26,
28, June 1, 18,
July 22, August
7, 11, September
22, October 20,
29, November
13-14, 17, 19, 21, 25, December 2, 7,
9, 16, 19-20, 28, 30-31

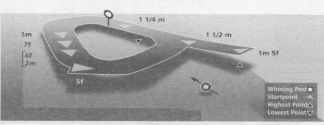

Racing Post standard times

5f	57.5	1m2f	2min1.8
6f	1min9.6	1m4f	2min28
7f	1min22.2	1m5f	2min40.5
1m	1min35.3	2m	3min16

Trainers	Wins-Runs	%	2yo	3yo+	£1 level stks
David Evans	61-493	12	3-45	58-448	-161.42
Mark Johnston	59-359	16	5-42	54-317	-102.11
Richard Hannon Snr	47-255	18	13-93	34-162	-63.19
John Gosden	47-215	22	10-64	37-151	-7.96
David Simcock	39-189	21	3-12	36-177	+15.14
Andrew Balding	38-225	17	9-36	29-189	-25.01
Jeremy Noseda	38-120	32	6-21	32-99	+6.19
Gary Moore	36-309	12	4-31	32-278	-101.03
Ronald Harris	29-245	12	3-16	26-229	-65.58
William Haggas	29-114	25	4-41	25-73	-13.85
Marco Botti	27-186	15	5-41	22-145	-52.84
Ralph Beckett	27-126	21	8-38	19-88	+9.11
William Knight	26-170	15	4-16	22-154	-24.24

Jockeys	Wins-Rides	%	£1 level stks	Best Trainer	W-R
Adam Kirby	123-620	20	+64.22	David Evans	20-95
Jim Crowley	107-627	17	-84.33	Ralph Beckett	21-78
Luke Morris	100-844	12	-250.71	Ronald Harris	22-129
George Baker	96-573	17	-84.78	Gary Moore	17-116
Joe Fanning	64-427	15	-27.81	Mark Johnston	36-228
Ryan Moore	62-201	31	+20.18	Sir Michael Stoute	17-35
Shane Kelly	57-410	14	-67.38	Daniel Mark Loughnane	7-34
Liam Keniry	48-498	10	-108.01	J S Moore	8-53
Hayley Turner	48-380	13	-97.73	Conor Dore	16-103
David Probert	47-378	12	-82.84	Andrew Balding	18-95
Andrea Atzeni	46-277	17	+21.36	Roger Varian	7-36
Jamie Spencer	45-250	18	-23.55	David Simcock	7-30
William Carson	43-433	10	-147.43	Richard Guest	5-20

Favourites

2yo	41.3%	-18.40	3yo	41.6%	-47.49	TOTAL	38.6%	-78.66

MUSSELBURGH

Linkfield Road EH21 7RG
Tel 0131 665 2859

How to get there
Road: M8 Jct 2,
A8 east, follow
Ring Road, A1
east. Rail:
Musselburgh
from Edinburgh
Waverley

Features RH, flat,
tight

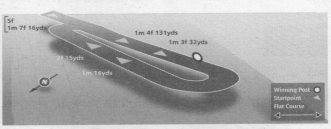

2015 Fixtures April 3, 5, May 1,
11, 22, June 6, 13, 29, July 21, 31,
August 7, 26-27, September 4, 12, 27

Racing Post standard times

5f	58	1m3f32yds	2min22
7f30yds	1min26.8	1m4f100yds	2min40
1m	1min38.8	1m6f	1min59.2
1m1f	1min51.1	2m	3min25

Trainers	Wins-Runs	%	2yo	3yo+	£1 level stks
Richard Fahey	40-174	23	11-48	29-126	+78.54
Mark Johnston	38-208	18	11-47	27-161	+5.56
Jim Goldie	29-328	9	0-8	29-320	-78.22
Keith Dalgleish	20-198	10	8-47	12-151	-27.15
David O'Meara	18-94	19	0-16	18-78	-5.59
Philip Kirby	15-60	25	0-2	15-58	+46.56
Tim Easterby	13-133	10	2-21	11-112	-35.40
Kevin Ryan	13-93	14	7-27	6-66	-25.46
David Barron	13-69	19	5-15	8-54	-10.00
Alan Swinbank	13-56	23	1-2	12-54	+15.25
Paul Midgley	12-86	14	0-10	12-76	-14.85
Bryan Smart	12-85	14	7-32	5-53	-20.88
Brian Ellison	11-92	12	2-7	9-85	-23.42

Jockeys	Wins-Rides	%	£1 level stks	Best Trainer	W-R
Joe Fanning	39-201	19	+8.70	Mark Johnston	30-117
Graham Lee	26-172	15	+7.86	Jim Goldie	13-97
Tom Eaves	23-223	10	+6.23	Keith Dalgleish	8-75
Paul Hanagan	17-69	25	+5.70	Richard Fahey	10-31
Robert Winston	16-76	21	+21.75	Alan Swinbank	6-21
Phillip Makin	14-116	12	-51.65	Kevin Ryan	6-36
Frederik Tylicki	14-65	22	+45.88	Saeed bin Suroor	2-3
Daniel Tudhope	13-91	14	-23.76	David O'Meara	8-42
Connor Beasley	11-51	22	-5.38	Michael Dods	5-8
Graham Gibbons	11-45	24	+12.88	David Barron	8-19
P J McDonald	10-125	8	-19.00	Alistair Whillans	3-16
Duran Fentiman	10-99	10	-23.42	Tim Easterby	3-38
Paul Mulrennan	10-97	10	-40.30	Paul Midgley	2-3

Favourites

2yo	37.5%	-7.24		3yo	34.4%	-9.27			TOTAL	33.8%	-33.79

Newbury, Berkshire, RG14 7NZ
Tel: 01635 400 15 or 01635 550 354

NEWBURY

How to get there
Road: M4 Jct 13
and A34 south.
Rail: Newbury
Racecourse

Features LH,
wide, flat

2015 Fixtures
April 17-18, May
15-16, June 11,
25, July 2, 9, 17-18, 23, August 14-15,
25, September 18-19, October 23-24

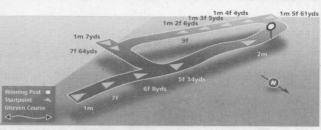

Racing Post standard times

5f34yds	59.6	1m1f	1min50
6f8yds	1min10.5	1m2f6yds	2min3
7f	1min22.8	1m3f5yds	2min17
7f64yds	1min28	1m4f4yds	2min30.3
1m	1min35.8	1m5f61yds	2min47.5
1m7yds	1min36.5	2m	3min23.5

Trainers	Wins-Runs	%	2yo	3yo+	£1 level stks
Richard Hannon Snr	44-382	12	33-215	11-167	-124.67
John Gosden	30-138	22	7-27	23-111	+39.04
William Haggas	20-101	20	3-33	17-68	+3.13
Roger Charlton	18-119	15	9-55	9-64	+40.21
Clive Cox	17-151	11	6-46	11-105	-38.45
Saeed bin Suroor	15-66	23	2-10	13-56	-0.51
Luca Cumani	15-64	23	0-3	15-61	-6.25
Ralph Beckett	14-93	15	1-24	13-69	-5.88
Richard Hannon	13-117	11	7-59	6-58	-56.05
Mick Channon	12-209	6	6-107	6-102	-83.50
Roger Varian	11-62	18	5-17	6-45	+59.83
Andrew Balding	10-120	8	4-44	6-76	-47.14
Mark Johnston	10-76	13	5-22	5-54	-17.75

Jockeys	Wins-Rides	%	£1 level stks	Best Trainer	W-R
Richard Hughes	49-298	16	-47.50	Richard Hannon Snr	29-167
William Buick	27-181	15	-48.18	John Gosden	16-75
Ryan Moore	20-161	12	-76.72	Sir Michael Stoute	8-53
James Doyle	20-154	13	-11.74	Roger Charlton	9-52
Silvestre De Sousa	20-119	17	+30.67	Saeed bin Suroor	8-24
Jim Crowley	19-161	12	+5.82	Ralph Beckett	11-62
Kieren Fallon	15-127	12	-29.58	Luca Cumani	5-26
Paul Hanagan	15-103	15	-2.57	William Haggas	4-14
Frankie Dettori	15-76	20	+34.96	Mahmood Al Zarooni	3-7
Adam Kirby	14-142	10	-30.00	Clive Cox	8-74
Dane O'Neill	14-113	12	+53.13	Henry Candy	4-25
Andrea Atzeni	12-74	16	+13.60	Luca Cumani	3-12
Tom Queally	11-106	10	-32.80	Sir Henry Cecil	6-31

Favourites

2yo	33.6% -14.98	3yo	28.1% -31.77	TOTAL	30.2% -56.85

NEWCASTLE

High Gosforth Park NE3 5HP
Tel: 0191 236 2020 or 236 5508

How to get there
Road: Signposted from A1. Rail:
Newcastle Central, metro to Regent Centre or Four Lane End and bus

Features: LH, galloping, 4f uphill straight

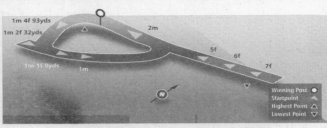

2015 Fixtures April 11, 28, May 13, 19, 29, June 6, 25-27, July 25, August 6, 14, 28, 31, September 4, October 1, 13

Racing Post standard times

5f	59	1m1f9yds	1min53.2
6f	1min12	1m2f32yds	2min7
7f	1min25	1m4f93yds	2min37.5
1m (Rnd)	1min40	1m6f97yds	3min4
1m3yds (Str)	1min38	2m19yds	3min26

Trainers	Wins-Runs	%	2yo	3yo+	£1 level stks
Richard Fahey	32-199	16	16-63	16-136	+2.83
Michael Dods	24-151	16	5-34	19-117	-1.29
David O'Meara	18-144	13	6-20	12-124	-29.84
Brian Ellison	17-150	11	0-24	17-126	-67.39
Kevin Ryan	15-106	14	4-35	11-71	-11.30
Tim Easterby	14-171	8	2-40	12-131	-90.17
Tracy Waggott	13-129	10	0-4	13-125	-24.00
David Barron	12-58	21	1-9	11-49	+2.68
Ruth Carr	11-110	10	0-3	11-107	+11.00
Richard Guest	11-103	11	1-9	10-94	-7.08
Mark Johnston	11-101	11	4-36	7-65	-41.38
Jim Goldie	11-100	11	0-1	11-99	-34.45
Keith Dalgleish	11-93	12	4-25	7-68	-13.63

Jockeys	Wins-Rides	%	£1 level stks	Best Trainer	W-R
Graham Lee	25-156	16	-21.75	Sir Michael Stoute	3-3
Paul Mulrennan	23-165	14	-28.25	Michael Dods	9-37
Tony Hamilton	20-147	14	-14.09	Richard Fahey	12-64
Graham Gibbons	20-129	16	-20.69	David Barron	9-37
P J McDonald	19-181	10	-4.17	Michael Dods	3-3
Barry McHugh	17-153	11	+38.50	Tony Coyle	5-31
Paul Hanagan	16-106	15	-36.28	Richard Fahey	6-38
Dale Swift	14-111	13	-41.55	Brian Ellison	8-43
Tom Eaves	13-247	5	-130.93	Keith Dalgleish	3-31
Joe Fanning	13-89	15	-7.19	Mark Johnston	3-41
Daniel Tudhope	12-137	9	-80.12	David O'Meara	8-77
Phillip Makin	12-117	10	-9.05	Kevin Ryan	3-27
David Allan	12-115	10	-5.92	Tim Easterby	5-52

Favourites

2yo	34.8%	-15.40	3yo	41.2%	+2.25	TOTAL 33.5% -30.59

Westfield House, The Links,
Newmarket, Suffolk. CB8 0TG

NEWMARKET

Rowley Mile

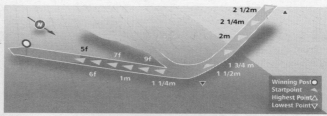

How to get there
Road: from south M11 Jct 9, then A11, otherwise A14 and A11. Rail: Newmarket

Features RH, wide, galloping, uphill finish

2015 Fixtures April 15-16, May 2-3, 14-16, 29-30, September 19, 24-26, October 3, 9-10, 21, 30-31

Racing Post standard times

5f	57.5	1m2f	2min0.5
6f	1min10.1	1m4f	2min28
7f	1min22.5	1m6f	2min53.5
1m	1min35.1	2m	3min19
1m1f	1min47.8	2m2f	3min45

Trainers	Wins-Runs	%	2yo	3yo+	£1 level stks
Richard Hannon Snr	32-247	13	16-129	16-118	+7.29
John Gosden	31-203	15	9-64	22-139	-5.39
Mark Johnston	25-200	13	7-62	18-138	+25.71
Mahmood Al Zarooni	23-95	24	10-44	13-51	+53.55
Saeed bin Suroor	18-125	14	5-35	13-90	-16.50
Andrew Balding	16-153	10	3-45	13-108	+2.88
William Haggas	16-153	10	8-65	8-88	-12.15
Roger Varian	14-97	14	5-39	9-58	-1.83
Richard Hannon	14-78	18	6-28	8-50	+51.41
Charlie Appleby	14-63	22	9-32	5-31	+40.73
Richard Fahey	13-122	11	2-28	11-94	-28.70
Charles Hills	12-144	8	7-67	5-77	-42.50
Roger Charlton	12-62	19	5-14	7-48	+24.25

Jockeys	Wins-Rides	%	£1 level stks	Best Trainer	W-R
Richard Hughes	31-206	15	+10.99	Richard Hannon Snr	15-94
Paul Hanagan	30-204	15	-48.10	Richard Fahey	8-41
Ryan Moore	26-219	12	-50.97	Sir Michael Stoute	6-61
William Buick	22-234	9	-82.45	John Gosden	14-114
Silvestre De Sousa	20-120	17	+84.07	Mark Johnston	6-26
Frankie Dettori	19-144	13	-12.68	Mahmood Al Zarooni	7-35
Mickael Barzalona	19-113	17	+6.14	Mahmood Al Zarooni	10-37
Tom Queally	16-177	9	-67.67	Sir Henry Cecil	8-41
Andrea Atzeni	16-129	12	+9.41	Roger Varian	5-33
Kieren Fallon	16-126	13	+67.09	Luca Cumani	4-33
Joe Fanning	15-155	10	-11.90	Mark Johnston	12-95
Jim Crowley	13-119	11	-12.43	Ralph Beckett	6-38
Michael Hills	11-68	16	+11.25	Charles Hills	6-35

Favourites

2yo	39.2% -1.08	3yo	35.6% +11.08	TOTAL	34.3% -4.68

NEWMARKET

Westfield House, The Links,
Newmarket, Suffolk. CB8 0TG

July Course

How to get there
See previous
page

Features RH,
wide, galloping,
uphill finish

2015 Fixtures
June 19-20,
25-27, July 9-11,
17-18, 24-25, 31,
August 1, 7-8,
14-15, 28-29

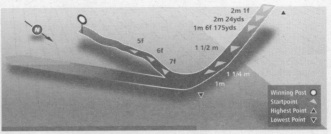

Racing Post standard times

5f	57.2	1m110yds	1min43	1m6f175yds	3min3
6f	1min10.1	1m2f	2min1.5	2m24yds	3min20
7f	1min23	1m4f	2min26.5		
1m	1min36	1m5f	2min40		

Trainers	Wins-Runs	%	2yo	3yo+	£1 level stks
Richard Hannon Snr	35-264	13	23-139	12-125	-19.96
John Gosden	34-200	17	9-68	25-132	+27.31
Saeed bin Suroor	30-137	22	13-50	17-87	-3.53
Mark Johnston	29-185	16	4-41	25-144	+17.58
Mahmood Al Zarooni	23-104	22	15-74	8-30	+77.50
Richard Fahey	16-117	14	3-34	13-83	-0.38
Sir Michael Stoute	16-106	15	1-34	15-72	-37.02
William Haggas	15-120	13	3-28	12-92	-63.39
David Elsworth	15-103	15	5-39	10-64	+39.00
Richard Hannon	15-100	15	11-56	4-44	-7.75
Brian Meehan	14-133	11	7-69	7-64	-59.87
Charlie Appleby	14-81	17	9-40	5-41	-11.22
Jeremy Noseda	14-68	21	5-24	9-44	-5.48

Jockeys	Wins-Rides	%	£1 level stks	Best Trainer	W-R
William Buick	42-194	22	+34.44	John Gosden	21-82
Ryan Moore	39-192	20	-3.41	Sir Michael Stoute	7-47
Mickael Barzalona	39-144	27	+67.37	Saeed bin Suroor	13-40
Richard Hughes	27-138	20	-3.47	Richard Hannon Snr	12-69
Paul Hanagan	25-157	16	-6.43	Richard Fahey	4-26
Kieren Fallon	21-158	13	-39.67	Luca Cumani	7-38
Neil Callan	17-116	15	-11.30	Mark Johnston	5-14
Tom Queally	15-151	10	-19.50	Sir Henry Cecil	4-25
Jamie Spencer	15-123	12	-49.71	Michael Bell	3-26
Silvestre De Sousa	14-116	12	-35.17	Mark Johnston	6-28
Dane O'Neill	14-113	12	+18.23	Mark Johnston	4-7
Frankie Dettori	13-145	9	-76.63	Mahmood Al Zarooni	3-21
James Doyle	11-96	11	-32.34	Richard Hannon	3-3

Favourites

2yo	35.6%	-8.77		3yo	35.8%	-8.07		TOTAL	32.7%	-54.86

GREGORIAN: another July Course winner for John Gosden and William Buick

NOTTINGHAM

Colwick Park, Nottingham, NG2 4BE. Tel 0115 958 0620

How to get there
Road: M1 Jct 25, A52 east to B686, signs for Trent Bridge, then Colwick Park.
Rail: Nottingham

Features LH, flat, easy turns

2015 Fixtures April 8, 18, 28, May 8-9, 19, 21, 31, June 1, 11, 15, 25, July 4, 17, 30, August 3, 11, 14, September 30, October 7, 14, 28, November 4

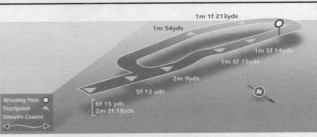

Racing Post standard times

5f13yds	58.4	1m2f50yds (Inner)	2min8.6
5f13yds (Inner)	59.8	1m6f15yds	2min57
6f15yds	1min12.2	2m9yds	3min24
1m75yds	1min42	2m9yds (Inner)	3min32
1m75yds (Inner)	1min43.5	2m2f18yds	3min55
1m2f50yds	2min6		

Trainers	Wins-Runs	%	2yo	3yo+	£1 level stks
Michael Appleby	20-96	21	1-6	19-90	+77.13
Saeed bin Suroor	14-63	22	5-23	9-40	-14.20
Richard Fahey	12-94	13	6-24	6-70	-23.13
Richard Hannon Snr	12-71	17	8-39	4-32	+10.82
Clive Cox	12-49	24	2-14	10-35	+22.95
Luca Cumani	11-49	22	2-16	9-33	+6.18
John Gosden	10-63	16	2-18	8-45	-21.60
Mark Johnston	9-120	8	4-48	5-72	-75.79
Mick Channon	9-82	11	4-35	5-47	-28.92
Kevin Ryan	9-59	15	5-22	4-37	-6.90
Mrs K Burke	9-23	39	2-9	7-14	+17.81
Ralph Beckett	8-54	15	2-18	6-36	-13.98
Roger Varian	8-52	15	1-16	7-36	-4.25

Jockeys	Wins-Rides	%	£1 level stks	Best Trainer	W-R
James Doyle	16-85	19	-10.75	Roy Brotherton	2-2
Silvestre De Sousa	15-105	14	-14.10	Saeed bin Suroor	7-20
Tom Queally	15-99	15	+26.86	Sir Henry Cecil	5-21
Paul Mulrennan	12-75	16	+18.83	Michael Dods	3-12
Hayley Turner	12-68	18	+29.75	Michael Bell	3-24
Jamie Spencer	12-57	21	-18.07	Michael Bell	3-11
Luke Morris	11-94	12	-20.40	Michael Appleby	2-3
Paul Hanagan	11-77	14	-14.29	John Gosden	2-3
Andrew Mullen	11-58	19	+31.00	Michael Appleby	9-38
Jim Crowley	11-43	26	+22.29	Ralph Beckett	6-20
Frederik Tylicki	10-70	14	-3.67	Saeed bin Suroor	2-4
Andrea Atzeni	10-70	14	-6.75	Marco Botti	3-10
Adam Kirby	10-59	17	+2.00	Clive Cox	3-16

Favourites

2yo	39.2% -6.08	3yo	30.7% -50.15	TOTAL	31.4% -81.14

33 Ropergate, Pontefract,
WF8 1LE. Tel 01977 703 224

PONTEFRACT

How to get there
Road: M62 Jct
32, then A539.
Rail: Pontefract
Monkhill or
Pontefract Baghill
from Leeds

Features LH,
undulating, sharp
home turn, last
half-mile all uphill

2015 Fixtures April 7, 20, 29, May 22,
June 8, 21, 29, July 7, 17, 26, August
5, 16, September 17, 24, October 5,
19

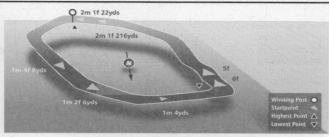

Racing Post standard times

5f	1min1.8	1m4f8yds	2min35.5
6f	1min14.6	2m1f22yds	3min41
1m4yds	1min42.6	2m1f216yds	3min51
1m2f6yds	2min9.4	2m5f122yds	4min41

Trainers	Wins-Runs	%	2yo	3yo+	£1 level stks
Richard Fahey	32-175	18	12-46	20-129	+35.60
Mark Johnston	25-167	15	2-40	23-127	-56.22
Tim Easterby	14-147	10	3-40	11-107	-40.17
Paul Midgley	12-93	13	0-5	12-88	+45.50
William Haggas	12-41	29	3-13	9-28	-0.41
Kevin Ryan	11-90	12	4-35	7-55	+22.33
Micky Hammond	10-111	9	0-11	10-100	-9.75
David O'Meara	10-92	11	0-10	10-82	-22.25
David Barron	10-49	20	2-8	8-41	+13.46
Alan Swinbank	9-65	14	2-9	7-56	-15.75
Jedd O'Keeffe	9-46	20	2-15	7-31	+39.25
Tom Dascombe	9-44	20	3-19	6-25	+9.33
Alan McCabe	8-56	14	1-17	7-39	+21.73

Jockeys	Wins-Rides	%	£1 level stks	Best Trainer	W-R
Silvestre De Sousa	39-162	24	+45.02	Mark Johnston	13-54
Robert Winston	18-126	14	+5.60	David Barron	3-4
Paul Hanagan	16-134	12	-41.38	Richard Fahey	9-53
Franny Norton	15-77	19	+59.88	Mark Johnston	5-22
Paul Mulrennan	14-106	13	+40.00	James Given	3-7
Tony Hamilton	12-82	15	-18.15	Richard Fahey	10-48
David Allan	11-97	11	-0.17	Tim Easterby	8-62
Graham Lee	11-93	12	+9.75	Jedd O'Keeffe	2-4
Phillip Makin	10-86	12	-29.68	Kevin Ryan	3-31
Joe Fanning	10-84	12	-28.97	Mark Johnston	5-56
P J McDonald	9-109	8	-47.00	Ann Duffield	3-18
Tom Eaves	9-102	9	-8.00	Bryan Smart	2-16
Kieren Fallon	9-65	14	-14.17	Luca Cumani	2-6

Favourites

2yo	36.7%	+0.07	3yo	37.9%	-2.43	
				TOTAL	33%	-13.33

REDCAR

Redcar, Teesside,
TS10 2BY. Tel 01642 484 068

How to get there
Road: A1, A168, A19, then A174.
Rail: Redcar Central from Darlington

Features LH, flat, galloping

2015 Fixtures
April 6, 13, 30, May 18, 25-26, June 19-20, July 19, 29, August 8, 29, September 8, 23, October 3, 16, 26, November 3

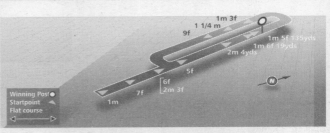

Racing Post standard times

5f	57	1m3f	2min16
6f	1min9.5	1m5f135yds	2min51
7f	1min22	1m6f19yds	2min57.5
1m	1min35	2m4yds	3min22
1m1f	1min48	2m3f	4min8
1m2f	2min3		

Trainers	Wins-Runs	%	2yo	3yo+	£1 level stks
David O'Meara	28-176	16	5-39	23-137	+6.79
Richard Fahey	26-159	16	12-74	14-85	-24.14
Tim Easterby	25-312	8	7-103	18-209	-119.17
Bryan Smart	15-115	13	5-46	10-69	+48.93
Michael Dods	14-118	12	2-31	12-87	-35.45
John Quinn	14-78	18	2-28	12-50	-25.68
Kevin Ryan	13-94	14	8-45	5-49	-8.67
Paul Midgley	12-137	9	0-22	12-115	-70.08
David Nicholls	12-113	11	3-17	9-96	-51.15
Ruth Carr	12-93	13	0-1	12-92	+1.63
David Barron	12-51	24	2-10	10-41	+33.50
Keith Reveley	10-58	17	0-5	10-53	+5.25
Jim Goldie	10-44	23	0-2	10-42	+51.25

Jockeys	Wins-Rides	%	£1 level stks	Best Trainer	W-R
Daniel Tudhope	26-114	23	+54.96	David O'Meara	19-71
Graham Gibbons	20-105	19	+18.37	David Barron	8-20
David Allan	19-179	11	+10.83	Tim Easterby	11-105
James Sullivan	17-147	12	+34.38	Ruth Carr	8-51
Graham Lee	17-113	15	-14.23	Jim Goldie	3-8
Paul Mulrennan	16-128	13	+5.43	Bryan Smart	3-19
Paul Hanagan	16-71	23	-10.00	Richard Fahey	7-25
Tony Hamilton	14-122	11	-60.90	Richard Fahey	10-66
Phillip Makin	14-109	13	+0.71	Kevin Ryan	4-19
Tom Eaves	13-219	6	-148.88	Michael Dods	5-25
P J McDonald	13-157	8	-47.90	Noel Quinlan	2-3
Michael O'Connell	12-71	17	-19.83	John Quinn	5-22
Adrian Nicholls	11-77	14	-32.65	David Nicholls	9-50

Favourites

2yo	48%	+23.42	3yo	31%	-13.67	TOTAL	35.2%	+19.09

77 North Street, Ripon, N Yorkshire
HG4 1DS. Tel 01765 602 156 or 01765 603 696

RIPON

How to get there
Road: A1, then
B6265. Rail:
Harrogate, bus to
Ripon centre, 1m
walk

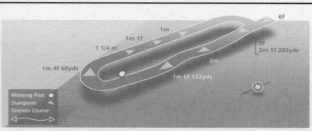

Features RH,
sharp

2015 Fixtures
April 16, 25, May
8, 17, June 2-3, 17-18, July 6, 18,
August 3-4, 15, 18, 31, September 26

Racing Post standard times

5f	58	1m2f	2min4.5
6f	1min10.3	1m4f10yds	2min33.4
1m	1min38.1	2m	3min26.5
1m1f	1min52	2m1f203yds	3min53
1m1f170yds	2min1.3		

Trainers	Wins-Runs	%	2yo	3yo+	£1 level stks
David O'Meara	34-185	18	3-29	31-156	+15.90
Tim Easterby	29-323	9	11-100	18-223	-26.09
Richard Fahey	28-206	14	11-61	17-145	-35.32
Mark Johnston	18-158	11	1-28	17-130	-71.65
David Barron	18-105	17	1-15	17-90	+1.10
William Haggas	12-37	32	3-10	9-27	-5.54
Ruth Carr	10-93	11	0-0	10-93	-23.00
Paul Midgley	10-87	11	2-17	8-70	-24.29
Ann Duffield	10-61	16	7-32	3-29	+19.66
Mick Channon	10-58	17	5-24	5-34	-13.69
David Nicholls	9-148	6	1-17	8-131	-84.88
Kevin Ryan	8-119	7	2-34	6-85	-65.88
Richard Whitaker	8-69	12	0-11	8-58	-20.25

Jockeys	Wins-Rides	%	£1 level stks	Best Trainer	W-R
Daniel Tudhope	24-116	21	+27.34	David O'Meara	20-86
Graham Gibbons	20-126	16	-22.76	David Barron	8-49
Tony Hamilton	20-103	19	-7.07	Richard Fahey	18-80
P J McDonald	18-164	11	-27.63	Ann Duffield	4-25
Graham Lee	15-108	14	-37.49	William Haggas	2-4
Phillip Makin	13-105	12	-18.88	William Haggas	2-4
David Allan	12-159	8	-58.59	Tim Easterby	11-138
Adrian Nicholls	12-102	12	-31.17	David Nicholls	7-68
Silvestre De Sousa	12-80	15	+10.81	Mel Brittain	3-4
James Sullivan	11-116	9	-43.00	Ruth Carr	7-48
Tom Eaves	10-107	9	-26.67	Michael Appleby	1-1
Paul Mulrennan	9-112	8	-69.71	Paul Midgley	2-10
Robert Winston	9-82	11	+12.60	David Barron	2-2

Favourites

2yo	37.8%	+1.14	3yo	41%	+7.49	TOTAL 36.8%	+8.69

SALISBURY

Netherhampton, Salisbury, Wilts
SP2 8PN. Tel 01722 326 461

How to get there
Road: 2m west
of Salisbury on
A3094. Rail:
Salisbury, bus

Features RH,
uphill finish

2015 Fixtures
May 3, 14, 23,
June 9, 14, 24,
July 11, 25, August 4, 12-13, 21,
September 3, 11, 30, October 12

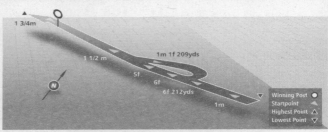

Racing Post standard times

5f	59.8	1m1f198yds	2min5.8
6f	1min12.3	1m4f	2min33
6f212yds	1min26.5	1m6f21yds	3min
1m	1min39.5		

Trainers	Wins-Runs	%	2yo	3yo+	£1 level stks
Richard Hannon Snr	57-265	22	35-146	22-119	+11.16
Ralph Beckett	20-121	17	7-45	13-76	-5.22
Andrew Balding	17-126	13	4-38	13-88	-32.45
David Evans	14-100	14	5-35	9-65	+85.66
Rod Millman	13-106	12	3-23	10-83	+14.80
Richard Hannon	13-88	15	10-44	3-44	-13.97
Mick Channon	12-108	11	4-47	8-61	-22.76
Clive Cox	8-86	9	4-34	4-52	-49.00
Hughie Morrison	8-66	12	0-14	8-52	-22.75
Roger Charlton	8-60	13	3-24	5-36	-7.36
Saeed bin Suroor	8-44	18	2-10	6-34	+2.78
Roger Varian	8-36	22	3-10	5-26	-3.02
David Simcock	8-31	26	3-4	5-27	+2.48

Jockeys	Wins-Rides	%	£1 level stks	Best Trainer	W-R
Richard Hughes	56-240	23	-7.11	Richard Hannon Snr	33-116
James Doyle	20-92	22	+88.42	Roger Charlton	4-25
Pat Dobbs	17-116	15	+17.19	Richard Hannon Snr	11-55
Jim Crowley	17-112	15	+52.35	Ralph Beckett	9-58
Dane O'Neill	10-113	9	-25.03	Henry Candy	4-28
Andrea Atzeni	10-54	19	-9.75	Luca Cumani	3-4
Tom Queally	10-52	19	+18.43	Lady Cecil	4-4
Kieren Fallon	10-44	23	+9.73	Luca Cumani	3-14
William Buick	9-45	20	-2.31	John Gosden	5-15
Jimmy Fortune	8-95	8	-57.20	Andrew Balding	4-35
Paul Hanagan	8-36	22	+3.53	Roger Varian	2-2
Liam Keniry	7-89	8	-47.00	Ed de Giles	2-3
George Baker	7-66	11	-6.88	Ed Walker	2-4

Favourites

2yo	44.4%	+3.11		3yo	33%	-28.61	
					TOTAL	35.2%	-47.49

Esher, Surrey, KT10 9AJ.
Tel 01372 463 072 or 01372 464 348

SANDOWN

How to get there
Road: M25 Jct 10
then A3. Rail:
Esher from
Waterloo

Features RH, last
7f uphill

2015 Fixtures
April 24, May 21,
28, June 12-13,
July 3-4, 15, 22-23, 29, August 6,
21-22, September 11, 16

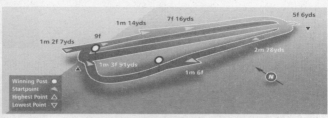

Racing Post standard times

5f6yds	59.8	1m2f7yds	2min5.8
7f16yds	1min27	1m3f91yds	2min23
1m14yds	1min39.9	1m6f	2min58.3
1m1f	1min52.9	2m78yds	3min34

Trainers	Wins-Runs	%	2yo	3yo+	£1 level stks
Richard Hannon Snr	35-220	16	19-82	16-138	-9.72
Sir Michael Stoute	25-130	19	3-27	22-103	-13.96
Andrew Balding	24-137	18	4-30	20-107	+37.94
John Gosden	21-128	16	6-28	15-100	-32.51
William Haggas	11-55	20	0-10	11-45	+6.63
Saeed bin Suroor	10-76	13	2-12	8-64	-40.07
Brian Meehan	10-69	14	4-25	6-44	+0.40
Richard Hannon	10-65	15	6-25	4-40	-9.66
Clive Cox	9-82	11	3-16	6-66	-36.35
Jeremy Noseda	8-42	19	4-8	4-34	-5.77
Mark Johnston	7-86	8	1-18	6-68	-45.50
Mick Channon	7-85	8	5-31	2-54	-21.50
Henry Candy	7-44	16	1-5	6-39	-1.42

Jockeys	Wins-Rides	%	£1 level stks	Best Trainer	W-R
Ryan Moore	48-226	21	-27.50	Sir Michael Stoute	16-77
Richard Hughes	34-192	18	-31.17	Richard Hannon Snr	19-97
William Buick	27-179	15	-67.47	John Gosden	14-85
James Doyle	19-122	16	-18.42	Roger Charlton	7-29
Jamie Spencer	14-63	22	+5.71	David Brown	2-2
Jimmy Fortune	13-113	12	+8.00	Andrew Balding	9-44
Pat Dobbs	13-77	17	+28.27	Richard Hannon Snr	8-34
Dane O'Neill	12-113	11	-51.42	Henry Candy	5-26
Kieren Fallon	12-111	11	-36.93	Luca Cumani	4-25
Jim Crowley	12-89	13	+35.50	Ralph Beckett	3-26
David Probert	12-74	16	-2.06	Andrew Balding	10-45
Adam Kirby	10-102	10	-47.68	Clive Cox	5-43
Tom Queally	10-91	11	-46.88	Sir Henry Cecil	3-21

Favourites

2yo	44.2%	+2.32	3yo	28.1%	-54.76	TOTAL 34%	-38.37

SOUTHWELL

Rolleston, Newark, Notts
NG25 0TS. Tel 01636 814 481

How to get there Road: A1 to Newark, then A617 or M1 to Nottingham, then A612. Rail: Rolleston

Features LH, Fibresand, sharp

Please note there are no turf fixtures scheduled for 2015 Stats relate to all-weather only

2015 Fixtures March 31, April 9, 14, 23, 27, May 18, July 27, August 6, November 3, 12, 24, 26, December 8, 12, 15, 17-18, 22, 27, 29

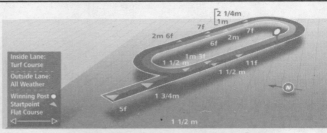

Racing Post standard times

5f	58	1m4f	2min35
6f	1min14	1m5f	2min50.5
7f	1min27	1m6f	3min2
1m	1min39.8	2m	3min34
1m3f	2min22.3	2m2f	4min4

Trainers	Wins-Runs	%	2yo	3yo+	£1 level stks
Michael Appleby	64-323	20	1-17	63-306	-3.16
Mark Johnston	57-233	24	10-45	47-188	-13.16
Alan McCabe	50-361	14	8-47	42-314	-19.21
Brian Ellison	43-235	18	4-18	39-217	-55.29
Kevin Ryan	42-190	22	8-35	34-155	-16.03
David Nicholls	38-211	18	2-27	36-184	+34.97
J R Jenkins	37-262	14	1-8	36-254	-42.08
Bryan Smart	31-209	15	2-29	29-180	-8.32
David O'Meara	28-199	14	2-22	26-177	-77.59
Derek Shaw	28-199	14	0-20	28-179	+10.40
Roy Bowring	27-203	13	0-2	27-201	-2.90
Hughie Morrison	27-110	25	2-9	25-101	+22.95
Scott Dixon	25-230	11	2-22	23-208	-34.00

Jockeys	Wins-Rides	%	£1 level stks	Best Trainer	W-R
Joe Fanning	74-367	20	-41.32	Mark Johnston	39-136
Luke Morris	51-380	13	-65.33	Ronald Harris	9-56
Andrew Mullen	46-256	18	-37.19	Michael Appleby	31-145
Tom Eaves	43-375	11	-14.51	Bryan Smart	15-102
Hayley Turner	32-164	20	+4.33	Conor Dore	15-84
Barry McHugh	29-200	14	-7.68	Brian Ellison	12-50
Dale Swift	29-178	16	-13.88	Derek Shaw	11-45
Phillip Makin	29-121	24	+14.94	Kevin Ryan	23-59
Frederik Tylicki	28-157	18	-7.22	J R Jenkins	19-82
Robert Winston	27-183	15	-31.82	Alan Swinbank	5-19
Graham Lee	27-169	16	-64.69	James Given	9-41
Silvestre De Sousa	27-125	22	-19.35	Mark Johnston	9-31
Graham Gibbons	21-149	14	-16.94	David Nicholls	3-9

Favourites

2yo	46.7%	-4.81	3yo	39%	-57.39	
				TOTAL	39.7%	-44.87

Station Road, Thirsk, N Yorkshire,
YO7 1QL. Tel 01845 522 276

THIRSK

How to get there
Road: A61 from
A1 in the west
or A19 in the
east. Rail: Thirsk,
10min walk

Features LH,
sharp, tight turns

2015 Fixtures
April 18, May 2, 9,
16, 27, June 8, 16, July 1, 14, 24, 31,
August 1, 10, 17, 28, September 5

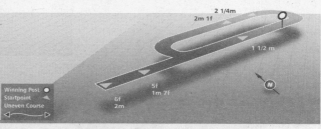

Racing Post standard times

5f	58	1m	1min36.5
6f	1min10.6	1m4f	2min32
7f	1min24	2m	3min23

Trainers	Wins-Runs	%	2yo	3yo+	£1 level stks
Richard Fahey	27-189	14	10-65	17-124	-22.34
Tim Easterby	23-286	8	8-85	15-201	-123.14
David O'Meara	21-153	14	5-18	16-135	-10.47
Kevin Ryan	19-153	12	6-49	13-104	-14.93
David Barron	16-105	15	4-20	12-85	-20.11
Michael Dods	14-143	10	1-27	13-116	-26.10
Ruth Carr	14-132	11	0-1	14-131	-2.92
David Nicholls	13-191	7	1-26	12-165	-104.75
Michael Easterby	10-131	8	0-30	10-101	-34.25
Alan Swinbank	10-66	15	0-6	10-60	+10.13
Mick Channon	9-45	20	5-16	4-29	+0.83
Richard Guest	8-90	9	0-16	8-74	+7.00
Jim Goldie	8-55	15	0-1	8-54	+0.70

Jockeys	Wins-Rides	%	£1 level stks	Best Trainer	W-R
Graham Gibbons	24-128	19	+32.94	David Barron	9-41
Daniel Tudhope	24-121	20	+69.48	David O'Meara	14-59
Paul Mulrennan	19-181	10	-66.10	Michael Dods	4-40
Robert Winston	17-132	13	+2.15	Mel Brittain	3-13
P J McDonald	16-186	9	-46.50	Ruth Carr	6-35
David Allan	14-135	10	-63.02	Tim Easterby	9-91
Phillip Makin	12-130	9	-38.31	Kevin Ryan	6-42
Tom Eaves	11-181	6	-76.38	Keith Dalgleish	3-12
Tony Hamilton	11-121	9	-40.38	Richard Fahey	8-74
Barry McHugh	11-106	10	+24.50	Kevin Ryan	2-5
Frederik Tylicki	11-59	19	+28.50	James Given	2-7
Adrian Nicholls	10-107	9	-44.35	David Nicholls	7-88
Graham Lee	10-99	10	-23.63	Ann Duffield	2-5

Favourites

2yo	37.2%	-6.91	3yo	35.3%	-7.16	TOTAL 32.1%	-14.71

WETHERBY

York Road, Wetherby, West Yorks
L22 5EJ. Tel: 01937 582 035

How to get there Road: A1, A58 from Leeds, B1224 from York. Rail: Leeds, Harrogate, York.
Features LH
2015 Fixtures April 26, June 22, July 13, 21

WETHERBY: soon to be the backdrop to more than just National Hunt racing

Maidenhead Road, Windsor, Berks
SL4 5JJ. Tel 01753 498 400

WINDSOR

How to get there
Road: M4 Jctn 6,
A355, A308. Rail:
Paddington to
Windsor Central/
Waterloo to Wind-
sor Riverside

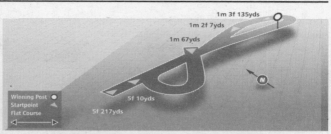

1m 3f 135yds
1m 2f 7yds
1m 67yds
5f 10yds
5f 217yds
Winning Post
Startpoint
Flat Course
N

Features Figure
of eight, flat, long
straight

2015 Fixtures April 13, 20, 27, May
4, 11, 18, 25, June 1, 8, 15, 22, 27-29,
July 6, 13, 20, 27, August 3, 9-10, 17,
29, September 7, October 5, 12, 19

Racing Post standard times

5f10yds	59.2	1m2f7yds	2min5
6f	1min10.5	1m3f135yds	2min25
1m67yds	1min41.1		

Trainers	Wins-Runs	%	2yo	3yo+	£1 level stks
Richard Hannon Snr	51-282	18	33-132	18-150	-74.81
Andrew Balding	27-108	25	8-21	19-87	+48.34
Ralph Beckett	20-105	19	5-37	15-68	+2.35
Jeremy Noseda	18-71	25	1-9	17-62	-1.60
Roger Varian	18-62	29	1-9	17-53	+24.75
Sir Michael Stoute	17-85	20	1-10	16-75	-9.17
David Evans	16-137	12	7-45	9-92	-18.00
Gary Moore	16-86	19	3-10	13-76	+30.12
Roger Charlton	15-79	19	2-26	13-53	+29.77
Richard Hannon	13-98	13	9-40	4-58	-53.85
William Haggas	13-47	28	3-12	10-35	-4.88
John Bridger	11-111	10	0-1	11-110	-44.75
John Gosden	11-67	16	1-8	10-59	-20.35

Jockeys	Wins-Rides	%	£1 level stks	Best Trainer	W-R
Richard Hughes	70-315	22	-72.59	Richard Hannon Snr	33-134
Ryan Moore	53-210	25	-23.04	Sir Michael Stoute	12-53
Jimmy Fortune	25-162	15	-13.83	Andrew Balding	10-35
Andrea Atzeni	23-83	28	+62.42	Roger Varian	6-14
Jim Crowley	22-189	12	-34.55	Ralph Beckett	8-61
James Doyle	22-146	15	+34.67	Roger Charlton	9-39
Adam Kirby	21-145	14	-30.23	Clive Cox	3-44
George Baker	19-114	17	+49.35	Roger Charlton	3-11
William Buick	16-107	15	-23.08	Jeremy Noseda	5-9
Dane O'Neill	14-151	9	-30.92	Henry Candy	7-43
Jamie Spencer	12-70	17	-15.78	Ralph Beckett	2-4
Pat Cosgrave	11-104	11	+18.50	Jim Boyle	4-26
David Probert	10-111	9	-49.32	Andrew Balding	7-31

Favourites

2yo	52.5%	+32.96	3yo	40.9%	+32.23	TOTAL 39.4% +44.46

WOLVES

Dunstall Park, Gorsebrook Road, Wolverhampton,
West Midlands. WV6 0PE. Tel 08702 202 442

How to get there
Road: A449,
close to M6, M42
and M54. Rail:
Wolverhampton

Features LH,
sharp, relaid with
Tapeta in 2014

2015 Fixtures
April 2, 6, 10-11,
18, 21, 25, 27-29, May 11, June 2-4,
22, 29, July 7, 13, August 10, 21, 27,
September 5, 14, 19, 25, 29, October
2-3, 9, 13, 16-17, 20, 23, 27, 30-31,
November 3, 10, 13-14, 16, 20-21,
27-28, 30, December 1, 4-5, 11-12,
14, 18, 21-22, 26

Racing Post standard times

5f20yds	1min0.5	1m1f103yds	1min57.3
5f216yds	1min13.2	1m4f50yds	2min35.3
7f32yds	1min27	1m5f194yds	2min58.5
1m141yds	1min46.7	2m119yds	3min36

Trainers	Wins-Runs	%	2yo	3yo+	£1 level stks
Mark Johnston	96-475	20	7-86	89-389	-66.66
David Evans	94-771	12	24-153	70-618	-136.18
Marco Botti	76-337	23	23-110	53-227	+32.17
Richard Fahey	53-459	12	12-116	41-343	-80.47
Tom Dascombe	51-323	16	18-123	33-200	-64.29
Jamie Osborne	48-255	19	19-83	29-172	+9.85
Richard Guest	44-445	10	1-30	43-415	-103.50
Kevin Ryan	44-286	15	8-74	36-212	-27.92
Keith Dalgleish	43-262	16	5-44	38-218	-14.05
Michael Appleby	42-382	11	1-15	41-367	-114.79
Tony Carroll	40-415	10	1-9	39-406	-154.72
Michael Easterby	40-365	11	1-38	39-327	-57.72
Ian Williams	39-276	14	1-19	38-257	+35.23

Jockeys	Wins-Rides	%	£1 level stks	Best Trainer	W-R
Luke Morris	161-1338	12	-379.32	Sir Mark Prescott Bt	19-88
Adam Kirby	131-653	20	-111.39	Marco Botti	28-72
Joe Fanning	130-769	17	-8.54	Mark Johnston	57-279
Graham Gibbons	74-591	13	-112.57	Michael Easterby	19-107
Shane Kelly	72-597	12	-195.08	Daniel Mark Loughnane	15-91
Silvestre De Sousa	70-364	19	-44.96	Saeed bin Suroor	14-29
Richard Kingscote	68-452	15	-17.35	Tom Dascombe	46-216
Martin Harley	62-377	16	+54.64	Marco Botti	17-66
Jamie Spencer	60-309	19	-67.00	Ian Williams	9-38
George Baker	58-289	20	+16.77	David Lanigan	4-9
Tom Eaves	52-676	8	-275.06	Bryan Smart	13-96
Graham Lee	52-384	14	-114.06	James Given	6-38
Robert Winston	51-357	14	-16.86	Charles Hills	7-28

Favourites

2yo	37.9%	-68.54	3yo	39.9%	-51.16	TOTAL	36.6%	-246.15

North Denes, Great Yarmouth, Norfolk
NR30 4AU. Tel 01493 842 527

YARMOUTH

How to get there
Road: A47 to
end, A1064. Rail:
Great Yarmouth,
bus

Features LH, flat

2015 Fixtures
June 26, July 2,
8, 14, 23, 28,
August 5-6, 13,
25, 30, September 15-17, October
20, 27

Racing Post standard times

5f43yds	1min0.5	1m2f21yds	2min5
6f3yds	1min11	1m3f101yds	2min23.5
7f3yds	1min23.6	1m6f17yds	2min59
1m3yds	1min36.5	2m	3min24.5
1m1f	1min50	2m2f51yds	3min56

Trainers	*Wins-Runs*	%	2yo	3yo+	£1 level stks
William Haggas	29-94	31	8-35	21-59	+31.75
Chris Wall	25-110	23	0-14	25-96	+11.75
Luca Cumani	18-69	26	5-20	13-49	+8.19
Michael Bell	16-131	12	5-31	11-100	-30.73
Julia Feilden	16-126	13	0-8	16-118	-19.88
Mark Johnston	16-99	16	6-31	10-68	+1.80
Phil McEntee	15-118	13	1-6	14-112	+30.63
Roger Varian	15-60	25	5-23	10-37	-3.39
J R Jenkins	14-129	11	0-12	14-117	+12.25
Mick Channon	14-105	13	5-27	9-78	-9.56
Mark H Tompkins	13-142	9	1-26	12-116	-42.00
Marco Botti	13-84	15	7-25	6-59	-9.48
Rae Guest	13-64	20	1-10	12-54	-1.18

Jockeys	*Wins-Rides*	%	£1 level stks	*Best Trainer*	W-R
Kieren Fallon	32-152	21	+35.04	Luca Cumani	4-20
Ryan Moore	29-120	24	-11.07	Sir Michael Stoute	6-31
Paul Hanagan	27-110	25	+18.63	William Haggas	5-13
Ted Durcan	24-176	14	-47.22	Chris Wall	14-52
Frederik Tylicki	23-145	16	+136.35	J R Jenkins	6-41
Luke Morris	21-158	13	-25.10	Sir Mark Prescott Bt	6-23
Jamie Spencer	21-150	14	-55.67	John Weymes	2-4
William Buick	20-113	18	-50.81	John Gosden	7-41
Tom Queally	18-160	11	-15.49	Sir Henry Cecil	5-15
Andrea Atzeni	18-132	14	-43.50	Roger Varian	5-15
Chris Catlin	17-89	19	+82.45	Rae Guest	6-19
Silvestre De Sousa	16-84	19	-9.40	Mark Johnston	6-25
Hayley Turner	15-99	15	+1.08	Michael Bell	7-37

Favourites

2yo	49.6%	+15.99	3yo	39.4%	-2.64	TOTAL 36.6%	-55.36

YORK

Knavesmire Road, York, YO23 1EX
Tel 01904 620 911

How to get there
Road: Course
is south of city.
From north, A1,
A59 to York,
northern bypass
from A19 to A64.
Otherwise, A64.
Rail: York, bus

Features LH, flat

2015 Fixtures May 13-15, 30, June
12-13, July 10-11, 24-25, August
19-22, September 6, October 9-10

6f 214yds
6f
7f 202yds
5f
1m 205yds
1m 2f 85yds
1m 3f 195yds
1m 5f 194yds
1m 7f 195yds
Winning Post
Startpoint
Flat Course

Racing Post standard times

5f	57.5	1m208yds	1min49
5f89yds	1min2.7	1m2f88yds	2min7
6f	1min10	1m4f	2min28.1
7f	1min22.3	1m6f	2min57
1m	1min37	2m88yds	3min29

Trainers	Wins-Runs	%	2yo	3yo+	£1 level stks
Richard Fahey	35-532	7	13-157	22-375	-193.01
David O'Meara	28-249	11	1-17	27-232	-28.75
Kevin Ryan	26-217	12	16-86	10-131	-11.94
William Haggas	26-116	22	6-29	20-87	+51.85
Tim Easterby	19-311	6	6-77	13-234	-96.00
Sir Michael Stoute	15-70	21	1-3	14-67	-10.71
Michael Easterby	13-201	6	3-42	10-159	-71.00
Luca Cumani	12-53	23	1-5	11-48	+35.50
Brian Ellison	11-135	8	0-14	11-121	+6.75
Mick Channon	10-95	11	7-43	3-52	-42.58
Saeed bin Suroor	10-92	11	1-8	9-84	-40.85
John Gosden	10-64	16	0-4	10-60	-7.88
Mark Johnston	9-198	5	5-65	4-133	-147.40

Jockeys	Wins-Rides	%	£1 level stks	Best Trainer	W-R
Ryan Moore	30-153	20	+25.06	Sir Michael Stoute	11-38
Paul Hanagan	27-211	13	-5.48	Richard Fahey	17-127
Kieren Fallon	22-146	15	+31.25	Luca Cumani	5-25
Daniel Tudhope	20-166	12	-32.25	David O'Meara	16-127
William Buick	17-109	16	+42.38	John Gosden	7-43
Silvestre De Sousa	15-148	10	-44.40	Saeed bin Suroor	3-23
Phillip Makin	14-132	11	-37.33	Kevin Ryan	9-62
Jamie Spencer	14-125	11	-2.17	David Barron	3-8
David Allan	13-176	7	-38.50	Tim Easterby	12-143
Frankie Dettori	13-78	17	-1.45	Mahmood Al Zarooni	4-17
Graham Gibbons	12-170	7	-80.33	David Barron	4-56
Robert Winston	11-107	10	+17.50	Dean Ivory	3-4
Paul Mulrennan	11-105	10	+29.00	Michael Easterby	3-22

Favourites

2yo	30.9%	-11.71		3yo	32%	+10.71	TOTAL 29.2% -16.18

MUBTAGHAA: another big-priced York winner for William Haggas, who was born in Yorkshire and loves to send one to the track from his Newmarket base

Win - free form!

THIS YEAR'S QUIZ could hardly be more simple, and the prize should prove invaluable to our lucky winner. We're offering a free subscription to The Flat Form Book, the BHA's official form book – every week from May to November, you could be getting the previous week's results in full, together with Notebook comments highlighting future winners, adjusted Official Ratings and Racing Post ratings. The winner will also get a copy of last year's complete form book.

All you have to do is this: identify the three horses pictured on the following pages. And the clue is they were all French-trained Group 1 winners in Britain last season. If you think you know the answer, write their names in the box below in the order in which they appear.

Send your answers along with your details on the entry form below, to:

**2015 Flat Annual Competition, Racing & Football Outlook,
Floor 23, 1 Canada Square, London, E14 5AP.**

Entries must reach us no later than first post on April 24. The winner's name and the right answers will be printed in the RFO's April 28 edition.

Six runners-up will each receive a copy of last year's form book.

Name

Address

Town

Postcode

In the event of more than one correct entry, the winner will be drawn at random from the correct entries. The Editor's decision is final and no correspondence will be entered into.

BETTING CHART

ON	£1	ODDS	£5	AGAINST
50		Evens		50
52.4	1.10	11-10	5.50	47.6
54.5	1.20	6-5	6	45.5
55.6	1.25	5-4	6.25	44.4
58	1.37	11-8	6.95	42
60	1.50	6-4	7.50	40
62	1.62	13-8	8.10	38
63.6	1.75	7-4	8.75	36.4
65.3	1.87	15-8	9.35	34.7
66.7	2	2-1	10	33.3
68	2.12	85-40	10.60	32
69.2	2.25	9-4	11.25	30.8
71.4	2.50	5-2	12.50	28.6
73.4	2.75	11-4	13.75	26.6
75	3	3-1	15	25
76.9	3.30	100-30	16.50	23.1
77.8	3.50	7-2	17.50	22.2
80		4-1		20
82		9-2		18
83.3		5-1		16.7
84.6		11-2		15.4
85.7		6-1		14.3
86.7		13-2		13.3
87.5		7-1		12.5
88.2		15-2		11.8
89		8-1		11
89.35		100-12		10.65
89.4		17-2		10.6
90		9-1		10
91		10-1		9
91.8		11-1		8.2
92.6		12-1		7.4
93.5		14-1		6.5
94.4		16-1		5.6
94.7		18-1		5.3
95.2		20-1		4.8
95.7		22-1		4.3
96.2		25-1		3.8
97.2		33-1		2.8
97.6		40-1		2.4
98.1		50-1		1.9
98.5		66-1		1.3
99.0		100-1		0.99

The table above (often known as the 'Field Money Table') shows both bookmakers' margins and how much a backer needs to invest to win £100. To calculate a bookmaker's margin, simply add up the percentages of all the odds on offer. The sum by which the total exceeds 100% gives the 'over-round' on the book. To determine what stake is required to win £100 (includes returned stake) at a particular price, just look at the relevant row, either odds-against or odds-on.

RULE 4 DEDUCTIONS

When a horse is withdrawn before coming under starter's orders, but after a market has been formed, bookmakers are entitled to make the following deductions from win and place returns (excluding stakes) in accordance with Tattersalls' Rule 4(c).

	Odds of withdrawn horse	*Deduction from winnings*
(1)	3-10 or shorter	75p in the £
(2)	2-5 to 1-3	70p in the £
(3)	8-15 to 4-9	65p in the £
(4)	8-13 to 4-7	60p in the £
(5)	4-5 to 4-6	55p in the £
(6)	20-21 to 5-6	50p in the £
(7)	Evens to 6-5	45p in the £
(8)	5-4 to 6-4	40p in the £
(9)	13-8 to 7-4	35p in the £
(10)	15-8 to 9-4	30p in the £
(11)	5-2 to 3-1	25p in the £
(12)	100-30 to 4-1	20p in the £
(13)	9-2 to 11-2	15p in the £
(14)	6-1 to 9-1	10p in the £
(15)	10-1 to 14-1	5p in the £
(16)	longer than 14-1	no deductions

(17) .... When more than one horse is withdrawn without coming under starter's orders, total deductions shall not exceed 75p in the £.

Starting-price bets are affected only when there was insufficient time to form a new market.

Feedback!

If you have any comments or criticism about this book, or suggestions for future editions, please tell us.

Write   Nick Watts/Dylan Hill
2015 Flat Annual
Racing & Football Outlook
Floor 23
1 Canada Square
London E14 5AP

email   rfo@rfoutlook.com

Horse index

All horses discussed, with page numbers, except for references in the Group 1 and two-year-old form sections (pages 81-111), which have their own indexes

Accession 46
Accra Beach 54
Aces 54
Acolyte 54
Adelaide 49
Agnes Stewart 23, 30, 31, 51
Aggression 31
Ainippe 51
Air Pilot 63
Aktabantay 8, 45
Al Kazeem 54
Al Naamah 23, 30
Angel Vision 31
Anthem Alexander 22, 32, 51, 76
Arab Spring 78
Arabian Queen 13
Archie 57
Ascription 8
Atab 54
Banzari 29
Basateen 62
Beat The Tide 75
Beautiful Romance 23, 29
Belardo 17, 43
Bellajeu 64
Bold 55
Boom The Groom 69
Brooch 50
Brown Panther 57
Burning Blaze 65
Burning Thread 13
Cable Bay 54
Camagueyana 64
Cappella Sansevero 32, 51
Captain Cat 54
Carntop 64
Cartier 29
Cascades 13
Caspian Prince 69
Charming Thought 18, 77
Chemical Charge 26, 64
Chief Spirit 46
Christophermarlowe 26

Cloud Seven 46
Cock Of The North 68
Commemorative 53
Connecticut 32
Consort 19, 26, 32
Convey 19, 26, 33
Cool Silk Boy 69
Cosmic Ray 53
Covert Love 8
Crisscrossed 66
Crystal Zvezda 30
Cursory Glance 22, 44, 76
Dancetrack 54
Danzeno 67
Dark Profit 54
Dashing Star 13
Demora 67
Donny Rover 67
Double Up 75
Dragon King 59
Due Diligence 49
Dutch Connection 54, 77
Easter 29
Edge Of Sanity 33
Elm Park 18, 25, 33, 52, 71, 78
Elysian Flyer 62
Encore D'Or 64, 71
Endless Drama 19, 33, 51
Engaging Smile 64
Epicuris 25, 34
Equitanus 53
Ervedya 23
Estidhkaar 18, 61, 77
Eternal 26
Extortionist 66, 79
Extremity 8
Fadhayyil 22, 76
Fannaan 18
Faydhan 16, 77
Fiftyshadesofpink 10
Flaming Spear 19, 56
Fontanelice 23
Forgotten Rules 34, 49

Forte 30, 64
Found 20, 27, 34, 48, 76
Free Eagle 49, 78
Freight Train 58
Full Mast 19, 25
G Force 57, 79
Gimlet 10
Giovanni Canaletto 24, 48
Gleneagles 16, 24, 48, 77
Gm Hopkins 34
Golden Horn 26
Goodyearforroses 27
Grandad's World 58
Great Glen 64
Green Door 66
Greyemkay 74
Hakam 54
Handiwork 74
Heatstroke 54
Here Comes When 53
High Admiral 53
High Celebrity 21, 76
Highland Castle 14
Highland Reel 17, 24, 77
Home Of The Brave 8
Hootenanny 18
Humphrey Repton 46
Hungerford 65
Ice Lord 55
Ice Slice 46
Intransive 35
Invisible Gold 45
Irish Rookie 23, 30
Ivawood 17, 61, 77
Jack Naylor 23, 29, 35
Jacob Black 59
John F Kennedy 16, 24, 48, 77
Judicial 54
Jumeirah Glory 59
Justice Day 14
Justice Good 14
Justice Well 14
Just The Judge 54
Kawaii 46
Kingston Hill 35, 43, 78
Kirkman 74
Kiyoshi 54
Kodi Bear 18, 55
Kodiva 54

La Fritillaire 69
La Superba 15
Lady Correspondent 23
Lady Eli 23
Lancelot Du Lac 66
Last Minute Lisa 74
Ledbury 54
Legatissimo 29
Libbard 55
Lightning Charlie 66
Lightning Moon 35, 45
Lightning Spear 65
Lightning Thunder 65
Likely 23
L'Ingenue 64
Loaves And Fishes 28, 55
Lobster Pot 8
Louis De Palma 55
Lucida 22, 50, 76
Lulu The Zulu 67
Maftool 18
Magical Path 10
Magic Dancer 64
Make Believe 19
Make It Up 53
Malabar 23, 71
Mange All 44
Marsh Hawk 61
Master Apprentice 53
Master Of Irony 64
Master The World 15
McCreery 26, 54
Mecca's Angel 59, 79
Melodious 15
Merdon Castle 15
Milky Way 66
Moheet 19, 26
Montaly 53
Moonlight Sonata 30
Muhaarar 53
Muraaqaba 23
Mutakayyef 44
My Twinkle 36
Nabatean 53
Nawaasy 54
New Providence 9
Niceofyoutotellme 63
Nidnod 10
Night Of Thunder 60, 79

Not Never 9
Nufooth.................................... 46
Odeon 68
Ol' Man River.......... 16, 24, 36, 48, 77
Only Joking 9
Ooty Hill.............................. 36, 54
Osaila 23, 60
Pacify..................................... 64
Parish Boy 18, 26, 36, 50
Pastoral Girl............................. 69
Peace And War 65
Peacock 62
Perrault.................................... 64
Pharmaceutical 54
Pillar....................................... 65
Pleascach 29, 50
Point Of Woods 65
Portage.................................... 37
Postponed......................... 72, 78
Pour La Victoire......................... 73
Prize Exhibit 23
Qualify 20, 76
Queen Nefertiti 23, 29
Raydara.......................... 22, 37, 51
Redstart............................. 27, 64
Richard Pankhurst........ 18, 26, 37, 77
Rideonastar 63
Rosalie Bonheur...................... 55, 75
Royal Altitude 46
Royal Warranty.......................... 53
Russian Ounch.......................... 68
Sacrament................................ 65
Salt Island................................ 54
Sandy Cove.............................. 46
Scooner.................................... 55
Secret Gesture 63
Secret Hint 53
Secret Pursuit........................... 37
Seve 57
Shalimah 55
Sheriff 10
She's Mine 10
Short Squeeze 10, 45
Short Work 65
Sightline 65
Silvery Blue 10
Sir Domino 56
Sir Isaac Newton 16, 24, 48
Sirius Prospect.......................... 66
Skate 54
Smaih 61
Smuggler's Cove 16
Sole Power 50, 79
Solow 79
Spanish Squeeze 10, 45
Spectator.................................. 53
Speculative Bid 15
Spirit Of Sound.......................... 10
Stake Acclaim 66
Star Of Seville........................... 27
Strath Burn 53
Sugar Lump 62
Sunset Glow............................. 23
Sur Empire 58
Sympathy 23, 27
Tall Ship 66
Tangba 65
Telescope................................. 78
Terror 23
That Is The Spirit 57
The Grey Gatsby 56, 78
The New Master 15
The Wow Signal 18
This Is The Day 46
Tiggy Wiggy 21, 60, 76
Timba 30
Together Forever 20, 28, 49, 76
Top Tug.................................... 72
Toumar 65
Truth 29
Tunnel Tiger 74
Vedouma................................... 77
Vert De Grece.................. 18, 26, 44
Wajeeh 62
War Envoy 16
Wee Frankie 59
Weld Al Emarat 56
Wet Sail 45
What Say You............................ 28
Windshear 62
Words.......................... 20, 28, 49
Ya Hade Ye Delil 62
Yaakooum 62
Yorkshire Dales 15
Zawraq 18, 25, 50
Ziggurat 10
Zuhoor Baynoona 58